Cajun
Country
GUIDE

Cajun Country

GUIDE

Macon Fry and Julie Posner

PELICAN PUBLISHING COMPANY

Gretna 1992

Library of Congress Cataloging-in-Publication Data

Fry, Macon.
   Cajun country guide / Macon Fry and Julie Posner.
     p.   cm.
   Includes bibliographical references and index.
   ISBN 0-88289-831-0
   1. Louisiana—Guidebooks. 2. Cajuns—Louisiana. I. Posner,
Julie. II. Title.
   F367.3.F79   1992
   917.6304'63—dc20   92-17360
                                         CIP

Information in this guidebook is based on authoritative data available at the time of printing. Prices and hours of operations of businesses listed are subject to change without notice. Readers are asked to take this into account when consulting this guide.

Maps and charts by Julie Posner unless otherwise indicated.

Cover photos by Greg Guirard

Manufactured in the United States of America
Published by Pelican Publishing Company, Inc.
1101 Monroe Street, Gretna, Louisiana 70053

Contents

Preface

Less than forty-eight hours after arriving in New Orleans, I found myself a bleary-eyed passenger in a packed car speeding across the Atchafalaya Throughway at 8 A.M. As the sun smoldered along the tops of the black willow and cypress, I looked down from the interstate at the blackness of the nation's largest freshwater swamp and pondered how different and beautiful South Louisiana was.

Our destination was the town of Mamou and the tiny bar, Fred's Lounge, that hosts a live radio broadcast every Saturday morning beginning at 9 o'clock. We stopped in Eunice and everyone piled out of the car and into a small grocery, where about a dozen people were lined up to purchase steaming links of Cajun boudin sausage for breakfast. Back in the car, clutching cold drinks and incendiary sausages, we screamed out across the prairie for the final 20 miles, our anticipation fired by the first strains of live Cajun accordion wheezing on the radio.

Had I not already been thrown into shock by waking before sunrise and spending an hour driving over water, or by consuming a boudin sausage and cold beer before 8:30 A.M., the surprise when we entered Fred's might have been lethal! In a room with about as much floor space as twenty phone booths, at least fifty country folks, men and women, were drinking and dancing about a postage-stamp-size band area. Through the smoke I could read a few signs on the wall—"No standing on the jukebox" and "No substitute musicians." The man in western wear by the bar was chatting in French with proprietor Fred Tate, and the singer was singing in Cajun French, but I had no trouble understanding the message here: *Laissez les bon temps roulez!* (Let the good times roll!) Despite the attempts of historians to deromanticize Cajun history, despite the efforts of folklorists to analyze the culture and the efforts of Cajuns throughout South Louisiana to destroy the stereotypes surrounding themselves, Cajun Country of South Louisiana remains one of the most intoxicatingly different and exotic places in America.

Hot boudin and cold beer sign. (Photo by Macon Fry)

Acknowledgments

Many people have helped bring this guide into being, and I could not even begin to thank all of them. However, I must express my appreciation to the following:

Reginald and Gerry Keller, who introduced me to Cajun Country and provided the years of hospitality that made this book possible.

Joe Sasfy, the best unpaid editor, inspiration, and pal an author could have.

The staff at all of the local and regional visitors' centers, who came through with hospitality and assistance time after time. Among these, special thanks are due to Kelly Strenge in Lafayette, Jane Breaux and Betty Guidry in New Iberia, and Betty Reed in Houma.

The dozens of others who have shared their knowledge, their homes, and their emotional support, including Lee Lavergne, Donna Wheaton, Frank ("Woody") Waulk, Jr., Tracy Santa, Eleanor Naquin, Anne Savoy, Glenn Pitre, Pat Rickles, Barry Jean Ancelet, Greg Guirard, Floyd Soileau, Alice Posner, Ed Neham, Kenneth Delcambre, Lucy and Dee DeHart, Dale Ladner, Michael Lach and the California Kids, Carol Wuchter, Rosemary Dennis, and Greg Smith.

Last but not least, special thanks is due to my editors Nina Kooij, who gave me the encouragement to embark on this project, and John Rogers, for his remarkable attention to detail.

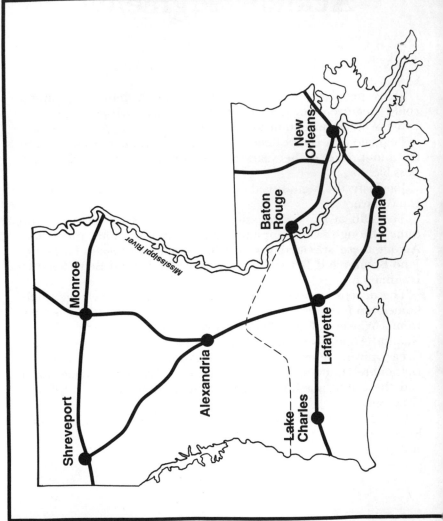

Louisiana's Major Highwa

How to Use This Book

In the introductory chapters you will find general information on the land, flora, fauna, people, and recreational opportunities found in Cajun Country. In the second half of the book, Cajun Country is broken into 6 regions. Each region is explored in a separate chapter which outlines the major towns and describes attractions in more detail. Within each regional chapter there are reviews of the best restaurants and dance halls in that region and a representative list of accommodations. For those planning on spending several days in the area, these chapters will allow you an opportunity to plan an itinerary in advance and to read about places as you go.

Because Cajun Country is such a small area (easily traversed in a day or two), it is also important to consider the area as a whole when planning an activity or itinerary for a given day or evening. For instance, if you are staying in Lafayette (Central Cajun Country), you may want to make a morning trip to Jefferson Island (Teche Country), go to the live Roundez Vous Des Cajuns dance in Eunice (Cajun Heartland) in the afternoon, and eat dinner at Hawk's Crawfish Restaurant (Western Cajun Country) in the evening. To facilitate planning such a trip across regions, the introductory chapters on food, music, and outdoor recreation include maps of Cajun Country that show the location of the most highly recommended attractions.

Symbols used in this text:

There are two types of icons used in the text. All attractions, restaurants, and dance halls that are highly recommended are denoted with a star (★). These are places that are worth driving out of your way to visit. Restaurant prices are denoted by dollar signs. One dollar sign ($) means a satisfying meal (usually at least a main dish and side order or dessert) may be purchased for $7 or less. Two dollar signs ($$) means the price will be $7 to $15, and three signs ($$$) means a meal will cost over $15.

11

Swamp. (Photo by Julie Posner)

1
The Land

What Is Cajun Country?

Cajun Country is a land of black coffee and bayous, steaming crawfish and swamps; it is a place where the wheezing push-pull of an accordion hangs in the air over the upland prairie like a blanket of humidity. Cajun Country is set apart from the rest of Louisiana and the country as a whole by a landscape that continues to confound road builders and a regional culture so distinct that until recently people of Anglo descent were often referred to as *les Américains*. On the state map the area has been dubbed Acadiana, in honor of the Acadian people who settled there in the mid-eighteenth century.

The "official" state boundaries of Acadiana roughly form a triangle-shaped region in South Louisiana, with a base extending along 300 miles (as the crow flies) of jigsawed Gulf coast. The east side of the triangle follows the Mississippi River north from just above New Orleans, while the west side slants in from the Louisiana and Texas border to an apex about 200 miles northwest of New Orleans in Avoyelles parish. The entire triangle composes less than half the state, or 22 mainly rural parishes (as counties are known in Louisiana), and contains none of the state's three largest cities. In fact, Lafayette, its biggest city, has a population of about 85,000 residents, a distant fourth behind New Orleans, Baton Rouge, and Shreveport. This guide focuses on areas where the food, music, language, and other expressions of the Cajun and Creole cultures are strongest.

The unique and enduring cultures of Cajun Country owe their survival in the twentieth century in no small way to geographic isolation. For years after most of the rest of the country was linked by superhighways, the jungle of the Atchafalaya Basin defied engineers and left Cajun Country unreachable by high-speed interstate traffic. Interstate 10, the main east-west route linking New Orleans and Baton Rouge with Lafayette, Lake Charles, and

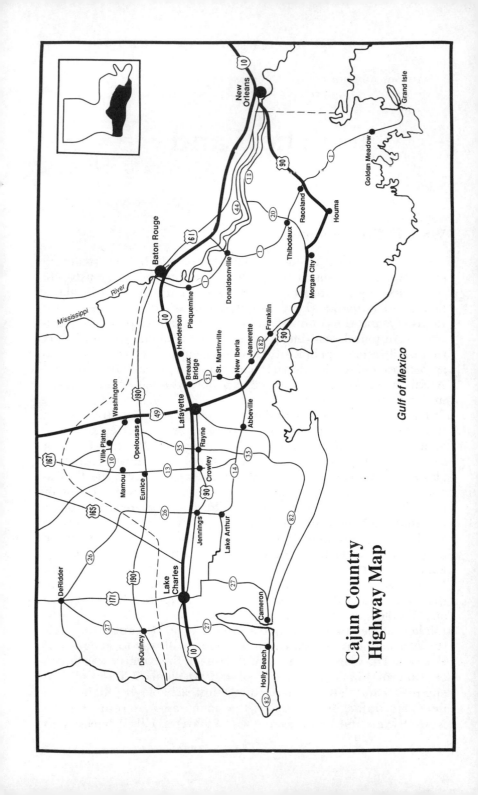

Cajun Country
Highway Map

Houston, was not completed until 1973. It took the most expensive stretch of interstate ever constructed to span the yawning Atchafalaya Basin Swamp and connect the state capital of Baton Rouge with the hub city of Cajun Country, Lafayette. Deeper into Cajun Country, difficulties in travel were even more marked. Until well into the twentieth century some towns were inaccessible by road and children traveled to school by schoolboat. When the oil industry began exploring the coastal wetlands south of Houma in the forties, they discovered Houma Indian communities whose residents spoke archaic French thriving in watery isolation.

Geography

When you talk about the geography of South Louisiana, two adjectives come to mind: "flat" and "wet." Driving down the moss-draped byways of Cajun Country, a glance out the window generally reveals a more liquid than solid landscape. Land in South Louisiana is a relatively recent occurrence, emerging from the receding waters of the last ice age about 6000 years ago. When the first humans came to the continent via the land bridge, all of Cajun Country was under water. Today the region has nearly 3000 square miles of water surface. Some places that appear to be solid are actually a barely congealed goo that will suck a leg in as far as the thigh and steal a sneaker on the way out.

Cajun Country is located entirely within the Gulf Coastal Plain. Along the southern edge of the region the Gulf Coast Marsh forms a roughly thirty-mile-wide band bordering the Gulf of Mexico. To the east are the fertile fields and swamps of the Mississippi Alluvial Plain, while the west is characterized by the vast flat lands of the Gulf Coast or "Cajun" Prairie. Even on the high and dry Cajun Prairie, however, water is visible everywhere, as mechanically flooded rice fields stretch to the horizon.

One calculation estimates that Louisiana's 400-mile-long coast measures 6,952 miles of actual shoreline if you trace the myriad indentations, bays, and sounds that etch its boundary with the Gulf of Mexico. Along this tattered coastline, the **Gulf Coast Marsh** contains over 30 percent of the coastal wetlands in the entire contiguous 48 states. In the eastern section of Cajun Country, the marsh is a drainage field for the Mississippi and Atchafalaya rivers and is laced with bayous and channels. In the west, the coast is more stable and less marked by the meanderings of these rivers. The only significant high ground in the western Gulf Coast Marsh is a series of ridges called *cheniers* (French for oaks) or "islands."

Coastal marsh. (Photo by Macon Fry)

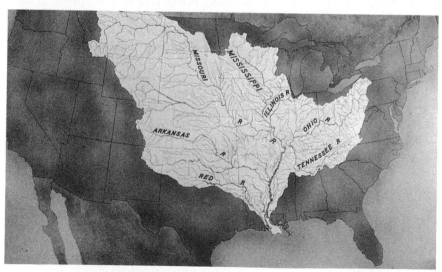

Drainage in the Mississippi Valley. (Courtesy of U.S. Army Corps of Engineers)

Even at times of low water, these tree-covered mounds appear as "islands" in the sea of surrounding marsh grass. Like fire ants clinging to the unsubmerged portion of a floating log, the *cheniers* form a string of tiny communities across southern Cameron and Vermilion Parishes that are inhabited by oil workers, fishermen, trappers, and ranchers, and frequented by bird watchers and recreational fishermen.

The **Mississippi Alluvial Plain** stretches from just east of the Mississippi to the western edge of Lafayette Parish. This wedge of land and water forms a gigantic funnel or basin which drains the runoff water from over half the continent through its two mighty rivers, the Mississippi and the Atchafalaya. The rivers ride high above surrounding plains for miles, confined between man-made embankments called levees (French for "raised up"). These levees prevent the rivers from covering a third of the state with water at flood stage.

For over 3000 years the Mississippi River, or Meche Sebe, as the Indians called it, has been the primary tool building and shaping South Louisiana. Its vagaries have etched themselves into the present map of the state in a tangle of old distributaries and former channels like Bayou Teche and Bayou Lafourche. The high land along these streams is hugged by roads, sugarcane plantations, and farming and fishing communities. In many cases, waterways, with their parallel roads, drop south into impenetrable marsh, leaving travelers to retrace their steps. From the levees on either side of bayous and rivers, the land drops away into a viscous muck the consistency of barely cooled jello.

Most of western Cajun country is occupied by the expansive **Cajun Prairie**. The Prairie, about twice the size of Delaware, stretches from the Vermilion River west of Lafayette to the Texas border above Lake Charles. From an elevation of about 70 feet above sea level at the top of the Cajun Prairie in Mamou, the West Gulf Coastal Plain tilts down at a slope of a foot a mile to the lakes and permanently wet prairie marsh along the coast of Cameron and Vermilion Parishes. It is covered with rice, crawfish, and soybean farms and dotted with cattle and rail towns. The Prairie is not a part of the state that folks hear about much, as Hollywood prefers images of gators and trappers to fields of rice and big Cajun or Zydeco dances. Little is left of the towering grasses and abundant wildflowers that greeted the first visitors, but the Prairie is one of the most romantic and culturally unspoiled areas of the state. Its open spaces and little communities offer an improbable number of dance halls and great eateries.

Fisherman in Atchafalaya Basin. (Courtesy of U.S. Army Corps of Engineers)

The **Atchafalaya River** (pronounced uh-chaf-uh-lie-uh), a primary distributary of the Mississippi and Red rivers, courses through the heart of the Mississippi Alluvial plain between New Orleans and Lafayette. Surrounding the Atchafalaya, at an average width of twenty miles and a rough length of 150 miles, is America's largest freshwater swamp, the Atchafalaya Basin. This vast jungle within levees is an area of natural beauty on the scale of the Grand Canyon. Unlike the canyon, however, the Basin (as it is referred to locally) is teeming with wildlife that has supported generations of Cajun trappers, hunters, moss pickers, lumbermen, fishermen, and most recently a burgeoning oil and gas industry. Today the Basin, which flows south between Lafayette and Baton Rouge before pouring into the Gulf below Morgan City, is mainly inaccessible by road, but is a wondrous place to visit by canoe or on one of the many swamp tours that ply its waters.

THE THREATENED BASIN

Most folks seldom see more of the Atchafalaya Basin than the tops of black willow trees as they speed across the elevated Atchafalaya Throughway. These motorists miss a plant and animal world unto itself where nature labors overtime producing fantastic blooms, lush foliage, and forage for a host of exotic animals, along with the accompanying richly oxygenated and pollinated air, the gentle hum of dozing insects, the lapping of water, and the cry of birds. In the evening a screaming cacophony of frogs and bugs fills the dark.

Unfortunately, the seemingly peaceful Basin is a region teetering on the edge of both natural and man-made disaster. If there were no controls in place at the town of Torras, the Atchafalaya River would have long ago captured the Mississippi River by offering a shorter and steeper route to the Gulf (142 miles vs. the present 315). The mighty Mississippi has made at least three such moves in the last 7000 years and tried valiantly to change its course again in the flood of 1973. Were this were to happen today, miles of Basin land would be inundated, including hundreds of gas and oil wells and Morgan City, which lies behind huge walls squarely in the middle of the floodplain. The impact such a switch would have on the factories and deepwater ports that cling to the Mississippi below Baton Rouge would be incalculable. These economic interests would be left on the banks of a sluggish stream and New Orleans' drinking water would be contaminated with salty Gulf water.

Tent City, for refugees of 1927 flood. (Courtesy of Lafayette Courthouse Archives)

Both to prevent this catastrophe and in immediate response to the mind-boggling sweep of waters in 1927 that is still referred to picturesquely (and hopefully) as the "hundred-year flood," the United States Corps of Engineers set about building new levees along the Basin. Entire regions that were once within the flood-plain were lopped off, residents were moved outside of the newly created banks, and a plan was developed for the "final" control of the flow of water between the Mississippi River and the Atchafalaya. The weir and overbank floodgate which were to accomplish this miracle were completed in 1963 and the Corps had not finished touting their invincibility before the flood of 1973 came along and undermined a large portion of the structure. Were it not for emergency measures, the final switch of the Mississippi's course would have been accomplished!

As mentioned, the threat to the Atchafalaya Basin is not solely a matter of natural catastrophe. In creating levees and controlling the flow of water into the area, the Corps of Engineers is also controlling the flow of alluvial sediment, channeling it into the now artificially walled area, and filling in old waterways at an alarming rate.

Some areas of the Basin are laced with a spider web of abandoned oil and natural gas pipes and wellheads. Once buried below water or sediment, these pipes hang rusting in the swamps; many of the companies that built and left them have been out of business for decades. Of course, this type of "cut and burn" mentality is not new to the Basin. The destructive power of the lumber industry that thrived in the Basin around the turn of the century is plainly visible in vast cemeteries of tombstone-like tree stumps, which were unusuable as lumber.

2

The People

From its language to its food and music, Cajun Country is a land defined by its people. High-speed interstates and bridges may have spanned the geographic barriers isolating the region, but the people of South Louisiana still possess an indomitable spirit of independence and self-sufficiency. Many still live life close to the land, not untouched, but unmarred by the opening of the countryside in the last half a century.

The most quantifiable difference between the folks in Cajun Country and their upstate neighbors is the predominance of the Catholic Church in the south and Protestant faith in the north. The northern boundary of Acadiana neatly divides the 22 predominantly Catholic parishes of the south from the 40 predominantly Protestant upstate parishes. The people of North Louisiana are mainly hard-working folks who are not too different from other rural Southerners, scrubbing sustenance from hard-scrabble farms and from the gas and lumber industries in the piney hills. The denizens of Cajun Country, however, are best known for their leisure skills. Whether they are cooking, making music, recounting a good story over a drink, or making a friendly wager, there is a marked value placed on the simple pursuit of "passing a good time." It is not indolence, but a zest for life or "joie de vivre" that separates South Louisiana from the rest of the state (and country) and makes it a paradise for anyone seeking to get away from the headlong pursuit of work and money for soul-satisfying indulgence in great food and music.

The largest, best known, and culturally predominant group in South Louisiana are the Cajuns, but the area is actually inhabited by many people of diverse ancestry. There are three surviving Indian tribes, a large black Creole population, many anglos, and significant numbers of people who trace their roots back to several different European countries. Some of the earliest immigrants to the area were Germans who settled on the banks of the Mississippi River at a place about thirty miles north of New

Chitimacha basketmaker. (Photo by Macon Fry)

Orleans that is now known as the German Coast. Other European nationalities include Italians, who arrived in the early twentieth century, and people of Spanish and French descent. Among those of French descent are three distinct groups—Cajuns, French nationals, and refugees from Saint-Domingue. All of these people have mixed with the Acadians and contributed to the unique food, music, philosophy, and way of life in Cajun Country.

Indian Tribes of Cajun Country

Most of the Indian people of South Louisiana suffered fates common to tribes around the country. Although the first European visitors were initially welcomed by most Louisiana tribes, the Indian populace was soon treated to disease, enslavement, and decimation by war.

The **Chitimacha** are the only tribe in South Louisiana still living on some of the same traditional lands they occupied in 1700. Originally the Chitimachas inhabited a wide area surrounding the Atchafalaya Basin from the Mississippi River at Bayou Plaquemine down Bayou Lafourche. During the early 1700s these otherwise peaceful people became engaged in armed conflict with the French that led to the enslavement and slaughter of the majority of the tribe. Most of the surviving members hid in the swampland between Bayou Teche and Grand Lake, near the present-day towns of Jeanerette and Charenton. By 1925, when the federal government officially recognized the tribe and established a reservation at the site, there were only about fifty members surviving. Today the tribe numbers about 500 members, with 250 living on the reservation. Their language and most of the customs and lore have been lost. Fewer than a half dozen older women are preserving the fine split cane basketry created by the Chitimacha. A selection of baskets and other artifacts are on display in a museum and tribal center operated by the park service at the Charenton reservation.

The **Coushatta**, also known as Koasati, moved to South Louisiana in the early 1800s and represent the most ethnically pure (nearly full blooded) tribe in the state. Three hundred or so tribal members now live on a reservation in Elton, where the northwest Prairie joins the pine hills of central Louisiana. While the Coushatta have been fortunate in preserving their language (the Coushatta language is still the first language of those living on the reservation) and many customs, their insularity has had a high price. Deprived of a good public education until the sixties, 90 percent of the population had incomes under 3000 dollars in the 1970s and only half the heads of families were literate (Fred B. Kniffen, Hiram F. Gregory, and George A. Stokes. *The Historic Indian Tribes Of Louisiana.* Baton Rouge, LA: LSU Press, 1987). Many of the Coushatta are now employed on farms in the Elton region and an effort is being made to establish several profitable industries on the reservation. A visitor and tribal center is open to the public with a small display of local crafts.

From a nadir of sixty countable members in 1803, the **Houmas** now represent the largest Indian group in Louisiana, with a tribal roll of about 11,000. Like the Coushattas, the Houmas were relatively late arrivals in South Louisiana. They were forced from prime agricultural lands along the Mississippi River and upper reaches of Bayous Lafourche and Terrebonne to the soggy southern reaches of Bayou Country, where they still extract their living from the fur, fish, and mineral wealth of the wetlands. The largest concentration still live in the wetlands south of the present-day city of Houma, where nearly 1000 members of the tribe are within walking distance of the village of Dulac on Bayou Grand Caillou.

It is ironic that Louisiana's most populous Indian tribe has yet to be recognized by the federal government. This recognition (which is likely to come in the near future) has been impeded by the adoption of the French language by most of the Houma people and by their extreme watery isolation. Several communities of Houmas existed on marsh islands for a century, virtually untouched by life in mainland Acadiana, until the oil industry began making inroads in the marsh during the late forties.

Cajuns

The Acadians in Nova Scotia: The ancestors of today's Cajuns were French pioneers who settled in Nova Scotia mainly in 1604 and 1632. The character and strength of the Cajun people today has its roots in their experience as colonists in the Acadia province of Nova Scotia, where they arrived at the beginning of a conflict between the British and French that was to stretch into nearly 100 years of war. This conflict between superpowers effectively isolated the colonists from support by either country and left them to fend for themselves against alternate Indian and British aggression.

The Acadians were a mainly poor and illiterate people. They led an agrarian life, gathering solidarity from a strong attachment to the land, a strong faith in the Catholic Church, and an esprit de corps born of family affiliation and political isolation. In 1713, when Acadia was formally ceded to England in the Treaty Of Utrecht, the British answered the colonists' pleas for neutrality with a demand for allegiance to the British Crown. The demand became an ultimatum in 1753; the French Acadians would either take an unconditional oath of allegiance or face confiscation of property and deportation to the British colonies. In what has been called The Grand Derangement of 1755, 16,000 French Acadians who had built a life in Nova Scotia for over a century were divested of their property and deported. Families and friends were separated and scattered throughout the British colonies, where some were pressed into servitude.

Acadians in Louisiana: When the British and French settled their differences in 1763, the Acadians who had spent the last ten years in scattered exile looked to reestablish their families, communities, and lives in freedom. The greatest numbers eventually found their way to South Louisiana, where they again became pioneers in new and unsettled lands. Ironically, when the Acadians began to arrive in Louisiana, the colony had just come under Spanish rule and they were again the subjects of a non-French crown. The Spanish government in New Orleans saw an opportunity to settle the area west of the Mississippi and offered Acadian and other immigrants of French descent a choice of lands on the frontier. The first settlers made homes on high lands along the "German Coast" of the Mississippi River, and then along bayous in the Lafourche, Teche, and Opelousas districts.

While New Orleans was a bustling cosmopolitan center, most of South Louisiana was still a rough-hewn territory occupied by Indians, trappers (known as *courir du bois*), and a few wealthy French plantation owners who relied on the protection of Spanish military outposts. The new immigrants adapted and thrived in South Louisiana, where most began raising cattle and subsistence crops. The ties of family and church were already in place, and the travail of displacement fostered a sense of solidarity and a desire for independence among the new settlers. By the end of the century the Acadian tradition of large families and the subdivision of early land grants had begun to stretch the seams of original settlements. Some of the settlers moved towards less fertile backlands, where they learned how to harvest the natural bounty of the swamps and marsh. Others sold their waterfront land to the growing Anglo and French planter class and headed for the prairie frontier west of the Atchafalaya Basin.

These movements began the pattern of Cajun communities that exist today. Large Acadian settlements were established on the banks of the Vermilion River at the present-day site of Lafayette and near the Spanish military Poste de Opelousas. During the 19th century the Acadians managed to continue as a group basically unenfranchised by the rest of the state or country. Although they had their statesmen, Civil War heroes, and an upwardly mobile urban class, for the most part the Acadians sought independence from larger political affairs and enjoyed an agrarian life of relative isolation.

Cajuns in the Twentieth Century: When the isolation of Southwest Louisiana began to crack at the turn of the century, the descendants of the Acadians were well established. The 1860 census counted over 18,000 Acadian-French surnames. The predominance of the Acadian way of life was such that they were actually absorbing many other ethnic groups in the region, forming a distinctive "Cajun" culture.

The frontier in Louisiana was opened by many of the same vehicles that opened other parts of the nation—the railroad, the radio, and the automobile. Perhaps the biggest harbinger of change was the discovery of oil at Jennings, Louisiana, in 1901. Along with the oil boom, the event which most impacted the Cajun culture was the implementation of a highly ethnocentric mandatory public education policy in 1916. When Cajun children began attending school, they were confronted with a policy that forbade speaking French on school grounds. This policy effectively deprived a generation of their native tongue and nearly eradicated the Cajun French language in South Louisiana. By the time the offshore oil boom brought thousands of newcomers to Acadiana in the fifties, "Cajun" was a deprecatory term and many had learned to be ashamed of their heritage and culture.

Cajun Renaissance: There are nearly a million French-speaking descendants of the Acadians living in South Louisiana today. Nowhere else in the nation has a single ethnic group been as successful in assimilating others while resisting total mainstream assimilation itself. It is not uncommon to find "Cajuns" with non-French surnames like Schexnieder, Robert, Allemand, and Fernandez. Today's Cajuns, from urban professionals to rice and crawfish farmers, fishermen, and oilmen, have found a new pride in their distinctive culture. Beginning with the interest of folklorists in the early sixties and continuing with the efforts of the Council on Development of French in Louisiana (CODOFIL) and the Cajun French Music Association, Cajuns have once again begun to appreciate and cultivate their rich heritage. Their success can be measured in the vibrant music scene on the Cajun Prairie, the great restaurants of Lafayette, and the reintroduction of French in many of the public schools. It would seem that the unique food, music, and language of the region will thrive for at least one more generation among the descendents of the Acadian people, providing visitors to the region an opportunity to enjoy a nearly lost way of life.

Creoles

Few words are open to as many interpretations as "Creole." From the Spanish word *criollo*, or "child of the colonies" (John Chase. *Frenchmen, Desire, Good Children*, 2nd Edition. New Orleans, LA: Robert L. Crager and Company, 1960), it has been used to describe almost anything unique to South Louisiana, from tomatoes to horses to yams. In New Orleans and the old European settlements of St. Martinville and New Iberia, the term "Creole" was used to differentiate people of French or Spanish parentage who were born in Louisiana. When the slave trade in Louisiana grew in the late 18th century, the term was used to differentiate slaves born in the colonies (*esclavos Criollos*) from those brought from Africa (*esclavos Africanos*).

The term "Creole" generally fell out of frequent use as a descriptor for those of European descent in the years prior to the War Between the States, but in regards to the black population it developed deeper connotations. Many Creole slaves became free men before the war. Some of these people had children by their owners or were of partial Carribean descent and were thus lighter skinned. They became known as Creoles of Color. Some went on to become prosperous businessmen and landowners, even plantation and slave owners, prior to the war, establishing a rich and largely undocumented culture of their own.

Today the term "Creole" in South Louisiana is usually used to describe Creoles of Color, or those brought up in the black French-speaking community. This group is sometimes incorrectly referred to as "black Cajuns," but the Creole people have a culture very much their own, including the distinctive Zydeco music. The French language has been best preserved among Creole people, as they were often isolated from the educational "opportunities" afforded the white populace after the War Between the States. Some of the biggest Creole communities today are in the St. Martinville and Opelousas areas, where Zydeco dance halls throw open their doors on weekends.

The Language and Expressions of Cajun Country

Despite the efforts of the Anglo state bureaucracy to eradicate the French language from public schools and courthouses over the last 75 years, it is estimated that over a million Louisianians still speak French as a primary or secondary language. Although it is unlikely that non-French-speaking visitors will encounter a language barrier in Cajun Country (as they might have thirty years ago), there are still 5th- and 6th-generation residents of the region who do not speak fluent English. In homes, bars, restaurants, and other places of relaxation (especially in the countryside), one can count on hearing Cajun French spoken, and a number of radio stations have introduced all French broadcasts. Those who speak standard French will find Cajun French understandable, but in many ways a very different language. The variation from standard is not nearly so surprising as the fact that the language is spoken at all, when you consider that it has existed exclusively as an orally transmitted tradition.

There are actually three distinct types of French spoken in South Louisiana: Acadian French, Creole French, and Standard Louisiana French (Hosea Phillips. "The Spoken French of Louisiana." In *The Cajuns: Essays On Their History and Culture*, edited by Glenn Conrad. Baton Rouge, LA: USL Press, 1983). The most common French used in Louisiana is Acadian French. This is strictly a spoken language which has maintained many archaic 17th-century forms while borrowing words from a number of other tongues. Although speakers from throughout South Louisiana have no trouble understanding each other, Acadian French varies widely from region to region. The distinct variant spoken along Bayou Lafourche has even been given the name "Lafourchaise." A second type of Louisiana French is Creole French, which is spoken mainly by the black population and was once referred to as Gumbo or Negro French. Like Acadian French, Creole French has been wildly altered during its transmission as a strictly spoken language. Creole French can vary widely between neighboring towns within the same region. The least-heard variant of the French language in Cajun Country is Standard Louisiana French, spoken primarily by an older, wealthier class who received an education at private French institutions. It is occasionally written and is used by few younger family members.

Although the impending loss of the distinctive forms of Cajun French is being justifiably lamented, it will be a long time before the language patterns, accents, and expressions of English-speaking Cajuns disappear. Cajun English will be as striking to many visitors as the often-heard Cajun French. Emphasis in Cajun English is often expressed by repetition. A fire can be merely "hot" or "hot hot!"; a strong cup of coffee may be dark or "black black!" In the casual way of the Cajun French that suggests that the good life comes without being tirelessly pursued, folks "pass a good time" rather than "have" one. A flirtatious gentleman would not be so bold as to "take" a look at a lady, but might "pass a look." As an expression of astonishment you will often hear the cry "Poo Yi!" Many lyrical expressions are drawn from the enchanting South Louisiana environment. The blustery weather of early March is often referred to as "The winds of Lent," and east and west may be referred to as "towards the rising sun" or "towards the setting sun."

There is no capturing the poetry of Cajun French or Cajun English in writing, perhaps because they have never been a written language. The best way to appreciate these forms is to visit the region and pass a good time with the people of Cajun Country.

Hurricane floodwaters. (Courtesy of U.S. Army Corps of Engineers)

3

The Climate

Cajun Country enjoys a semi-tropical latitude. Lafayette, its biggest city, is about 30 degrees north of the equator, about the same latitude as Shanghai and Cairo. The climate is moist, warm, and luxuriant through most of the year, moderated by the warm waters of the neighboring Gulf of Mexico. People down here talk about the humidity as if it were an entity, much the way Chicagoans decry the wind-chill factor. The correct response when you step into an air-conditioned restaurant in mid-July and the waitress asks, "Hot out there?" is to wipe your brow and assert, "It's not so much the heat but the humidity."

Summers can be drippingly hot and humid, with daytime temperatures ranging from 85 to 95 degrees and the mercury seldom dropping below 65 at night. Rainfall averages about 60 inches a year, with nearly a third of that coming in June through August. In these months silver clouds float in from the Gulf and turn into afternoon thunderheads.

Fall and spring are probably the most pleasant times to visit Cajun Country. Autumn is the dry season, with cool evenings and warm days. Rice mills send clouds of chaff from their driers and the air is filled with the sweet smell of the sugarcane harvest and smoke from marsh fires. Occasionally disturbing the serenity of late summer and harvest time are huge tropical storms that play intermittent target practice with Louisiana's Gulf coast.

Winters are short and characterized by rain squalls and cloudy but mild weather followed by clear, cold weather. Daytime temperatures range from 55 to 65 degrees, with nighttime lows seldom dipping below 40. Only a few days are likely to go below freezing, so snowfall is rare. Because the weather in these parts is "supposed to be" so mild, visitors are often surprised at the grousing that accompanies a 40-degree "cold snap."

Spring begins early in Cajun Country. It is not unusual to find azaleas blooming in January. By late February the squalls and chills of winter give way to more generalized wind and showers and warm weather. Many people like to visit in the late winter and early spring for the Cajun Mardi Gras celebration. The best advice is to pack for both warm and cold weather. I have been to Mardi Gras in January when people were sweltering so badly that they were discarding masks before noon; in 1988, when Mardi Gras fell on March 3, I had to wear a glove to keep a beer can from freezing to my hand.

Hurricanes

Hurricanes are the most feared climatic event in Cajun Country. While they are not unique to the area, South Louisiana's location on the northern rim of the Gulf of Mexico makes it a target for some of the most violent tropical storms to threaten the continent. The hurricane season runs June through early October. During these months a common South Louisiana pastime is "tracking" the storms on special maps given out as promotional items at fast-food outlets.

While the majority of hurricanes striking the Louisiana coast make landfall around the mouth of the Mississippi River, some of the fiercest, such as Audrey (June 28, 1957), Carmen (September 8, 1974), and Danny (August 15, 1985) have struck to the west in Cajun Country. Here the low elevation and huge expanses of marsh allow storms to surge forward unimpeded. The already sodden ground often floods from severe rainfall even before punishing winds push the tidal surge ashore. Waves twenty feet high can roar in from the gulf at speeds up to forty miles an hour, leaving cows in trees and trees in telephone lines as much as twenty miles inland from the coast. Lake Charles, Cameron, and Creole are left with grim reminders, in the form of mass graves, of the destructive powers of Hurricane Audrey, which slammed Cameron in 1957, claimed over 500 victims, and did in excess of 150 million dollars of damage.

4

Flora and Fauna

A temperate climate and long growing season (230-300 days) cloaks much of South Louisiana in luxuriant vegetation year round. Something is always blooming and (notable if you are an allergy sufferer) going to seed. Although there is little variation in climate within the region, there is wide variation in the wild flora corresponding to differences in elevation and proximity to the coast. Swamps and freshwater areas are naturally more verdant than the salt marshes and prairie.

Coastal Marshes

Perhaps the harshest environment in South Louisiana is the coastal marsh, where life is battered by storms and shriveled by salt. With the completion of the Hug The Coast Highway and Creole Nature Trail in Cameron Parish, some of this isolated domain of seabirds and cordgrass has become accessible to auto touring. Only the hardiest plants, such as **coarse wire** and **three-corner grasses**, prevail here. On sand and shell ridges that striate the marsh are natural growths of live oaks. These ridges have been dubbed *cheniers* (French for "oak") for their twisted sylvan canopy which rises above the windblown miles of marsh and beach.

Of the fifteen species of oak found in Louisiana, none is more grand than the **Live oak**, which grows wild in coastal Louisiana and in plantings throughout the state. The stately tree lends its dignity to hundreds of plantation grounds and an arbor of shade to countless backroads and highways in Cajun Country. Other oaks grow taller, but only the Live oak has branches that sweep out up to 200 feet in circumference. The trunks often measure over forty feet in girth, while each branch, large as an average tree trunk, supports its own small ecosystem of lichens, squirrels, birds, and strands of Spanish moss. The tree is so venerated that a Live Oak Society was created in 1934. To become a member, a tree must be at least 100 years old. Among the most famous of the

Live oaks on a coastal chenier. (Photo by Dr. E. L. Caze)

Live oaks in Cajun Country is the Evangeline Oak, located in St. Martinville near the site where legend places the landing of Longfellow's heroine.

Spanish moss ranks with the Bald cypress and Live oak as a botanical symbol of Cajun Country. Its solemnly hanging strands are no doubt responsible for the haunted air believed to permeate so many plantation homes, the languid quality attributed to the atmosphere, and the mysterious allure ascribed to the swamps of the region. It grows in profusion on the outstretched arms of Live oaks and festoons the borders of lakes, where the gray-green beards reach down to the soaring knees of the cypress.

This elegant plant has become the object of considerable legend. The Spanish dubbed it "Frenchman's wig," while the French supposedly called it *barbe espagnole*, or "Spanish beard." The current label is not botanically correct, as the plant is not a moss but a member of the pineapple family. It is not a parasite but an independent plant nourished by air which has no ill effect on the tree where it comes to rest. Indians and Acadian settlers used the "moss" as bedding and mixed it with mud for use as a construction material called *bousillage* by the French. Around the turn of the century Spanish moss was harvested and dried for use as upholstery stuffing. The black inner fiber filled the seats of many a Model T.

Fresh Marshes and Swamps

Whether you are entering Cajun Country from New Orleans in the east or the Texas border west of Lake Charles, the first vegetation you are likely to see is that of the saltwater marsh. Farther inland, in the brackish marsh and freshwater swamp, cattails, alligator grass, and marsh elder supplant the coarser salt vegetation. In the freshwater swamps and alluvial valleys between Lafayette and New Orleans lies Louisiana's richest plant growth. **Oak, pecan**, and **hickory** trees grow along ridges with an understory of **vines, wild muscadine grapes, blackberries, elderberries**, and **ferns**. **Tupelo** and **black gum, willow** and **Bald cypress** thrive in the permanently moist areas. These shelter **palmetto, hibiscus, rosemallow**, and various wildflowers like the **giant purple and yellow iris**. Among the most striking and prevalent plants in the permanently flooded regions are water flowers like **American lotus**, which displays towering yellow blossoms over floating pad-like foliage. **Duckweed** (the world's smallest flowering plant) forms a green carpet over slow-moving water, giving many of the bayous a "slimy" appearance.

Water hyacinths choke a bayou. (Courtesy of LA Department of Wildlife and Fisheries)

The most ubiquitous of all water flowers is the **purple water hyacinth**. In warm-weather months water hayacinths, with their delicate lavender blossoms fading into purple, form a solid carpet over many of the waterways in Cajun Country. This is one plant you will see in the summer wherever you go and regardless of how long you stay. From roadside ditches to bayous, rivers, and miles of swamp, the water hyacinth proliferates in mind-boggling numbers. The flowers can self-pollinate, with one plant generating up to 65,000 others in a season. Dormant seeds may germinate 20 years later. Despite its beauty, the reproductive capabilities of the water hyacinth have made it a major nuisance and threat to aquatic life across South Louisiana. The plants form a blanket that shades waterways and robs their oxygen content, at times becoming so thick as to prohibit navigation. The lovely and troublesome flower is not a native to South Louisiana, but was introduced to the state during the Cotton Exposition of 1884 in New Orleans. The Japanese reportedly brought a large quantity of the flowers (native to South America) to give away as souvenirs. They were carried forth and distributed across the state. By 1897 they had already become a threat to waterborne commerce and the Corps of Engineers was called in to eradicate the plants. Thus began what has become the ongoing battle of the bloom, with man tossing arsenic, oil, flames, threshers, and a variety of chemical weapons at the happy and still hardy flowers.

Bald cypress, found in the moist, alluvial valleys and swamps of Cajun Country, is the state tree of Louisiana. It is distinguished by a wide, flared base that tapers upwards and a dark feathery green foliage which browns and falls in the colder months. One of the most unusual features of the cypress are the vertical outgrowths or "knees" which rise from the roots, piercing the surrounding water and soil surface; these are assumed to be a sort of breathing apparatus for the tree.

The state legislature may have considered the poetic beauty of the Bald cypress bearded with Spanish moss when it appointed it state tree in 1964, but for years it was appreciated for its practical virtues as a building material. Cypress lumber became known as the "eternal wood." Unfortunately the lumber turned out to be a lot more eternal than most of the trees. In the late 1800s the lumber industry set about plundering the wetlands of South Louisiana. Some of the trees harvested in the 19th century were close to a thousand years old and big enough to provide enough lumber for a modest home. By the early twentieth century there were no longer enough harvestable trees left, and the mill owners packed it in.

Artisans continue to harvest cypress in the form of "sinker" logs. These are cut pieces of cypress that either sank or were lost in storms years ago. The most sought-after cypress is called "pecky." These logs have been eaten away inside by a mysterious fungal agent to create a lacy pattern when cut in cross-section. To see cypress more than 200 years old today, one must look at the floors and moldings of plantation homes, the vistas of decapitated stumps rising from roadside wetlands, or take a swamp tour that accesses hidden corners of the Atchafalaya Basin.

Cajun Prairie

If you travel on Interstate 10 between Lafayette and the Texas border or spend any time in the Cajun Heartland of Evangeline and St. Landry Parish, you will find a flat and nearly treeless terrain that fails to comply with any of the swamp stereotypes of Cajun Country. A few feet beneath the level prairie surface lies a nearly impervious layer of clay that holds water on the surface and deters the growth of trees and other large plants. At one time this region was covered with towering grasses and wildflowers. Now most of the prairie has given way to the plow. Farmers have taken advantage of poor drainage and flooded fields to grow rice and crawfish. Where bayous and creeks cross the prairie, small groves of trees have sprung up in the stream beds. Towns which have grown by the shelter of these trees are often called Coves or Islands, as the patches of trees seem to float on the open prairie. Scraps of wild prairie growth still exist along roadsides, rail beds, and scattered in far-flung locations in the form of wildflowers such as **Compass Plant, Blazing Star, Spiderwort, Clover**, and **Blue Star** (*see* Eunice Prairie Wildflower Refuge).

Notable Fauna

Birds: Over 375 species of birds have been observed within the boundaries of Louisiana. A temperate climate makes Louisiana a comfortable permanent residence for nearly all avian species common in the Southeast, but the main factor contributing to the plethora of our winged friends is the state's location across the Great Mississippi Valley Flyway. Louisiana is a landing pad for birds from both eastern and western regions. Some stop and winter here while others grab a nap or some seafood and continue on their migration. In the Christmas bird count of 1953, 153 different species were counted in one day on a 15-mile diameter

Egrets foraging in marsh. (Courtesy of LA Department of Wildlife and Fisheries)

Nutria. (Courtesy of U.S. Army Corps of Engineers)

chunk of marsh in Cameron Parish! Of special interest to hunters and bird watchers are the thousands of wild geese and ducks that visit the region each fall and winter.

South Louisiana sports about a half dozen varieties of **egret**. These members of the heron family are tall, slender birds with long legs and necks. The graceful egret may be distinguished from other species in flight, as they hold their necks bent into an S shape. Perhaps the most beautiful is the **snowy egret**. The lacy "nuptial feathers" on the back of the snowy egret are raised in a dazzling display during courtship. Once decimated by plume hunters, the population rebounded through the efforts of naturalist E. A. McIlHenny. They can now be seen anywhere in Cajun country, silent sentinels searching for minnows or crawfish or perched atop cattle. A favored spot for viewing these birds is at the rookery built by McIlHenny in the Jungle Gardens on Avery Island.

The **brown pelican** is the official state bird of Louisiana, which in turn is often called the "Pelican State." The pelican is one odd-looking bird. Adults are buff gray, stand about two feet tall, and have a large, scooplike bill. At one month old they use this bill to harvest five pounds of fish a day. In the 1950s colonies of over 5000 were reported on coastal islands, but by the mid-sixties the bird had disappeared from the state, a victim of pesticide runoff. The state seal adopted in 1902 shows a distinctly white pelican, but this was presumably artistic license and not a prophecy of a time when the whites would outnumber the browns. Brown pelican colonies are now being reestablished on Rockefeller Wildlife Refuge and Grand Terre with birds imported from Florida.

Fur Bearers: The wetlands of Cajun country support an enormous number of fur-bearing critters, from **otter** to **muskrat** and **nutria**. The Indians and the French trappers harvested large numbers of pelts. Although the fur-garment industry has taken it on the chin recently, there are still over 10,000 trappers who derive at least part of their livelihood from the sale of animal skins. Louisiana remains the top wild fur producer in the nation, harvesting more pelts during the 1980s than all of the Canadian provinces combined.

The nutria is the most unusual and plentiful of Louisiana's fur bearers, and one that will almost certainly be seen if you spend much time in the coastal marsh areas. They can even be seen sunning on the lakeside in front of the Governor's Mansion in Baton Rouge. The nutria is one in a long line of nuisance animals and plants which were introduced to Louisiana in the last hundred or so years. Brought to the state for experimental breeding by E.A. McIlhenny in the 1930s, it is actually an aquatic rodent that is native to South America, where it is called a *coypu*. It is a nine-pound cross between a beaver and a water rat, with huge, razor-sharp incisors and webbed hind feet for swimming.

From 13 pairs, McIlhenny's experimental group grew to an estimated 300 individuals before a hurricane loosed the entire population into the marshes of South Louisiana in 1940. By 1957 the shaggy footballs were so numerous that they were devouring acres of marshland and competing with the native muskrat. The legislature put out a 25-cent reward for each nutria and scored a bountiful take of 510,000 animals in less than a year. The bounty was removed in the sixties and the pelts (politely referred to as "Hudson Bay Beaver" in New York markets) became popular among furriers in the seventies. Louisiana's fur market has fallen on hard times and the nutria is again considered a pest by all except the alligator population, which loves to snack on them.

Fish and Shellfish: Possessing America's largest freshwater swamp, the drainage basin of the nation's largest river (sopping the runoff from two thirds of the country), and a thirty-mile-wide band of wetlands bordering on the Gulf of Mexico, it is not surprising that South Louisiana is home to an immense variety of aquatic and marine life. Although an aquarium was recently constructed in New Orleans, most people around Cajun Country still think about fish as something to either catch or eat (usually both). In fact, some assert that had the aquarium been constructed in Cajun Country, placards beside exhibits would have carried recipes rather than scientific names for each fish.

Louisiana produces a third of the nation's commercial fish catch and hosts nearly a quarter of the nation's marine recreational fishing activities (250,000 licensed recreational saltwater anglers). Among the most important commercial species are **shrimp, menhaden, crabs, oysters**, and **crawfish**—all categories in which Louisiana is a national leader. Favorites of recreational fishermen are **redfish, speckled trout, flounder, red snapper**, and **mackerel**. Freshwater anglers take their pick of **largemouth bass, bream, catfish,** and **crappie** (called *sac-a-lait* in Cajun Country).

If the alligator is the animal most closely associated with Cajun Country, it is closely followed by the **crawfish**. The crawfish, or "mudbug" as it is called locally, was elevated to star status and a major industry at the same time that the Cajun people were rediscovering a pride in their unique culture in the late fifties. For

Alligator and hide. (Courtesy of LA Department of Wildlife and Fisheries)

this reason it has been adopted by Cajuns as a symbol or mascot in a way the gator never was. Once considered a lowly critter eaten mainly by denizens of the Atchafalaya Basin, the crustaceans which resemble miniature lobsters were first commercially "farmed" in stocked ponds in 1959. It was not long before the tasty creatures had moved from camp tables and Basin-bars to restaurants across the region. In addition to the original Crawfish Festival in Breaux Bridge (the first weekend in April), Louisiana now celebrates the "mudbug" at an International Crawfish Tasting and Trade Show, an annual World Championship Etouffée Cook-off Contest, and dozens of other fairs and festivals. For more on eating crawfish read the Food chapter.

Crawfish is sometimes spelled, but never pronounced, "crayfish" in Cajun Country, where over twenty species exist in the wild. The two most popular food varieties are the Red Swamp and White River, which are harvested in profusion in the freshwater swamps of the Atchafalaya Basin. Crawfish are most active in the slow-moving freshwater swamps during warm weather. After breeding in April and May they generally leave the water and burrow in nearby mudflats, where they live two feet down until around October, when they seek water for their hatchlings. Thus, the crawfish season generally lasts from December until mid-June. During these months rice and soybean farmers flood their fields and harvest them with wire mesh traps. In early summer, fields are drained for planting and the crawfish burrow again, leaving towering mud castles over their subterranean homes. The crawfish industry now touches virtually every citizen of the small towns around the Basin and surrounding parishes where traps are made, bait is sold, boats are built and repaired, crawfish meat is processed, and the live ones are sold by the sack. Over 100 million pounds of crawfish are harvested in Louisiana each year, or almost 90 percent of the world's production!

A private zoo operator in Bayou Country once told me, "You just don't have a tourist attraction in South Louisiana without **alligators**." No other animal is more consistently associated with Cajuns than *Alligator mississippiensas*. It is difficult to find a movie filmed in the region where one of the protagonists is not wrestling, trapping, eating, or being eaten by one of the huge reptiles. Although a good number of people in this part of the country eat alligator, and a growing number trap them, it is strictly a figment of the Hollywood imagination that many people wrestle or are eaten by them. They are voracious predators, but seldom attack a human unless provoked. The American alligator is found through-

out Louisiana, with the greatest numbers living in coastal freshwater areas, where they seldom stray far from their nest (summer)
or underground den (winter). Alligators can grow to nearly twenty
feet long. The largest ever recorded in Louisiana was a 19-foot-long
gator observed in Vermilion Parish in January of 1890. In 1963,
with alligator populations dwindling, the reptile was temporarily
declared off limits for hunting and trapping. Populations recovered
by 1975 to the point where carefully regulated trapping was
permitted. Alligator trapping can be a very lucrative business for
the short fall season. During the summer months the alligator is
now ubiquitous in slow-moving freshwater areas of Cajun Country. (For information on alligator watching, see the Recreation
chapter).

5

The Economy:
Major Industrial and
Agricultural Products

Louisiana Oil and Gas Industry

Louisiana is the second leading producer of oil and natural gas in the nation. The industry is the backbone of the state's economy and has touched the lives of every individual in the predominantly agrarian Cajun Country. The first Louisiana oil well was "brought in" in 1901 shortly after oil was struck at the famous Spindletop gusher in Texas. In the year following that first strike at the Evangeline Field north of Jennings, 76 oil and gas companies began operating in the state. Unabated growth became a boom when the first offshore oil rig was brought in off the coast of Morgan City in 1947. Hundreds of companies moved their offshore offices to Lafayette.

In a state where anti-taxation sentiment is a religion, the oil and gas industry has pumped billions of dollars of lease and royalty income into health care, education, and capital improvement programs (not to mention politicians' pockets). Following the first oil strikes, major oil companies built refineries in Louisiana and thousands of support industry jobs followed. Airplane and helicopter mechanics and pilots, roustabouts, seamen, steel fabricators, engineers, surveyors, and countless other workers turn their labors to the extraction of oil in the state. In Cajun Country the cultural impact of the oil rush was severe. Oil tycoons and roustabouts from around the nation came to seek a share of the mineral wealth. Advanced programs in engineering and computer sciences were instituted at the University of Southwest Louisiana, but the oil boom lured many Cajun youth away from school and traditional pursuits to high-paying, unskilled labor.

The stage was set for disaster in Louisiana when world oil prices

47

Oil rig headed for the Gulf. (Courtesy of U.S. Army Corps of Engineers)

collapsed in the eighties. In 1982 crude oil averaged nearly $40 a barrel. By 1986 the price had fallen to $12.50. Royalty and lease income to the state withered from $624 million in 1982 to about $286 million in 1987. Funding for essential state programs disappeared and thousands of unskilled and uneducated laborers became unemployed. Lafayette and other industry hubs suffered bank closures whose numbers exceeded those of the Great Depression.

Although oil prices have rebounded some, the scars of an oil boom gone bust are still evident throughout Cajun Country in boarded-up businesses, flagging employment figures, lack of education, and general economic turmoil. With oil reserves as well as cash flow on the decline, folks are now examining more closely the benefits of extracting a nonrenewable resource from the earth and the social and environmental costs of that process (*see* section on Environmental Issues later in this chapter).

Petrochemical Industry

Louisiana's chemical industry is the fourth largest in the nation, and second to oil and gas in economic value to the state. In Cajun country, where most plants are located, chemical manufacture provides almost 20 percent of industrial employment. The greatest concentrations of plants are on the Mississippi River above New Orleans and the Calcasieu River around Lake Charles, where there is plenty of fresh water for processing and deepwater ports for shipping.

The growth of the chemical industry has earned the lower Mississippi Valley a reputation as the "Chemical Corridor," the "American Ruhr," and, more to the point, "Cancer Alley" (*see* section on Environmental Issues later in this chapter). Most of the companies use the state's plentiful oil resources to produce petrochemicals like polyvinylchloride (that's PVC for short), acetone, polytetrahydrofuran, and a wide array of solvents, starter chemicals, fertilizers, and bases. These chemicals are not generally converted to consumer products here, but are sold in bulk and shipped to other locations for processing and packaging. Anyone interested in the chemical industry should drive the Mississippi River Road, where they can see massive Vulcan, Dupont, and Hooker facilities and actually tour the plant at DOW (*see* the River Region chapter for details).

Plant and Animal Harvest

Seafood: Seafood, along with petroleum/natural gas and chemicals, is one of Louisiana's three major industries. The state pro-

Shrimpboat in the Gulf of Mexico. (Courtesy of U.S. Army Corps of Engineers)

duces a third of the nation's commercial fish catch, and leads the country in the harvest of shrimp, menhaden, crabs, oysters, and crawfish. Naturally the bulk of Louisiana's seafood is harvested from the estuaries and Gulf Coastal waters that fringe Cajun Country. Fishing has been a way of life for some Cajun communities for generations. It is perhaps the most picturesque of the state's leading industries. Shrimp boats with towering booms line narrow bayous, traps are stacked neatly in front yards, and crawfishermen can be seen from afar, reaping a solitary harvest from open rice ponds. Prizing independence and self-sufficiency, many Cajuns build their own boats and construct their own nets and traps.

Sugarcane: Louisiana is the top sugarcane-producing state, with over half of the nation's crop. Historically, sugarcane is probably the most important crop in Cajun Country. Just as oil and gas have wrought huge economic and social change in the twentieth century, sugarcane held sway in the nineteenth century. Prior to the War Between the States, sugarcane created vast wealth for a few Anglo and French planters, who decorated the landscape with magnificent plantation homes. Cane production in Louisiana is concentrated along the main bayous and rivers between New Orleans and Lafayette. The biggest and wealthiest planters were located along the Mississippi River Road, while others moved west to Bayous Lafourche and Teche. As they moved westward, Anglo planters displaced many Cajun landholders and created a distinct sugar culture that thrived on cheap labor. They levelled endless fields and planted green rows of cane, six feet wide, on the fertile alluvial soils.

Since Etienne de Boré, a Mississippi River Road planter, perfected a technique for granulating sugar in 1796, the growing and milling of cane have become highly mechanized processes. One machine now does the work of dozens of laborers. Where there were once thousands of mills, processing is now managed at fewer than thirty locations. Despite this change, row upon row of verdant cane still dominates the landscape of eastern Cajun Country, where over 15,000 workers are employed in the industry. Life moves to the pace of the planting and harvesting cycle and the small shacks of field hands and former cane cutters stand alongside grand plantation homes. In the fall the smoke of burning fields (the useless husks are burned off before the cane is loaded) and steaming mills cloud the sky, as trucks rumble through normally quiet towns like Jeanerette and Franklin.

Old Inger Superfund Site. (Photo by Julie Posner)

Cypress killed by saltwater intrusion. (Photo by Julie Posner)

Rice: Louisiana ranks third in the nation in rice production, with the largest amount grown on the Cajun Prairie between Lafayette and the Texas border. Although rice can survive without large amounts of water, it is usually grown in flooded fields in order to control weeds and pests. The level prairie, with its impervious clay subsoil, proved perfect for mechanical flooding and, in recent years, crawfish have been alternated with rice crops. The growth of the rice industry coincided with the western expansion of the railroad following the War Between the States. The major growers in the rice industry were not Cajuns, but people of mixed European descent. Germans, Danes, and Anglos were recruited from the Midwest by railroad men and land speculators to settle the open prairie. Most of the rail towns that stretch west from Lafayette are still rice towns and are marked by giant silos and driers. Many of these towns have a distinctly non-Cajun set of family names and a Victorian ambiance, reflecting early settlement patterns.

Cattle: The cattle industry in Louisiana predates that of neighboring Texas. In fact, the famous Texas longhorn originated in Louisiana. Early pioneers were allocated heads of beef to encourage settlement, and the first cattle drive in the United States is believed to have been along the Old Spanish Trail (roughly following the course of U.S. 90) in Southwest Louisiana. Folklorists have even traced some of the Western cattle songs (usually associated with Texas), with lines like "yippee-ki-yi," back to Cajun tunes with cries of "hipee-ti-yo." Among the unusual sights of Cajun Country are herds of hump-backed Brahmas (brought to the area for their resistance to insects) wandering unfenced on marshy pasture hemmed in by bayous. Along the coastal fringe, these unfenced herds are often tended by ranchers in small boats and brought to market by barge.

Environmental Issues

Louisiana's environment is suffering attacks from both the loss of land and damage to existing land, water, and atmosphere. Destruction and degradation of the environment in Cajun Country has become so severe as to concern not only residents and visitors to the area, but people throughout the nation. The wetlands of Cajun Country are among the most recent and the most rapidly disappearing soils in the country. Louisiana's coastline is disappearing at a rate of 45 to 60 square miles a year! In addition to that swept away in tropical storms, a large amount of marsh is simply subsiding, or sinking beneath the waters of the Gulf of

Mexico. The areas of greatest loss are the coastal wetlands between the Mississippi River below New Orleans and the Vermilion River south of Lafayette. In these areas, roads that were once above water are now submerged at high tide and bayou-side homes stand isolated on stilts.

Until 1984 Louisiana had no State Department of Environmental Quality. Oil and lumber interests exploring in the wetlands drilled, cut timber, and dug canals with little or no oversight. As ground cover was removed and new channels were created, erosion increased dramatically in the swamps and marshes, carrying valuable soil into the gulf. Places that were once narrow pipeline canals have become shallow ponds and lakes. The land loss has been rapid enough to confound the fishermen who rely on specific channels and landforms to navigate, as these landmarks often disappear from one season to the next. With the loss of land, saltwater encroaches further and destroys more natural land cover and habitat for animals like shrimp, crabs, and oysters that feed and breed in the marsh.

In addition to land loss, South Louisiana's oil and chemical industries have been pumping amazing amounts of toxic chemicals into the air, water, and land for most of a century. The state is now the nation's second leading toxic polluter (behind the vastly larger state of Texas). According to recent statistics (1988) published in New Orleans' *Times-Picayune*, Louisiana ranks first in surface water discharges, second in toxic underground injection, second in the discharge of known carcinogens, and fourth in toxic air discharges. The same data found the state to rank 48th in environmental programs. Damage through release of toxic chemicals is visible to the keen-eyed visitor in abandoned waste dumps, Superfund cleanup sites, and huge areas of swamp where cypress are devoid of foliage. Anyone taking a swamp tour below Houma or in the oilfields around Henderson in the Atchafalaya Basin will be struck by the miles of abandoned and rusting pipeline.

When royalty and lease income from South Louisiana's industry was paying all the bills for state services, there was little environmental outcry. Now that the halcyon days of oil exploration are over (onshore oil reserves peaked in the '70s), the state is realizing a staggering environmental price tag. The seafood industry is lamenting the loss of formerly productive fishing grounds, recreational sportsmen are decrying diminished takes, and even oil exploration companies are becoming involved in the fight to save the nation's most extensive wetlands area.

6

Food

Every country had its own 'Cajun cuisine,' a cuisine that depended on the local environment. We just happen to be the luckiest of people; nature gave us, when I think of our area, the greatest natural pantry God has given anyone.

Chef John Folse,
Lafitte's Landing Restaurant in Donaldsonville

In the mid-eighties, "Cajun" and "New Orleans-style" restaurants began cropping up all over the country, spurred by the success of Cajun chef Paul Prudhomme. Words like "Jambalaya," "Crawfish Pie," and "Filé Gumbo" became known as more than just lyrics to a popular song. Like the region's music, the best South Louisiana cuisine is still simmering around the plains and wetlands of Cajun Country, where cooks have access to a wondrous variety of fresh seafoods and tasty fresh and smoked meats. Where else can one find pungent smoked tasso and andouille sausage, rabbit and quail, alligator, crawfish, and large Gulf shrimp alongside fresh, uncut beef and pork at the market?

The mere presence of fine and exotic ingredients cannot explain the variety or far-flung abundance of great eateries in an area so rural. In Cajun Country food and music are integral parts and expressions of the regional culture. Nowhere else, except perhaps in New Orleans, is eating an experience of such intense and often ritualistic proportions. Folks spend a week talking about and anticipating a big feed, crawfish boil, or *boucherie*, but as soon as they are eating they begin discoursing on the last meal and the one to follow!

Splendid cooking and eating is an event, a celebration that needs no excuse. In fact, the food is often the object of celebrations. Be sure to consult the list of Fairs and Festivals in Acadiana and don't miss the opportunity to visit a small-town *boucherie* or harvest festival like the Opelousas Yambilee and Here's the Beef

Cookoff, Broussard Boudin Festival, Eunice Crawfish Etouffée Cookoff, or St. Martinville *Boucherie*. There are countless events where you can sample great food just as it is eaten in the homes of Acadiana.

The best dishes in many Cajun Country restaurants reflect traditions carried out on home dining tables for centuries. Fresh seafood is served on Fridays, fried fish and crawfish etouffée abound during the Lenten season, and hot gumbo or "duck camp stew" warms up chilly winter days. Around Mardi Gras you will likely find boudin sausage and hard-boiled eggs on the counter at cafes and bars out in the country, while Good Friday is universally celebrated with mounds of boiled crawfish. Throughout the year stews, rice dishes, and roasts and fowl stuffed with garlic or dressing are served at the humblest and grandest restaurants alike. Seek out the small cafes and lunchrooms and you will discover a variation in eats that goes far beyond the obvious seafood in coastal regions and crawfish on the Prairie. Houma is the only place you are likely to find the wonderful *tarte à la bouillie* confection. In Labadieville you will find Choupic Burgers, and in the heartland you will find barbecue basted with an oniony sauce. Try Steen's cane syrup (made in Abbeville) over morning biscuits with a dark cup of coffee. Visit the Steamboat Restaurant and get the traditional yams and gumbo. The variety is endless once you start to look and eat!

Cajun or Creole?

The food in Acadiana is often called "Cajun" or "Creole." With the growing popularity of Louisiana cuisine, these terms have often become confused. Both are French Louisiana-born but describe quite different preparations. Traditional **Cajun food** combines simple French country cooking with the whole realm of locally available ingredients such as bay leaves, filé powder, and cayenne peppers. It is a cuisine born of life close to the land, prepared by people who frequently did not have anything except for the abundance of their own fields or gardens. It is highly seasoned and spiced, often flavored with onion, sweet green peppers, and celery. Frequently these savory ingredients are slow-cooked in one large pot. Cajun food is not necessarily hot, but if a menu lists an item as such, be forewarned that by anyone else's standards it is probably a three-alarm dish!

Unlike Cajun food, **Creole cuisine** has its roots in the urban

Making sweet dough pies. (Photo by Julie Posner)

environments of New Orleans and the French and Spanish settlements of St. Martinville, New Iberia, and Opelousas. In this sense
Creole cuisine was the food of the wealthy, but it was often
prepared by black cooks who introduced their own recipes and
ideas. Creole dishes thus tend to be more complex and use a
broader variety of spices, herbs, and sauces than traditional Cajun
food.

Restaurant Guide

Many people will tell you they "have not eaten at a bad restaurant in Cajun Country." I wouldn't go that far, but there are an
improbable number of fine eateries for so small and sparsely
populated an area. A good rule of thumb is to eat simple fare at
the casual places and more elaborate and sauced preparations at
the upscale ones.

The following is a discussion of the different types of fantastic
regional eateries I have discovered in the cities, little towns, and
countryside of South Louisiana, as well as a list of my top favorites. The list is not meant to be complete, but represents places I
drive out of the way to visit. These are pinpointed on the map in
this chapter.

An effort has been made to establish meaningful and descriptive categories for use throughout the text, but many of the
fancier Cajun/Creole restaurants serve dishes that fall into several
categories, and some of the simpler places try their hand at more
complex dishes. All the restaurants listed here are reviewed along
with dozens of others in the regional chapters of this book. After
ten years of traveling in Cajun Country, I still find good new
places (that are not necessarily new) on almost every foray, so the
best advice is to be bold, go hungry, and eat a lot!

Restaurant Categories

Cajun/Down Home: If you want to eat the kind of country
cooking that Cajun and Creole people have enjoyed for centuries,
the best place to look is at humble diners and cafes listed in this
category. Sonny Prudhomme, Chef at Prudhomme's Cajun Cafe
in Carencro, put it this way: "Give me a good round or sevin steak
with potato salad or rice dressing, that's Cajun cooking. I got to
have that blue plate!" Tennessee has its loyalists among fans of
down-home cooking, but Cajun Country has got to be the Blue
Plate Capital of the world. You won't find any boring vegetable

Eating boiled crawfish. (Courtesy of LA Office of Tourism)

plates here, but mouthwatering stews, gravies, and gumbos seasoned like no other simple food you have ever eaten. These places are a real bargain, but many are only open at lunch; in fact, few serve dinner. For details consult reviews in the main text.

Cajun/Creole: Those restaurants we describe as Cajun/Creole serve food that is a combination of the two cuisines. These restaurants are not only among the finest in Cajun Country, but among the best anywhere. Their nationally and internationally recognized chefs marry regional ingredients with traditional Cajun, Creole, and classic French cooking to create simply incredible meals. You will find dishes such as crawfish fajitas, corn maque choux, Cajun caviar (made with choupic roe), Kahlua-grilled shrimp, and seafood-stuffed eggplant pirogues, in addition to the more typical etouffées, gumbos, and sauce piquantes. Some, like Joe's in Livonia and Prudhomme's Cajun Cafe in Carencro, are very moderately priced and offer a selection of hearty Cajun cooking at lunch. Others, like Vive la Différence, Lafitte's Landing, and Cafe Vermilionville qualify as splurges but also serve meals you will never forget. Cajun Country is determinedly casual; nothing fancier than clean sports clothes (long pants!) is required at any of these eateries, though men may want to wear a coat at dinner.

Seafood: Although most of the restaurants in all our categories serve seafood dishes, they also serve a large number of other regional foods. The restaurants we describe as seafood places specialize almost exclusively in salt- and freshwater fish and shellfish (boiled seafood spots are treated in a separate category). The most popular way to eat seafood in Cajun Country is fried, and for good reason—people down here really know how to fry! In case you are worried about turning your heart into a hockey puck, most of these places also serve excellent non-fried dishes. Not surprisingly, most of the restaurants recommended in this category are located along the coastal region. If the Coco Marina in Cocodrie were any closer to the Gulf, it would need an anchor. Black's and Dupuy's in Abbeville deserve special mention, as they serve mainly oysters or oyster preparations and rank as two of the best oyster bars in the world!

Boiled Crawfish and Crabs: Perhaps the most unique group of eateries in Cajun Country are places that specialize in fresh boiled crustaceans. In Cajun Country that usually means crawfish (for more on crawfish see the Flora and Fauna chapter). Crabs tend to be second-class citizens (even though Louisiana blue crabs are as good as any) which are mainly eaten in the late summer and fall when crawfish are not in season. For true crawfish lovers there is nothing like a simple, boiled "mudbug." The biggest and best crawfish never leave Cajun Country. Some of the crawfish you get at places like Hawk's (my personal favorite!) check in at seven to the pound and resemble small lobsters. They are piled on beer trays in steaming three- to four-pound mounds and carried piping hot from the kitchen. The most common seasonings are salt and cayenne (usually available in mild or hot).

Eating crawfish is easy once you get the knack and there are plenty of folks willing to give you pointers. The process is similar to eating boiled shrimp. Remove the head and peel the shell to get to the succulent tail meat. Once you get the hang of it they are actually easier than shrimp, as the meat may be pulled out with your teeth without peeling the whole thing.

While boiled crawfish are served at many of the finer restaurants in Cajun Country, the best are laid out at rustic seafood patios or "boiling points," as the serious boiled seafood spots are known. These are places with cement or plank floors and wooden chairs and tables covered with paper or plastic. A true mark of the old-fashioned boiling point is a sink in the dining area where you can wash your hands without, or before, entering the restrooms. Many crawfish patios are located way out in the country, so getting there can be half the fun. Just remember that crawfish (and most crawfish restaurants) are seasonal, usually open between January and mid-June.

Local Faves: The places in this category don't necessarily serve traditional Louisiana cuisine, but are local favorites you wouldn't find anywhere else. They range from old thirties roadhouses like Chester's, which specializes in pre-fast-food-outlet-style fried chicken and froglegs, to the glitzy Charly G's grill in Lafayette. Want a "Cajun pizza?" Try Deano's "Cajun Executioner!"

Meat Markets: It is hard to drive ten miles in Cajun Country without coming across a market, gas station, or grocery selling boudin and cracklins. Many small meat markets do their own slaughtering, cutting, smoking, and stuffing. They serve up a variety of goods found nowhere else: boudin, tasso, paunce, andouille, hog's head cheese, cracklins (fried morsels of pork fat, often with a strip of meat attached), garlic sausage, and beef jerky. Whether you are looking for a quick snack of seafood boudin, some beef jerky to nibble on while driving, hiking, or camping, or something to take home and cook, the meat markets of Cajun Country offer a variable bounty.

Surely the most popular meat item is a rice sausage known as boudin. The proper way to see Cajun Country is with a link of boudin in one hand and a cold beer in the other. Whenever I drive through Cajun Country, I take a cooler to pack with smoked meats and a glove compartment full of paper towels to clean up after hasty boudin stops.

The variety of meat preparations across Cajun Country is incredible. When I asked folklorist Barry Ancelet where the best meat markets were, he astutely advised, "The best boudin is always less than five miles from where you live!" In Dr. Ancelet's case this meant the Best Stop Grocery in Scott, where we had steaming links with a livery flavor. Boudin varies from livery (heavy on the giblets) around the Lafayette area, to spicy with plenty of lean pork in Sunset, Opelousas, and especially at Johnson's Meat Market in Eunice. South of Lafayette there are still markets selling boudin rouge, or blood sausage.

Regional differences in meats are not limited to boudin. The classic andouille sausage in LaPlace is made only with very lean and large chunks of pork, while in Opelousas it is made with chitterlings. The Prairie is the "smoke belt," whereas further south a fine variety of fresh meats and sausages dominate meat market shelves. Hebert's in Maurice and a few others in the south specialize in whole/deboned stuffed chickens, and stuffed chops. The list here will be a general guide, but don't hesitate to get a link of boudin at the gas station wherever you happen to fill the tank.

Food in Cajun Country

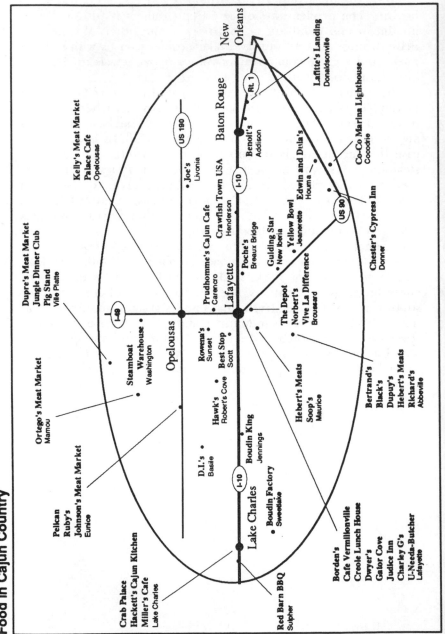

Restaurants Map.

Restaurant	Style	City	Cost	Comments
Benoit's	Meat Market	Addis	$	Cajun beef jerky
Bertrand's	Seafood	Abbeville	$$	Grilled oysters, view
Best Stop	Meat Market	Scott	$	Boudin, smoked boudin
Black's	Seafood	Abbeville	$ to $$	Oysters/seasonal
Borden's Ice Cream	Local Fave	Lafayette	$	Freezes and frappes
Boudin Factory	Cajun/Downhome	Sweetlake	$	Barbecue, plate lunches
Boudin King	Local Fave	Jennings	$	Fried chicken, gumbo
Cafe Vormilionville	Cajun/Creole	Lafayette	$$$	Seafoods and soups
Charly G's	Local Fave	Lafayette	$$$	Grilled seafood, salads
Chester's Cypress Inn	Local Fave	Donner	$$	Fried chicken, frog legs
Co-Co Marina Lighthouse	Seafood	Cocodrie	$$	Great view, great food
Crab Palace	Crawfish/Crabs	Lake Charles	$ to $$	Family style
Crawfishtown USA	Crawfish/Crabs	Henderson	$$	Family style
Creole Lunch House	Cajun/Downhome	Lafayette	$	Stuffed bread, soul food
D.I.'s Restaurant	Crawfish/Crabs	Basile	$$	Family style
Dupre's Grocery	Meat Market	Ville Platte	$	Cracklin's and boudin
Dupuy's	Seafood	Abbeville	$ to $$	Oysters/seasonal
Dwyer's	Cajun/Downhome	Lafayette	$	Hub City lunch favorite
Edwin and Dula's	Seafood	Houma	$ to $$	Stuffed potato, crawfish
Gator Cove	Crawfish/Crabs	Lafayette	$$	Family style
Guiding Star	Crawfish/Crabs	New Iberia	$$	Newspaper tablecloths
Hackett's Cajun Kitchen	Meat Market	Lake Charles	$	Smoked boudin, lunch
Hawk's	Crawfish/Crabs	Robert's Cove	$$	Best crawfish!/seasonal
Hebert's	Meat Market	Maurice	$	Deboned stuffed chickens
Hebert's	Meat Market	Abbeville	$	Boudin rouge
Joe's	Cajun/Creole	Livonia	$ to $$	Superb food and value
Johnson's	Meat Market	Eunice	$	World's best boudin
Judice Inn	Local Fave	Lafayette	$	"No two alike" burgers
Jungle Dinner Club	Crawfish/Crabs	Ville Platte	$$	Unique--flavored crawfish
Kelly's	Meat Market	Opelousas	$	Boudin, lunch
Lafitte's Landing	Cajun/Creole	Donaldsonville	$$$	Upscale & unforgettable
Miller's Cafe	Cajun/Downhome	Lake Charles	$	BBQ, Sweet Dough Pie
Norbert's	Cajun/Downhome	Broussard	$	Soulful plate lunch
Ortego's	Meat Market	Mamou	$	Tasso
Palace Cafe	Cajun/Downhome	Opelousas	$	Fried Chicken Salad
Pelican	Cajun/Downhome	Eunice	$	Sunday lunch spectacular
Pig Stand	Cajun/Downhome	Ville Platte	$	BBQ & plate lunch/dinner
Poche's	Meat Market	Breaux Bridge	$	Cracklin's near I-10
Prudhomme's Cajun Cafe	Cajun/Creole	Carencro	$ to $$	Great food! Great value!
Red Barn BBQ	Local Fave	Sulpher	$	"All U Can Eat" BBQ lunch
Richard's	Crawfish/Crabs	Abbeville	$$	Old place on river
Rowena's	Meat Market	Sunset	$	Meaty boudin
Ruby's	Cajun/Downhome	Eunice	$	Plate lunch central
Soop's	Cajun/Downhome	Maurice	$ to $$	Stews, gumbos and lunch
Steamboat Warehouse	Cajun/Creole	Washington	$$	Sweet potato and gumbo
The Depot	Cajun/Downhome	Broussard	$	Fabulous lunch buffet
U-Needa-Butcher	Meat Market	Lafayette	$	World's best cracklin's
Vive La Différence	Cajun/Creole	Broussard	$$$	Full meal, set price
Yellow Bowl	Seafood	Jeanerette	$$ to $$$	Crawfish specialties

Restaurants Chart.

Food Glossary

Andouille (say, *and-DO-we*) is a spicy (but not usually hot) smoked sausage which is usually stuffed with large pieces of lean pork. The Mississippi River Region between LaPlace (Andouille Capital of the World) and Gramercy is famous for andouille so lean you can slice it off and eat it as a snack, though most people use it for flavoring chicken or seafood gumbos. At several places around the Carencro and Opelousas area north of Lafayette you will find a "poor man's andouille" that is stuffed with spices and small bits of chitterlings.

Crawfish Bisque (pronounced *bisk*) is a rich, roux-based crawfish soup filled with sweet crawfish tail meat, often served with a bowl of rice on the side which you may add to taste. The treasured morsel in crawfish bisque is a crawfish shell stuffed with chopped crawfish meat, herbs, and breadcrumbs which rests at the bottom of the bowl and soaks up the flavor of the soup. Nowadays some places substitute a crawfish *boulette* for the stuffed shell.

A **boucherie** (pronounced *boo-share-REE*) is the traditional slaughtering and preparing of a hog, where the hard work offered by many neighbors is rewarded by generous samplings of cracklins, backbone stew, *cochon de lait* (suckling pig), and other products of the day's labor. Before refrigeration a *boucherie* was not only a social event but a means of distributing the meat to avoid spoilage. Each family with an animal for slaughter would take turns hosting the event. Refrigeration and modern slaughterhouses have removed the need for such gatherings, but they still continue as social events, accompanied by music and cold beer.

Boudin (*BOO-dan*) is a rich and well-seasoned rice and pork sausage which sometimes includes varying amounts of giblets. Boudin is sold precooked and still warm at thousands of places in Cajun Country. To eat boudin, cut the link in half and squeeze the stuffing out of its casing right into your mouth. These links are so popular that it has been said a seven-course Cajun meal is a six pack of beer and a pound of boudin. You can find boudin at meat markets or just about anywhere else! If you don't like it one place, try another, as there is a wide variety of preparations, including the newfangled "crawfish boudin" and "seafood boudin," which have no meat. For the brave there is the traditional "boudin rouge" or blood sausage (made just as the name suggests). I have seen signs advertising "Rubber Boots, Hardware, Boudin" and others proclaiming "Fishing Tackle, Bait, Kerosene, Boudin," but the best places to get boudin are little meat markets, where it is made fresh every morning.

Boulette (*BOO-let*) is a ball-shaped fritter similar to a hush puppy, but usually seasoned with onion and pepper and often spiked with tender crawfish tails.

Chaudin (*SHOW-dan*) is basically the same as paunce, only made with pork stomach.

Cracklins, also known as Gratons, are fried strips of pork skin which often have thin strips of meat and fat attached. This is not exactly health food, but it is one heck of a great snack if properly seasoned and consumed with a cold beverage. Hey, George Bush likes the stuff. How can you go wrong?

Crawfish Etouffée (pronounced *eh-two-FAY*) is a dish in which the peeled crawfish tails are smothered in a stew of fresh chopped peppers, onions, and garlic which have been simmered in butter. There are hundreds of variations served in homes and restaurants around Cajun Country. Some have tomato in the stew. Some are thickened with butter, while others add a roux or corn starch to bind them. The best versions of this dish use the crawfish fat for extra richness and flavor.

The terms "**Dirty Rice**" or "**Rice Dressing**" refer to the same dish, which is made from a blend of rice cooked in broth, chopped chicken giblets, and sometimes bits of pork.

Filé (pronounced *FEE-lay*) is a seasoning and thickening agent made from ground sassafrass leaves and used in gumbos. The ingredient was introduced to the French by local Indian tribes. It is only added at the end of the cooking process and may be found on many restaurant tables. It is not used as often in seafood gumbos as in chicken, sausage, or wild game varieties. Just shake a bit into your bowl and stir it in.

Gumbo is a Cajun/Creole dish of epic stature. The term is so evocative it is used to describe music, art, people, and just about anything else that can have a rich blend of ethnic ingredients. From immigrants of African descent came the name and the use of okra (a popular thickening agent), the French gave the dish a roux and delicate seasonings, local Indians contributed the filé and hot peppers, and Acadians hunted the wild game or seafood that became the object of each soup. The end result is a soup that warms the whole body, starting with the palate and ending with the soul. There are an endless variety of gumbos served in Louisiana, their recipes guided more by what is "on hand" than any hard-and-fast rules. Among the most popular are Chicken and Andouille (or other smoked sausage), Shrimp and Crab, and basic Seafood Gumbo.

Jambalaya (pronounced *jum-buh-LIE-uh*) is a poor boy's dish of South Louisiana origin. In a traditional jambalaya, chicken, sausage, ham, and chopped vegetables are cooked and added with seasonings and liquid to an iron pot full of rice. Like gumbo, the ingredients to jambalaya depend only on what the chef has on his shelf. Some glamorous versions include shrimp or crab meat. Accomplished chefs sometimes add all the partially cooked ingredients to the pot before starting the rice, but most now cook them separately. At the last minute the rice and other ingredients are combined, stirred, and allowed to finish over a low flame.

Maque Choux (pronounced *mock-shoo*) is a corn dish that varies in consistency from a stew to a chowder or soup. It always contains corn and frequently features tomato and bits of caramelized onion, tomato, and cayenne pepper.

Pain Perdue is called "lost bread" in New Orleans and French toast just about everywhere else. In Louisiana it is most often made with leftover French bread, which gives the toast a firmer and richer flavor.

Paunce is stuffed calf stomach. It may be smoked or simply fresh and ready to cook in the oven.

A **Po-boy** is a New Orleans-style sandwich made on crusty French bread. The best Cajun Country varieties come stuffed with fresh fried seafood.

Roux (pronounced *roo*) is flour browned in butter or oil which may be used as a thickening, coloring, and flavoring agent in pot food like stews and gumbos.

Sauce Piquant (*pee-CAHNT*) can be made in many ways with any number of central ingredients from alligator to chicken or tasso. The common characteristic of these varieties is a fiery hot reddish gravy.

Tasso is a lean, smoked seasoning meat quite similar to beef jerky, only more highly spiced, more moist, and usually cut into thick ropes. It may be made from either pork or beef. Tasso is typically used to flavor pot food, but is sometimes sliced thin and cooked in a sauce to be served on rice or pasta.

Yam is the popular name for the bright orange and golden sweet potatoes grown mainly around Opelousas.

7

Music

Be it Cajun, Zydeco, or Swamp Pop, the native music of Acadiana is the antithesis of the planned-out, self-conscious, commercial pap piped onto TV screens at urban discos and rock clubs. It is the music of working people, young and old, who love to dance and have a special knack for having fun.

The most astonishing thing about the traditional music of Cajun Country is how vibrant and how much a part of life it continues to be. Finding great regional music in Acadiana is almost as simple as rolling down the car window or spinning the dial on the radio. On weekends music pours from aging dance halls and bars in tiny Prairie towns like Lewisburg, Basile, and Mamou. It is played at festivals, Cajun restaurants, and church socials where the entire family can come and dance. It can even be heard in a smattering of country bars at nine o'clock in the morning on Saturdays! While a few Cajun and Zydeco artists have gained acclaim through Grammy nominations and club perform-ances outside the state, the vast majority never leave the flat-pan Cajun Prairie where their records, recorded for tiny regional record labels, are played on radio and jukeboxes.

Cajun Music

Despite its current popularity, Cajun music has evolved through some lean years. Around the turn of the century Cajun was a predominantly fiddle-based music played at house dances (*bals de maison*) and *fais-do-dos* (named for the separate room where chil-dren could be rocked to sleep). In the early 1900s, the diatonic accordion was adopted and by the thirties the music began to move out of homes and into dance halls and bars.

Traditional Cajun music suffered its first major blow at this time, when popular swing and country styles heard on the radio supplanted the older styles. The accordion was abandoned in favor of electric and steel guitars. In the late forties accordion-

Front-porch musicians in Opelousas. (Photo by Julie Posner)

based music enjoyed a brief renaissance, spurred by Cajun hero Iry Lejeune. The boom was short-lived, however, as the banning of French in public schools, the oil boom, and improved roads and communication began to take a toll on traditional Cajun folkways. By the Eisenhower era "Cajun" had become a mainly deprecatory term and the music, like the Cajun-French language, was shunned by socially conscious Cajuns and non-Cajuns alike.

The flowering of Cajun music in the past 25 years can be attributed to many influences: folklorists who brought artists like Dewey Balfa before a national audience, stubbornly independent Cajun record men, the Council for the Development of French in Louisiana, and the musicians who never gave up. Due to the efforts of these people, the music can now be heard in a wide variety of styles and venues. Whether it is a fiddle and squeeze-box waltz, pounding piano-accordion rock, or pedal-steel swing, Cajun music is still dance music made by working people who play as hard as (perhaps harder than) they labor.

Old-Style Cajun Dance Halls

Many of the dance halls and dance hall traditions of the '40s and '50s survived the lean years and are alive for anyone willing to look off the beaten path. Halls like Borque's and Guidry's in Lewisburg or Snook's in Ville Platte maintain bars separate from the dance area. There is no charge to sit at the bar or listen from the open windows that look onto the dance floor, but a dollar admission is charged to get into the low-slung dance area. Smiley's Bayou Club in Erath has its own variation on this tradition. Admission is free, but if you want to dance you first pay a dollar and the waitress then staples a red dance-ticket to the shirt collar. Men are the only ones required to buy tickets, but a sign over the bar cautions, "No same-sex dancers!" Because the music is played for dancing it is rare for anyone to applaud; appreciation is shown on the dance floor, where waltzes and two-steps are most popular.

Cajun Music for the Family

One important ingredient in the revival of Cajun music has been the growth of places where the whole family can go to dance and hear the music. During the '30s and '40s bars and dance halls which barred minors began to supplant house parties and fais-do-do's as the main site for Cajun dances. In 1974 CODIFIL sponsored the first annual Tribute to Cajun Music Festival. Since that time

The late Cleveland and Clifton Chenier. (Courtesy of Ann Savoy)

the Festivals Acadiens in Lafayette and the Zydeco Festival in Plaisance have become the two biggest music events of the year in Cajun Country, offering a chance for young and old to enjoy great regional music. Most of the other harvest and food festivals in small towns around Acadiana have also begun featuring Cajun and Zydeco bands.

Cajun music can also be heard at new restaurant/dance halls like the world-famous Mulate's in Breaux Bridge, D.I.'s in Basile, and Lurcy's in Elton. These places have found clientele among locals and visiting tourists who are looking for a place to hear Cajun music and take the kids. One great thing about the restaurant dance halls is that they often have music on weeknights. Surely the biggest regular Cajun music events directed at the entire family are the Saturday night *Cajun Roundez Vous* broadcast from the Liberty Theater in Eunice which begins at a convenient 6 P.M. (not to be missed!) and the daily shows at Vermilionville theme park in Lafayette. More adventuresome families should try visiting out-of-the-way spots such as Toby's in Opelousas.

Zydeco Music

If you want to have fun you got to go way out in the country to the Zydeco.

Clarence ("Bon Ton") Garlow
from "Bon Ton Roule," 1950

You no longer need to go to Cajun Country at all to hear the highly rhythmic dance music of South Louisiana's black Creole population. Still, when you pull up behind the strip of cars and pickups lining a narrow blacktop and hear the grating of the rubboard or sound of an accordion drifting from the open door of a hunkering old hall like Levi's in Abbeville, you will know why Clarence Garlow directed everyone "way out in the country to the Zydeco." There is no place like the sprawling dance halls and ramshackle bars of South Louisiana to catch a big Zydeco dance.

Although several Creole musicians recorded in the 1920s and 1930s (in a style quite similar to Cajun musicians of the era), Zydeco music did not become a commercial entity until the years following World War II. Until that time Zydeco, like Cajun music, was played mainly at house parties and community social events across the countryside. The word "Zydeco" is believed to be phonetically derived from the French words *les haricot*, which were used in an old French blues song popularized by Clifton Chenier,

"*Les Haricot Sont Pas Salés,*" translated as, "The snap beans have no salt." The song was about times so hard that there was no seasoning meat for the pot. Like Cajun music, Zydeco has evolved since the early days, moving from house parties to dance halls and bars and adopting such non-traditional instruments as the saxophone, electric guitar, bass, and drums. If anything the Zydeco scene today is even more vibrant than its Cajun counterpart. The success of Rockin' Sidney with his quasi-Zydeco national hit, "My Toot Toot," and the adulation heaped on the late Clifton Chenier have made the music attractive to a new generation of musicians. These youngsters have brought new ideas to Zydeco while maintaining its pounding Afro-Caribbean dance groove. Today the fiddle is seldom heard, as most songs are powered by a piano-style accordion and rasping *frottoir*, or rubboard. The rubboard is easily the most distinctive instrument in Zydeco music and a source of much of its energy. Fashioned after the old corrugated washboards, they are crafted in sheet-metal shops with curved metal shoulder straps. The rubboard hangs down over the chest and leaves both hands free to strike and scrape the surface with bottle openers.

In a region that has changed remarkably little in the last twenty-five years, Zydeco dance halls still dot the countryside and clubs featuring Zydeco can be found in many towns. Today's dance halls maintain strong ties to the community; when you first walk into a dance you are more likely to feel like you have entered a big house party than a nightclub. Halls like PaPa Paul's in Mamou and Hamilton's in Lafayette are holdovers from an earlier era and are operated by the same families that ran them thirty or more years ago. Often the proprietors live adjacent to the hall and maintain barbecue pits out back that serve up spicy chops or chicken while the band plays. I remember the first dance I went to at PaPa Paul's; by the time Marcel Dugas had finished his set, the smoke from PaPa's Barbecue next door was literally wafting into the dance hall. Admission to a big dance is usually $4 or $5 and most places roll out the welcome mat to "outsiders." Just remember that a big dance is often a special occasion and folks tend to dress up just a little bit (clean sports clothes or nice denims are okay), and remember the best way to show your appreciation is to get up and dance!

Swamp Pop

Although Swamp Pop artists have sold millions of records (far surpassing their Cajun and Zydeco counterparts), Swamp Pop remains the least recognized and respected of South Louisiana's indigenous musics. Swamp Pop is a new term used to describe the distinctive South Louisiana rock-and-roll ballad style popularized in the late fifties and early sixties. The music is a blend of New Orleans R&B, Country, and Gulf Coast Blues sung with a Cajun French accent. Between 1959 and 1963 over fifteen of these distinctive records climbed onto the Billboard Top 100, while hundreds of others filled jukeboxes and radio playlists across the Gulf South. Although the name "Swamp Pop" may be unfamiliar to many, hits like "Mathilda," by Cookie and the Cupcakes; "This Should Go On Forever," by Rod Bernard; "Sea Of Love," by Phil Phillips; "I'm Leaving It Up To You," by Dale and Grace; and "Sweet Dreams," by Tommy McLain, remain some of the best-loved songs of the rock-and-roll era.

Incredibly, many of the great singers and musicians of Swamp Pop are still making music in the obscurity of the Lafayette and Lake Charles lounge scenes. In motel lounges and hideaway bars, artists like Warren Storm, Tommy McLain, Charles Mann, T.K. Hulin, and Willie Tee are still performing their own songs and country hits in front of packed dance floors. These are among the true unsung heroes of South Louisiana music, plugging away five to six nights a week in smoky bars while people rub bellies on the dance floor. This is music to jitterbug and clutch to. Although songs like "Mathilda" have become veritable Cajun anthems, there is no new generation picking up the Swamp Pop torch. If you get the opportunity be sure to see one of these fine singers; they are the last of a breed.

Music Guide

Although there are hundreds of places to hear South Louisiana music in Cajun Country, finding and getting to a dance still poses a problem for the casual tourist. First, many dance halls have truly inscrutable locations. Some, like the Double D Cotton Club in Parks, Borque's in Lewisburg, and Caffery's Ranch in Au Large, are located in towns that do not even appear on some state maps!

During the Lenten season (between Mardi Gras and Easter), entertainment in this predominantly Catholic region comes to a near halt. At other times traditional dances (Zydeco and Cajun) are usually held on weekends because most of the musicians and clientele are working people with demanding day jobs. There are quite a few Cajun dances held on Sunday afternoon or early evening. Zydeco dances tend to be less predictable than Cajun ones. Some Zydeco dance halls only have music one weekend a month, and switch between Friday and Saturday night. The saddest fact impacting the search for a traditional dance is the fact that many of the venerable old halls are closing down. The Evangeline, The Bon Ton Roule, and dozens of others have packed it in over the past ten years. During the writing of this text two of the best music spots, The Blue Goose Lounge in Eunice and Champagne's Grocery near Lafayette, closed their doors. Times are just as hard at newer venues.

Despite the difficulties, there is a bounty of music out there for the listening. The Music Map and accompanying chart in this chapter list the best places to hear traditional South Louisiana music. These and dozens of other locales are reviewed in the main text, with phone numbers (it is highly recommended that you call to verify times and days of music!), addresses, and directions on how to get to them. The object here is to depict where the different types of music can be heard during a typical week and how easy it is to find music by simply making a short drive into the countryside. Although the map is not to scale, it will hopefully show that there are many music spots distributed throughout Cajun Country that will be just a short drive from where you are staying.

South Louisiana Music Meccas

Record Stores & Studios of Cajun Country: Remember the days when you could walk into a record store, pick out a forty-five, and listen to it before you bought it? How many people remember when records were sold from TV repair shops, instrument stores, and retail outlets tacked onto the front of primitive recording studios? For those who do remember, South Louisiana will offer a step into the past.

Since the late forties a handful of stubbornly independent local "record men" (producers, distributors, and retailers) have catered to the musicians and music fans of Acadiana from little shops and studios. The continued operation of four of these homegrown enterprises (within a 150-square-mile area!) in an era dominated by huge record companies, MTV, and mass marketing speaks volumes about the special nature of the regional music scene. Although all of these tiny companies have had a glimmer of national success, it is the recording and sales of records never distributed outside of the region that has sustained them. South Louisiana is still an area where strictly local records get played on

Music in Cajun Country

Music Map.

Venue	Music	City	Comments
A'Bear's Cafe	Cajun	Houma	Cajun & all-u-can-eat catfish on Fri.
Belizaire's	Cajun	Crowley	Family dine & dance, Wed.--Sun.
Bourque's Club	Cajun	Opelousas	Old Time Dance on Sat. night
Caffery's Alexandria Ranch	Zydeco	Breaux Bridge	Outdoor screened-in dance pavillion
Clifton's Club	Zydeco	Loreauville	Huge dance hall
D.I.'s Restaurant	Cajun	Basile	Family Dine & Dance on Tues.
Davis Lounge	Zydeco	Cecilia	Old Time dance hall
Double D Cotton Club	Zydeco	Parks	Old wood frame and floor hall
Dup's	Cajun	Eunice	Old bar, Sat. a.m. radio broadcast
El Sido's	Zydeco	Lafayette	Urban hall, dance most Fri.--Sun.
Fred's Lounge	Cajun	Mamou	Famous broadcast, Sat. a.m. since 1957
Frenchmen's Wilderness Cpgd	Cajun	Butte La Rose	Saturday, 8 p.m.
Friendly Lounge	Zydeco	Cecilia	Old dance hall
Gilton's Lounge	Zydeco	Eunice	New hall, biggest in state
Guidry's Friendly Lounge	Cajun	Opelousas	Wonderful old--time dance, 5 p.m. Sun.
Hamilton's	Zydeco	Lafayette	Old wood hall, great vibes
Harold's	Cajun	Duson	Pool hall, dance hall, Sat. 8 p.m.
Harris's	Cajun	Hayes	Wednesday--Saturday
Harry's Lounge	Cajun	Breaux Bridge	Sunday, 5 p.m.
Kaiser's Place	Cajun	Breaux Bridge	Old Time Dance hall, Sat. 10 a.m.
La Poussiere	Cajun	Breaux Bridge	Saturday, 8 p.m.
Lakeview Campground	Cajun	Eunice	Tavern & dance hall, Sat. 8 p.m.
Levy's Place	Zydeco	Abbeville	Funky & way out in the country
Liberty Theatre	Cajun	Eunice	Big event! 6 p.m. Sat. broadcast
Lloyd's Lounge	Cajun	Lake Charles	Western-style saloon & hall
Lurcy's Restaurant	Cajun	Elton	Small dance & dine, Mon. & Fri. 7 p.m.
Mulate's	Cajun	Breaux Bridge	Dance & Dine, 7 days, lunch & dinner
Offshore Lounge	Zydeco	Lawtell	Thur. night jam, Roy Carrier's place
Papa Paul's	Zydeco	Mamou	Way out in the country! Fri.--Sun.
Ponderosa Lounge	Zydeco	Abbeville	Rough and tumble urban hall
Prejean's	Cajun	Lafayette	Family dine & dance, 7 nights
Rainbeaux Club	Cajun	New Iberia	Big hall, Cajun Sat. 8 p.m.;Ctry. Sun. 4 p.m.
Richard's Lounge	Zydeco	Lawtell	Big old hall, big name performers
Savoy's Music Shop	Cajun	Eunice	Front--porch--style jam 10 a.m. Sat.
Slim's Y Ki Ki	Zydeco	Opelousas	Big old hall, big name acts
Smiley's Bayou Club	Cajun	Erath	Old club, Fri. 7 p.m.;Sat. 9 p.m.;Sun. 2 p.m.
Smiley's Bon Amie	Cajun	Delcambre	Big hall, Cajun Sun. 6 p.m;Ctry. Sat 9 p.m.
Thibodeaux's	Zydeco	Lake Charles	Unusual old two-story hall
Toby's Little Lodge	Cajun	Opelousas	Wed.--Sat., Cajun Thur.
Vallot's	Zydeco	Abbeville	Rough & tumble urban Zydeco
VFW	Cajun	Lake Arthur	Public dance Sat. 8 p.m., Sun. 2 p.m.
VFW	Cajun	Lake Charles	Public dance Sat. 8 p.m.
Yesterday's Gateway	Other	Lafayette	Swamp Pop lounge

Music Chart.

Live radio broadcast from Church Point. (Photo by Julie Posner)

the radio and there is still such a thing as a "regional hit record" or a "jukebox hit."

Most South Louisiana record men do mail-order business, but a real treat awaits those who make the pilgrimage to visit the storefronts that invariably adjoin small studios or offices. Not only do these places offer a chance to find recordings unavailable anyplace else in the world, they often afford the opportunity to meet and chat with the enterprising men who have helped make forty years of South Louisiana music. Like the pot-bellied stoves in country stores, the counters at these shops are often pulpits for bull sessions, but of a musical nature. There is usually a stereo available to play any of the obscure goodies you find, and you are likely to get a dose of gossip on how the record was made (and how drunk the musicians were at the time). Guys like Eddie Shuler, who operates Goldband Records out of his Quick Service TV Repair Shop, can tell you about legendary musicians like Iry LeJeune or Cleveland Crochet. Jay Miller at Modern Music in Crowley will recall early recording sessions with Clifton Chenier, or you can go to Ville Platte and talk to Floyd Soileau about the year he had two records in the Billboard Top Twenty! A visit to one or all of these stores is essential for the fan of South Louisiana music.

Cajun and Zydeco Radio Shows: While DJ's elsewhere in the nation are bound to rigid playlists, many shows in Cajun Country cater to the distinctive local populace. Regional hits are still made on the power of radio shows beaming locally produced records across the Prairie. Many shows are broadcast entirely in French, with only nonconforming words like "McDonald's," "Ford," and "rock and roll" popping out in English. Most interesting are the live broadcasts from dance halls (listed on the music chart in this chapter). The best time to tune in a French or Zydeco broadcast is on Saturday morning, but there are shows throughout the week. If you are trying to find out who is playing at a particular club and can not reach the club owner, try calling a local D.J. The biggest Cajun and Zydeco broadcasts are listed with times, phone numbers, and dial positions in the appendices to this book.

8

Recreation

Swamp Tours

The most exotic of Cajun Country's sights are its freshwater swamps. To visit South Louisiana and not get a close-up view of its wetlands is like staying in a camp on the rim of the Grand Canyon and not looking out the window! Over a dozen tour companies now offer inexpensive excursions into places where you will find a profusion of jungle life such as alligators, nutria, snakes, turtles, and all manner of creatures that are equally comfortable on land or water. In the deeper swamp, where palmetto and muscadine vines darken shadows beneath ancient cypress trees, one can hear the questioning call of horned owls and the cry of an eagle. Cypress knees touch tendrils of hanging moss. The turn of a bayou can display miles of bristling marsh or an open lake studded with cypress stumps and carpeted with American lotus blossoms.

The best swamp tours not only offer a glimpse into a flowering wilderness, but also provide an insight into the history and people who make a living in Louisiana's wetlands. Ancient cypress mills stand abandoned in thickets of rosemallow and muscadine, old fishing vessels are sunk in the muck, while nearby oil platforms and fishermen extract the bounty of the swamp. In some places you may see the vestiges of once thriving swamp communities and pass the camps and houseboats of trappers, fishermen, and other part-time swamp dwellers. Most of the men who will guide you into the wetlands come from families who have lived by or in the swamps for generations. They are often people who hunt, fish, or trap for a living and really seem to enjoy sharing their knowledge with visitors.

Each tour offers something different depending on the guide, type of boat, and particular route. Many are aimed at families and tour buses. These tours glide through bayous and lakes on big, covered pontoon boats. A few tour operators offer trips for the more adventurous, using airboats (small, flat-bottomed craft powered by car engines equipped with airplane propellers) and specially designed swamp boats. These unique craft can access regions impassable by larger boats, and get there fast. Many tours engage in the questionable practice of feeding alligators chunks of chicken, doughnuts, or even marshmallows. The way I see it, if God had meant for alligators to eat marshmallows, he would have given them coat hangers to toast 'em on. In case you really want to see gators eat, those tours which feed them have been noted.

When to Go: What you see in the swamps depends largely on what time of day and what season you visit. A few tours offer flexible departure times. These are recommended, as they will allow you to leave in the especially serene morning and evening hours. If you are looking for alligators, any warm-weather month should do. Late fall and late spring are ideal times for viewing migratory birds. Something is always blooming except in the cold months of December through February. In March you will see wild iris, spider lilies, and dogwoods. By early spring millions of hyacinth blossoms begin to choke off smaller waterways. In midsummer the towering stalks of American lotus produce gigantic yellow blossoms.

Remember, even if a tour operator offers regularly scheduled excursions, it is always recommended to CALL FIRST! High water, weather conditions, or the sudden booking of a couple tour buses could mean a long drive for no tour unless you make reservations. For an in-depth review of each tour consult the regional chapters.

Self-Guided Swamp Tours (Boat Rentals): The best way to find solitude in the swamp is to rent a boat and go out on your own. You may not see as many alligators as you would with the trained eye of a tour guide, but you can usually find a quiet bayou or slough away from the traffic of tour boats and commercial fishermen. It is easy to become lost in the wetlands, but with a modicum of care (and the maps provided at some locations) you can enjoy a private excursion of your own choosing. Remember, if you rent a pirogue use extra caution, as these boats have a very shallow draft and tip easily. A somewhat exaggerated warning suggests that "if you have never paddled a pirogue, part your hair down the middle and don't chew gum" in order to keep the craft balanced! Take drinks, bug spray, and something to sit on so you can stop and picnic in the forest. Look under Boat Rentals in the index to find a rental location nearby.

Swamp Tour List
Prices are per person. **Call first.** ★Recommended

★Airboat Tours, Inc.; Loreauville, (318) 229-4457. Departs any time by appointment. Cost: $10 for 1-hr. tour, $40 min. $20 for 2-hr. tour, $60 min. Type: Airboat.

Angelle's Atchafalaya Swamp Tours; Henderson, (318) 667-6135 (H), 228-8567. Cost: $7. Type: Pontoon boat.

★Atchafalaya Backwater Tours; Gibson, (504) 575-2371. Cost: $20 for 2-hr. tour, $40 min. Type: Small boat. Pirogue rental available.

★Blind River Swamp Tours, Inc.; Hwy. 61, Gramercy, (504) 869-4765. Departs any time by appointment. Cost: $15. Type: Pontoon or small boat.

Cajun Airboat Tours; Henderson, (318) 228-7670. Departs any time by appointment. Cost: $10 for one-hour tour, $30 min. Type: Airboat.

★Cajun Man Swamp Tours; Houma, (504) 868-4625. Cost: $15 to $20 for 2-hr. tour. Type: Pontoon. Feeds gators.

McGee's Landing; Henderson, (318) 228-2384 or 228-8519. Cost: $8.50, children $5. Type: Pontoon.

Munson's Cypress Bayou Swamp Tour; Houma, (504) 851-3569. Cost: $15. Type: Pontoon. Feeds gators.

Annie Miller's Swamp Tour; Houma, (504) 879-3934. Cost: $14. Type: Pontoon. Feeds gators.

★Scully's; Morgan City, (504) 385-2388. Cost: $20; more than 2 people $15 ea. Type: Small boat or pontoon

★Torres' Cajun Swamp Tour; Kraemer, (504) 633-7799. Cost: $10 to $15. Type: Pontoon.

★Errol Verret's Swamp Tour; Henderson, (318) 394-7145. Cost: Roughly $25 an hour plus gas. Type: Small skiff.

Zam's Bayou Swamp Tours; Kraemer, (504) 633-7881. Cost: $10. Type: Pontoon.

Fishing, Crabbing, and Castnetting

For the recreational fisherman Louisiana lives up to its motto, "The Sportsman's Paradise." Cajun Country has the widest variety of fresh- and saltwater fishing anywhere in the world. There are far too many fishing places to ever list even the best ones! The city of Houma alone has over 25 boat launches and as many fishing charters. A good day or morning of fishing, crabbing, or castnetting can be as simple as pulling your car over, stepping out the door, and wetting a line. You don't need a bunch of bucks, a boat, or fancy gear to spend a day filling the cooler with fish, shrimp, or blue crabs. Fishing from the coast and the banks of rivers and bayous is a daily routine for thousands of Louisianians. A few hours with a fishing or crabbing line in hand can make time stand still as you watch egrets land nearby and alligators sunning themselves on mudbanks.

Fishing Charters: There are three basic types of charters: freshwater (swamp), inside water (marsh), and offshore. Offshore fishing usually means excursions to the oil rigs that dot coastal waters. These rigs have legs reaching hundreds of feet down to the bottom which form man-made reefs that attract everything from red snapper to sharks. Offshore charters are generally the most expensive, as they must use bigger boats, more gas, and heavier tackle. Costs may range from $60 to $150 per person depending on charter company, size of group, whether it is a half- or full-day trip, and whether tackle must be rented. You will want to ask the charter operator what is included in the cost (tackle, food, etc.), how big the boat is, if there is a shaded or air-conditioned area on board, if the crew will help inexperienced fishermen, whether they combine parties, and what happens if there is a forced cancellation.

Inside water (marsh) and freshwater expeditions are quicker and less expensive. Inside trips afford a chance to latch onto Louisiana's most popular saltwater fish, redfish and speckled seatrout. You will be less windblown and wave-tossed than offshore and will get a good look at miles of marsh fringe and sea birds. In the freshwater swamps you can catch bass, *sac-a-lait*, and bream while getting a close-up view of the reptile and amphibious denizens of the swamp. Costs may range from $30 to $100 per person.

Finding a Charter

There are hundreds of charters operating in Cajun Country. Unless you want to call an agency like Provost Adventures (listed below), your best bet for finding a reputable operator is to call the local Chamber of Commerce or Tourism Office. These offices usually have a list and can provide assistance in selecting and making reservations. Below is a list of agencies that will help.

Louisiana Department of Wildlife and Fisheries: (504) 765-2496.

Louisiana Department of Recreation and Tourism: 1-800-33-GUMBO.

Southwest Louisiana Visitors Commission: These folks can help you with launches and charters accessing the Calcasieu and Sabine rivers and marsh regions. 1-800-456-SWLA.

Lafourche Department of Recreation and Tourism: Here you will find information on launches and freshwater, inside water, and off-shore charters leaving out of Leeville, Grand Isle, and elsewhere south of Raceland on Bayou Lafourche. Most of these charters are less than 2 hours from New Orleans.

Houma-Terrebonne Visitors Commission: Charters from this area range from swamp to offshore. All are within 3 hours of New Orleans. 1-800-688-2732.

Iberia Parish Tourist Commission: Most of the charters in this area are freshwater excursions into the Atchafalaya Basin Swamp. (318) 365-1540.

Provost Guide Service is an outdoorsman's "travel agent." Provost arranges fishing charters throughout Cajun Country with no commission charged. This is the place for "one-stop shopping" when it comes to fishing charters (and hunting trips) of all types, including overnight adventures at secluded fishing camps. (318) 837-2831.

  Shore Fishing, Crabbing, & Castnetting: Most of Louisiana's saltwater species, including fierce five-pound redfish and silvery speck-led trout, may be caught year-round right from the roadside. All you need is a fishing license, a $15 rod and reel combo, and about $5 worth of tackle and lures or bait; all of these may be obtained at groceries, discount department stores, and sporting goods stores throughout the area.

  Crabbing is the great family pastime of coastal Cajun Country. All you need are several 5-foot lengths of cotton or nylon string, a $5 dip net, a package of chicken necks, and a cooler, bucket, or trash can to stow your catch in. Crabs shouldn't be put in ice or water, but stored in a shady container until boiled. At any of the places listed below you will probably find someone who can give you a few pointers, but here is the basic procedure: Find a clearing by a shallow saltwater beach or stream (off a pier works fine, but you need a longer string). Tie one end of your string to a stick and tie the other to a chicken neck. Throw the chicken neck into the water close to shore. By the time you have baited and tossed a half dozen lines you can begin the harvest. Gently check

A roadside catch. (Courtesy of LA Office of Tourism)

each line for the tell-tale gnawing and tugging of a big blue crab. When you get one on the line, pull it in very slowly, with your dip net ready. Folks catch hundreds of crabs in one morning using this procedure! No license is required.

Using a cast net takes a bit more practice and money (a four-foot net costs about $20 and you must have a basic fishing license), but when you see netters pulling in fifty shrimp per throw, you will be itching to give it a try. All you need is a net and a cooler from a local discount store. The same places that are good for crabbing are often fine for using a cast net. Find a clearing where there are not a lot of snags on the bottom and give it a toss.

Shore Fishing, Crabbing, and Castnetting Spots

For more information see index.

Grand Isle	*Rockefeller Refuge*
Point Aux Chenes	*Creole Nature Trail*
Cypremort Point	*Holly Beach*
Salt Point	*Cocodrie*

Fishing Rules and Regulations: Size limits, creel limits, the cost of fishing licenses, and other regulations pertaining to recreational fishing are subject to frequent change and should be verified before you plan a trip by calling the State Department of Wildlife and Fisheries. As a point of reference, the basic recreational fishing licenses for 1992 were as follows:

No license is required for crabbing with a baited line. Anyone fishing with a pole, hook and line, rod and reel, or cast net must purchase a fishing license (with the exception of military personnel, nonresidents under 16 years old, and Texas residents over 65).

A Resident Fishing License for fresh and salt water costs $11. It expires on June 30, regardless of when it is purchased.

A Nonresident 2-day Saltwater Fishing License costs $8.50.

A Nonresident 7-day Saltwater License ($15.50) plus the required 7-Day Trip License ($10.50) costs a total of $26.

A Nonresident Full-Season Saltwater Anglers License ($25.50) and required seasonal Nonresident Basic Fishing License ($15.50) cost a total of $41.00.

A Nonresident Freshwater Trout License costs $15.50.

Breeding fighting cocks. (Photo by Julie Posner)

Wagering Sports

Louisiana has a history of tolerance for gambling that coincides well with its reputation for political hijinks. For years after organized gambling was outlawed in most other states, houses of chance operated openly here. Even after gambling was declared illegal in Louisiana, casinos did a brisk business under gubernatorial protection. Although the last casinos were closed by the fifties, a tolerance and affinity for wagering has remained strong in Cajun Country. There was little surprise when Gov. Edwin Edwards (the only Cajun governor in the 20th century) organized a gambling spree to Monte Carlo to help pay off his campaign debts. Aside from your basic "friendly bet," the most common recreational objects of gambling in Cajun Country are horse racing, cards, and cockfighting. All three of these are traditional pursuits that date back to the colonial period.

Horse Racing: Kentucky is most famous for producing fine racehorses, but South Louisiana breeds championship jockeys. Eddie Delahoussaye (a two-time Kentucky Derby winner), Randy Romero, and Ray Sibille are just a few of the great Cajun jocks who have emerged on the national scene. Until Evangeline Downs opened in 1966, most horse-racing activity in Cajun Country took place on weekends at "bush tracks" behind country estates. These rude tracks were the proving grounds for the paddock of jockeys who have risen through the ranks at Evangeline Downs to national prominence, and were vital community gathering spots for most of a century. Of the dozens of bush tracks that proliferated in Cajun country as recently as 1970, the only track we found still operating regularly was Clem's in Abbeville which has races every Sunday morning.

The bush tracks of Cajun Country disappeared mainly as a result of the opening of Evangeline Downs Thoroughbred Track and Delta Downs Quarterhorse and Thoroughbred Track, both of which have pari-mutuel betting and offtrack windows. Evangeline Downs is the premier track in Cajun Country, located just north of Lafayette in Carencro. It is a first-class facility, with Thoroughbred races Friday through Monday, from the first week in April to the first week in September. The smaller Delta Downs has the good-time, informal ambiance of a bush track. Some folks carry in lawn chairs. Delta Downs is located in Vinton, northwest of Lake Charles in Western Cajun Country. Races are held at Delta year round. Thoroughbreds are generally run September through March, and Quarterhorses are run April through August, Thursday through Sunday. For more information on these tracks, consult the index.

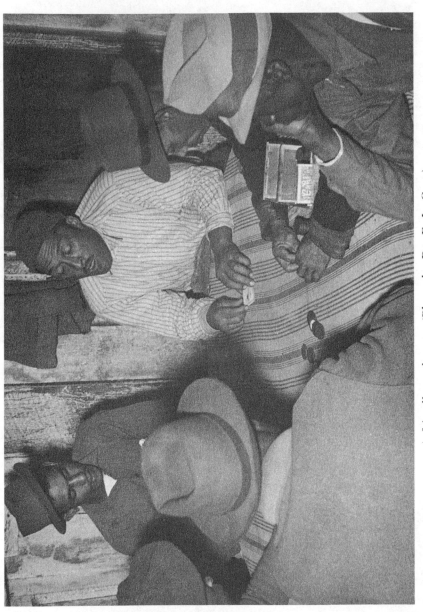

A friendly card game. (Photo by Dr. E. L. Caze)

Cockfighting: Louisiana is one of six states in the nation that still permit cockfighting in some areas. Naturally there has been an outcry by animal rights activists against the activity, but state legislators (using the political savvy for which Louisiana politicians are famous) managed to declare that game fowl are not animals and therefore not subject to animal cruelty laws! Cockfighting is a particularly strong tradition in the rural parishes of Cajun Country, where the techniques of breeding, raising, conditioning, and fighting have been passed along within families from generation to generation.

Whether you visit a cockpit or not, you are likely to see game fowl being raised throughout the region. Because the birds are prone to attacking each other they are kept tethered to individual domiciles. A cock breeder can be identified by a yard covered with small teepees made of corrugated steel with cocks leashed to them.

A typical cockpit has a bar and lounge in the front. The pit itself can be as primitive as a barn, but is usually a small arena with bleacher seating. Most people figure a cockpit is a place where men go to drink, swear, gamble, and beat each other up. In fact, violence is generally confined to the birds in the fenced ring, and most pits attract a wide array of couples, families, and cockfight fanatics who come to make private wagers. These wagers are conveyed before and during the fight in indecipherable yells and hand gestures across the pit.

Cockfighting is definitely not for everyone, but the curious who decide to attend a fight may be surprised to find that the event is not particularly gory. Fights are held in tournaments where trainers are required to enter a certain number of birds, which are paired by weight. The birds are equipped with razor-sharp spurs that are affixed to their natural heel spurs by leather thongs. The fights are presided over by a referee and follow clearly established written rules. A fight is over after one of the fowls attacks and the other refuses to fight for a specified number of consecutive pairings. Thus, the fights do not necessarily end in the death of a bird.

Due to the controversy over animal rights, cockers and pit owners are naturally a bit suspicious of outsiders, and forbid cameras in the pit area. There are, however, several pits which are open to the public without membership (usually for a $5 to $10 admission). For more information on these, refer to the index.

Cards: Nearly every town in Southwest Louisiana has a card bar. Many times I have entered a crowded club expecting to find a band playing and instead discovered a half dozen tables of card sharps. By far the most popular game played at these bars, and in household gatherings around Cajun Country, is Bourré. There are a few popular variations on this game. Around Upper Lafourche country there are a half dozen bars where a variation called Pedro is the only game in the house.

Biking

You don't have to be an olympic athlete to take a bike tour in Cajun Country. The terrain is predominantly flat, so the main concern is climate. The best time to tour the region on bike or otherwise is in fall or spring, with fall being the drier of the two. The *Cajun Country Guide* should be equally useful to bicyclists and motorists. Many of the same areas and routes that are attractive for auto touring are also excellent on two wheels. These include the **Creole Nature Trail** in Southwest Louisiana (for vistas of the coastal marshes), the **Cajun Heartland** (for an abundance of good music and food), and **River Road** or the **Old Spanish Trail** (the Route 182 section) in Teche Country (for a look at the grandest manors of the antebellum South).

For a combination biking and camping trip you can travel the **Atchafalaya Basin Levee** between Morgan City and the flood control structure at Simmesport. Camping is allowed on the grassy land beside the levees and at Lake Fausse State Park. Unfortunately most of the roads in Cajun Country are narrow, substandard, or have very little shoulder. If you are traveling the River Road or Atchafalaya Basin routes and have an all-terrain or other "fat-tire" bike, you may ride atop the levees, which are alternately shell, gravel, and packed dirt. Atop the levee you can view commerce on the river or the swamp without the worries of auto traffic.

Biking Gear, Rentals, Maps, and Information: **Pack and Paddle;** 601 E. Pinhook Rd., Lafayette, La. 70501. (318) 232-5854. Joan Williams, the owner and manager of this outdoors store, is the #1 biking enthusiast in Cajun Country. She offers guided group tours to all the regions mentioned above except the Atchafalaya route. These bike tours include meals at restaurants, accommodations, and entrance fees at plantations. (Costs range from $179 for a two-day tour to $389 for a 4-day trip). Pack and Paddle also offers equipment and bicycle rentals ($15 a day, $55 a week). A brochure detailing the Pack and Paddle Tours is available free upon request. For the rider who wants a book with exact miles between each attraction and each turn, Joan Williams has published a bicycle guide to Cajun Country, *Backroad Tours Of French Louisiana.*

Bicycle Michael's; 618 Frenchman St., New Orleans, LA 70130. (504) 945-9505. This all-purpose bike shop located just below the French Quarter rents bikes for $12.50 a day, $50 for 5 days, and $60 for a full week.

Hiking

With the exception of trails at Chicot State Park, none of the hiking paths in Cajun Country is over four miles. The landscape is either too wet or given over to agricultural development. Most of the "hiking" referred to in this text is therefore of the casual day-trip variety. For a variation on the basically flat terrain, try Chicot Park or the State Arboretum just north of Ville Platte. Refer to hiking in the index for more detailed information.

Bird Watching

It is not uncommon for birding parties in Cajun Country to record a day's total of 100 to 150 bird species. Louisiana possesses several attributes which combine to make it one of the best states in the union for bird watching. It is located on the Mississippi Flyway, a busy thoroughfare for migrating birds, and it gets plenty of traffic from the Central Flyway. Cajun Country encompasses a wild and wide variety of habitat types: open water, marshes, swamps, bottomland forests, prairies, and beaches. The state regularly hosts a multitude of species that are just passing through. All of these attributes have added up to a total of over 400 species of birds frequenting the region.

South Louisiana is eminently "birdable" all through the year, but is especially rewarding during the spring. A cold front in April or early May often forces birds migrating north across the Gulf of Mexico to land in the first available trees. In this type of "fall out" the coastal woods and *cheniers* are boiling with warblers, vireos, tanagers, buntings, grosbeaks, and other perching birds, while the mudflats and marshes are carpeted by migrating shorebirds.

Cameron Parish is generally considered to be the best bird watching spot in Louisiana. It contains the coastal woods needed for the "fall out" phenomenon plus lakes, marsh, beach, and mudflats. There are observation decks, piers, and walkways along the Creole Nature Trail for bird watching. Places to stop and try along the route include the freshwater marsh at Gibbstown, Rutherford Beach near Oak Grove, the East Cameron Jetties in the city of Cameron, Holly Beach, the Hollyman Sanctuary near Johnson's Bayou, Sabine Refuge Nature Trail, and the deck and trails at Rockefeller Refuge. Between Cameron Parish and New Orleans one can try the highways south of Houma, the levees of the Atchafalaya Basin, coastal salt domes at Avery and Jefferson islands, and Chicot Park. For information on the places listed above, consult the index or request a copy of the *Birding Guide to Southwest Louisiana* from the Southwest Louisiana Visitors Center. (Above bird watching text supplied by noted Louisiana expert Bill Vermilion. Used with permission.)

Louisiana Bird Watching Information Sources

Southwest Louisiana Visitors Bureau; Lake Charles, 1-800-456-SWLA

Louisiana Ornithological Society; Baton Rouge (LSU)

Louisiana Science and Nature Center; New Orleans, (504) 241-9606

Orleans Audubon Society; New Orleans, (504) 246-2473

Acadiana Audubon Society Chapter; Live Oak Gardens, Jefferson Island, (318) 235-6181. Jim Foret

Acadiana Park Nature Station; Lafayette, (318) 235-6181

Gulf Coast Bird Club; Lake Charles, (318) 477-2360. Winston Caillouet, editor

Alligator Watching

The Louisiana alligator has become a symbol of Cajun Country and has wound up in some pretty strange places in the process. The reptiles have been found wandering across the horse track at Evangeline Downs, in the pond on the median adjacent to the Gateway Lafayette Visitors Center, and in Cypress Lake beside the Student Union Building at the University of Southwest Louisiana. Probably the closest alligator to Interstate 10 (a dubious distinction) resides in a small concrete-and-glass cell at the Chateau des Cocodrie beside the Jennings Oil and Gas Park and Visitors Center. There is no point in looking for gators in zoos or at these bizarre locations, as they abound in the wild during warm-weather months.

Alligators grow about a foot per year for the first ten years. To figure the size of a gator, estimate the number of inches between the tip of the nose and the bulge at the eyes. If it is five inches between these points the reptile is about five feet long, or five years old. Spotting the creatures is the hard part. They don't move much and blend in well with the marshy environment. They can be resting invisibly in the sun just a few feet from where you are standing. The key is to be patient, but a set of binoculars may help. Look for crushed marsh grass and troughs in the mud where they have lumbered from the water. If you don't see any, don't be disappointed; they probably saw you!

The best way to see a gator in the wild is to take a swamp tour. Many of the tour guides trap them during the alligator season, and others feed them. They all know the best places to look, since the alligators seldom roam far from their nests. If you are searching on foot, try the nature trails at the Sabine Wildlife Refuge, Rockefeller Wildlife Refuge, Avery Island, and Lake Chicot at Chicot State Park. For more information on these spots consult the index.

Louisiana alligator. (Courtesy of LA Department of Wildlife and Fisheries)

9

Getting Around

Air Connections

Most visitors arrive in Cajun Country by way of New Orleans or Houston, cities with busy international airports. **From Houston International**, Continental Airlines (1-800-231-0856) and L'Express (1-800-344-1970) operate several commuter flights daily into the Cajun Hub City of Lafayette. **From New Orleans**, the only direct air connection is offered by L'Express, which has 3 flights daily, Monday through Friday. **From Dallas/Fort Worth** Delta and Continental both operate commuter flights into Lafayette. All commercial flights to Lafayette arrive at Lafayette Municipal Airport, which is about 3 miles from downtown. Southwest Limo Service (318-234-7976) offers shuttle transportation to downtown and local hotels for $5. Rental car and cab service is also available from the airport (*see* car rentals below).

Train Service into Cajun Country

Amtrak's Sunset Limited Line runs between Los Angeles and New Orleans, bisecting the lower half of Cajun Country, with stops in Shriever, New Iberia, Lafayette (133 E. Grant St.), and Lake Charles. There is one westbound train on Monday, Wednesday, and Saturday. One eastbound train operates on the same route on Tuesday, Thursday, and Sunday. Round trips from New Orleans to Lafayette are around $50. The train station in Lafayette is convenient to downtown, but not within walking distance of any accommodations. (1-800-872-7245).

Bus Routes through Cajun Country

Greyhound-Trailways (315 Lee St. in Lafayette, Tel. (318) 235-1541.) operates nine buses between New Orleans, Lafayette, and Houston each day. Two of these take the longer southern route (U.S. 190) through Houma; the others follow the interstate through Baton Rouge. Buses depart New Orleans (Tel. (504) 525-9371) for Lafayette every 3 hours. There are connections from New Orleans and Lafayette accessing Opelousas and Eunice in the Cajun Heartland. None of the bus stations on these routes (except in New Orleans) is convenient to motels.

Automobile Travel in Cajun Country

However you get there, you will want a car in Cajun Country. The area is rural, the population dispersed, and many attractions are well off the beaten path. Folks arriving in New Orleans or Houston by plane would be advised to rent a car in one of those cities and drive into Cajun Country. There will be many interesting sites along the way and a car will again be a necessity upon arriving at your Cajun point of destination. There are numerous car rental companies in Lafayette. The major rental companies have offices at the Lafayette airport, while several budget outfits are located around town. Taxi service in Lafayette is provided by Acadiana Yellow Cab (318-237-5701) and Bayou Cab (318-235-7515).

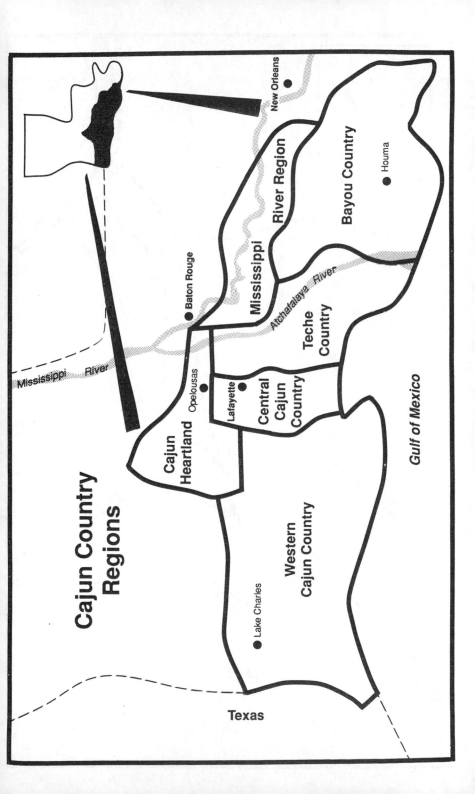

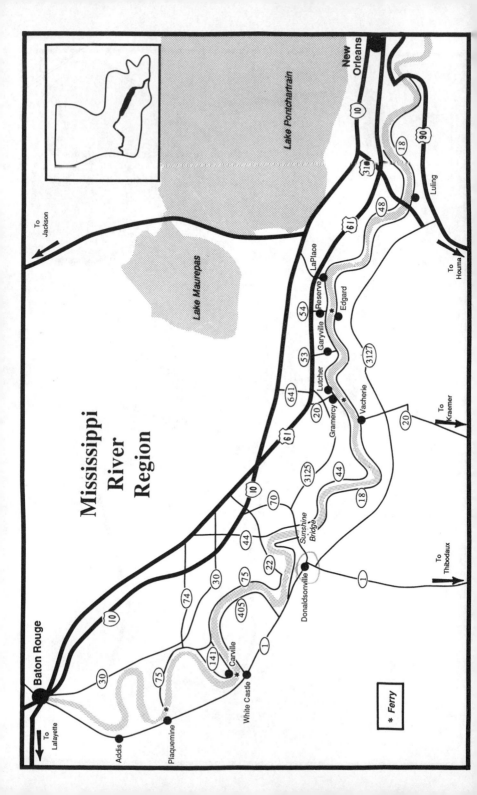

Mississippi River Region

To Jackson

To Lafayette

Baton Rouge

Lake Maurepas

Lake Pontchartrain

New Orleans

To Houma

Addis

Plaquemine

White Castle

Carville

Donaldsonville

Sunshine Bridge

To Thibodaux

To Kraemer

Vacherie

Gramercy

Lutcher

Garyville

Reserve

Edgard

LaPlace

Luling

To Houma

* *Ferry*

(30)
(10)
(74)
(75)
(141)
(30)
(405)
(1)
(75)
(22)
(44)
(70)
(10)
(3125)
(61)
(641)
(20)
(53)
(54)
(61)
(310)
(10)
(48)
(18)
(90)
(44)
(18)
(3127)
(20)
(1)

10

Mississippi River Region

The Great River Road offers an opportunity to go from a plantation tour to a plant tour, to sample rich Creole and Cajun cuisine, take a swamp tour, and stay the night in some of the grandest domiciles ever constructed in America. There are many mythical stretches of highway in America, but none with the allure of this ancient road, clinging to the banks of America's mightiest stream. Indians, steamboat captains, and planters (who were at one time the nation's wealthiest class) have all coveted River Road addresses. Even today the narrow two-lane route is second in popularity only to New Orleans as a Louisiana tourist attraction. Because the river's main course is southward, its banks and the two adjacent River Roads are defined as "east" and "west." This makes sense, except in Cajun Country. Between New Orleans and Baton Rouge the river actually follows a mainly west-to-east course. Thus, attractions heading upriver from New Orleans are described as "west," despite the fact that the banks of the stream are still known as "east bank" and "west bank!"

The Mississippi, one of the three great rivers of the world, is the dominant force shaping life along the eastern border of Cajun Country. Since Indian times the river has been the focus of trade and industry and its natural levees have provided the high ground for successive waves of settlement. When the first white settlers arrived in New Orleans, they quickly moved upriver, establishing farms along the narrow swaths of raised earth on either side of the mighty stream. Among the early settlers were the first wave of Acadian immigrants, who arrived in 1765 and made their homes on the West Bank of St. James Parish along what became known as the Acadian Coast. The Acadians did not last long on this prized ground, and like the Indians were swept into the swamps to the west by the growth of the sugarcane and lumber industries and the influx of a wealthy European and Anglo planter class.

In the late eighteenth century, the river was the arterial highway of the western frontier and planters took advantage of busy riverboat traffic to ship raw goods to market in New Orleans. After the War Between The States, the planter class, like the Acadians, was pushed aside by the arrival of lumber, petroleum and the petro-chemical industries. The remnants of these waves of settlement are everywhere, visible as you drive along the River Roads and Airline Highway (Rt. 61). There are old abandoned Acadian homes, stately plantation houses, and crumbling share-croppers' shacks. The area is mainly rural and poor. Towns like Lutcher and Garyville, once lumber mill communities, still sport company-built houses and networks of rail beds once used to pull cypress from the swamps. Dwarfing them are the stacks of huge chemical plants that have given the area its latest notoriety as "the cancer corridor of America."

Travel Tips

This chapter is organized in a linear fashion, tracing each river road from New Orleans to just south of Baton Rouge, with the few attractions on the adjacent Airline Highway (east bank) in-cluded in the continuum. At the end of this chapter you will find a list of restaurants and accommodations reviewed within. For those planning to take the River Roads all the way to Baton Rouge, then drive west on Interstate 10 to Lafayette, it is impor-tant to remember that these are winding and twisting routes which can take over three hours to drive without any stops! To budget your time, plan no more than three plantation tours in one day with stops for lunch and leg stretching. For expediency and a varied view, it is recommended that travelers switch between the four main routes of the region; Interstate 10, Airline Highway (Route 61), and the east-bank and west-bank courses of River Road. The River Roads change route numbers along the way, but generally follow the fifteen- to twenty-foot-tall river levees. There is no view of the river from your car, so you may want to take advantage of the frequent ferry service between the two banks or walk the levee for a glimpse of river traffic.

RIVER ROAD EAST BANK

This section is arranged in a linear east-to-west format traveling up River Road from New Orleans. At the end of the section you will find a list of restaurants and accommodations reviewed. The quickest way to access the lower reaches of the River Roads at this time is to take Route 61 (Airline Highway) north from the New

Orleans Airport about 3 miles, then cut over to the river on Route 50 (Almedia Road). Go 1 mile to reach River Road, which is labeled as Route 48 at this juncture. A new branch of Interstate 10, called Interstate 310 (scheduled to open in late 1992), will intersect I-10 just west of the New Orleans International Airport, cross the river at St. Rose, and provide even faster access to both east and west River Road.

*Destrehan Plantation River Road just above St. Rose.

Destrehan is located just 2 miles above St. Rose and a half mile south of I-310. Built in 1787, it is the oldest plantation home left intact in the lower Mississippi Valley. Twin wings were added to either side of the house in 1810 and a Greek Revival facade was built about ten years later, but otherwise the structure is in its original configuration. A forty-five-minute tour of the house begins with a short video depicting its history and appearance before current renovations began. Downstairs the house has brick floors and is scantily furnished. Upstairs living quarters are elegantly furnished with period antiques. One room has been left unfinished, its walls and ceilings opened to expose original construction techniques.

The history of Destrehan speaks of the changing character of the region. Sugarcane supplanted indigo as the primary crop in 1802. Following the War Between the States, the plantation was bought by Mexican Petroleum and was the site of an Amoco refinery through the mid-twentieth century. When Amoco closed the refinery, they let the house fall apart. In an attempt to make amends, the petroleum giant (which still owns the grounds) has been instrumental in restoring the plantation. A Spring Plantation Festival is held the first weekend in May. The $2 admission allows entrance to the house and opportunity to visit food and craft booths on the grounds. A Fall Festival has also been instituted the second weekend in November. Destrehan is open for tours from 9:30 A.M. to 4 P.M. daily, except major holidays. The tour costs $5 for adults, $4 for seniors, $3 for children 6 to 11, and children 5 and under are admitted free. The last tour begins at 4 P.M. (504) 764-9315.

Ormond Plantation River Road just above St. Rose.

Ormond Plantation is 1.5 miles north of Destrehan (.5 miles above I-310). This place is a good example of how owners go about destroying the original character of a plantation home. Like Destrehan, Ormond was a colonial structure (built in 1787), but it has lost all resemblance to its former appearance. Mr. and Mrs. Alfred Brown, owners of the Brown's Velvet Dairy in New Orleans,

Building the Bonnet Carre Spillway. (Courtesy of U.S. Army Corps of Engineers)

enclosed the carriageways and added a rear east and west wing in 1942. In 1968, Ormond was purchased by real estate developers who planned to turn it into the clubhouse of a golf course. They poured cement over the brick floors, and destroyed much of the woodwork. Despite its wildly amended state, Ormond will be of interest to antique and artifact hounds, as it is stuffed with a mind-boggling collection of miscellanea from the past two centuries. There is an antique doll room, many artifacts from the War Between the States, and a large cane collection on display.

Ormond has daily tours from 10 A.M. to 4:30 P.M. The tour costs $5 for adults, $4 for seniors, and $2.50 for children 6 to 12. Bed and Breakfast accommodations are available by reservation at $125 for double occupancy. A carafe of wine and a fresh fruit and cheese tray are served on the veranda in the evening. In the morning, hot coffee will be placed outside your bedroom, followed at 8:30 A.M. by a Continental-style breakfast. (504) 764-8544.

*Bonnet Carre Spillway

Five miles north of I-310, River Road passes the industrial complex of Norco and one mile later crosses a levee and drops into the Bonnet Carre Spillway. The spillway is one of the huge and seemingly miraculous structures built by the United States Corps of Engineers to control the waters of the Mississippi at time of flood. The Bonnet Carre, constructed in 1935, is a floodgate and guide levee system built into the river levee wall. When the river threatens to flood areas to the south, the gates can be opened to allow water to escape through a mile-and-a-half wide channel from the Mississippi into Lake Pontchartrain, seven miles to the north. This site was chosen for construction of the spillway based on the proximity of the lake and the demonstrated proclivity of the Mississippi to jump its banks at this point. In 1850 a crevasse occurred in the river levee here that remained open for six months, allowing water to spread across a 7000-foot-wide area.

The folks at the Corps don't like to stir up the political muck that moves when large amounts of water are diverted, so it is unlikely you will find the gates open. Instead you will drive along the spillway bed below the surface of the river. A drive through the bottom of the 1.5-mile-wide floodbed provides a startling view of the placid pursuits that continue in the face of man's struggle against nature. At high water, there is always someone netting bait or fishing alongside the road. At extreme high water, the spillway road closes and traffic is diverted to Airline Highway. Most of the spillway is covered with bushes, trees, small streams, and ponds, fading to cypress swamp towards Lake Pontchartrain. Around

March and April, the spillway is a popular spot for blackberry picking, picnicking, canoeing, fishing, and other recreational pursuits. **Bonnet Carre Spillway Recreation and Camping Area** Airline Hwy. Where Route 61 (Airline Highway) crosses the spillway there is a boat launch, picnic area, and free campground. A number of trails head out into the underbrush from this point. The camping is primitive. Porta-potties are provided for folks in tents (there is a maximum-stay limit of two weeks). To get to the recreation area, take Airline Highway west from New Orleans (9.2 miles from the airport). From River Road cut over to Airline at the town of Norco. The campground is beside the Spillway Bridge.

LaPlace

From the west side of the Bonnet Carre Spillway, River Road passes five and a half miles of industrial development and rubble before entering the town of LaPlace (10.5 miles from I-310 by way of River Road). Here the road veers away from the levee and becomes Route 44 (in town it is called 5th Street). LaPlace is located near the site of the biggest slave revolt in American history. The revolt occurred in 1818 at Woodland Plantation and involved nearly 600 slaves, who were defeated by the militia just west of New Orleans. Following their defeat, the slaves who were not dead were beheaded and their heads were placed on stakes along the River Road. Today LaPlace, the largest town on the river between Baton Rouge and New Orleans (population about 17,000), is a bedroom community for folks who work in the Crescent City. It is known as the Andouille Capital of the World. The history of this lean pork sausage has been clouded, but it apparently goes back to a settlement of Germans in the region in the eighteenth century. Andouille is different from other sausage varieties in Acadiana, having no filler, just big chunks of fatless pork seasoned with pepper and garlic, and smoked to an almost fully cooked state. **Wayne Jacob's Smokehouse** 2550 West 5th St. (River Road), LaPlace.

Jacob's is located 1.5 miles past the convergence of Route 44 and River Road in LaPlace. Although they have moved from the funky country store just down the road, the andouille is the same recipe that has been passed down in the Jacob family for generations. At least three branches of the family produce andouille at separate locations, but Wayne's is my pick of the litter. The country sausage and hog's head cheese are also excellent. Wayne

Jacob's has a variety of dry goods, homemade jellies, and desserts for sale, too. The andouille sells for about $3.99 a pound. Jacob's is open (October through April) Monday through Saturday, from 8:30 A.M. to 5 P.M. (504) 652-9990.

Airline Motors Restaurant Cajun/Down Home, $$. 221 E. Airline Hwy.

Built in 1939, Airline Motors Restaurant is one of the few thriving landmarks of the days when Airline Highway was the only "fast" route between New Orleans and Baton Rouge. The restaurant is actually an oversized example of classic American diner decor. Festooned with curved corners, glass bricks, and plenty of neon, this place just sucks you in off the road. Inside there is a long counter, bar area, and large dining room. There are a dozen seafood and steak dinners for $7 to $13, but I recommend the gumbos, which are made with LaPlace's famous andouille. The fried food is well prepared and includes a variety of seafood po-boys and onion rings. While you are waiting for your food you can get your appetite going by studying the placemat maps of the River Region. Instead of the usual drawings of tourist attractions, they are festooned with a complete list of every petrochemical plant along the river. Airline Motors Restaurant never closes. (504) 652-9181.

ABA (canoe) Rentals 1221 W. Airline Hwy., LaPlace.

If you want to explore the many streams and ponds around the Bonnet Carre Spillway, ABA Rentals in LaPlace is the closest place to rent a canoe. A canoe, two paddles, life jackets, roof pads, and tie downs cost $20 for 24 hours. You can rent a canoe (or flat-bottomed boat) here and within 15 minutes be paddling through the spillway (*see* Bonnet Carre Recreation Area above). ABA is open Monday through Saturday from 8:30 A.M. to 5:30 P.M. In the summer they also open on some Sundays. (504) 652-7937.

Bailey's Smoke House Meat Market/Andouille. 1413 W. Airline Hwy., LaPlace.

Bailey's has great andouille with more garlic than the standard blend. They also sell smoked sausage, hog's head cheese, and some of the best tasso east of the Cajun Heartland. They are open Monday through Saturday from 8 A.M. to 6 P.M. (504) 651-2956.

Lodging

Holiday Inn 3900 Main St., $60 to $75 double. (504) 652-5544.
Millet Motel 1525 W. Airline Hwy., $32 to $35 double. (504) 652-4401.

San Francisco Plantation. (Photo by Julie Posner)

Reserve

*Cox's Meat Market Andouille. River Road and 9th St., Reserve.

Cox's is 17 miles from I-310, and 5 miles above LaPlace. This is the ultimate andouille palace. No one prepares a leaner or tastier sausage than Cox's. A tribute to their superlative meat came from the *Chef's Source Book,* which described it as "America's best andouille" in 1986. Cox's andouille is the choice of dozens of New Orleans' finest restaurants. It is a bit less cooked than others and therefore holds together well in a gumbo. Unfortunately this means you won't be able to cut off a thin slice to nibble on in the car. From Airline Highway, go west (towards the river) on Route 53 just north of LaPlace. When you get to River Road head south 1/4 mile. Cox's is open from 8 A.M. to 5 P.M., Monday through Saturday. (504) 536-2491.

Reserve to Edgard Ferry Rt. 53 (Central Ave.) and River Rd.

If you are doing a short trip up River Road and want to get a look at the Waterford Three Nuclear Plant or Oak Alley (*see* West Bank River Road section), you can cross the river here by way of the Ascension Ferry. This will also give you a fantastic view of the river and its heavy commerce. The ferry operates from 5 A.M. to 9 P.M., crossing approximately every 15 minutes. The last trip is at 8:45. There is a $1 fee for travel from the west to east banks.

Don's Country Store Meat Market/Andouille, po-boys. 318 Central Ave., Reserve

If you are making a day trip up River Road, Don's is your first convenient lunch stop. This unusual store sells meats, groceries, a full line of hardware, fish or shrimp boxes, and po-boys to go! If you are looking for a good, fully cooked andouille that you can carve a smokey taste off of, this is the spot. There is a recipe board by the butcher case with 24 free Cajun recipes to help you prepare the meat. From River Road, turn onto Route 53 (Central Avenue), go about 1.5 miles, and Don's is on the right. They are open Monday through Saturday from 7 A.M. to 7 P.M., and Sunday from 8 A.M. to noon. (504) 536-2275.

*San Francisco Plantation

Only 4 miles from Route 53 in Reserve (21 miles from I-310), San Francisco is the most perfectly restored of all the plantation

Cypress cut by Stebbins Lumber Company. (St. James Historical Society Museum)

homes in Acadiana. Unlike Ormond and Destrehan downriver, San Francisco is not a colonial home, but was built at the height of River Road's grandeur in 1853. Builder Edmond Marmillion reportedly spent every cent he had making this home a jewel. From the paint to the drapes and furnishings, everything inside and out is either original or modeled after descriptions in Marmillion's inventories. Among the preserved details are seven deceptively painted faux marble mantles, a crushed brick floor that resembles a rich, red carpet, and most spectacular, five ceiling frescoes. Outside, the home has the appearance of a gingerbread steamboat with Gothic windows, galleries, and ornate woodwork. The roof is graced with a small windowed room called a "widow's walk" from which residents could watch traffic on the river.

The tour guide pointed out the wavy original glass in the enclosed gallery to the rear, but politely ignored the expansive view of Marathon Oil Company's not-so-original field of storage tanks. San Francisco has developed a weird symbiotic relationship with the hulking petroleum giant. Marathon bought the place and its extensive properties in 1974 and, though they desecrated its once immaculate grounds, they also sunk two million dollars into restoring San Francisco to the showpiece of River Road's eastern course. Tours are scheduled from 10 A.M. to 4 P.M. daily except holidays. Tours cost $6 for adults, $3.75 for 12- to 17-year-olds, and $2.50 for children 6 to 12. (504) 535-2341.

Garyville

The best place for a glimpse of the River Region's once booming lumber industry is one mile north of San Francisco Plantation in the town of Garyville. The Chicago-based Stebbins Lumber Company mapped out, built, and populated Garyville. Between 1903 and the 1930's, the company harvested every twig of usable cypress from the nearby Blind River Swamp (*see* Blind River Swamp Tours in Gramercy for a close-up look at the remnants of the logging operation). Garyville is only three blocks wide and about eight blocks deep heading back from the river. East Street was built to accommodate black workers, Main Street housed the whites, and West Street was lined with homes for mainly Italian immigrants. Over 60 of the company homes are still standing and are listed on the historic register.

Little in these cottages suggests the vast sums that were earned

Lutcher Moore lumber train in cut swamp. (St. James Historical Society Museum)

when the mill was in business. Most of the money went to administrators in Chicago, not to the local laborers who slaved in the mill. The company office and mill yard were located a couple of miles back from the river. The office has been restored and turned into a museum (*see* review below). Across from the office is the Garyville State Bank, the only other commercial building to survive since the lumbering days.

*Garyville Timbermill Museum Main St. and Railroad Ave.

When I visited the Timbermill museum in the spring of 1991 it was not complete, but there were harbingers of an amazing attraction on the way. In the midst of a room full of dusty artifacts and papers, project director Norman Marmillion was beaming in delight at having just discovered all the original blueprints for the building. Aside from saving many thousands of dollars in architect's fees, the find was like a needle in the haystack of meticulously preserved company documents, photos, and machinery. The Stebbins Lumber Company actually constructed and hired the entire town, so the artifacts here cover every phase of life in Garyville. They tell the story of the birth and death of a company town, as well as the details of lumbering and milling operations. The museum is being funded by several chemical companies (not the state), and is projected to open in August of 1992. From River Road, turn away from the river on Route 54, about 1 mile above San Francisco Plantation. Stay on Route 54 for about 1.5 miles, and after you cross the railroad tracks take the first right. The museum is at the corner of Main Street and Railroad Avenue (504) 535-3202.

Gramercy and Lutcher

Between Garyville and Gramercy (27 miles north of I-310), there are 5 miles of hideous industrial scenery, courtesy of Nalco, DuPont, and LaRoche chemical companies. One of the more unusual sights here is the amazing "bridge to nowhere," which has been hanging unfinished over the river for several years. Even the roads and ramps on either side are incomplete. Stalled by a lack of funds and an old-boy contract-bidding scandal, the bridge will one day provide folks a faster route (of dubious value) between the vacant fields and factories on one side of the river and those on the other. Past the bridge, Gramercy and Lutcher run together in an indecipherable grid of small streets. Like many other towns on River Road, they have narrow frontage on the river but stretch for several miles back towards Route 61 (Airline Highway).

Gramercy is an old sugar town, and home to the Colonial Sugar Mill. Many residents are now employed at the nearby Kaiser Aluminum and Chemical Plant, and other River Road industries. Route 20, the main route perpendicular to the river, forms a rough boundary with neighboring Lutcher and provides a 3.5-mile link between River Road and Airline Highway.

Lutcher, like Garyville downriver, is a former lumbermill town. It was built and populated around the turn of the century by the Lutcher Moore Cypress Lumber Company. The mill and offices were located right on River Road, and the business district and residential areas were (and still are) located several blocks back from the river. In addition to sugar, lumber, and chemicals, this part of St. James Parish is noted as the only place in the country where Perique tobacco is grown. Perique is a strong, fermented tobacco that is usually blended with other milder leaves, but it is occasionally smoked unadulterated by locals.

Veron's Super Market Meat Market. Rt. 641, Lutcher.

Veron's is the only manufacturer I have found of "boudin blanc". Like the French sausage from which Cajun Boudin developed, Veron's is a riceless product. In consistency and flavor, the sausages more closely resemble a hot dog than your typical Cajun boudin. They are sold chilled in shrink-wrapped packages. Turn away from the river onto Route 20 and go 1.2 miles. Take a left onto Route 641. Veron's is .5 miles ahead on the left. They are open Monday through Saturday from 7 A.M. to 7 P.M. and Sunday until 1 P.M.

Zapp's Potato Chip Factory 307 Airline Hwy. (Rt. 61), Gramercy.

Zapp's is located just south of Route 20 on Route 61. Since opening in the mid-eighties Zapp's has become a local snack food favorite, producing fresh, spiced (and plain) chips at its tiny factory. Any potato chip junkie knows that the fresh, local chip is always best, but Zapp's has a unique product. They slice their chips thick and cook them in small, hand-stirred batches in vats of peanut oil. When they emerge from the fryer, the most popular variety is dusted with Ron Zappe's own "cajun spice" mixture. The plant offers fifteen-minute "drop-in" tours whenever possible. The best time to visit is on Monday through Wednesday mornings, when the chips are being made. Zapp's t-shirts and caps are sold. Out-of-town chipaholics may mail order by calling 1-800-HOT-CHIP. Zapp's Potato Chips, 307 East Airline Hwy, P.O. Box 1533, Gramercy, LA 70052.

★Blind River Swamp Tour Airline Hwy. (Rt. 61), Gramercy.

This tour provides a wonderful view of the historic lumber

operations in the River Region. It departs from Billy Fauchex's houseboat on Airline Highway just above the Route 20 intersection. Much of the tour is spent on the lovely Blind River, with a couple excursions up small bayous where you will see a beautiful cypress and tupelo forest full of wildlife. Cuts and troughs are still evident in the woods where the Lutcher Moore Lumber Company ran its railroad spurs. One of the unique stops on this tour is at the **Blind River Chapel**. This tiny chapel, which sits in watery isolation four miles from the nearest road, was built in 1983 by Marthe DeRoche (who lives in the camp next door) "in Honor of Our Lady of Blind River."

Guide Billy Fauchex grew up on the banks of the river and has dozens of stories about each bayou. He is knowledgeable, but cultivates a relaxed attitude. He will go when you want to go (early morning to late evening), he will go where you want to go (whether it's the Blind River Chapel or the "Bayou Bar"), and you can stock his cooler with whatever type of beverages or food you like. Fauchex runs a party barge, but groups of three or less can go on his small and quick flatboat and get to very remote areas. Two-hour tours cost $15 a person ($40 a trip for 2 or less). Fauchex operates 7 days a week, with regularly scheduled tours at 9 A.M., noon, and 3 P.M. Take Route 20 north to Airline Highway. Turn left on Airline Highway and the entrance to Blind River Tours is 1 block ahead on the right. (504) 869-4765.

*St. James Parish Historical Society Bonfire Museum
One mile north of Route 20 on the River Road you will find this fine one-room museum that is operated by the St. James Historical Society. The museum has vintage photographs, documents, and artifacts relating to Perique tobacco, the lumber and sugar industries, and the Christmas Bonfire tradition (*see* review of Bonfire Festival later in this chapter). There is a wall of photographs of plantation homes (many no longer standing), with captions explaining their fate. Many of the lumber artifacts here came from the office of the Lutcher Moore Mill, which is still standing on a lot behind the museum. One display contains Indian artifacts removed from a mound a few miles away on Route 3125 (*see* Indian Mound below). Like the Timbermill Museum in Garyville, this collection provides a striking look at the changing industries and cultures along the River Road. Admission is free. The museum is open from 8 A.M. to 4 P.M. Monday through Friday. (504) 869-9752.

*Festival of the Bonfires Weekend before the Winter Solstice.
During the weeks before Christmas, civic groups from the

Bonfires on the levee. (St. James Historical Society Museum)

communities along the river construct towering wooden structures on the crown of the levee. Spaced about 50 yards apart, the bonfire stacks resemble a two-mile row of log steeples. On the last evening of the festival, the bonfires are torched, shedding a raging light on a host of revelers, and a brilliant reflection across the river. Country and Cajun bands perform under a big tent, crafts are sold, and tons of typical festival food (funnel cakes, hot dogs, and beer) are consumed.

The bonfires have been a tradition in St. John, St. Charles, St. James and Ascension Parishes for over 200 years. The tradition can be traced back to German and French settlers, and historians point out that a similar tradition is still strong in the Alsace region of France and along the Rhine in Germany. Some trace the roots back to Druid celebrations of the Summer and Winter Solstice. The bonfire tradition had nearly died out by the 1930s, when it was practiced mainly at home by blacks in the river parishes. The annual torching is now fully revived. In 1989 there were 100 bonfires torched between Gramercy and Donaldsonville. Call the Bonfire Museum (above) for information.

Lutcher to Vacherie Ferry River Road, Lutcher.

One and a half miles above Route 20, and a half mile past the Bonfire Museum, is the Lutcher-Vacherie Ferry. This is the place to cross the river if you are heading for Oak Alley Plantation on the West Bank. Passengers on this ferry had a wild ride one January day in 1989, when the ferry became lost in the winter fog for two hours before finding its way to the opposite landing! Barring incident, the ferry crosses every half hour, daily, from 6 A.M. to 11:45 P.M. There is a $1 charge for travelers from the west to east bank.

Stockpile Restaurant Cajun/Down Home, $ to $$. Rt. 3125 in Grand Point.

The Stockpile Restaurant and Tavern is my favorite eatery on the East Bank of the Mississippi above New Orleans (there are not many choices). It is a new place with a studied "rusticity," but owner Eric Larouque knows how to satisfy a working man's appetite. Plate lunches, like white beans and hamburger steak and crawfish bisque with potato salad, are served every day. On Thursday nights, workers from the nearby chemical plants flock in to feed on the Stockpile's "all you can eat" fried catfish. During crawfish season, there is often an "all you can eat" crawfish special, too. The Stockpile is a couple of minutes off River Road in the heart of the Perique tobacco-growing region above Lutcher. Two and a half miles above Route 20 on River Road, turn onto

Bed-and-breakfast cabin at Tezcuco. (Photo by Julie Posner)

Route 642. The Stockpile is 1.4 miles north, at the intersection of Route 642 and Route 3125. They are open Saturday and Monday from 3 P.M. to 10 P.M. Tuesday through Friday and Sundays they are open from 10 A.M. to 10 P.M. (504) 869-9917 or 869-3529.

Indian Mound Rt. 3125 in Grand Point.

Just over 2 miles west of the Stockpile Restaurant on the river side of Route 3125, a thirty-foot-high Indian mound rises from the middle of a cultivated field. The mound was partially excavated (you can see artifacts in the Bonfire Museum) and found to be built before A.D. 400. Interestingly, the soil in the mound is not native to the region, but seems to have been brought from about 75 miles upriver in the Tunica Hills region.

Gramercy to the Sunshine Bridge (Rt. 70) and Donaldsonville

By way of River Road, it is 18 miles from Gramercy to the Sunshine Bridge (45 miles from I-310). The bridge connects a very rural portion of the east bank with the city of Donaldsonville on the west bank. There are no attractions open to the public in this section of East River Road, but you do pass through about 8 miles of pleasant scenery before hitting the huge and smelly industrial complex at Agrico.

NORTH OF THE SUNSHINE BRIDGE (RT. 70)

*Tezcuco

Just over a mile above the Sunshine Bridge, across the river from Donaldsonville, is Tezcuco plantation and "village." Tezcuco was built in the Greek Revival style in the 1850s. The plantation tour was not nearly as interesting as roaming the yard and gardens. A number of slave quarters, overseers' cottages, and other outbuildings were salvaged from other plantations and moved to Tezcuco. These give the grounds the feel of a Victorian village. Several of the buildings are open, including the old commissary (which now has antiques and collectibles for sale), a small chapel, and an old carriagehouse. A half dozen of the outbuildings are used as Bed and Breakfast accommodations. Tours (every 45 minutes) cost $5 for adults, $3.50 for teens, and $2.50 for kids. (504) 562-3929.

*Tezcuco Bed and Breakfast

Tezcuco has the best Bed and Breakfast accommodations on River Road. Guests stay in cabins that are located within a hundred yards of the main house. All have working fireplaces (stocked with firewood) and most have porches. They are available with lavish antique furnishings or decorated with simple country charm. Even the least expensive are warm and homey. After a day of plantation hopping up River Road, this is a great place to unwind with the complimentary bottle of wine and a walk on the grounds after the last tours leave. You can stay at Tezcuco as cheaply as in New Orleans. Smaller cottages rent for $60 and $75 double occupancy, and the larger places for $85 and $95 (7.5% tax on all rooms added). A "General's Suite" on the third floor of the main house is available for $185. In the morning, a tray of scrambled eggs, hot homemade biscuits, grits, sausage, and fresh fruit (Louisiana strawberries in season) is delivered to your door. Check-in time is 2 P.M. (504) 562-3929.

Travel Tip

In the 2.5 miles between Tezcuco and Houmas House, Route 44 turns north towards Burnside and River Road becomes Route 942.

The Cabin Restaurant Cajun/Down Home, $ to $$ Rt. 44 in Burnside.

This is an area of few eateries and the simple fare here, like beans and rice, fried seafood, and po-boys is merely serviceable. The big disappointments were the "World-Famous Gumbo" and "Legendary" buttermilk pie, which was mostly sugar. The main attraction is the quaint decorating and architecture, which seems to appeal to tour-bus guides. The restaurant is a conglomeration of slave cabins from the Monroe Plantation which have been stuck together in ramshackle fashion. In one cabin, the walls are papered with old newspapers fixed in place with flour paste. My favorite room is the bathroom, fashioned from a huge cypress rainwater cistern and materials from the Old Crow Distillery in New Orleans. The Cabin is located at the corner of Route 22 and Route 44 (two miles east of River Road). They are open Monday through Wednesday from 8 A.M. to 3 P.M., Thursday and Friday until 9 P.M., and Sunday until 6 P.M. (504) 473-3007.

Houmas House 40136 River Rd. (Rt. 942).

Just short of 4 miles above the Sunshine Bridge on River Road is the oldest tourable plantation in the area. Alexandre Latil purchased the land from the Houma Indians and built a small, two-story structure in 1790. This original 4-room house with outside stairways is now adjoined to the rear of a massive Greek Revival Plantation built in 1840. In the years just before the War Between the States, Houmas House was the biggest sugar producer in the nation. Maybe we got the wrong guide, but I found the formal tour of the house a bit pedantic. Members of the huge group touring the house (which is very popular with tour-bus operators) seemed to drift off, and one offered to pay the guide NOT to talk and just let him look! There is an excellent view of the river from the upstairs gallery. Daily tours are offered on every half hour from 10 A.M. to 4 P.M. in winter and until 5 P.M. other months. The tour costs $6.50 for adults, $4.50 for 13-17-year-olds, and $3.25 for kids. (504) 473-7841.

Travel Tip

There are two notable drive-by antebellum homes above Houmas House. Bocage Plantation, 2 miles above Houmas House, is a beautiful Greek Revival structure built in 1801. A mile farther up River Road is the stately Louisiana classic, Hermitage Plantation.

★Ashland Belle Helene Plantation 7497 Ashland Rd., Geismar.

Ashland Belle Helene Plantation, 14 miles above the Sunshine Bridge, is not on the list of homes published by the River Road Preservation Society. In terms of antebellum plantations, this crumbling Greek Revival manse constructed in 1837 is the great secret of the river's east bank. After the careful restorations and staid tours of lower River Road, it is awe-inspiring to see an unadorned giant like this in such pristine disrepair. It is obvious that Ashland is a little different when you pull up to the drive and, instead of a dull brown historical marker, you see a jungle of signs bragging "Don Johnson Oak Tree" and "Site of Eight Movies" (various other signs advertising Ashland boast 11 and 14 movies). Plaster and paint are peeling from the 28 thirty-foot high columns surrounding the big house and boards are missing from the 15-foot-wide gallery that encircles the second floor. Horses and cows graze in the parking area.

No tour guides will bend your ear at Ashland. Simply follow the homemade informative markers as you wander through the mansion. On the first floor, renovations have progressed to the point where all the flooring has been removed in most rooms, exposing brick piers and dirt beneath. After climbing a spiral staircase, you may walk through floor-to-ceiling windows onto the gallery. The upstairs rooms are mostly restored and are decorated with furniture original to the home. There are a few areas where the ever-present decay is cosmetically created by designers working on films like *The Beguiled, Band Of Angels,* and *Long Hot Summer.* Ashland does not face the river, but sits a few hundred yards off

Ashland Belle Helene Plantation. (Photo by Julie Posner)

River Road on Ashland Road. The turn-off is well marked. Between Darrow and Geismer, head east one block on Ashland Road and look for the Belle Helene entrance on your left. From I-10 take exit #177 onto Route 30 west. Proceed 3/4 mile, then turn left onto Ashland Road. Go 3 miles and Ashland Belle Helene Plantation is on the right. The plantation is open daily from 9 A.M. to 5 P.M. Admission is $4.50. (504) 473-1328 or 473-1207.

Travel Tip

Route 75 turns away from the river for two miles at Carville (7.5 miles above Ashland Belle Helene) and cuts off a 9-mile oxbow bend in River Road (which becomes Route 141). The shortcut through the town of St. Gabriel misses the White Castle Ferry and National Hansen's Disease Center, which offers free tours (*see* review below). After the Hansen's Center, River Road passes through farmland and pecan groves owned by the state prison system and becomes gravel for 4.5 miles before intersecting Route 75 at the upriver bend of the oxbow.

Carville-White Castle Ferry

Two miles from the intersection of Route 141 and Route 75 is the Carville Ferry. The ferry runs from 5:30 A.M. to 8:30 A.M. and 3:30 P.M. to 7:30 P.M. and hits the west bank of River Road near Nottoway Plantation.

*National Hansen's Disease Center

The National Hansen's Disease Center rests in a verdant oxbow bend of the Mississippi River, 85 miles north of New Orleans. Originally the site of Indian Camp Plantation, the land was purchased by the state of Louisiana in 1894 for the establishment of a "leper colony." The land was bought under the pretense of opening an ostrich farm, and the first seven residents were delivered from New Orleans in the dark of night on a coal barge. Our tour guide said bluntly, "This was a place where people came to stay, and to die." Believed to be highly contagious, the afflicted were forced into a life of isolation at the quiet, decaying plantation.

Because the 350-acre center was operated as an isolated "colony," it has all the trappings of a small village, including 100 buildings, two churches, a fire station, general store, 350-seat movie theater, golf course, tennis courts, and 20-acre fishing pond. The administrative offices are in the old plantation house. Today the center leads the world in research and treatment of Hansen's Disease (as leprosy is now known). Since the development of sulfone therapy at Carville in 1941, Hansen's can be rendered completely noncontagious. The 6000 Hansen's Disease patients in the United States no longer need to be confined for long periods and the resident population at the Carville facility has dwindled from nearly 500 to less than 200. The center is being transformed into a federal prison for low-security inmates, and is scheduled to cease operations in 1994.

A tour of the facility, which begins with a 9-minute video, is absolutely fascinating. Joe, a former patient, has been the sole tour guide at the Center for over 20 years and provides eloquent commentary in a lilting St. Croix accent. The buildings on tour, constructed mainly in the early 1900s, are connected by 4 miles of two-story-high masonry walkways with screened sides that afford a view of tranquil grounds and gardens. Many remaining patients glide quietly along the passageways on antique bicycles and wheelchairs. The solitude of the place is soothing, but inspires reflections on historically grim health-care policies.

The use of the facility as a minimum security prison raises a new set of questions. When I asked Joe if the workers on the grounds were building a fence, he exclaimed, "Oh, no! These are judges, lawyers, stock people. They are building new tennis courts and a swimming pool!" It is ironic that a place deemed satisfactory as a residence for Hansen's Disease patients for nearly a century is not comfortable enough for our white-collar criminals. When the change from health care facility to prison is complete in 1994, tours are likely to be halted.

Free drop-by tours are offered Monday through Friday at 10 A.M. and 1 P.M. (minimum age 16). From I-10, take Exit #177 onto Route 30 west. Go 4 miles and turn left onto Route 73. Go 1.6 miles and you will hit River Road. Turn right on River Road for 4.8 miles. (504) 642-4755.

J.A. Barthel's Store

Four miles from the northern intersection of Route 75 and Route 141, on River Road in Sunshine, is Barthel's, a country store right out of a Norman Rockwell painting. After 110 years in business, the store is still owned by a Mr. Barthel (who lives next door) and still sells the Sunshine community anything they could possibly want, from hardware to ham sandwiches. The tidy little cross-cut sandwiches (available in double-decker) on white bread make a nice picnic to carry to the top of the levee, or eat while you are waiting for the Plaquemine Ferry just five miles up the road.

Plaquemine Ferry

This ferry, 32.5 miles from the Sunshine Bridge and 78.5 miles from I-310, is the northern terminus of the East River Road tour.

It is one of the oldest operating ferries on the lower Mississippi and the northernmost point on the Cajun Country tour of the eastern side of River Road. Cross the river here and you wind up in the old lumber and rail town of Plaquemine. The ferry operates daily from 5 A.M. until 9 P.M., departing on the half-hour. There is a $1 toll.

RIVER ROAD EAST BANK FOOD AND LODGING

For information on the restaurants and accommodations in this list, consult the text for the East Bank of River Road.

Lodging

Ormond Plantation Bed and Breakfast River Road, St. Rose.
Holiday Inn 3900 Main St., LaPlace.
Millet Motel 1525 W. Airline Hwy., LaPlace.
★Tezcuco River Rd. 1.2 miles above the Sunshine Bridge, across from Donaldsonville.

Food

Wayne Jacob's Smokehouse Meat Market/Andouille. 2550 West 5th St., LaPlace.
Airline Motors Restaurant Cajun/Down Home, $$. 221 E. Airline Hwy., LaPlace.
Bailey's Smoke House Meat Market/Andouille. 1413 W. Airline Hwy., LaPlace.
★Cox's Meat Market Andouille. River Road and 9th St., Reserve.
Don's Country Store Andouille, po-boys. 318 Central Ave., Reserve.
Veron's Super Market Meat Market. Rt. 641, Lutcher.
Zapp's Potato Chip Factory 307 Airline Hwy. (Rt. 61), Gramercy.
Stockpile Restaurant Cajun/Down Home, $ to $$. Rt. 3125 in Grand Point.
The Cabin Restaurant Cajun/Down Home, $ to $$. Rt. 44 in Burnside.

WEST BANK OF RIVER ROAD

This section is organized in a linear fashion, moving upriver from New Orleans. There is a list of accommodations and restau-

Holy Rosary Cemetery. (Photo by Julie Posner)

rants at the end of the section. The west bank tour of River Road begins at the intersection of the I-310 (Hale Boggs) Bridge and River Road, about one mile north of Luling. From New Orleans, take I-310 south from I-10 (the exit is just west of the New Orleans International Airport). You may also catch the Reserve ferry from the east bank to Edgard (17 miles north of I-310), or hit River Road at U.S. 90, just west of the Huey P. Long Bridge. The west bank features the same bizarre mixture of plants and plantations as the east side of the river. Attractions are fewer and farther between on the west bank, but include two of the most famous plantations of the River Region, easy access to a couple of swamp tours, and one of the finest restaurants in the state.

Union Carbide-Taft Plant and Holy Rosary Cemetery

The juxtaposition of this sprawling industrial center 6 miles above I-310 and the tiny Holy Rosary Cemetery speaks volumes about the history and future of the River Region. The cemetery was established in 1878, but is now surrounded by the erupting stacks of Union Carbide, Agrico, and Louisiana Power and Light plants.

Waterford 3 Nuclear Plant and Visitors Center Rt. 3127, Taft.

Waterford 3, Louisiana's first nuclear power plant, is located 7 miles above I-310. A controlled nuclear reaction within an 882,000-pound reactor vessel heats water, and the resulting steam is used to power electricity-producing turbines. For safety and security reasons, the reactor area is closed to the public. A visitors center houses a model of the plant and a dozen or so "hands on" exhibits. You can test your own ability to produce current on an exercise bicycle wired to a display board. Pedal easy and a light bulb comes on. Pedal harder and you can create enough juice to power an electric hair dryer. Among the more sophisticated displays are a nuclear control room simulator and a Geiger counter test that measures the effectiveness of various materials in shielding radioactivity. One mile north of the Nuclear Unit on River Road, turn left on Route 3141. Go 1 mile and turn left (east) onto Route 3127. Continue about a mile to the entrance. The visitors center is open from 8 A.M. to 4:30 P.M., Monday through Friday. (504) 739-6075.

Edgard to Reserve Ferry

The Edgard Ferry is located 16.7 miles from I-310 and about 9 miles upriver from the nuclear plant. This ferry connects the andouille area of the east bank with a heavily industrialized portion of the west. It provides a view of the river and its heavy commerce. The ferry is located at the intersection of Route 53 and River Road. It operates from 5 A.M. to 9 P.M., crossing every 30 minutes. The last trip is at 8:30. A $1 fee is charged heading to the east bank only.

Evergreen and Whitney Plantations

A battleground has been formed six miles upriver from the Edgard ferry, in which environmentalists and historic preservationists are pitted against an industrial giant and St. John Parish officials. In 1990, Formosa, a huge plastics manufacturing corporation with offices in Taiwan, quietly announced plans to build a $2 billion rayon and polyvinyl chloride plant at the 1700-acre Whitney Plantation. Whitney's fate appears to be sealed, but the biggest outcry came in 1991 when Formosa began negotiations on the purchase of neighboring Evergreen Plantation. Activists want to preserve the plantation, which is one of a few that still has slave cabins and other outbuildings intact. However, the owners of Evergreen reportedly see little value in owning a property adjacent to a stench-producing rayon factory. Look for the wounded when you pass this war zone.

Bridge to Nowhere

As yet unnamed, unfinished, and unconnected with any existing roads, part of this span has been hanging over the river 1.5 miles above Whitney Plantation for several years.

Vacherie and Lutcher Ferry

This ferry (27 miles above I-310) disappeared in the fog for two hours one January day in 1989. Barring incident, the ferry crosses every half hour daily. The ferry operates from 6 A.M. to 11:45 P.M. A $1 fee is charged heading to the east bank only.

St. Phillip Bar and Lounge; Confectionery

The clapboard confectionery located directly across from the Vacherie Ferry is closed, but the St. Phillip Bar is still an operating River Road landmark. Mounted antlers and fish adorn the walls of this aging watering hole.

Route 20 to Kraemer Swamp Tours and Boudreaux's Restaurant

Route 20 intersects River Road about 30 miles above I-310 in the town of Vacherie (French for "ranch"). This is the best place to access the swamps between the Mississippi and Bayou Lafourche. The narrow road drops quickly from River Road into the wetlands around Lake Des Allemands and Lake Boeuf. Within 5 miles you are no longer in the province of the wealthy sugar culture, but in the domain of Cajun fishermen and trappers. To get to Boudreaux's Cajun Restaurant, head west 9 miles to the intersection of Route 307. Bear right on Route 307 and it is 3 miles to Chackbay. To get to Kraemer (site of two swamp tours), turn left on Route 307 and travel 10.5 miles (*see* Bayou Country chapter for more on Kraemer and Chackbay).

Oak Alley Plantation River Rd. above Vacherie.

Six miles above the Vacherie to Edgard Ferry (33 miles from I-310), Oak Alley is one of the best-known houses on River Road, named for the quarter-mile oak-lined carriageway leading from the mansion to the river. The 28 trees on either side of the drive were planted by an unknown French settler in the early 1700s, before the big house was constructed. The mansion was built in 1837 by wealthy French sugar planter Jacques Telesphore Roman. In 1925, Andrew and Josephine Stewart rescued the place from decay and left it to the non-profit group that operates tours today. The house contains many period antiques, but is not the grandest of River Road manses. Its reputation, like its name, is owed to the beautiful ensemble of proud columns and stately grounds. Bed and Breakfast accommodations are offered in the old cottages behind the plantation and a restaurant (not recommended) on the grounds serves lunch from 11 A.M. to 3 P.M. daily. Tours are offered daily from 9 A.M. to 5:30 P.M. (5 P.M. from November to February). Tours cost $6 for adults. (504) 265-2151.

Oak Alley Plantation Bed and Breakfast

Overnight accommodations at Oak Alley are in small cottages behind the main house. These wooden tenant houses built around 1880 have been restored and are very sunny and bright, with new kitchens, baths, and central air and heat. Not surprisingly, they don't have a very "lived in" feel, but the main attraction is the plantation grounds, which you may wander at will. A small creek runs through the yard. Walk out your door and see the sun set over miles of sugarcane. There are six cottages; two are shotgun doubles. Double occupancy rates are $75 to $100 a night. A small breakfast (included in the price of the room) is served at the restaurant from 9 A.M. to 11 A.M. Tours of the plantation cost an additional $6.

Strategic Petroleum Reserve/First Acadian Settlement

Seven miles above Oak Alley you will find another of the strange contrasts which have become the rule on River Road. Across from a marker denoting the point where the Acadians established their first settlement on the Mississippi (known as the Acadian Coast) are the pipes and storage tanks of a National Strategic Petroleum Reserve facility. Over the next two miles you will pass two of the River Region's industrial giants, Chevron Chemical and Agrico Faustina.

Oak Alley Plantation. (Courtesy of LA Office of Tourism)

*Lafitte's Landing Restaurant Cajun/Creole, \$\$\$ or \$\$ (lunch). Donaldsonville.

In the shadow of the Sunshine Bridge, 16 miles above Oak Alley (48 miles from I-310), is one of the most renowned eateries in South Louisiana. The restaurant is located in the old Vialla Plantation House where the son of pirate Jean Lafitte was married. John D. Folse, the owner and chef of Lafitte's Landing, has won hundreds of international awards for his creative Creole, Cajun, and classic French cooking. No chef, including Paul Prudhomme, has more completely mastered the use of all the wonderful ingredients to be found in Cajun Country. The menu changes daily, reflecting the availability of fresh ingredients and the whims of Folse's skilled staff, but make a point of trying the Cajun Caviar. Gathered from a native Louisiana fish known as a choupic or "cypress trout," this caviar was introduced by Folse and plays an important part in several of his appetizers. If it is not on the menu, ask about the crabmeat crepe. This delicate pancake is filled with crab, topped with the choupic roe, and dressed with fresh warm mayonnaise and fresh herbs.

There is no telling what may be offered on the menu when you visit, but the soups and appetizers are transcendental. We ordered the savory Oyster Rockefeller Soup and Red Bean Gumbo. The gumbo is an amazingly simple and tasty soup, strong and rich, seasoned with thyme, and naturally thickened by the beans. The sweetbreads are as tasty as any on earth. For a main course you may select from a dozen seafood, beef, and veal preparations. The fried flounder with broiled shrimp, caramelized onion, apple, and garlic was our favorite. I could write a book on the desserts prepared at Lafitte's Landing, but will simply suggest that you don't leave without eating one. Sweets like The Decadent (also known as "death by chocolate") and the Mandarin Orange Cheese Cake are criminally delicious. They arrive on chilled plates with chilled forks and are served in small ponds of decorative sauces.

A dinner at Lafitte's Landing is a bit expensive (entrees with salad and soup included cost \$16 to \$20), but unforgettable. Many dishes are almost as stunning to look at as they are to taste! If a stay at one of the plantations on River Road does not leave you feeling like a wealthy plantation owner, a meal at the Landing should do the trick! Lafitte's Landing may be reached in an hour and a half from New Orleans by taking I-10 to Route 70 and crossing the Sunshine Bridge. It is open for lunch Monday through Saturday from 11 A.M. to 3 P.M. Dinner is served Tuesday through Saturday from 6 P.M. to 10 P.M., and Sunday from

11 A.M. to 8 P.M. Reservations are suggested, but the atmosphere is informal. (504) 473-1232.

Sunshine Bridge

Like the Gramercy Bridge (which will be finished at some unknown point in the future) downriver, the Sunshine Bridge hung uncompleted for most of a decade, and developed its own reputation as "a bridge to nowhere." Now that it is finished, a lot of folks still call it by that name, based on the lack of any development on either side of the river here. It is a sweeping span that provides immediate access to Lafitte's Landing Restaurant, and connection to Donaldsonville (4 miles up the road) by way of Route 70. Unless you are interested in seeing the Triad Chemical plant, it is recommended that you leave River Road at this point and take Route 70 into town. This cuts off a 7.5-mile oxbow in River Road.

Donaldsonville

Donaldsonville, with a population of about 8000, is one of the three largest towns on either side of the river between New Orleans and Baton Rouge. Its quaint historic district of about 12 square blocks sandwiched between the railroad and the river has over 600 buildings constructed between 1865 and 1930. The city is located at a point where the Mississippi at one time turned and flowed southward toward the Gulf. After the river jumped to its current course in A.D. 1200, an Indian settlement grew at the intersection of the Mississippi and its former channel. When La Salle arrived at the juncture, he called the Indian camp *Lafourche de Chetimachas* (fork of the Chetimachas) and the former course of the Mississippi became known as Bayou Lafourche. Following (strangely enough) the eviction of the Indians, the site became a major trading post and destination of a large number of Acadian immigrants in 1758. Sam Donaldson founded the city of Donaldsonville in 1806 on lands purchased from Acadian settlers. It became the seat of Ascension Parish and, for the year of 1830, functioned as the state capital.

Downtown Donaldsonville Walking Tour

The interesting commercial buildings in Donaldsonville lie along Mississippi Street (Route 18) and Railroad Street (Route 307). Mississippi Street, which faces the river levee, was the old business district when most goods were moved by steamer. Railroad Street intersects Mississippi Street and runs to the railroad depot about

10 blocks away. The city was burned by Union troops, so few of its buildings predate the war. In the 1870s, the railroad arrived and business began to grow towards the depot. Near the intersection of Railroad and Mississippi is a good place to bail out of the car for a short stroll. You can walk across the street, over the levee, and enjoy the view from a public observation platform overlooking the river, or check out a few of the downtown buildings and Italian eateries.

B. Lemann & Brothers, Inc. Mississippi and Railroad St.

The city brochure proclaims B. Lemann and Brothers, built in the mid-thirties, to be the oldest department store in Louisiana. Incredibly, the store remains open, selling an impressive collection of hardware and dry goods.

Louisiana Square

When Sam Donaldson mapped out the city in 1806, this little park across from Lemann and Brothers was part of the plan. Along with the public observation platform on the river, the square is a prime spot to relax and enjoy a po-boy or sub from nearby Ferris Restaurant.

Ruggiero's Restaurant Local Fave, $ to $$. 206 Railroad Ave.

After most of the original Acadian settlers left Donaldsonville in the early 1800s, the city remained a destination for many immigrants, and a large number of Italians settled in the area. Ruggerio's is one of 3 spaghetti houses along Railroad Avenue, and my favorite. Of course, they sell a lot more than spaghetti. This is Louisiana-Italian food. Try the garlic fries or hot shrimp salad. For a real splurge, attack a plate of Premier Garlic Shrimp and Spaghetti. There are a variety of po-boys, gumbos, seafoods, and steaks available, too. Carry-out orders are available. Ruggiero's is open Tuesday through Thursday from 7 A.M. to 9:30 P.M., and Friday through Saturday until 10 P.M. (504) 473-8476.

Ferris Restaurant Local Fave, $. 212 Railroad Ave.

Ferris Restaurant reflects the melting pot that the River Region became in the early twentieth century. Margie and Victor Ferris, Jr., operate this sandwich and ice cream shop just two doors down Railroad Avenue from where Victor, Sr., a Lebanese immigrant, opened a fruit and vegetable stand during the Depression. Victor, Jr., tends bar while Margie dispenses sandwiches and ice cream on the other side of this very unusual restaurant. What can you say about a place that "specializes in Po-boys, Ice Cream, Domestic and Imported Wines"? They bake their own meats for sandwiches and the combo po-boys are excellent, especially the "Triple De-

Nottoway Plantation. (Courtesy of LA Office of Tourism)

light" (ham, roast beef, and swiss, fully decked on a french loaf), and the "Italian Po-boy." For a meal with a view, take your sandwiches a few blocks down to the river. Ferris is open Monday through Saturday from 7 A.M. to 7 P.M. (504) 473-8513.

Travel Tip

In Donaldsonville, River Road (Route 18) converges with Route 1 for a short distance. The river and River Road curve wildly between Donaldsonville and Plaquemine. You may turn off of Route 1 onto Route 405 to intersect River Road again. To the south, Route 1 follows Bayou Lafourche 100 miles to the Gulf Coast town of Grand Isle (*see* Bayou Country for more on the Lafourche area). To the north, Route 1 turns to follow the river. Here it is a four-lane highway with a 55-mph speed limit. It cuts the distance between Donaldsonville and Plaquemine in half (to 21 miles). There is an entrance to Nottoway Plantation (the primary attraction on upper River Road) from Route 1.

White Castle-Carville Ferry

This ferry, 13 miles from the intersection of Route 405 and Route 1 in Donaldsonville, connects the two premier attractions of upper River Road, Nottoway Plantation on the west bank and the National Hansen's Disease Center on the east side in Carville. It departs every half hour from 5:15 A.M. to 7:45 A.M., and 3:45 P.M. to 7:15 P.M. There is a $1 fee for traffic heading to the east bank.

White Castle

White Castle (population 2000) is located amongst acres of sugarcane, 15 miles above Donaldsonville by way of River Road. The town got its name from a sugar plantation which was moved and finally disassembled when the U.S. Corps of Engineers chopped off part of the city to build a new line of levees. The huge Cora-Texas sugar mill rises above the fields as you enter town. Founded in 1817, Cora is one of the oldest operating mills in the state.

*Nottoway Plantation

The most stunning and imposing of River Road plantations stands about 2 miles above the town of White Castle on Route 1 (17 miles from the Sunshine Bridge). Nottoway was built in 1859 at the height of opulence in the River Region, and its 50 rooms make it the largest antebellum plantation house in the south. The dimensions are startling. The home has 53,000 square feet of floor space and one curved wing has 22 square columns. No expense was spared in this jewel of the river. A bowling alley was built downstairs, two 5000-gallon water cisterns in the attic provided ample running water, and a gas producing plant was built in the back to light the house.

The planters of River Road engaged in a costly and proud game of one-upmanship. The builder of Nottoway was John Randolph of Virginia, who allegedly was determined to outdo another Virginia planter, John Andres, who had built Belle Grove Plantation nearby.

An exacting restoration was begun in 1980, and the house has been open for tours since that time. Nottoway is of the scale and proportions of a castle. Among the most impressive of its rooms is the downstairs ballroom. This parlor is in the semicircular west wing of the mansion and is painted glowing white, including the floors. The view from the upstairs gallery is equally amazing. At one time the house had acres between its front gate and the river. The levee has been moved to within throwing distance of the gallery and river traffic is plainly visible.

Many houses along the river boast ghost stories but, in character with its grandeur, Nottoway's most memorable claim to fame is how the house was saved by Southern hospitality. The manse had been selected for bombardment by Yankee gunboats until a commanding officer recognized the structure as a place where he had once been welcomed and entertained, and spared it from destruction. Nottoway has a large gift shop, a restaurant (not recommended) and regular tours daily. Tours are scheduled on the half hour from 9 A.M. to 5 P.M. and cost $8 for adults and $3 for children. (504) 545-2730 or 545-2409.

Nottoway Plantation Bed and Breakfast

With their cheapest rooms priced at $125, Nottoway is not for budget travelers. A bellhop handles your bags, a personal-size bottle of sherry appears in each room, and wakeup coffee and muffins arrive before breakfast. Despite this pampering, the best thing about a night at Nottoway is the opportunity to roam the house and its galleries alone at night. Moonlight sets the all-white downstairs ballroom aglow and you can relax on the upstairs balcony and watch ships passing on the river. There are 13 rooms available, with 9 in the main house and attached wings. All are furnished with period antiques and discreetly equipped with televisions. The four rooms in the 1839 overseer's cottage have a quiet view of the gardens. There is a small swimming pool for hot summer evenings.

Probably the biggest disappointment here was the food. From the wake-up muffins and coffee to breakfast and dinner at the restaurant (not included in the price of a room), the food quality was poor. Check-in time is 2:30 P.M. with check-out at 11 A.M. Rooms in the mansion and wings range from $175 to $125; accommodations in the overseer's cottage are $125, and 3 suites in the mansion cost $200 to $250. (504) 545-2730 or 545-2409.

Chapel of the Madonna River Rd., Bayou Goula.

Have you ever noticed the plethora of privately constructed shrines and chapels around the country that claim to be "the smallest church in the world?" Cajun Country has at least three such edifices, but the Chapel of the Madonna is probably the most diminutive. If such arcane attractions interest you, look for this pine-sheltered place of prayer 4.5 miles north of Nottoway on River Road.

Plaquemine Ferry

The Plaquemine Ferry is located on River Road (Route 405) on the far east end of town. River Road turns away from the levee here and joins Route 75. To continue into Plaquemine turn west on Route 1. The ferry operates from 7 A.M. until 9 P.M. daily, departing on the half hour. There is a $1 toll.

Plaquemine

River Road and Route 1 converge in the city of Plaquemine, 24 miles above the Sunshine Bridge. This formerly booming lumber, steamboat, and rail town is named for Bayou Plaquemine, which intersects the Mississippi here. New Orleans founder Iberville reportedly called the bayou "River Plaquemine" (from the Indian word for persimmon) in 1699, after sampling the fruits of the trees along the stream. At its heyday around the turn of the century, steamers and trains converged at the Plaquemine locks, hauling lumber cut in the swamps of Iberville Parish onto river and rail. Five sugar mills operated near town, and 16 trains passed through Plaquemine daily. On Sundays, a horse track below town attracted several thousand spectators. By the 1940s, the lumber had been mostly depleted, and in 1961 the Plaquemine lock connecting the bayou to the river was permanently closed. Like the locks, many of the downtown buildings are now closed, and the railroad tracks through the heart of town seldom creak with

Plaquemine Lockhouse Visitors Center. (Courtesy of LA Office of Tourism)

cargo. New businesses have grown along Route 1 east of town, where you can find fast food, supermarkets, and discount stores.
*Plaquemine Locks State Commemorative Area Rt. 1 and Main St.

The Plaquemine Lock complex, which includes a visitors center, museum, riverfront park, and observation tower, should be the first stop on any tour of Plaquemine. It is worth a detour if you are traveling the upper reaches of either side of River Road. A self-guided tour of the whole area should take about 45 minutes. Park your car here and you can walk to the major attractions and best restaurant in town. The lockhouse was built by a Dutch architect, using white ceramic brick and red roof tiles. Here you can get maps, brochures, directions, and see an 8-minute video history of the town and locks with some spectacular flood footage. The museum is filled with lockhouse artifacts and still photos of the steamer days, but most impressive is a small-scale working model of the locks and downtown area. Push a button and you can watch the entire process that allowed ships to drop from the higher Mississippi into the bayou. Push another button and the important buildings and landmarks of Plaquemine light up one at a time as a recorded voice gives their history.

After an information stop at the lockhouse you can walk outside and get a close-up view of the huge concrete-and-steel locks. The bayou had been widened and dredged since the first settlers arrived, but locks were not constructed until 1895. Built by Colonel George W. Goethals (the main designer of the Panama Canal) and completed in 1909, the Plaquemine Locks had the highest freshwater lift in the world (51'). The locks operated on a unique gravity principle until hydraulic pumps were added. In 1961, when larger locks were installed upriver at Port Allen, the Plaquemine facility was permanently closed. In 1972, the lock was placed on the National Register of Historic Places. Across from the lock there is a small park on the river levee with a display of various types of boats used in the area, and an observation tower forty feet above the river. From this tower you can see ships for miles in each direction. A soon-to-be-installed radio transmitter will allow observers to listen in on the conversations of ship captains. At the park area across from the lockhouse, there is a walkway leading down into the historic Turnerville residential district. The tower, locks, and other outdoor areas are open every day. The lockhouse is open Monday through Friday from 8 A.M. to 4 P.M. (504) 687-0642

Captain Joe in the Plaquemine locks. (Photo by Dr. E. L. Caze)

*City Cafe Local Fave, $. 435 Main St. (near the Plaquemine Lock).

The City Cafe has been operated by the Miranda family since 1919, and remains the overwhelming lunch and dinner favorite of old-timers around Plaquemine. This is one of those places where everyone knows one another and conversation is exchanged freely between tables. Like family-run Italian restaurants in New Orleans, the City Cafe serves a variety of seafood, blue-plate specials, and spaghetti and meatballs in their two small dining rooms. The house special is catfish or chicken-fried steak with white gravy. Wednesday night you can order "all the catfish you can eat" with trimmings for $6. Other noteworthy fried dishes are fresh, thin-cut onion rings and fried dill pickle chips. Saturday night's spaghetti and meatballs with garlic bread draws a crowd. Tasty broiled catfish, red snapper, shrimp, and steaks are also available. If you are not very hungry, half orders of all dishes are available upon request. Save room for the "three-in-one" dessert, the Cafe's own version of Mississippi Mud Pie. A crumb crust packed with pecans is layered with chocolate pie filling and covered with whipped topping. The City Cafe is open Monday through Thursday from 10 A.M. to 8 P.M., and Friday and Saturday until 9 P.M. They are closed Sunday. (504) 687-7871.

*DOW Chemicals Plant Tour Rt. 1 and Rt. 1148, Plaquemine.

DOW Chemical Corporation's Plaquemine Plant is located 1.6 miles above the city on Route 1. After driving past dozens of plants along River Road, it is fascinating to finally get inside the gates for a close-up look at one. DOW began operating at the site in 1956. Today it is the largest petrochemical plant in Louisiana, with 18 separate production units on 1400 acres of former cane fields. The DOW complex is like a small city, with its own fire department, 44 miles of railroad track, and a power generating system. The coal gasification plant is the largest of its type in the world, generating enough power to supply Baton Rouge with electricity.

All of these resources are dedicated to the production of a number of base or "feeder" chemicals, which are shipped elsewhere for conversion to retail products. Among the substances routinely produced are chlorine, vinyl chloride, chlorinated polyethylene, and methocel, a wood pulp product which is "used to thicken McDonald's milkshakes" (yum yum).

Displays at the conference center diagram the chemicals manufactured here and their common uses (no appointment necessary). Call in advance to view a short video and get a tour through one of three non-hardhat areas: Environmental Operations, Polyethylene Plant, or Research Laboratories. Probably the most impressive part of the tour is simply traveling around the facilities, which bristle with power and hiss with steam. You will drive down avenues with such quaint names as Chlorine and Caustic roads, below pressurized storage tanks, and past blazing flares which are constantly lit to burn off escaping wastes.

As you tour the plant, below you lies a pool of toxic chemical waste, more than 46,000 tons of it, that now covers over thirty underground acres. DOW dumped the chemicals, liquid, and sludge into 15-foot-deep unlined pits between 1958 and 1973 and is now investing huge sums of money to try to pump them back to the surface before they reach the drinking-water aquifer for the city of Plaquemine. The old dumping area and 224 pumps are not on the public tour.

To get to DOW from Route 1 in Plaquemine, turn right at the stoplight onto Woodland Road. Go about a half mile and take a left towards the plant at the DOW sign. Before you pass the guard's gate, take a right to the visitors' parking lot and the conference center. Although the conference center display is open every weekday, to be sure of getting a tour it is suggested that you call a couple of days in advance. Tours are often conducted on Wednesdays, but the DOW staff is very accommodating. (504) 389-6623 or 389-8136.

Benoit's Meat Block Meat Market/Plate Lunch. Rt. 1 in Addis.

This meat market 5 miles above Plaquemine and 15 miles south of I-10 is the last stop on the River Road west bank tour. Benoit's has a complete selection of Cajun meats, from fresh whole rabbits to homemade sausages and stuffed chickens. Everything is smoked or prepared on the premises. The specialties are tasso, andouille, and thick ropes of delicious Cajun beef jerky. I recommend visiting at lunch time so you can try one of Benoit's heavy lunch plates (take-out service only) or well-stuffed po-boys. Lunch is sold Monday through Friday from 11 A.M. to 2 P.M. The market is open Monday through Friday from 8 A.M. to 6 P.M., and Saturday until 1 P.M. (504) 749-3869.

RIVER ROAD WEST BANK FOOD AND LODGING

Lodging

Oak Alley Plantation Bed and Breakfast River Rd., above Vacherie.

Nottoway Plantation Bed and Breakfast Rt. 1, 2 miles above White Castle.

Food

*Lafitte's Landing Restaurant Cajun/Creole, $$$ or $$ (lunch). River Road, Donaldsonville.

Ruggiero's Restaurant Local Fave, $ to $$. 206 Railroad Ave., Donaldsonville.

Ferris Restaurant Local Fave, $. 212 Railroad Ave., Donaldsonville.

*City Cafe Local Fave, $. 435 Main St., Plaquemine.

Benoit's Meat Block Meat Market/Plate Lunch. Rt. 1, Addis.

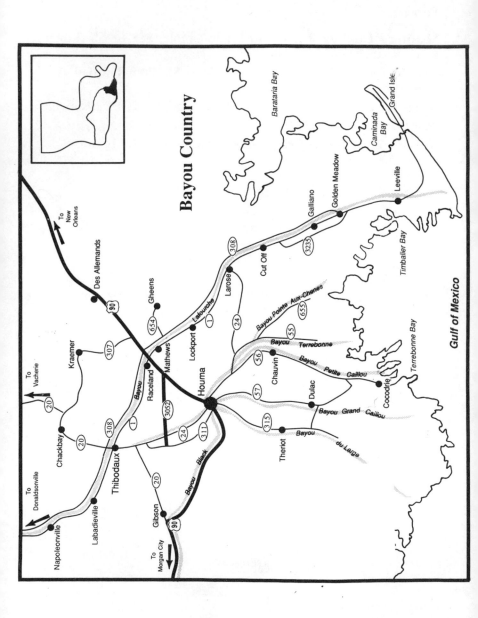

Bayou Country

11

Bayou Country

Bayou Country is a vast sodden expanse of land sandwiched between the Mississippi River and the Atchafalaya Basin just west of New Orleans, where the southeastern tip of Acadiana dips its frayed toe into the Gulf of Mexico. It is comprised of the coastal parishes of Lafourche and Terrebonne, which are connected to New Orleans and Teche Country by U.S. 90 in the South and accessed from River Road by Route 1 in the north. Nearly three quarters of the area is open water or wooded swamp, but its nickname arises from the dozens of bayous that meander southward towards the gulf.

Bayou Country begins less than an hour west of the Crescent City. While it correctly bills itself as "the closest Cajun Country to New Orleans," many of its towns, which cling to narrow bayou levees and ridges, are among the most remote and unspoiled places in all of South Louisiana. Watery isolation has made the region a favorite destination among fishermen, wildlife watchers, and those interested in traditional Cajun language and folkways. Unfortunately, few places remain where one can hear Cajun music, and Zydeco is nonexistent in this predominantly white region.

Travel throughout Bayou Country is a truly unique experience, as roads cling to natural ridges. The coastal town of Grand Isle is 55 miles from New Orleans "as the crow flies" and about 100 miles by car. Port Fourchon on Bayou Lafourche is about 30 miles from Cocodrie on neighboring Bayou Terrebonne, but is separated by 80 miles of road. Throughout much of the nineteenth century, the only way to get from Bayou Country (and other points farther west) to New Orleans was by boats traveling up Bayou Lafourche to the Mississippi, then back down the river to the city. Early ranchers developed trails for moving livestock from western ranges to market in New Orleans. These trails formed the basis for what is now the primary east-west route, U.S. 90 or the Old Spanish Trail. Even modern U.S. 90 has its surprises. Decades since construction commenced, engineers are still slogging through the swamp west of Houma. Just past Raceland the four-lane ends and motorists have the choice of going 12 miles south through Houma or heading as many miles north before continuing west on Route 20.

NEW ORLEANS TO LAFOURCHE

Des Allemands

The first Bayou Country town you will encounter driving west from New Orleans on Route 90 is Des Allemands. Named for the adjacent bayou and lake, this community, just 30 miles outside the Crescent City, is best known for catfish, which are plentiful in the surrounding freshwater bogs. It calls itself The Catfish Capital of the Universe and is home of the Catfish Festival (first weekend in July) and Spahr's Catfish Pond Restaurant.

Spahr's Catfish Pond Seafood/Local Fave, $. U.S. 90 W., Des Allemands.

Spahr's has a fried catfish platter with fries and a tasty catfish sauce piquant. The regular lunch special of catfish filets and catfish sauce piquant is a steal. The dining room of this former service station has floor-to-ceiling windows that look south onto the Des Allemands marsh, where a family of goats wander unfenced on a small island of grass. Spahr's is located about a mile west of Bayou Des Allemands. They are open 7 days a week from 9 A.M. to 9 P.M. (504) 758-1602.

Kraemer

About 9 miles past Des Allemands, a sign marks the turnoff for Route 307 to the swamp village of Kraemer. Even if you are not planning on taking one of the swamp tours emanating from Kraemer, this is a great route for seeing the terrain and wildlife of Bayou Country. The drive north from U.S. 90 on Route 307 drops from cane fields to enchanting swamp in less than 10 miles. The present-day town of Kraemer (if you can call a place whose only two businesses are swamp tours and alligator processing a "town") was a cluster of homes called Bayou Beouf (for the adjacent stream) until a few years ago when the postal service decided to move the Kraemer post office to this location. On the banks of cypress-shrouded Bayou Beouf you will find Torres' and Zam's swamp tours. Also on the banks beside the bridge are the now-closed trading post and tiny wood-frame theater of old Bayou Beouf. How did a community this size support a theater?

Attractions: Torres' Swamp Tours and Zam's Swamp Tours are two of the most interesting wetlands excursions in the state. Both leave from the banks of Bayou Beouf (pronounced "buff") at the tiny settlement of Kraemer. Both tours are on pontoon boats big enough to accommodate a busload. The tours travel up and down Bayou Beouf, affording a view of several types of wetlands filled with snakes, gators, and nutria. They don't penetrate the swamp beyond the banks of the bayou, but excellent guides make them special.

★Torres' Swamp Tours Rt. 307, at Bayou Beouf Bridge.

Guide Raymond Torres' family has lived on the banks of Bayou Beouf for five generations of lumbermen, trappers, and hunters. Like his ancestors, he enjoys a life close to the water, hunting alligator and deer and fishing on the miles of surrounding swamp. He remembers traveling by boat across Bayou Beouf to go to school, but proudly asserts, "I got my Ph.D in the swamp." Nobody can spot a snake on a tree branch or alligator in a thicket faster than Torres. Many big tour guides talk a lot of "bull" for tourists. Torres just uses his life in the swamp, his twenty years as a Fish and Game Agent, and his honest warmth to make the trip come alive. He has a small zoo of alligators, nutria, turtles, and birds in his back yard, and a sheltered picnic area with restrooms. Torres usually operates one tour in the morning and two in the afternoon. The cost is $10 to get on with a group or $15 if there are no other passengers ready to go. (504) 633-7799.

Zam's Swamp Tours Rt. 307, at Bayou Beouf Bridge.

Zam's is operated by "Papa Gator" Tregle, who has an alligator-hide- and fur-processing business out back. Zam's tour covers the same stretch of Bayou Beouf as Torres', but the highlight is a stroll through his yard, where you will see dozens of hides, feet, heads, and other gator parts hung out to dry. The best time for this tour is in the late fall when the alligator season is winding down and his processing business is gearing up. On one visit he let us hold a baby nutria and showed us its mother's freshly cleaned pelt! Even if the processing business is not in full swing, there are plenty of the reptiles to be seen in Zam's own gator pond. You can purchase souvenir alligator parts (great for key chains and conversation pieces) from his eccentric gift shop for a fraction of what they cost in New Orleans. Zam usually schedules

Tour guide Zam ("Papa Gator") Tregle. (Photo by Julie Posner)

one tour in the morning and two in the afternoon. The tour costs $10 a person to get on with a group. (504) 633-7881.

Chackbay

There is not much to see in Chackbay, but the town, just ten miles from River Road and Kraemer on Route 20, is a good food stop on a day trip from New Orleans. In early September Chackbay hosts a Gumbo Festival with Cajun bands.

Boudreaux's Restaurant Cajun/Down Home, $. Rt. 20, Chackbay. This working man's eatery occupies half of an old service station. It is a prime spot for sampling the bounty of the surrounding swamp. Whole fried alligator legs with all the trimmings are around $9, and a small serving of alligator or turtle sauce piquant is under $6. More delectable are the crawfish etouffée and stew. I recommend the homemade onion rings and (when it is available) *tarte à la bouillee*. *Tarte à la bouillee* is a Cajun dessert unique to this region, comprised of a boiled milk custard in a sweet dough pie shell. It's delicious with a dark cup of blackeye coffee. Boudreaux's is located at 507 Route 20 in Chackbay. From Kraemer take Route 307 10 miles to the intersection of Route 20. Turn onto Route 20 west and Boudreaux's is about 3 miles up on the right. They are open daily from 10 A.M. to 11 P.M. (504) 633-2382.

INTRO TO LAFOURCHE

The grand stream of Bayou Country is Bayou Lafourche (French for fork). A former course of the Mississippi River, Lafourche snakes southward for over a hundred miles from its severed junction with the Mississippi at Donaldsonville before reaching a terminus at the coastal fishing resort (and former pirate haven) of Grand Isle. Once the province of several Indian tribes, the bayou was settled by Germans and Acadians in the mid-eighteenth century. On the upper reaches are dozens of plantations, which give way to small truck farms and fishing communities in the south.

The uninterrupted stretch of communities along the more densely settled west bank of the bayou has earned Lafourche the nickname "the longest Main Street in America." To drive the full length of Lafourche on the narrow roads (Route 308 and Route 1) that parallel each bank can take most of a day. There are bridges

Shrimpboat on Bayou Lafourche. (Photo by Julie Posner)

at each small town to permit access to either bank. Most travelers intersect Bayou Lafourche on U.S. 90 just below Raceland and head down Route 1 through the fishing villages of south Lafourche to spend time surf casting, beach combing, birdwatching, or camping at Grand Isle State Park. Those interested in visiting the new Acadian Cultural Center or the Laurel Valley Village Plantation can head 20 minutes north to Thibodaux.

SOUTH BAYOU LAFOURCHE

South Lafourche is an easy day trip from New Orleans or side trip for travelers heading to Houma. Along the 65-mile stretch of bayou between U.S. 90 and the coastal village of Grand Isle, the French Cajun language and culture are vibrant. Residents speak in a distinctive accent, and indulge their own variety of French known as Lafourchaise. The best drive follows Route 1 down the west side of the stream. A short drive south takes visitors to Adam's Market (and mounted animal menagerie), Golden Ranch Plantation (on the east side) and the Louisiana Catalog Store in Cut Off. Land narrows to a thin strip on either side of the bayou, and cane fields give way to pasture. You may purchase handwoven garlands of fresh garlic, baskets of Creole tomatoes, or fresh Gulf shrimp. At Golden Meadow, the land plays out on the east side and traffic is funnelled onto Route 1. Shrimp boats line the bayou and little bars accommodate offshore oil workers. From marinas and roadside vantage points, recreational fishermen ply some of the most productive waters in the state.

The history of settlement in southern Lafourche has been one of retreat. With the same disregard for brooding nature that sees men building condominiums on sea islands, and mansions on seismic faults overlooking the Pacific, the earliest settlers of south Lafourche arrived in the early 19th century and established themselves directly on the Gulf. They bypassed higher land to nest on coastal *cheniers* (low-lying oak ridges) with access to prime fishing. Nature was kind until 1893, when a fierce hurricane drove 4 to 12 feet of water over most of Chenier Caminada. Two thousand lives were lost, the majority of homes were destroyed, and the *chenier* itself was wiped from the map. Most of the hardy survivors scavenged what remained of their homes, floated them northwest to Leeville on Bayou Lafourche, and rebuilt. In 1909 and 1915, two more catastrophic storms inundated the coast. The last of these erased Leeville and sent survivors fleeing northward again.

Lafourche Parish Tourist Commission Rt. 1, just south of U.S. 90.

The Lafourche Visitors Center has information on all the attractions of the upper and lower bayou. They are right below the U.S. 90 bridge on the south side. The center is open Monday through Friday, from 9 A.M. to 4 P.M. (504) 537-5800.

Adam's Fruit Market 5013 Rt. 1 South. Mathews.

Adam's Fruit Market is a fine introduction to life on the southern bayou. Since 1939 this store has been serving Raceland and Lockport. You will find fresh local produce, cane syrup, honey, and an assortment of dry goods housed in a large room decorated with fishing pictures and mounted trophies. The owner does his own taxidermy work and has created a crazy exhibit of stuffed alligators, nutria, and snakes scattered among the shelves of food. Fishing licenses, supplies, and souvenirs are available along with advice on fishing spots, tides, and weather. Adam's is about 1.5 miles south of U.S. 90. They are open 7 days a week from 6:30 A.M. to 6:30 P.M. (504) 532-3165.

Golden Ranch Plantation Rt. 654, Gheens.

Golden Ranch Plantation is one of the few attractions on the east bank of Southern Bayou Lafourche. Here you can see a number of turn-of-the-century outbuildings, the ruins of the old sugar mill, and the oldest brick slave cabin in South Louisiana (one of very few in the state still in existence). The only building open to the public is the original plantation store, with yards of empty shelves and a deserted post office counter. The lady who tends the store grew up near the plantation, but like the many workers who once lived there, has moved to the banks of the bayou. Her last regular customers were kids who stopped by for penny candies. You can still purchase snacks and work clothes.

The Golden Ranch rests amid one of the largest freshwater swamps south of U.S. 90. It was purchased in 1744 by Claude Dubreivl, who traded cattle to Indians for the property. John Gheens, for whom the community is now named, bought the ranch in 1879. As many as 100 families lived on the plantation, which had its own lumber and sugar mills, blacksmith, butcher, and boarding house. During the 1940's, the land was used primarily for cattle and trapping. It was deeded to the Gheens Foundation in 1982 for "philanthropic" purposes. Getting off the beaten path and over to the plantation is half the fun. The Golden Ranch may be reached from U.S. 90 by traveling 3 miles down the bayou on Route 308 (east side). From Route 1 and U.S. 90 on the west bank, go south 2 miles and cross the Mathews Bridge. Turn right onto Route 308, continue 1 mile, and take a left onto Route 654. The plantation is 6.5 miles east of the bayou. (504) 532-2524.

Lockport

Route 1 crosses a former channel of the Intracoastal Waterway at this community of 3000, about 5 miles south of U.S. 90. Lockport is one of three incorporated towns in Lafourche. Most of its 2500 citizens find work in the oil, marine, or fishing industries. Some travel 5 miles south to the Bollinger Shipyard. There is a cluster of turn-of-the-century businesses on the west side of the bayou and a modern supermarket.

Blackie's Po-Boy Local Fave, $. Rt. 1 in Lockport.

This is one of the popular plate lunch and po-boy stops along the bayou. (504) 532-5117.

Plaisance Meat Market Rt. 1, south of Lockport in Valentine.

This meat market is one of a few remaining in South Louisiana that serves blood boudin (also known as *boudin rouge*). The boudin is sold cold, so you will have to find a place to heat it up before eating. They also have regular boudin, cracklins, and hog's head cheese. The market is open from 8 A.M. to 5 P.M. Tuesday through Friday and until noon on Saturday. (504) 523-3123.

Larose

At this small farming and fishing community 16 miles south of U.S. 90, the arable land on either side of the road begins to significantly diminish. Here you will find a modern supermarket and discount chain store as well as a couple of fast-food franchises. At the north end of town, Route 24 intersects Route 1 from the west, providing a shortcut to Houma and the Pointe Aux Chenes Wildlife Area (*see* South of Houma section). I recommend the coffee from McDonald's or Jenny's Balcony Restaurant as an accompaniment to the delicious sweets from nearby Dufrene's Bakery.

Cut Off

Is there another village with a more prosaic name than "Cut Off?" Like many of the "line villages" along Lafourche, Larose and Cut Off seem to just run together. It takes a local to distinguish between which businesses are located in which town. The small shrimping community stretching along both sides of the bayou about 19 miles south of U.S. 90 has earned some attention among sports fans who recognize it as the home of Bobby Hebert, wayward quarterback of the New Orleans Saints. It is now home to the biggest clearinghouse for printed material on South Louisiana in the country.

*Dufrene's Bakery 1706 A W. Main St., Cut Off

The original Dufrene's location in Golden Meadow has been serving the people of south Lafourche for half a century. At this newer shop you will find the same tasty selection of sweets, as well as hot loaves of french bread. The most unique item at Dufrene's is hardtack, a brittle flat loaf of bread sold by the bag to folks going out on boats. A better buy for hungry travelers are the pecan tarts, custard pie slices, and crisp pecan cookies. For the last twenty or so years, one old lady has come into the Cut Off shop to fix homemade chocolates. Chocoholics will be sent to paradise with the pecan bars and rocky road clusters made fresh each day. There is no seating, so get a cup of coffee at McDonald's (upstream) and enjoy your treats by the bayou or while browsing at the Louisiana Catalog Store. Dufrene's is open daily, from 5 A.M. to 7 P.M. They are located just south of the Cut Off Bridge at 50th Street. (504) 798-7780.

*Louisiana Catalog Store Rt. 1 and 70th St.

Author and film director Glen Pitre (best known for *Belizaire the Cajun*) operates the nation's biggest clearinghouse for printed material on Louisiana from a small store on the west bank of Bayou Lafourche. The store also carries a good selection of videos, gifts, and other quality materials relating to Cajun Country. Pitre is a native of Lafourche and you can get help finding local attractions by consulting his staff. They had no difficulty directing us to one of the houses that was floated up from Leeville after the hurricane of 1915, and turned us on to a couple of good places to eat. Anyone interested enough in the area to drive down from U.S. 90 should make a point of stopping and browsing here; those with a special interest in the people and places of South Louisiana will want to make a special trip to visit this amazing store. The store is expanding to a 2500-square-foot showroom at Route 1 and W. 70th Street. They are open Monday through Saturday from 10 A.M. to 6 P.M. To get a copy of their mail-order catalogue, write: Route 3, Box 614, Cut Off, Louisiana 70345. (504) 632-4100 or 1-800-375-4100.

Cut Off Net Shop Rt. 1 at Cote Blanche Bridge.

If you want to see nets being made and repaired, netmaker Troy Terrebonne is at work every weekday and accommodates curious travelers who want to stop by for a snoop. Look for the bayou-side Cut Off Net Shop, just south of the Cote Blanche Bridge. (504) 632-3248.

Cajun Pecan House Rt. 1 and W. 67th St., Cut Off.

It seems like the Cajun Pecan House is always closed when I pass by, but the King Cake (available between New Year's and Mardi Gras) and pecan pralines from this sweet shop have been highly recommended. They are only open from October to Easter. (504) 632-2337.

Travel Tip/Shortcut

Route 3235 is a 4-lane by-pass around the towns of Galliano and Golden Meadow (notorious speedtraps). At the South Lafourche Bridge (120th Street), go right on Route 3162. Less than 1 mile west, turn onto Route 3235 (known locally as the "New Highway 1 Road").

Chaisson's Meat Market Rt. 1, north of Golden Meadow.

Chaisson's is one of a few places that still sells *boudin rouge*, made with pork blood. They only sell it cold, but if you are renting a camp in Grand Isle you can buy a few links to heat up for an eye-opener the next morning. Chaisson's is open 7 A.M. to 5 P.M., Monday through Friday, and until 11 A.M. on Saturday. (504) 475-7770.

Golden Meadow

Talk about getting down! The fishing town of Golden Meadow, at 2 feet above sea level, might be more appropriately called Golden Marsh. It was reportedly named for the fields of golden-rod that early settlers found in the area. This village was not even on the map in 1915 when a great hurricane uprooted residents from homes farther south in Leeville. Many of the refugees packed their belongings and some actually moved their homes upstream to this scrap of "high" ground, and began the settlement of what is now Golden Meadow. Be aware (and beware!) —Golden Meadow is serious about its speed limit!

*Dufrene's Bakery 648 Bayou Dr. (Rt. 1), Golden Meadow.

Since 1929 Dufrene's has made french bread and sweets for the

denizens of lower Lafourche. A new store is open on the Rt. 3235
bypass. Open from 4 A.M. to 7 P.M., daily. (504) 475-5450.

*Randolph's Cajun/Seafood, $$. 806 S. Bayou Dr. (Rt. 1), Golden
Meadow.

Randolph's has been around at least as long as their neighbor,
Dufrene's Bakery. At lunch, men linger over cups of black coffee
and chat in French. The walls are decorated with fishing pictures and
fifty-year-old photos of the original dining room. Randolph's is an
economical place to get tasty home-cooked-style food. A plate of
catfish with white beans and gumbo costs under $6. Try the million-
aire pie. This concoction of whipped cream, cream cheese, and
pecans will definitely leave you feeling richer. Randolph's is open
from 11 A.M. to 9 P.M. Wednesday through Sunday. (504) 475-5276.

Petit Corporal In the heart of Golden Meadow.

This small wooden boat on a platform beside the bayou (just
south of Randolph's Restaurant) is described as the "oldest boat in
Southern Lafourche." Built in the mid-1800s, it remained in the
Theriot family for a century, first powered by a sail and then a
3.5-horsepower engine. The boat was donated to Golden Meadow
as a historical landmark and has been on display here since 1969.
As I read the descriptive marker, a guy barreling past in a pick-up
hollered out his window, "That's my grandfather's boat!"

Leeville

When Leeville (about 57 miles south of U.S. 90) was settled by
refugees from nearby Chenier Caminada around the turn of the
century, it was an oak-covered "island." These people had barely
reestablished themselves when storms erased Leeville Chenier
from the map. There was so little ground left to build on that
most of the twice-displaced residents moved north and established
themselves at present-day Golden Meadow. Leeville remained
largely unsettled until oil was discovered in the area in 1931.
Today it is marked by a couple of shrimp docks and the oil field.
A large bridge spans Bayou Lafourche here, providing an expan-
sive view of the mostly uninhabited coastal wetlands.

Smith Shrine Rt. 1, Leeville.

Another entry in the list of places claiming to be the World's
Smallest Chapel was established just north of the Leeville Bridge
in 1971. Noonie and Abraham Smith built the shrine commemo-
rating their children's untimely death across the road from their
gift shop "so we would remember to close it when it rains."

Port Fourchon

Just south of Leeville, Route 1 turns southeast to Grand Isle and Route 3090 heads west to the industrial superport of Fourchon. This is a primary jumping-off point for offshore oil industry workers, who head out for 2-, 3-, and 4-week stints in the Gulf of Mexico. Three and a half miles from the turnoff there is a free boat launch, and 4 miles west of Route 1, Fourchon Road ends on a desolate stretch of sandbagged Gulf beach. You can drive your vehicle along the sandbag line, find a place to park and picnic, or cast a fishing line in the surf.

Chenier Caminada

Just west of the bridge into Grand Isle, Route 1 crosses three small passes (excellent bridge-fishing spots). This watery area is the former site of Chenier Caminada. In the early 19th century, Caminada was a thriving community. Today there are a few camps on stilts beside a canal, but the community, like the land it was built on, was demolished by the hurricane of 1893.

Elmer's Island Rt. 1, west of Caminada Bay Bridge.

This is a privately owned fishing and camping compound, open for a $5 fee. See description under Grand Isle Recreation. (504) 787-2509.

*Cigar's Store & Restaurant Rt. 1, west of Caminada Bay Bridge.

Launch, live bait, camping, tackle, and restaurant. See Grand Isle section.

Grand Isle

Since the late 1800s, Grand Isle has been the major attraction on Louisiana's Gulf Coast. Too battered by storms to support an upscale resort, the island is instead a destination for fishermen, birdwatchers, and anyone who likes the salt air and warm water of Gulf beaches. All of Grand Isle's beaches are public. Swimmers, sunbathers, and surf-casting fishermen find easy access to the sand by way of short paths and decks extending over dunes from Route 1. Elmer's Island and Grand Isle State Park provide an opportunity to camp, fish, and watch the thousands of migratory (winter) and tropical (summer) birds that nest on the island. For those looking for the comforts of home, there are motels and cottages which rent by the day, week, or season. It gets hot and

Grand Isle. (Courtesy of U.S. Army Corps of Engineers)

humid on Grand Isle, and the Gulf water is warm, so the best time to visit is in the fall and spring. This is the off season for local vacationers, so rates are lower and crowds thin. Fortunately, the off season is also prime time for birdwatching and fishing!

Grand Isle is 74 miles south of U.S. 90, an almost two-hour drive by way of Route 1. It is a barrier island about 8 miles long and one mile wide. Stretching east to west along the Gulf Coast, it protects Caminada and Barataria bays and their surrounding marsh. The northern or bay side is covered with oak and chinaberry trees and is home to most of the permanent residents of the island, while the coast side is lined with camps and commercial establishments. Grand Isle was connected to the mainland by the Caminada Bay Bridge in 1930. When the offshore oil industry took off in the 1950s, it became an important oil terminal. Route 1 leading to Grand Isle is now a veritable drag strip of oil workers heading home from weeks at sea, and vacationers burning the pavement to get to their waterside retreats.

The island was first settled in the late eighteenth century. By the early 1800s it had a population of about 75. It was at this time that pirate activity in the area was at its most brazen. Jean Lafitte's buccaneers, known as Baratarians, developed a black market trade with New Orleans' markets. They shipped goods through the shallow bays and bayous above Grand Isle to the swamps just west of the city.

Until shortly after the War Between the States, the island remained devoid of significant commercial development. Following the war, an unsuccessful sugar plantation was bought by banking interests in New Orleans, who began the development of a resort complex. Just one year after the grandest beachside hotel and recreation facility (the Ocean Club) was completed, the 160-room structure and other new resorts were smashed to smithereens in the hurricane of 1893.

Recreation and Fishing

Those looking for a refreshing swim may be disappointed by the lukewarm waters of the Gulf. They may also be put off by the spectre of dozens of oil rigs within sight of the beach and a plethora of flotsam. Most people come here to enjoy the sun, birdwatch, and especially to fish. There are plenty of opportunities to do all of these at surfside recreation areas on the island. Some of the best birdwatching is at the far east end of the island near the Coast Guard Station, where Route 1 dead-ends into Barataria Pass.

Fishing the surf at Grand Isle. (Courtesy of LA Department of Wildlife and Fisheries)

The three primary areas to fish on Grand Isle are the surf, the roadside, and from bridges or piers. The warm Gulf waters are perfect for surf-casting. You don't need a huge rig or fancy tackle to load up on speckled trout and small redfish (called "rat reds") along the shore. The late spring and summer are prime trout-fishing times. High-pressure systems hold the Gulf flat and still and the brilliant sun reveals dark forms of schooling fish just 15 to 30 feet offshore. To latch onto speckled trout all you need is a medium-weight saltwater rod and reel and a couple of sparkle-beetle jigs from a local bait shop. Toss the jigs out and retrieve them in a jerky motion. Redfish action heats up as the weather cools. The same fishing technique works for reds but a little piece of fresh shrimp helps to sweeten the hook. The best beach fishing is along the stretch of sand in front of the Grand Isle Public Library on Route 1 and off of Elmer's Island (fee charged) on the west side of the Grand Isle Bridge.

If the surf is rough or unproductive, try bridges and roadside overlooks. From Leeville to the end of Grand Isle, there are countless inland fishing places where you may catch redfish, trout, drum, and croaker. The same technique may be used from these vantage points as in the surf, or try throwing shrimp beneath a weighted cork (available at local bait shops). Look for spots where current is flowing under the road and cast so that your bait is carried away from you. With a small cast net, you can fill a cooler with shrimp. The most popular fishing structures are the three passes at Chenier Caminada, the west side of the wooden bridge leading onto Grand Isle (now closed to vehicular traffic), and the pier at Grand Isle State Park. You will need heavy rods and tackle to deal with the current and bull-reds at the latter two.

★Grand Isle State Park Rt. 1, east end of Grand Isle.

Whether you are visiting Grand Isle for the day or overnight, Grand Isle State Park is an essential stop. The park has a shaded pavilion with a descriptive display on the geology and history of the island. There is a 3-story observation tower with a view of the entire island, a 400-foot fishing pier, and a number of bathhouses for swimmers. When the Gulf is rough, fishermen and crabbers can enjoy a small pier on the quiet bay side of the park. The wide beach is great for shelling, sunning, and picnicking.

Up to 100 overnight campers can pitch tents right on the beach, but there are no hook-ups. On summer weekends and holidays, the park gets a lot of pressure and camping spaces fill up. Call in advance to check availability. The park is near the far east end of the island. Take Route 1 east about 6 miles from the bridge to the caution light. Stay to the right at the caution light and continue one block to the entrance. Admission is $2 a vehicle for up to 4 people. It costs $2 for adults and $1 for kids to fish from the pier. Camping is $10. The park is open from 6 A.M. to 10 P.M. in the summer, and 8 A.M. to 7 P.M. in the winter (on Friday and Saturdays during the winter it remains open until 10 P.M.). (504) 787 2559.

Elmer's Island Fishing & camping. Rt. 1 west of the Caminada Bay Bridge.

Elmer's Island is a privately owned fishing area and campground located on a spit of beach and marsh striated with canals. The island is totally undeveloped. A dirt road leads across several lagoons which provide excellent trout and redfishing action on a high but falling tide. Find places where water is rushing under the road bed and throw your lures into the current. The road ends at a barren strip of beach, where you may fish for trout in the surf and camp out. Primitive areas like this appeal most to serious fishermen who are not troubled by a lack of electricity, running water, or sanitary facilities. It costs $5 a day to enter Elmer's whether you plan on fishing, camping, or both. (504) 787-2509.

Supplies for Fishing & Camping

Blue Water Sports, Fishing and beach gear. Corner of Rt. 1 and Santiny.

This is one of a couple of excellent supply stores on Route 1 in Grand Isle. You can purchase fishing licenses, rods and tackle, bait, camping gear, and anything you would want during a hot day on the beach. Blue Water is open from 8 A.M. to 5 P.M. daily. (504) 787-2212.

*Cigar's Fishing gear, launch, camping, & seafood bar. Rt. 1 West.

Whatever you need pertaining to fishing you can get here, including live bait, tackle, rod and reel combos, and food. A boat launch provides access to Caminada and Barataria bays. In the evenings, fishermen and locals belly up to the counter for beers and boiled seafood. You can order a tray of crabs or crawfish to eat at the bar, or take back to your camp. The store opens around 5 A.M. and closes around midnight daily. (504) 787-2188.

Food

There are not many places to eat in Grand Isle. Those spending a night might want to eat one meal at Cigar's and pick up (if you can't catch any) some fresh seafood or boiled crabs to take back to your camp. If you are spending the night, there is a large grocery store on Route 1.

Cigar's Cajun Cuisine Seafood, $ (lunch), $$ (dinner). Rt. 1 at the bridge.

This is the best eatery in Grand Isle, serving a variety of fresh seafood and Cajun fare. Cigar's is an informal place with nautical decor that caters to locals as well as the vacation crowd. A salad is delivered with even the most humble meal of soup and crackers. We got the oyster artichoke soup and gumbo and a couple of well-stuffed po-boys, but the fried seafood platters are most popular. For around $5, you can purchase a lunch special of stew, salad, vegetable, bread, and dessert. Cigar's is located on the west end of the Caminada Bay Bridge. They are open from 10 A.M. to 10 P.M. daily except Wednesdays. (504) 787-2188.

Cigar's Store Boiled seafood. Rt. 1 by the bridge.

Cigar's Store sells the same boiled seafood as the restaurant, for a good bit less. You can get a tray of hard crabs ($1 each) or crawfish to eat at the bar, or to take back to your camp. They are open daily from about 5 A.M. to midnight. (504) 787-2188.

Lodging

Motels and Cottages: Grand Isle has hundreds of rooms, apartments, and cottages for rent. Most of these either cater to vacationers from Louisiana or attract overnight or weekend fishermen. Few of these are very modern or luxurious. We have either visited or stayed at all of the ones listed below and found them to be clean and comfortable. Many are cute old cottages or rooms in older homes which have screened patios with cooking facilities so you can have an outdoor fish fry or crab boil. Off-season rates are usually offered October through April 30.

Rainbow Inn Apartments .9 miles east of the bridge. $50 to $60 double. Off-season rates are $35-$45. (504) 787-3515.

Sun and Sand Cabins 1 mile east of the bridge. $50 double. Everything but towels is furnished. (504) 787-2456.

Tropical Motel, Inc. 3.5 miles east of the bridge. $45 double ($30 off-season). Cabins are $55. (504) 787-3321 or 787-2898.

*Shady Rest Cottages Rt. 1 and Apple St. Individual cottages come with a kitchen equipped with basic utensils. TV and A/C. There is a shady fish cleaning and seafood boiling area. Summer rates for 1 to 4 people are $50; larger cottages for 5-6 people are about $66 a night. Off-season rates are $35 for two people. (504) 787-3367.

★Bill's Shady Lawn Santiny Lane, 1 block off Rt. 1. The proprietors of the Shady Lawn, Curtis and Kathleen LeBlanc, are old-timers on Grand Isle and veteran fisherfolk. People who come to the island to wet a line often drive up and down Route 1 looking for their green pickup as a sure sign of a hot fishing spot. Their five apartments are among the nicest on the island. Most come with a couple of double beds and a few cots. They rent for $50 for 4 people and $5 each additional guest ($35 for off season). There is a cottage with 2 double beds and 5 cots for $67. The best feature of Bill's is the shady lawn. There is a full set-up to cook fish or boil crabs, picnic tables, and a swing. Turn off Route 1 beside the Bluewater Sports Store. (504) 787-3170.

★Bruce Apartments Landry St., 1 block off Rt. 1. The cottages are about 50 years old, and some of the coziest on Grand Isle. Each camp is a double house with screened-in front porch and camp-style furnishings. Turn off of Route 1 by the supermarket on Landry Street, and look for Bruce's white wood-frame cabins on the left. Doubles cost $40 ($35 a night for a week's rental). Two-bedroom cottages are $60. (504) 787-3374.

Collins Motel Rt. 1, east end of the island. $45 double. (504) 787-2893.

Camping: There are quite a few small lots on the island with full hook-ups for RV campers (none of which take reservations). Cigar's Marina and the Offshore Campground are two of the more popular among the camp-and-fish crowd.

Elmer's Island Rt. 1 west of the Caminada Bay Bridge.
See description under Recreation and Fishing section.

★Grand Isle State Park Rt. 1, east end of Grand Isle.
See description under Recreation and Fishing section.

NORTH BAYOU LAFOURCHE

For 50 miles between U.S. 90 at Raceland and its headwaters in the town of Donaldsonville on the Mississippi River, Upper Bayou Lafourche is adjoined by cane fields which slope gradually into swamp. The bayou has been dammed at its intersection with the river and plantation homes along its banks look out on a sluggish stream choked with water hyacinths. Small sugarmill towns like Labadieville, Supreme, and Napoleonville form an almost continuous "line village" on the western side of the stream. This is a historic route travelled by early settlers as they moved down the bayou from the Mississippi River. Similar to the Mississippi and Bayou Teche, many early land grants on Lafourche went to Acadians, but were bought up by Anglo planters during the antebellum sugar boom.

Like the waters of the bayou, the towns along Upper Lafourche are quiet and darkly reflective. Even Thibodaux, a college town and the biggest population center on the bayou, seems more like an old trading post and mill town than a social or economic hub. The small farming communities of the area offer little in the way of food and entertainment, but Route 1 provides a good look at the "sugar bowl" of Louisiana and the unleveed bayou offers a scenic route between River Road and Bayou Country. The new Acadian Cultural Center and Louisiana Boat Building Museum in Thibodaux and nearby Laurel Valley Village sugar plantation are easy side trips from U.S. 90.

Lafourche Parish Tourist Commission Rt. 1 just south of U.S. 90.

The Lafourche Visitors Center has information on all the attractions of Bayou Lafourche. They have a brochure with six self-guided driving and walking tours and maps of the region and its towns. They are right below the Route 90 Bridge on the south side, so folks planning on traveling Upper Lafourche will have to make a very short detour south. The center is open Monday through Friday from 9 A.M. to 4 P.M. (504) 537-5800.

Raceland

Three miles north of U.S. 90 on Bayou Lafourche, Raceland (population about 5000) allegedly got its name from horse races that were held on the surrounding meadows in antebellum times. Nothing so exciting as horse racing transpires here now. The business area on the west bank is almost entirely closed. During the summer months, this is a good area to find farmers selling fresh vegetables from the backs of pickups or at roadside stands.

★Rouse's Bakery Local Fave/Dessert. 3880 Rt. 1.

Rouse's Supermarket is one of few places where you can still purchase a *tarte à la bouillee*. The *tarte à la bouillee* is a traditional Cajun confection which I have not found sold anywhere except Bayou Country. It is rich boiled milk custard in a sweet dough pie shell. I would stack this up against any similar poor boy's dessert in the South. Although Rouse's is a chain grocery with several locations in the region, don't let that put you off; they prepare all their baked goods fresh on the premises. The best time to get your *tarte à la bouillee* is in the morning when they are still hot from the oven and are more easily eaten with a spoon than a fork (num-num). If you are not up for sweets at breakfast, pick one up for dessert; get a fork from the deli department and scarf down in the car! An 8" pie costs about $3. Rouse's is one mile north of U.S. 90. They are open daily, from 7 A.M. to 10 P.M. (504) 537-6666.

Sauce Piquante Festival First weekend in October.

Thibodaux

Thibodaux, 20 miles north of U.S. 90 and 30 miles south of the Mississippi River, is the largest town on Bayou Lafourche, with a population of 15,000. The site was originally settled in the mid-1700s by French and German people moving down from the river. It grew into an important trading post at a time when goods traveling between New Orleans and the Teche frontier moved to and from the Mississippi by way of Bayou Lafourche. The town became the seat of government in 1808 and was incorporated as Thibodauxville (after local planter Henry Schuyler Thibodaux) in 1830.

Thibodaux is one of several cities in Cajun Country that proudly claim to be a former home of Jim Bowie. Today, the old downtown area, with its two-story businesses and iron balustrades, looks like a weary French Quarter. New motels, fast-food restaurants, and shopping centers stretch along Route 20 to the east and west, away from the old bayou-side community. The center of activity, however, is Nicholls State University on the southern edge of town.

Thibodaux Chamber of Commerce 100 Green St.

You can get a walking tour map for Thibodaux at the Chamber offices in the old downtown area. They are located less than a block off Route 1 on Green Street and are open Monday through Friday from 9 A.M. to 5 P.M. (504) 446-1187.

Attractions

Old Thibodaux Walking Tour

The Thibodaux Walking Tour (map available at Lafourche Tourist Commission or Thibodaux Chamber of Commerce) emanates from the downtown area near the Chamber of Commerce at Route 1 and Green Street. There is plenty of free and inexpensive street parking in the area. Even without the brochure, which lists only bare-bones information for about fifty buildings, you can enjoy a walk through the downtown area, which sports a mixture of antebellum and turn-of-the-century homes and businesses. Most of the listed structures are in a ten-block swath stretching west from the bayou between Narrow Street on the south and Jackson Street on the north.

The eastern edge of the tour is highlighted by the *Lafourche Parish Courthouse* (at the corner of 2nd and Green streets), built in 1861. It is one of a handful of antebellum Louisiana courthouses still in use. Cornerstones of the western edge of the tour are two old churches. *St. Joseph Cathedral* (at Canal Boulevard and East 7th Street) was built in 1819 and was originally housed in a wood building which burned in 1916. The "new" building was constructed in 1923 using many details copied from churches in Europe, including a vaulted ceiling and stained glass window modeled after the rose window of Notre Dame Cathedral in France. *St. John's Episcopal Church* (at 718 Jackson on the corner of 7th St) is the oldest Episcopal Church in Louisiana, and one of the oldest west of the Mississippi. It was consecrated in 1845 and is a rare example of Georgian church architecture. Visitors are admitted to the sanctuary, where they can see an old slave gallery which now functions as a choir loft.

Laurel Valley Village 2 miles south of Rt. 20 on Rt. 308.

Laurel Valley Plantation is described as "the most intact turn-of-the-century sugar plantation complex in the country." There are many plantation homes on tour in South Louisiana, but this is one of very few places where you can actually see a variety of outbuildings. The original land here was deeded to an Acadian in the late 1700s, but was subsequently bought by a wealthy planter from Mississippi. Laurel Valley became the most productive sugar plantation in the parish prior to the War Between the States. After the war it was stripped of furnishings, equipment, livestock, and slaves. It rebounded to become a nearly self-sufficient village by 1900. Much of the forage for livestock and food for its laborers was grown on the grounds. Cane was carried to a mill located on the premises via 15 miles of private (small gauge) rail.

Although the grounds of Laurel Valley are open to drive or walk, all but one of the buildings are closed. The general store faces Bayou Lafourche and serves as a visitors center, museum, and gift shop. Volunteers provide information and brochures on the history of the plantation, and you will find photographs and old farm equipment on display. There is local honey and cane

Laurel Valley Village outbuildings. (Courtesy of LA Office of Tourism)

syrup and interesting items like bags from the old Thibodaux Sugar Co-op for sale.

After browsing, drive down the 2-mile plantation road which leads past rows of century-old laborers' cabins built of graying cypress. In a wooded area at the end of the road are the wooden schoolhouse, blacksmith and cooperage shops, overseer's cabin, one-room school, and the crumbling mill, built in 1845. Although these buildings are preserved, they have not undergone substantial renovation and thus are closed to foot traffic. A visit to the store and grounds takes 45 minutes. There is no admission charged. It is open daily, 10 A.M. to 4 P.M. (504) 446-8111.

Nicholls State University 1 mile South of Thibodaux on Rt. 1.

Nicholls State University, with its 166-acre campus overlooking Bayou Lafourche, is the biggest employer in the city of Thibodaux. The school was founded in 1948 and named for Thibodaux resident and two-term governor, Francis T. Nicholls (1834-1912). The school has grown to encompass 88 degree programs offered through 4 senior academic colleges.

The *Allen Ellender Memorial Library*. The Louisiana Collection, located on the third floor of the library, contains over 200,000 volumes pertaining to the people, geography, and history of the state. It is open during the fall, Monday through Thursday, from 7:30 A.M. to 11 P.M., Fridays until 4:30 P.M., Saturday from noon to 4 P.M., and Sunday from 3 P.M. to 11 P.M.

The *Center for Traditional Boat Building*. The Center for Traditional Louisiana Boat Building is located in the Allen Ellender Memorial Library at Nicholls State University. The Center conducts research on wooden boat building throughout South Louisiana and has a small exhibit in the first floor lobby of the library. Several boats are on display, along with a case full of pictures, artifacts, and models. Fishermen and outdoorsmen are constantly turning up old craft or portions thereof in the swamps of Cajun Country. The Center accepts donations, provides information, and will often send out personnel to examine artifacts. The bulk of the dugouts, pirogues, luggers, and rowing skiffs at the Center are housed in a barn on campus which is open for tours by appointment on Fridays from 1 P.M. to 4:30 P.M. (504) 448-4626.

★Acadian Cultural Center 315 St. Mary St. (Rt. 1).

This is one of three facilities under development by the Jean Lafitte National Park Service with displays, demonstrations, and film presentations on Cajun culture. The focus of the Thibodaux branch is on the Wetlands Cajun. There is a traditional Louisiana boat and boat-building display as well as exhibits on hunting, trapping, and fishing lifestyles. A film on Wetland Cajun Culture is shown in a 50-seat theater. (504) 447-4119.

Drive-by Plantations: There are several private antebellum homes on the banks of Bayou Lafourche just south of Thibodaux. *Acadia Plantation* is comprised of three cottages (later joined into one home) built in the 1820s by members of the Jim Bowie family. It is located south of Nicholls State University on Route 1. *Rienzi Plantation*, two tenths of a mile south of Route 20 on Route 308, was built in 1796. Legend has it that it was constructed by order of the Spanish queen, Maria Louisa, as a possible sanctuary in the event of her defeat by Napoleon.

Food

Try not to get hungry in Thibodaux. You will find plenty of fast food here and a couple of local favorites, but the choices are very limited. If you are just ravenous, I recommend stopping at Rouse's Grocery to get picnic fixings from the deli and a *tarte à la bouillee* from their bakery (*see* description at Raceland store).

Politz's Local Fave, $ to $$. 535 St. Mary (Rt. 1) north.

Politz's is the favorite lunch spot in Thibodaux. They serve everything from plate lunches to seafood, burgers, and gumbos. The big drawing card is Le Petit Menu, offered Tuesday through Friday from 11 A.M. to 1:30 P.M. Few items on the "little menu" are over $3, including a selection of salads, poboys, and gumbo. Fried okra or garlic bread is under a buck. Politz's gives the almost exclusively local clientele what they want—large servings at low prices. I can't highly recommend the food, but Politz's offers a good value and is the one place in town to sit down and eat. They are open for lunch Tuesday through Friday from 11 A.M. to 1:30 P.M. and Sunday until 2 P.M. Dinner is served Tuesday through Saturday from 5 P.M. to 9 P.M. (504) 448-0944.

★Rouse's Bakery Local Fave/Dessert. Rt. 1 north.

Rouse's Supermarket has a full-service deli and is one of a few places where you can purchase a *tarte à la bouillee*, a traditional Cajun confection indigenous to Bayou Country. For details see description of Rouse's in Raceland. Rouse's is open from 7 A.M. to 11 P.M. on weekdays and until midnight on weekends. (504) 447-5998.

★Bourgeois Meat Market 519 Rt. 20 (Schriever Hwy.), Schriever.

This meat market has been in the Bourgeois family for three

generations, long enough to develop a loyal following throughout Bayou Country. They have a variety of fresh and smoked meats, but their specialty is the chewy strips of spicy Cajun beef jerky (smoked for 10 hours each day). This isn't the leathery, hard jerky you find on the snack rack at your neighborhood convenience store, but a thicker and more tender meat. It is a well-seasoned treat, so be sure to get a cold drink to go with it. Also be sure to get twice as much as you think you want because it will likely disappear in a hurry. The jerky costs around $10 a pound, and Bourgeois will ship it UPS anywhere in the states. They are open from 7 A.M. to 5:30 P.M. weekdays, and until 3 P.M. on Saturday. Bourgeois is located just south of Thibodaux at 519 Schriever Highway (Route 20). (504) 447-7128.

Nearby Food

Boudreaux's Restaurant Cajun/Down Home, $. Rt. 20, Chackbay (7 miles north of Thibodaux). See New Orleans to Lafourche section.

Nubby Duck's Restaurant Cajun/Down Home, $. Rt. 1, Labadieville (9 miles northwest of Thibodaux). See Labadieville section below.

Nearby Recreation

Torres' Swamp Tours Rt. 307, Kraemer (17 miles northeast of Thibodaux). See New Orleans to Lafourche section.

Zam's Swamp Tours Rt. 307, Kraemer (17 miles northeast of Thibodaux). See New Orleans to Lafourche section.

Lodging

Holiday Inn 400 E. First St., $43 to $48 double. (504) 446-0561.

Sheraton Inn 201 N. Canal Blvd., $46 to $52 double. (504) 447-9071.

Labadieville

This village of about 2000 residents and the surrounding area were the site of the first settlements on Bayou Lafourche. The town, 9 miles north of Thibodaux, was originally called Star, for nearby Star Merchandise and Red Star Plantation. It was later changed to Labadieville in honor of the plantation owner, a

French colonist named Jean Louis Labadie. The town landmark is the spire of St. Philomene Church, built in 1888.

More unusual are the several little lunch counters advertising "Choupic Burgers." I can't strongly recommend these sandwiches, but can promise you will not find them anywhere but in Assumption Parish. Elsewhere, choupic (known under the euphemism "cypress trout") is considered a "trash" fish. It is, however, plentiful in the freshwater streams around these parts, where it is served chopped, seasoned, made into patties, and fried.

Another unusual characteristic of Labadieville is the three old card bars that line Route 1. Here the most popular card game is not the traditional bourré, but a variant similar to spades called Pedro.

*Nubby Duck's Restaurant Cajun/Down Home, $. Rt. 1, Labadieville.

Nubby Duck's has the misfortune to be located in an old fast-food building. Their name is not exactly a zinger either, but this is my favorite eatery on Upper Bayou Lafourche. Fried chicken is the self-proclaimed specialty at the Duck. I go for their meaty jambalaya and plate lunch specials. Jambalaya is always served on Saturdays, but is sometimes available during the week. It is dished out in mountainous scoops for under a dollar, or as part of a monumental plate lunch with chicken, salad, beans and dessert for about $4. On Sunday you can get a big midday meal of baked chicken with cornbread dressing. They are open from 2:30 A.M. to 8 P.M. (504) 526-8869.

Bayou Dairy Bar and Grill Rt. 1, Labadieville.

If your curiosity is just running wild (mine was!), this old-fashioned burger stand is about the best place to break down and try a choupic burger. The less adventuresome can go with an inexpensive cup of shrimp and okra gumbo, or beans and rice.

Madewood Plantation Rt. 308, 2 miles south of Napoleonville.

Madewood plantation was built in 1846 for Colonel Thomas Pugh and took 8 years to complete. The 21-room columned Greek Revival structure was built of wood gathered exclusively from the plantation's 3000 acres. It has a huge, free-standing staircase carved from walnut, and 25-foot-high ceilings. At the time of construction, interior wash rooms were rare, but Madewood had two. When the house was purchased by Mr. and Mrs. Harold Marshall in 1964, it had been vacant for 15 years, was devoid of furnishings, and was in disrepair. The Marshalls completely restored the house and installed period antique furnishings. Since that time the house has been featured in two films, *Sister, Sister* and *A Woman Called Moses*. The Marshall family still owns the Madewood and has opened Bed and Breakfast accommodations in the main house, an outbuilding, and another small house built in 1820. Tours are offered daily from 10 A.M. to 5 P.M. Admission is $5 for adults and $3 for kids. (504) 369-7151.

Madewood Plantation Bed and Breakfast

Brace yourself for pampered luxury should you decide to stay at Madewood. The glamor experience is a night in the main house which includes a candlelight dinner and full breakfast for $150 per double. Because the house is on tour, the rooms are available only from 5 P.M. to 10 A.M. If you are like me and get agoraphobic in a place this big, there are accommodations available in two smaller antebellum outbuildings for $85 per double including breakfast. Guests receive a complimentary wine and cheese tray and a tour of the house. (504) 369-7151.

Napoleonville

Although it has scarcely more than 1000 residents, Napoleonville (18 miles north of Thibodaux) is the seat of the Assumption Parish government. Located just 15 miles south of the Mississippi River at Donaldsonville, the town site was first settled by Spanish and Acadians moving down the bayou from the German Coast of the river.

Glenwood Sugar Factory Tour 5065 Hwy. 1006.

Glenwood is one of only a couple sugar mills that will still give tours of their facility during sugar milling season (roughly mid-October to mid-December). The tours are not formal or regularly scheduled. Just call in advance to make sure someone is available to show you around. Glenwood markets a unique product sold under the name Cajun Crystals. While they are partially refined sugar and are therefore labeled "turbinado" rather than "unrefined," these crystals are brown and retain some of their molasses coating. This unique Louisiana product is available at several grocery chains in the region. (504) 369-2941.

North of Napoleonville

Above Napoleonville, Route 1 continues 15 miles to the town of Donaldsonville (*see* Bayou Country chapter). About 3 miles north of Napoleonville, Route 402 cuts westward across the swamp to

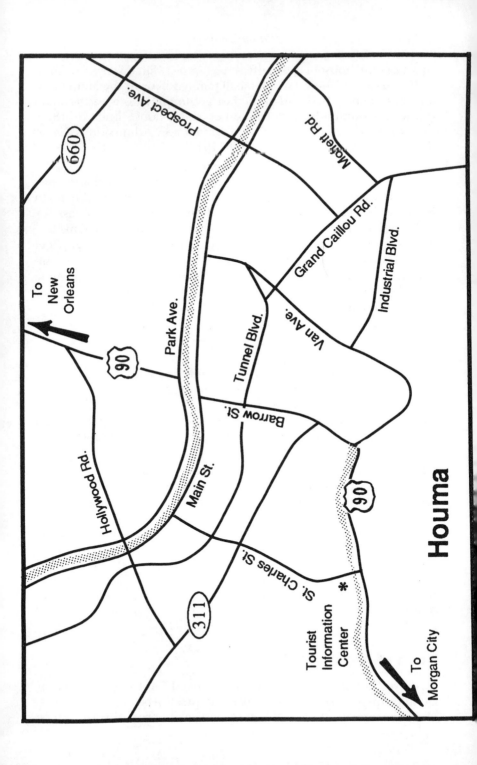

Lake Verret. This lake was once part of the Atchafalaya Basin and is a popular freshwater fishing spot. There is a bar, tackle shop, and launch on the lake at the end of Route 402. About 6 miles north of Napoleonville, Route 1 intersects old Route 70. This highway follows the levee of the Atchafalaya Basin south past the fishing community of *Pierre Part* to Morgan City.

HOUMA

Located at the geographic center of Bayou Country, about an hour and a half southwest of New Orleans by way of U.S. 90, Houma calls itself the Venice of America. Bayou Black, Little Bayou Black, Bayou Terrebonne, and the Intracoastal Waterway all converge at this city of bridges, with almost twice as many bayous fanning out in the old delta to the south. Houma (population 30,000) is the seat of the Terrebonne Parish government and the economic and social hub of the bayou region. Here plantation and farm country abuts the marsh and provides visitors a look at the varied economy of Cajun Country. The city has a large number of bargain-priced accommodations, including several Bed and Breakfasts, as well as major motel chains. You will find supermarkets, fast-food franchises, and three movie houses.

Houma was established on the banks of Bayou Terrebonne in 1834 and incorporated in 1843. The earliest recorded denizens of the region were Houma Indians, for whom the town is named. The Houma (which means red) use the red swamp crawfish as their tribal emblem. They made their way into the area in the early eighteenth century and were followed shortly by a wave of Acadian immigrants, who pushed the Indians into the wetlands to the south (where most still live). Early settlers relied largely on hunting, fishing, and trapping for sustenance. When the process for refining and granulating sugar was perfected in 1794, sugarcane became the predominant crop. Several antebellum sugar plantations may still be seen in the Houma area, and the stately Southdown Plantation Home is open to visitors.

While thousands of acres of sugarcane still fill the landscape, for the last 60 years Houma's fortunes have been inextricably tied to the oil and gas industry operating in the wetlands to the south. Barges, crew boats, jack-up rigs, and other petroleum vessels make their way down the Houma Navigation Channel and southern bayous to rich coastal oil fields. Like other oil centers in South Louisiana, Houma was economically pounded by the collapse of oil prices in the eighties. While boarded-up downtown windows are a legacy of these hard times, the city has diversified its economy and now enjoys an influx of adventurous tourists who come to explore the surrounding wetlands paradise via tour boats, charter fishing expeditions, and automobile.

Houma-Terrebonne Tourist Information Center U.S. 90 and St. Charles.

This is the first place to visit before exploring the Houma area. Aside from getting the usual walking tour info, maps, and brochures, you can find out what special events are scheduled. The folks here can help map out driving tours of the wetlands to the south or plantation country to the north, make reservations for swamp tours, or connect you with a fishing charter. If plantations and historic homes are your bag, you will want to drive a few blocks north on St. Charles Street to Route 311, which sports some of the most elegant old homes in the area. To get to the Visitors Center from New Orleans you must drive through downtown on U.S. 90 before turning north on St. Charles. From the west the visitors center will greet you before entering town. 1-800-688-2732 or (504) 868-2732.

Attractions

Before you tour downtown, budget time to see the outlying wetlands, which are the main attraction of the region. There is not a lot to see in downtown Houma, but there is no denying the charm of this town that tangles like a child's first Etch-A-Sketch drawing along the banks of a half dozen or so streams. Many streets are one-way avenues split down the middle by bayous. The main streets are Route 24 (Main Street), which follows Bayou Terrebonne, and U.S. 90 (Barrow Street), which traces the banks of the Intracoastal Waterway.

Walking Tour of the Houma Historic District Corner Rt. 24 and U.S. 90.

A map of historic buildings on the downtown walking tour is available at the Houma-Terrebonne Visitors Center. The tour can be completed in half an hour if you park near the intersection of Route 24 and U.S. 90. A metered parking space here costs 5 cents an hour. From this corner you can scope out the odd mixture of Victorian and turn-of-the-century storefronts (largely deserted), and the Art-Deco-style *Parish Courthouse*. Actually, the best reason to stop here is to grab a plate lunch at *Bob's Cafe* (*see* review in the food section). Among the scenic buildings are the *Old Post Office* on Main Street, which was used for the clandestine burial of Union soldiers killed in an ambush during the War Between the States (it now houses a restaurant), and the Art-Deco *People's Drug* building.

Houma Indian Festival Last weekend in August.

This is a very small but soulful festival. The event gets underway with a blessing of the festival grounds. Dances and chants are performed by visiting tribes and Houma baskets are sold. Coinciding with the festival is the crowning of the beautiful winner of the Miss Houma Indian Nation pageant.

ROUTE 311—HOUMA TO THIBODAUX

Route 311 arcs northwest from Houma to Thibodaux following the natural levee of Little Bayou Black. From a point just north of the visitors center, it skirts a couple of the city's main attractions before blazing into the cane fields of plantation country.

Southdown Plantation/Terrebonne Museum Rt. 311 and St. Charles St.

Southdown is the only plantation house in Bayou Country open to individual visitors (as opposed to large groups/bus tours) and is conveniently located within the Houma city limits. The plantation was constructed in 1859, with a second floor added in 1893. There is a room full of historical photos and artifacts of local industries such as fishing, seafood packing, shrimp drying, lumber milling, sugarcane, and petroleum. The Senator Allen J. Ellender Room on the second floor houses a replica of his senate office packed with souvenirs of a 36-year tenure (a record) in the U.S. Senate. Ellender was born in the tiny community of Bourg, south of Houma. His career stretched from days as floor leader in the State House during the Huey Long administration to a term as President Pro Tempore of the U.S. Senate before his death in 1972. The Ellender Room is filled with autographed pictures of political figures and celebrities received during his 36-year reign. There are a couple of super shots of President Kennedy and Jackie. Southdown is just a few blocks north of the Houma-Terrebonne Visitors Center. Admission is $4 for adults. The plantation and museum are open daily from 10 A.M. to 4 P.M. (except holidays). (504) 851-0154.

Waterland USA Rt. 311, just north of Southdown Plantation.

Waterland USA is located on Highway 311 in Houma just north of St. Charles Street. This 7-acre water amusement park is a veritable oasis on a humid summer day. Waterland may not be the type of place you expected to visit in Cajun Country, but 95-degree heat and 90 percent humidity can change vacationing perspectives a lot! Concessions, a game arcade, and miniature golf are available. Admission is $8 for all day, $5 after 5 P.M. Waterland is open daily from 10 A.M. to 8 P.M. (504) 876-3887.

Wildlife Museum Rt. 311, 3 miles north of Southdown Plantation.

This is the most unusual museum to ever crop up in anyone's back yard! Behind a brick home facing Little Bayou Black, the Wildlife Museum is a 6600-square-foot compound housing one of the largest private collections of mounted exotic animals in the world. Two ten-foot Alaskan brown bears are posed in claw-to-claw combat; a sixteen-foot-tall giraffe peers down from the rafters; and an Alaskan moose does a Bullwinkle impression under a set of antlers weighing nearly 100 pounds. There is nothing more striking than the sheer size of the larger animals when seen at close range.

The 750 full-size mounts in the Wildlife Museum were collected by big game hunter Curley Miller, who traveled to some of the most inhospitable regions on the planet to get his mounts. You are invited to handle the glasslike, softball-size ostrich eggs and the twenty-inch bone that guide Sherry Hebert swears is from a walrus penis! Curley Miller died in 1989, just a year after opening his dream museum, but his wife is working hard to keep the non-profit collection open to the public. The museum is open Tuesday-Saturday from 10 A.M. to 6 P.M., and from 1 P.M. to 6 P.M. on Sunday. Tours are held every hour. Admission is $4 and $2 for children ages 3 to 12. (504) 851-7674.

Drive-by Plantations: Between the Wildlife Museum and the intersection of highways 311 and 24 in Schriever are four plantations which may be viewed from the road but are privately owned and currently closed to the public.

Crescent Farm Plantation Rt. 311, 3½ miles north of Houma.

This raised Creole cottage (across from the Wildlife Museum) was built in 1834. It is noted for its square wooden columns and wide gallery.

Ellendale Plantation Rt. 311, 7 miles north of Houma.

Ellendale Plantation was built in the early 1800s, but has been altered significantly by several additions. There is an old brick sugar house still located on the grounds.

Ardoyne Mansion 1726 Rt. 311, 8 miles north of Houma.

Ardoyne is a fabulously ornate, high-Victorian plantation built in 1897 and patterned after a photograph of a Scottish castle. It is fitting that this gingerbread jewel was copied from a photo, as it is truly a storybook home with soaring eaves, a railed gallery, and moss-draped yard. Large group tours (15-20 persons) may be arranged by contacting Mrs. Margaret Shaffer at (504) 872-3197. Tour cost is $4 per adult.

Magnolia Plantation 628 Rt. 311 in Schriever, 12 miles north of Houma.

This plantation takes its name from several large magnolia trees on the grounds. The two-story Greek Revival-style structure was built in 1854 and was used as a hospital by Union soldiers. Pre-arranged group tours for 10 or more are available by contacting Mrs. Marlene Shaffer at (504) 446-1493. Tours cost $3.50 per person.

Food

A-Bear's Restaurant Cajun/Down Home, $ to $$. 809 Bayou Black Dr.

You won't find any bears lurking about the entrance to this tiny cafe; "A-Bear" is the phonetic spelling of Hebert, the proprietor's last name. The food here is hearty fare. Po-boys, red beans with sausage and potato salad, plate lunches, and bowls of gumbo for under $4 are recommended. To enjoy A-Bears at its good-timing best, stop by on a Friday night for the "all you can eat" fried catfish, which is served to the strains of acoustic Cajun music by "Cajun Man" Black Guidry and his wife, Sondra (*see* music listings below). The music and catfish are popular among locals, so be sure and get there before 7 P.M. or you may not get a seat! Don't pass up a chance to sample the heartbreakingly good icebox pies. The lemon and coconut are refreshingly chilled cream pies, while the pecan is served hot with ice cream. You can get a slice of pie and coffee to go and enjoy them at neighboring Jim Bowie Park on the Intracoastal Waterway. A-Bear's has good breakfasts, too. They are located at the intersection of U.S. 90 and Route 312, and are open Monday through Thursday from 7 A.M. to 5 P.M., Friday until 10 P.M., and Saturday until 2 P.M. (504) 872-6306.

Bob's Cafe Cajun/Down Home, $. 308 E. Main St. (Rt. 24).

Every city should have a lunch spot like Bob's. This downtown diner is a no-frills place to gorge on rib-sticking pot food like stews, gumbos, beans, and sauce piquantes. You have four tables to choose from and even fewer entrees on the changing menu, but this is the best home-style cooking to be found within the

Houma city limits. A typical lunch selection is veal roast, greens or white beans, scalloped potatoes, and cobbler for under five dollars. The chicken gumbo is fabulous and comes with three pieces of chicken afloat in the broth. Bob's is located on Main Street in the center of the downtown walking tour. They are open Monday through Friday from 7:30 A.M. to 1:30 P.M. (504) 872-6113.

Dave's Cajun Kitchen Seafood, $ to $$. 2433 W. Main St. (Rt. 24).

Dave LeBeuf dishes up generous servings of fresh fried seafood at moderate prices. All of LeBeuf's seafood dishes and platters (except the "large," which serves two) are priced under $10, including a softshell platter of two crabs with salad and fries for $9. My favorite is the fried catfish, which is cooked so that the center is just tender and the edges are crisp. Try one of the fried seafood po-boys or stop by for a lunch special. One recent lunch plate featured a softshell crab, white beans, beets, and a salad for $4. If you visit Dave's after the weather cools down, try the chicken andouille gumbo, redolent with smoked sausage and seasoned to warm more than your soul. Dave's is located just northwest of town. They are open Tuesday through Saturday, 11 A.M. to 9 P.M., and Friday until 10 P.M. Breakfast is served weekdays from 5:30 A.M. to 10 A.M. (504) 876-0270.

Dula and Edwin's Restaurant Seafood, $ to $$. 2426 Bayou Blue Rd.

The boisterous level of conversation and visiting between tables marks D&E's as a favorite among the locals, who line up for boiled crawfish, seafood gumbo, and the special seafood-stuffed potatoes. Dula and Edwin have a "Tourist Special," which is a sampler of all their best dishes ($10 each or $25 for three). They enjoy sitting down and demonstrating how to peel those crawfish and get into the hard-shell crabs. You know the boiled seafood is coming to you directly from the pot because you can see Edwin dumping the baskets of steaming crustaceans into serving bins at the rear of the dining area. Try to visit Dula and Edwin's for an early supper on Fridays so you can make it to the Cajun Man's show at A-Bear's. D&E's is located just north of Houma on Bayou Blue Road (Route 316). They are open Tuesday through Friday and Sunday from 10 A.M. to 10 P.M., and Saturday from 4 P.M. to 10 P.M. (504) 876-0271.

*Rouse's Supermarket Bakery Local Fave/Dessert. 2737 W. Main St.

This is the only place in Houma where you can still purchase a *tarte à la bouillee*. The *tarte à la bouillee* is a traditional Cajun confection which I have not found mentioned or sold anywhere except Bayou Country. It is a rich boiled milk custard in a sweet dough pie shell. See description in Raceland section. The Rouse's "Superstore" is at the corner of W. Main Street and Martin Luther King, Jr., Dr. They are open from 7 A.M. to 11 P.M. daily. (504) 868-5033.

Nearby Food

Sportsman's Paradise Seafood, $ to $$. See South of Houma.

★Coco Marina Seafood, $ to $$$. See South of Houma.

★Chester's Cypress Inn Local Fave, $$. See Houma to Morgan City.

La Trouvaille Cajun/Down Home, $$. See South of Houma.

Music

A-Bear's Restaurant Cajun food & music, $$. 809 Bayou Black Dr.

This little restaurant features the music of Black and Sondra Guidry every Friday night from about 7 P.M. to 9:30. Black performs Cajun and country classics plus a handful of his own compositions celebrating life on the bayous of Louisiana. A respectable accordionist and guitar picker with a deep voice, Black is a born entertainer. This is the only Cajun show in the Houma area. While you won't hear bona fide traditional music (Sondra plays a decidedly non-Cajun electric keyboard), the goodtime vibes are irrepressible. A-Bear's is located at the intersection of U.S. 90 and Route 312 just south of town. (504) 872-6306.

Nearby Recreation

The main forms of recreation in the Houma area are swamp tours and fishing in the surrounding wetlands.

Annie Miller Swamp Tour Located 8 miles west of Houma on U.S. 90. See Houma to Morgan City.

★Atchafalaya Basin Backwater Adventure Located 21 miles west of Houma on Rt. 20. See Houma to Morgan City. Pirogue rentals.

★A Cajun Man's Tour Located 16 miles west of Houma on U.S. 90. See Houma to Morgan City.

Munson's Swamp Tours Munson's is about 8 miles south of Houma on Grand Caillou Rd. See South of Houma.

Bayou Neuf Swamp Tour See South of Houma listing.

La Petite Maison du Bois. (Photo by Julie Posner)

Lodging

Hotels and Motels:

A-Bear's Motel U.S. 90 E., $25 double. (504) 872-4528.

Benedict House 1381 W. Tunnel Blvd., $33 to $37 double. (504) 868-0500.

Holiday Inn Holidome 210 South Hollywood Rd., $41 to $49 double. (504) 868-5851.

Houmas Red Carpet Inn U.S. 90 W., $34 double. (504) 876-4160.

Nan King Motel 224 S. Hollywood Rd., $21 double. (504) 851-6041.

Lake Houmas Inn U.S. 90 E., $30 double. (504) 868-9021.

Ramada Inn of Houma 1400 W. Tunnel Blvd., $43 to $47 double. (504) 879-4871.

Sugar Bowl Motel Corner of U.S. 90 and Rt. 24, $29 to $31 double. (504) 872-4521.

Bed and Breakfasts:

Cajun House of Hospitality 48 Killarney Ct.

Lucy and Dee Dehart welcome travelers into their small home in suburban Houma with open arms and hearts. These are folks that really enjoy entertaining and directing guests. Lucy grew up on the southern reaches of Bayou Dulac and can recall (in a thick Cajun accent) many trips to the family's trapping and fishing camp near Lake Theriot. Dee has a vast store of information on the coastal region too, having worked in the oil patch as a shrimper and as a sheriff's deputy. One of the highlights of our stay was listening to Dee recount stories of hurricanes, fishing trips, and local politics while Lucy sewed fluorescent panties (which she sells as Carnival throws). The Deharts' home is modern (located in a new subdivision). They accommodate groups of three or less and the bath is shared with the hosts. If you want the experience of joining a local family for a couple of days, the Deharts can adopt you by reservation! You will leave with memories of Lucy's seafood-stuffed potatoes and (if you're lucky) a pair of the most outrageous Mardi Gras panties ever made! The cost for 1 or 2 people is $35, and 3-4 people costs $45. (504) 872-2384 or 872-0465.

Chez Maudrey 311 Pecan St.

In the Houma style, this is a B&B that offers more in the way of hospitality than fancy digs. Maudrey rents a couple of rooms in her brick rambler by the side of the Intracoastal Waterway.

Shrimp and oil boats cruise past the front door. The rooms have private baths, but you share the rest of the house with the hostess. Maudrey will show videos about Cajun people, music, or Mardi Gras while she fixes breakfast and dinner. Maudrey is a fixture in the local tourist industry, helping coordinate bus tours and special events, so she has plenty of contacts and can help arrange an itinerary. You don't get plantation luxury here, but you will be mothered. Before sending guests out on a car tour, she always packs their coolers with ice, cold water, and fruit. The cost for one person is $25; two people are $35, and 4 people cost $45. Breakfast, dinner, and laundry facilities are included. (504) 868-9519 or 973-7897.

*La Petite Maison du Bois 4084 Southdown Mandalay.

The Little House of the Woods (as the name translates) is located amidst cane fields beside Bayou Black, about 8½ miles west of Houma. Guests get a small Cajun cottage built around the turn of the century completely to themselves. The cottage has two baths, a kitchen, laundry room, two bedrooms, a small T.V. room, and a front porch overlooking the quiet bayou. This is sugarcane country and the air is sweet and still in the evenings.

The hosts, Mr. and Mrs. Duplantis, were apologetic that they had not completed removing such modern interior adornments as paneling in a couple of rooms, but no excuses were necessary. The little house is a charming and homey cottage, perfect for a peaceful weekend or week-long getaway. Guests frequently use La Petite Maison as a base for fishing trips (there is a fenced yard to park your boat and car in), or as a point of departure to tour Bayou Country. The Duplantises live next door and can help plan your trip if you need guidance. Double occupancy is $35; 3-4 people cost $50; and 5-6 people are $55. To get to La Petite Maison, take U.S. 90 west from Houma. Cross the bayou at Annie Miller's Swamp Tours and proceed west less than a mile on Southdown Mandalay. (504) 879-3815 or 876-1582.

SOUTH OF HOUMA (COASTAL WETLANDS TOUR)

The area south of Houma is true Bayou Country. Four main bayous radiate out in a crow's-foot pattern through the coastal marsh. From east to west, Bayous Terrebonne/Pointe Aux-Chenes, Petit Caillou, Grand Caillou, and Bayou Du Large carry shrimp and oil industry boats to the Gulf and support long, narrow communities on their banks. Each bayou has a distinct character and set of family names and loyalties. In some places there is a notable friction between folks on one side of a bayou and those on "the other side." The west side of Bayou Grand Caillou is settled mainly by Houma Indians and had no paved road until recently, while the east has been paved for decades and is inhabited predominantly by Cajuns. Many bayou dwellers remember the days when a boy or girl could start a minor feud by consorting with a partner from "the other side." The diverging pattern of settlement has preserved many of the customs and much of the Cajun French dialect of the region. Linguists have found different varieties of French spoken on neighboring streams and the Houma Indians have a variety all their own.

Most residents south of Houma extract a living from the marsh in the form of oil or seafood. Driving south you will see seafood processing plants, shrimp boats, and miles of rozo cane (tall marsh cane) under mottled Gulf skies. The towns here are line villages that stretch for miles, but are often only one block deep. To drive the length of all of the bayous below Houma takes a full day if you stop for a swamp tour. Although you can't make a simple loop by car, you need not drive all the way back to Houma to complete a driving tour, as the roads are intermittently connected by east-west routes. I recommend driving only two or three of the bayous in a day. Start either on the east side with Bayou Pointe Aux-Chenes (fabulous scenery) or on the west with Bayou Grand Caillou (Indian communities, burial mounds, and swamp tour). Wherever you begin, plan on finishing the trip at Cocodrie at the south end of Bayou Petit Caillou on Route 56. Here you can see the aquarium and climb the observation tower at LUMCON. The perfect close to any bayou tour is a seafood dinner at the CoCo Marina in Cocodrie (*see* South of Houma food section).

Bayou Pointe Aux-Chenes

This is the easternmost bayou in the crow's foot south of Houma and perhaps the loveliest of all the streams in Bayou Country. Take Route 55 south to Route 665 (about 4 miles south of Bourg). Turn left on Route 665. From this point the road follows the natural levee of Bayou Pointe Aux-Chenes for 14 miles before ending abruptly at the old Indian community of Isle De Jean Charles. Along the side of the bayou you will see small herds of unfenced cattle grazing by the water in the shade of gnarled oak trees. There is a gas station, convenience store, and bait shop along the way.

Isle de Jean Charles Road at high tide. (Photo by Julie Posner)

The most spectacular leg of the drive begins 8.5 miles from the turnoff at Route 55. Here you turn right on *Isle de Jean Charles Road*. Until about 20 years ago there was no road here at all and the Houma Indian community at Isle de Jean Charles was isolated from "civilization" by 6 miles of marsh and water! At high tide the road is covered with about 4-8 inches of brackish water and fishermen pull in shrimp, crabs, trout, and redfish from the roadside. During a hurricane, the water could be well over the roof of your car. At the end of the road the homes of Isle de Jean Charles rise 15 and 20 feet above permanently flooded "yards" on the spindly support of telephone poles. As you drive past you may look up at the floorboards of these camps and trailers, but is hard to imagine the storm surge they await. A boat launch is located near the end of the Isle de Jean Charles Road. If the wind is down, there are hundreds of acres of pristine wetlands that may be explored by small, flat-bottomed boat, canoe, or rowboat. The launch fee is $5 for large craft and $3 for small boats. To return to Route 55 you have no choice but to backtrack.

Bayou Terrebonne

Route 55 veers south from Houma and hugs the east side of Bayou Terrebonne for about 20 miles before literally submerging in the marsh. From the junction of Route 55 and Route 665 (the Pointe Aux-Chenes road), it is a mile south to the fishing community of Montegut. Below Montegut, it is 8 miles to the end of the road. The last two miles are dirt and the last 3/4 mile is submerged. The road actually resembles a canal at this point, and some folks near the end have jonboats tied by the road to carry them across "front yards" to their doorsteps! You can often find seafood for sale at the docks here. To continue your bayou tour, cross Bayou Terrebonne on Route 58 in Montegut and head west about 1.5 miles to the town of Chauvin on Bayou Petit Caillou.

Bayou Petit Caillou

This is the busiest of the streams south of Houma and the corresponding road, Route 56, is the most settled and commercially developed of the bayou-routes. The road skirts the west side of Bayou Petit Caillou, or "little stones," a name reportedly derived from a pile of ballast stones which developed at the mouth of the bayou, left here by boats that had to lighten the load to make it through the shallows. It connects with Bayou Terrebonne and Route 55 via Route 58 at Chauvin and with Bayou Grand Caillou via Route 57 at Cocodrie in the south. Whether you begin your bayou driving tour in the east or west, you will want to finish on Petit Caillou, where you can dine on some of the finest and freshest seafood in Bayou Country.

Chauvin

Route 58 intersects Route 57 in the middle of the line village of Chauvin. The town was founded by a French hunter who settled on the high ground here and it was dubbed Petit Caillou after the adjacent bayou. In 1912 a post office was built and the town was named after the postmaster. Like other bayou towns of the region, shrimping became the primary industry in the twentieth century. Since the thirties, Chauvin has celebrated the bounty of the sea and its main industry with an annual blessing of the shrimp fleet.

"Lagniappe on the Bayou" 2nd weekend in October.

This festival brings the whole area together for drinking, music, games, dancing and shrimp.

La Trouvaille Restaurant Cajun/Down Home, $$. Rt. 56 in Chauvin.

About ten years ago Wylma Dusenberry bought this little Cajun cabin by Bayou Petit Caillou, 2 miles north of the Route 58 crossover, and began cooking for neighborhood folks. Today visitors from around the world arrive by tour bus to join the throngs of locals eating at La Trouvaille (which means "lucky find"). Cotton tablecloths adorn simple wood tables and the dinnerware is mix and match. The best seats in the house are the four tables in the kitchen, where you can watch the family at work. Wylma and two of her five daughters do all the cooking and you will hear cries of "Hey, Mama!" coming from over by the stove.

The food is very simple "blue plate" fare like pork roast, dirty rice, gumbo, and vegetables for a set price of about $8. The servings are not very large, but folks don't come here for the food so much as the country ambiance, the Dusenberry hospitality, and the singing. On the first Sunday of each month during the fall, a large contingent of the Dusenberry family gathers outside after lunch and sings to accordion and guitar accompaniment. The Dusenberrys are a Cajun Von Trapp family. Their music is far from traditional, but they perform favorites in back-porch sing-along harmony for the folks who gather on lawn chairs and benches. La Trouvaille is open for lunch on Wednesday through Sunday between October and May, but the best time to stop by is for the singing on the first Sunday of each month during the fall months. Call for reservations. The restaurant is located on Route 56 in Chauvin, 5 miles south of Houma. (504) 594-9503 or 873-8005.

Bayou Neuf Swamp Tours, Launch, Camping, Fishing, & Picnic Area

The Bayou Neuf recreation area is located beside La Trouvaille Restaurant in north Chauvin. This is a fine place to stop whether you are looking for a waterside picnic spot, a swamp tour, or overnight camping. Picnic tables and tent spaces are located well off the road in the shade of oak and cypress trees. The cost for day use is $3 per person. Tent camping costs $7 for 2 adults. For full RV hookups the charge is $15. Swamp tours are available by appointment at $15 per person. (504) 594-2628 or 594-3033.

Sportsman's Paradise Restaurant/Marina/Motel Rt. 56 in Chauvin.

The restaurant at Sportsman's Paradise Marina is a casual setting for a fried seafood dinner. The bargain-priced fried sea-food platter is among the best I've eaten. By lunchtime, sunburned fishermen are returning from half-day charters with big smiles and big appetites. The food and super-cold beers keep 'em smiling. Behind the restaurant is a small fisherman's motel (no-frills lodging for anglers who want to leave early, get back late, or have a place to wash the salt off). (504) 594-2414.

Lapeyrouse Seafood, Camping, and Fishing Rt. 56 south of Chauvin.

This is a hangout for commercial and recreational fishermen (in other words, just about everyone down here), who stop by for a drink at the bar and some tall tales. You can get bait, fishing tips, and groceries in the store. A flat fee of $10 covers a camping space with hook-ups, boat launch, and bank fishing privileges. Day use costs $2. The store and bar are open from 4 A.M. "until." Lapeyrouse Seafood is located on Route 56 at the Old Robinson Canal (1 mile north of the Route 56 and 57 T). (504) 594-2600

Lapeyrouse Store Junction of Rt. 57 and Rt. 56, south of Chauvin.

This community gathering spot has been in the Lapeyrouse family for over 75 years. Current owner Cecil Lapeyrouse used to work offshore, but when the oil industry bottomed out he took over the store. Now he dispenses fishing tips, bait, fuel, dry goods, and other essentials from the back room of the old grocery.

Louisiana Marine Conservatories Research Center. (Courtesy of LUMCON)

Lapeyrouse relates stories that have been passed down through the family, like the time that water was four feet deep inside the store and waves crashed against the roof during the mighty storm of '26. In addition to groceries and fishing stuff, the shelves at Lapeyrouse Store are laden with products from its 75 years in business, like a shiny Bakelite radio, fiesta-ware plates, and sundries whose practical purposes have been obscured by age. The store is 5 miles north of the Co-Co Marina.

Cocodrie

Cocodrie is at the southern end of Route 56. The name means alligator in French, but the main attraction down here is fish, not reptiles. Whether you like your fish cooked and served with savory side dishes, swimming in an aquarium, or struggling at the end of a fishing rod, Cocodrie is a prime destination.

★LUMCON Rt. 56, Cocodrie.

LUMCON is an acronym for the Louisiana Universities Marine Consortium, a marine research facility in Cocodrie with a brilliant display and video presentation on the wildlife, history, and development of the Gulf Coastal Wetlands. You can't miss this sleek structure rising from the waving patches of marsh grass beside Route 56, just south of the Route 57 intersection. LUMCON is an essential stop for anyone who was curious enough about Louisiana's lovely wetlands to drive all the way down to Cocodrie. In addition to the Gulf exhibit, there are aquaria displaying the fauna of the salt and freshwater marshes, as well as the tropical fishes that live around many offshore oil platforms. Eighty feet above the exhibition hall is a public observation tower with a panoramic view of the surrounding delta. A boardwalk into the marsh is under construction. LUMCON is open 7 days a week until 4:30, but the security guard will allow you inside to see the public exhibits until dark. (504) 851-2800.

★Co-Co Marina & Motel Rt. 56, end of the road in Cocodrie.

This is the ultimate fishing facility. Here you find very nice and inexpensive motel rooms, classy and moderately priced condominiums, fishing charters, boat hoists, supplies, a new "Tiki Bar," and a seafood restaurant. The Tiki Bar is owner Johnny Glover's latest creation. It sports a wood bar with all types of fishing lures shellacked into the surface and a thatched-roof patio. Rooms in the Co-Co's deluxe condo cost $100 a day for 4 ($10 for each additional person) and some have jacuzzis. One- and two-bedroom studios are $70 a night, double occupancy. Rooms in the less luxurious, but comfortable, motel are $30 a night, double occupancy. (504) 594-6626.

*Lighthouse Restaurant at Co-Co Marina Seafood, $$ to $$$.

A sunset dinner in the Lighthouse Restaurant at Co-Co Marina is perhaps the most exquisite dining experience in all of Bayou Country. From the second-story dining room one can gaze through a wall of windows and watch the sun fall over a patchwork of marsh and water stretching south into the Gulf of Mexico. Fishing videos play quietly in an uninterrupted stream on the television over the bar, providing the rare opportunity of watching fish being caught while eating them. As evening darkens, fishermen who are staying in the Co-Co's deluxe accommodations trickle in and stand at the bar to trade stories and plan the next day's excursions.

Co-Co serves the freshest seafood anywhere. The broiled snapper I had on a recent visit had been caught that morning. Unless you are a fisherman or know one, you may never have eaten seafood so fresh, firm, and sweet. The broiled fish of the day is an obvious choice, but once you have tried the Co-Co's Wine Island Shrimp, it will be hard to order anything else. Grab a hunk of crusty French bread from the "bottomless" basket and sop up some sauce. Tasty po-boys are available at $4 for shrimp, oyster, or fish, and $6 for the soft-shell crab. Johnny Glover's restaurant will forever shatter the image of grubby dockside counters where fishermen gulp cold beers and burgers. It is a casual place with good food and a sensational view. The restaurant is located in the marina at the end of Route 56, about 5 miles south of the Route 57 T. Just look for the thatched roof. (504) 594-6626.

Bayou Grand Caillou

Grand Caillou has two very distinct communities stretching along its east and west banks. On the east side, Route 57 breezes past miles of tidy bayou-side homes and shrimp boats belonging mainly to Cajuns. Twenty miles south of Houma, Route 57 intersects Route 56 in Cocodrie. On the west side a smaller road, known as Shrimper's Row, passes homes and stores owned by members of the United Houma Indian Nation. There is no reservation, sign, or boundary denoting the presence of Louisiana's largest Indian tribe, but the greatest concentration of these people live between Houma and Dulac on the west side of Bayou Grand Caillou.

Munson's Cypress Bayou Swamp Tour Rt. 57, 8 mi. below Houma.

When we pulled up at the cabin which serves as bar, boat launch, and headquarters for Munson's Swamp Tours, Mr. Munson was standing in the parking lot with the local Wildlife and Fisheries agent, Cecil DuPlantis. They were eyeballing a twenty-foot, barnacle-encrusted dugout boat, over a century old, that DuPlantis had just rescued from a muddy bank below Munson's launch.

Munson's tour follows a course past an abandoned oil platform, across the Houma Navigation Channel, and into a logging camp canal. We did not find any ancient boats on the trip, but got a close-up view of a wide variety of animals, including owls, armadillos, snakes, nutria, and gators. Once you have seen a gator eat, the whole thing gets a little routine, but Munson adds a twist by feeding his alligators doughnuts. He explained that the doughnuts have two notable advantages over chicken; they cost less and they float. Nutrias, as well as gators, wait for the arrival of the chuck wagon.

Munson's tour operates mostly in his own 18,000-acre compound of canals fenced off to the general public. This means that the area is inaccessible to hunters and fishermen and is a hotbed of wildlife. We visited in the late summer and saw three alligator nests filled with babies, each presided over by a tough-looking mother. There is also a chance to disembark, walk a canal levee, and look for armadillos and vistas of the surrounding swamp. When you get back to the launch, grab a beer or soda, drop some dough in the jukebox, and enjoy the view from Munson's screened patio. Munson's is located about 8 miles south of Houma on Grand Caillou Road. Tours are conducted at 10 A.M. and 3:30 P.M. daily. Munson will take as few as one person and as many as twenty with an admission price of $15 for adults and $10 for children (6-12). The tour lasts 2½ hours. (504) 851-3569

Coastguard Road

Below Dulac, Route 57 turns east to join Route 56 on neighboring Bayou Petit Caillou. To the south, Route 57 becomes Route 3011. Within a mile you will come to an old Houma Indian settlement. Though not as large as the community across the bayou, it is home to the Houma Nation Tribal Leader, Kirby Verret, and a number of fine artisans (including Mrs. Verret) who make cane baskets. The 11,000 members of the Houma Nation have not yet been federally recognized as a tribe (although this action is expected soon); thus, you will not find a reservation, fancy visitors center, or crafts display. Verret ascribes the lack of recognition to the fact that the Houmas never waged a war

Houma artisan with moss doll. (Photo by Macon Fry)

against whites and, thus, never entered into a formal treaty with them. The Indians just kept moving southward and were mainly ignored until oil and gas were found in the area. Francophiles delight in visiting the area, as a large number of Indians, including many children, still speak an archaic variety of French.

West of Bayou Grand Caillou/Cypress Cemetery
The west or "Indian" side of the bayou is considerably less developed than the east. There are Indian mounds at a couple of locations along the road. Just north of the bridge over Bayou Grand Caillou at Dulac, the Falgout Canal Road heads west to intersect Route 315 on Bayou Du Large. The Falgout Canal Road crosses the Houma Navigation Channel, and a 5-mile swath of eerie wetlands. As far as the horizon, bleached and blackened trunks and limbs of dead cypress protrude from the water. When the navigation channel was dredged out, salt water rushed into this freshwater swamp. The salinity destroyed sweetwater plant life and painted the ghostly landscape you see today.

Houma to Morgan City

The main east-west route in Houma is U.S. 90. Construction is inching along on a four-lane Houma bypass, which will cut a direct path to Morgan City north of the existing highway. The current course of U.S. 90 dips to the south as it follows the natural levee of Bayou Black. After crawling through downtown Houma, it passes a few old sugar plantations, rows of modest bayou-side homes and a large number of decrepit shacks and houseboats. The road is shadowed by immense arms of ancient oak trees. Settlements along Bayou Black are only as wide as the small ridges of high ground along its banks. Several swamp tours depart from Bayou Black west of Houma.

Wildlife Gardens U.S. 90, 16 miles west of Houma, near Gibson.
In 1975, James and Betty Provost had six parakeets and a new home with a natural swamp in the back yard. Now their swamp is a sculpted garden with raised trails, and houses a spectacular collection of native Louisiana wildlife. There are bobcats, red fox, otter, nutria, and alligators. The alligators are a relatively recent addition to the collection. Mrs. Provost explains, "You just don't have a tourist attraction in this area without alligators." Depending on when you visit, you may have an opportunity to handle baby alligators (they had 33 hatchlings crawling over each other on my visit). In the late summer you can see alligators on their nests.

Cajun Man guide "Black" Guidry and Gator Bait. (Photo by Julie Posner)

Chester's Cypress Inn. (Photo by Julie Posner)

More impressive than the gators were the 90-year-old Loggerhead turtles (now an endangered species), the great horned owls, and an extremely rare albino nutria.

The twenty-acre garden includes three acres of preserved swamp, enclosed animal habitats, a simulated trapper's cabin (originally created for a movie set), and a duck pond. According to Provost, the zoo has been a learning experience for her as well as her guests. It took her a while to discover it was not a stray gator gobbling up her ducklings but giant largemouth bass that lurk in the pond! Provost explains the difference between her "Cajun Zoo" and a big city zoo this way: "At those big city zoos the animal identification plates provide the scientific and the common names for each animal. Here we provide the given name and the recipe!" Guided tours begin at 10 A.M., 1 P.M., and 4 P.M. daily, except Sunday. The gardens are on the north side of Bayou Black about 16 miles west of Houma. Cross the bayou on the bridge at Greenwood School and continue west a couple of miles. Admission is $7 for adults and $2.50 for children. (504) 575-3676.

Annie Miller's Swamp Tours U.S. 90, 8 miles west of Houma.

No doubt about it, this is the most popular swamp tour in South Louisiana. If your main objective is to see alligators fed hunks of rotten chicken, you won't be disappointed. Annie Miller has been running this tour for a long time and her gators are well conditioned. She makes a show of calling them "by name", but when those guys hear the rumble of the outboard motor at the same time each day, they come like cats at the sound of a can opener. Annie Miller is a certified character; just listen to her warn passengers as the boat glides beneath an overpass, "This bridge would not only knock your head off, it would knock your brains out!" The problem with her tour is that it spends half of its duration getting to and from gator holes, which aren't located in the swamp at all but in man-made canals cut through marshland near the Intracoastal Waterway. Miller offers bilingual tours for French-speaking guests and her dock is conveniently located on Route 90 about 8 miles west of Houma. She has three large party barges (with uncomfortable center seating) which go out every day. Call for tour times and reservations. The 2 1/2-hour trip costs $15 for adults and $10 for children ages 3 to 12. (504) 879-3934.

*A Cajun Man's Swamp Tour U.S. 90, 16 miles west of Houma.

How does the idea of cruising the swamps and marshes of the Houma area with a Cajun musician and his Catahoula cur (the state dog) named Gator Bait strike you? Whether he is holding forth while piloting a comfortable party barge through the marsh, or picking and singing a Cajun favorite like "Big Mamou," "Black" Guidry is a consummate entertainer. Once Guidry gets past cautioning everyone that the tour fee is only "one way" and reminding folks to keep track of which way they are heading, he comes up with the comforting assurance, "If you have any questions, I'll answer them. If I can't answer them, I'll make something up!"

Kidding aside, Guidry is a conscientious and knowledgeable guide who makes sure everyone enjoys the trip as much as he so plainly does. The wetlands south of Houma are not the most scenic in Cajun Country, but Black has a good route, twisting through natural bayous draped with Spanish moss and blazing down wide oil-field canals. He edges up to tupelo swamps tangled with the white flowers of elderberry vines and red muscadine grapes and slowly skirts open marsh where thousands of waterbirds coat the distant horizon like snow.

Black carries a bag of old chicken which he dangles over the side at intervals for alligators that await his regular visits. This is the part of the trip that really excites the dog Gator Bait, who charges fearlessly to the railing, snarling and flashing his blue Catahoula eyes at the oblivious reptiles below. If you have never seen a Catahoula hound, or "spotted leopard dog," as they are sometimes called, the playful Gator Bait is one of the down-home attractions of this trip. The climax of the Cajun Man tour comes at a lost bend of a bayou where Guidry cuts the engines and unpacks his guitar and homemade accordion for a set of Cajun tunes. The shade is cool under the boat awning as Guidry winds up a song with, "Son of a gun we'll have big fun on the bayou!" Cajun Man leaves from the Bayou Black Marina 16 miles west of Houma on U.S. 90. Several tours go out each day for 1½ to 2 hours. Call first to confirm times and availability. For two people, the cost is $20 each, but usually there is a group to join and the fee is only $15 for adults and $10 for children. (504) 868-4625.

Route 20 to Morgan City

An alternative to taking U.S. 90 to Morgan City is to head north on either Route 311 (*see* the Drive-by plantation tour listed under Houma in this chapter) or Route 24, then take Route 20 west. This route is ideal if you are planning a side trip to the plantation country around Thibodaux or want to drive down a small piece of the original Old Spanish Trail. It also passes the great Chester's

Cypress Inn Restaurant. For years environmental, political, and engineering problems have prevented the construction of a four-lane highway connecting the wide spans of Route 90 that end on the east and west sides of Houma. In 1990, construction finally began on a U.S. 90 bypass that follows the present-day course of Route 20. It is scheduled for completion in late 1993.

*Chester's Cypress Inn Local Fave, $$. Rt. 20 in Donner.

Nestled in a stand of cypress trees halfway between Houma and Morgan City, this little hideaway has the best fried chicken this side of grandma's kitchen table. A sign boasts, "If the Colonel had our recipe he'd be a general." You won't find any nouveau Cajun cuisine here, just plates piled high with fried chicken, fish, froglegs, and mounds of crispy onion rings. Chester Boudreaux has passed away, but his children, Calvin Boudreaux and Bobbie LaRose, have kept the Inn much the same as it was when he opened in the forties. The tables are still covered with plastic, and the waitresses still carry cardboard plates laden with golden fried food from the adjacent building that houses the kitchen. Crowds drive the twenty miles from Morgan City and Houma (past dozens of new fast-food franchises) to eat in the homey dining room that once housed a dance hall. The onion rings, which arrive in towering portions that will serve three, are sweet and sliced to order. The Cypress Inn is a perfect stop after a weekend swamp tour. Chester's is on Route 20, about 3.5 miles east of the intersection with U.S. 90 (25 miles west of Houma). Their hours are Friday and Saturday from 5 P.M. to 10 P.M., and Sunday 11 A.M. to 10 P.M. (504) 446-6821.

Donner Park and Cypress Greens Golf Course Rt. 20 in Donner.

Don't let your ball sail into the cypress around this course or you may have to do battle with a gator to get it back. This is only a miniature-size course, but it is free and the setting is idyllic. Talk about small—the park's oval track is 464' around, or 11½ laps per mile! You might as well stand in one spot and spin in circles. The park is located on Route 20 in Donner about 2.6 miles east of the intersection with U.S. 90.

Old Spanish Trail/Deadwood Road

Although U.S. 90 is referred to throughout Cajun Country as "The Old Spanish Trail," the highway's path only approximates that of the trail in most places. West of Houma the trail actually veers north and crosses Route 20, following a ridge that now accommodates Deadwood Road. There is not much to see here but swamp scenery, but it is fun to trace this forgotten loop of the historic trail. One entrance to Deadwood Road is .3 miles east of the intersection of Route 20 and U.S. 90. About 3.8 miles to the east, Deadwood Road rejoins Route 20 (a tenth of a mile from the Cypress Greens Golf Course).

*Atchafalaya Basin Backwater Adventure N. Bayou Black Dr., Gibson.

Among tours for the seriously adventurous, Atchafalaya Backwater is in a class by itself! While other "swamp" tours in the Houma area wend through the open marsh, canals, and navigation channels to the south, Backwater Adventure operates solely within the commercially unnavigable waterways of the Great Chacahoula Swamp. Tours are limited to 6, the most that will fit in a small swamp boat. When we arrived at guide Jon Faslun's home and headquarters in Gibson, he emerged and called off his pack of pit bulls. Stroking a white beard, he gave a hard look at the folks that dared to show up late! After a few words with Faslun and the dogs, they mellowed out and we headed for the swamp. Faslun won't bend your ear with pat jokes and rehearsed hospitality, but his knowledge of the history, wildlife, and waterways in this part of the Basin is awe-inspiring. You get the feeling that no two trips with him are going to be alike.

I took the short (2½-hour) adventure, which began with a brief bayou tour of the historic village of Donner before spinning into the swamp. About 30 minutes away from the launch, Faslun beached the boat on a narrow wooded levee and helped his guests ashore. Ensconced on a tiny strip of land in a quiet backwater of the Chacahoula Swamp, Faslun settled in like Brer Rabbit in the briar patch. In a quarter-mile nature hike, he casually explained what type of snake was hanging overhead, plucked berries to taste, and crushed leaves to smell. Of the plants he commented, "A few are good to eat, a few aren't, and a few are here in case you eat the wrong thing." The climax of the tour was a short trek to the abandoned site of a century-old cypress mill (the second largest in the state in its heyday). It's overgrown with vines and still littered with artifacts of the lumbering operation.

Atchafalaya Backwater offers an experience that is more an adventure than a tour. It is a trip that will leave you talking as much about what you have done and learned as what you have seen. If you want to explore on your own, you can rent a pirogue, pack a cooler, and paddle about 45 minutes to the old mill site. The 2½-hour tour of the swamp surrounding Donner and Gibson costs $20 per person, with a $40 minimum. A more costly 4-hour Deep Swamp Tour, wilderness camping, and night trips may be arranged by appointment. Tours are offered at 11 and 3 daily. Pirogue rental is $10 for a twelve-hour day (maps and instructions are furnished). From Houma take Route 90 west to the bridge by the water tower in Gibson. After crossing the bayou, double back east two blocks on N. Bayou Black Dr. The fastest way to get there from New Orleans is by way of Route 20. Gibson is 11 miles west from the intersection of Route 311 and Route 20. About 150 yards past the Gibson sign on Route 20, turn left on Caroll Street. Turn left again on N. Bayou Black Road. Atchafalaya Backwater Adventure is .2 miles down on the left. (504) 575-2371.

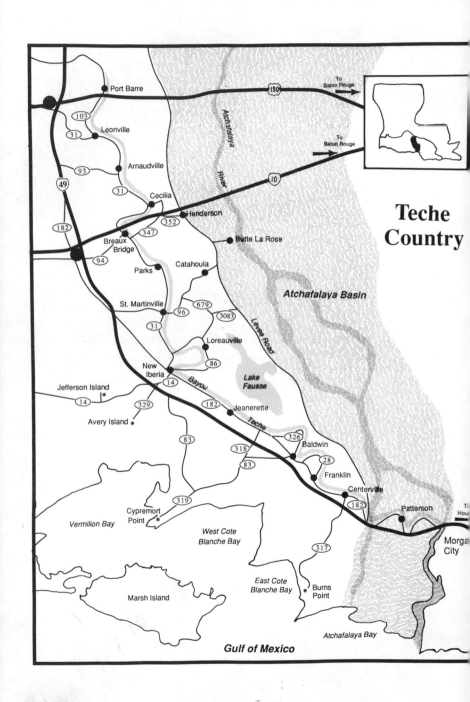

Teche Country

Port Barre

103
31
Leonville

93
Arnaudville

49
31
Cecilia

182
347
352 Henderson

Breaux Bridge
94
Parks
Catahoula

Butte La Rose

Atchafalaya River

Atchafalaya Basin

St. Martinville
96
679
31
3083

Levee Road

Loreauville
86

Lake Fausse

New Iberia
14

Jefferson Island
14 *

329
Avery Island *

182
Jeanerette

Bayou Teche

83

318
326
Baldwin
28
Franklin
Centerville
83

319
182
Patterson

Cypremort Point *

Vermilion Bay

West Cote Blanche Bay

317

Morgan City

To Baton Rouge
190

To Baton Rouge
10

East Cote Blanche Bay
* Burns Point

Marsh Island

Atchafalaya Bay

Gulf of Mexico

12

Teche Country

For centuries the main route for transportation in the Teche region was the bayou from which it derives its name. From headwaters in Port Barre, Bayou Teche (pronounced "Tesh") travels 130 miles through canopies of live oaks and acres of gleaming cane fields before pouring into the Atchafalaya River above Morgan City. The area was once occupied by the reputedly cannibalistic Attakapas Indians, who were eradicated when the first Europeans arrived. The name Teche was derived from the Indian word *tenche* (snake), which accurately describes the stream's twisting course through the geographic center of South Louisiana. The stream formed the main channel of the Mississippi River until about 3000 years ago when the river jumped its banks, seeking a shorter outlet to the Gulf. The quiet bayou now divides the soggy regions of the Atchafalaya Basin from the prairie to the west and marshes along the coast. Thanks to the poetry of Henry Wadsworth Longfellow, the region surrounding the bayou is often referred to as Evangeline Country in deference to the poet's Acadian heroine.

Although the Teche long ago faded from preeminence as an arterial highway, the romanticism of Longfellow only begins to scrape the surface of the diversity of attractions in the area today. The main route through the region is the Old Spanish Trail (U.S. 90 and Route 182), which mostly follows the course of the bayou. Teche Country is divided into two subregions which roughly reflect the different cultures and terrain along its banks. The Lower Teche (below St. Martinville) is dominated by the Anglo sugar culture which blossomed in the early 1800s. The less navigable Upper Teche (between St. Martinville and Port Barre) is a swampy area settled primarily by Cajuns and Creoles in the eighteenth century. The Europeans who settled the Upper Teche enjoyed a life of opulence and high culture when the rest of Cajun Country was a wild frontier. Teche Country remains an area largely disconnected from the Mississippi River and the rest of the nation, isolated by miles of swamp and marsh. A drive along the bayou on the Old Spanish Trail provides a longer (3.5 hour) but more scenic route into the Central and Cajun Heartland Regions. Side trips access the Atchafalaya Basin, Indian communities, fishing towns, and Gulf Coast beaches and wetlands.

THE LOWER TECHE

From the industrial port of Morgan City west to Jeanerette, the Lower Teche is dominated by the sugar culture. Miles of cane fields reach the horizon and the temple-like edifices of sugar plantations grace the higher west bank of the bayou. With the Louisiana Purchase and arrival of steamboats in the early 1800s, a wealthy planter class supplanted the few Cajun ranchers and farmers who had settled here. The Anglos established lumber mills and leveled thousands of acres of land for cane cultivation. They built massive houses and populated mill towns and trading posts along the bayou, which was the major route of transportation at the time. The dominance of Yankee settlers on the Lower Teche is evident today in the succession of decidedly non-French towns like Patterson, Franklin, and Baldwin. Anyone but the hurried traveler will want to forsake the four-lane rush of U.S. 90 for a drive down Route 182 (the Old Spanish Trail), which closely follows the bayou. On this venerable oak-shaded highway you will pass through the heart of the sugar belt, see turn-of-the-century towns and antebellum homes, and find opportunities for short side trips to coastal recreational areas and the Chitimacha Indian Reservation.

Morgan City

Located at the confluence of the Atchafalaya River, Bayou Teche, and the Intracoastal Waterway, Morgan City (The Shrimp and Petroleum Capital of Louisiana) is a bustling Gulf port with a huge oil and fishing fleet. This city of 16,000 is a decidedly prosaic gateway to the enchanting world of Teche Country. Entering from the east, one is greeted by miles of shipyards and oil industry facilities. Offshore oil platforms, hundreds of feet tall, rest on their sides on barges, awaiting transport to the Gulf. You will pass mounds of shredded steel at Southern Scrap Yards, stacks of massive wooden spools at Hercules Wire Rope Company, and hundreds of jack-up barges docked at the McDermott Industries Shipyards. When you hit town you are greeted by establishments like Foxy Lady Lounge, Mister Lucky's Club, and a host of night spots that cater to offshore workers who depart from and arrive here from long stints in the Gulf.

This is not the place to look for traditional French folkways. The town's founding fathers were Thomas Berwick (of Pennsylvania), Dr. Walter Brashear (of Kentucky) and Charles Morgan (of New York). The city was incorporated in 1860 after the arrival of the rail line from New Orleans, and named for Dr. Brashear, who owned the vast Tiger Island sugar plantation which occupied the site. When Charles Morgan purchased the railroad and steamship lines after the War Between the States, Morgan City was renamed in his honor. It was an honor well bestowed, as Morgan's dredging of the Atchafalaya Bay in 1872 opened the city to major industrial traffic. The port quickly became a hub for fishing and lumbering interests. Although Morgan City dubbed itself "Shrimp Capital of the World" following the first harvest of jumbo Gulf shrimp in the 1930s, the most significant economic development was the drilling of the nation's first producing offshore oil well nearby in 1947. The city celebrates its twin industries in the unusual Shrimp and Petroleum Festival held on Labor Day weekend each year (*see* description below).

Morgan City Tourist Information Center 725 Myrtle Street.

Despite its heavy industrial base and the blight that has struck town since the decline in oil prices in the eighties, there are several worthy attractions and lovely wetlands vistas in the Morgan City area. The best place to get up-to-date information is from the Visitors Center. The Center, located a block north of U.S. 90 beside the Swamp Gardens, has rest rooms, maps, and brochures on important local events and sites. It is open from 8 A.M. to 4 P.M. on Monday through Friday, and from 9 A.M. on weekends. (504) 384-3343.

Attractions

Swamp Gardens and Wildlife Zoo U.S. 90 East at Myrtle St.

Across the street from the Morgan City Tourist Information Center in downtown Morgan City are the Swamp Gardens and Wildlife Zoo. A guide leads visitors along a raised shell path through the 3.5-acre park. You'll see supposedly life-like replicas of people who inhabited the swamp. There is an audio system throughout the park with individual speakers at each exhibit. One display that discusses the cypress industry features a talking cypress tree, others discuss the animals and trapping industry. Deer

McDermott facility outside Morgan City. (Courtesy of U.S. Army Corps of Engineers)

Morgan City riverfront. (Courtesy of U.S. Army Corps of Engineers)

roam freely, and in one area of the park, alligators, nutria, raccoons, and a black bear are kept behind bars. The whole place has the ambiance of a miniature golf course with a swamp theme. It ranks with Christ of the Ozarks, Dinosaur World, and The Dells of Wisconsin as a supremely cheesy roadside attraction. Guided tours are offered Monday through Friday at 10:30, 1:30, 2:30, and 3:30. Saturday and Sunday tours are at 10:30, 1, 2, and 3 (except no morning tour on Sunday or Monday). Tours cost $2. (504) 384-3343.

Turn-of-the-Century House 715 Second St.

The oldest neighborhood in Morgan City is located southeast of the Atchafalaya Bridge, where the U.S. 90 up ramp begins its ascent. Most of the homes here, like the commercial district beside the river, were built in the early 1900s during the halcyon days of the lumber industry. The Turn-of-the-Century House was built in 1906 and lay squarely in the path of the new U.S. 90 Bridge, constructed in 1970. It was disassembled and moved a few blocks to its present location, where it operates as a small museum. Most of the millwork in the house is cypress, but the floors are long-leaf yellow pine. The first floor is decorated exclusively with period furniture of mahogany and oak, while the upstairs houses a display of Mardi Gras costumes and photographs. Dozens of antebellum homes in South Louisiana have been restored, but this is one of few turn-of-the-century houses open for tours. The house is open weekdays from 9 A.M. to 5 P.M., and weekends from 1 P.M. Admission is $2 for adults and $1 for students. (504) 380-4651.

Tarzan and Thunder Bay Video Presentations

The Turn-of-the-Century House Visitors Center is a screening room for two film classics (shown in video) made in Morgan City. The very first film adaptation of Edgar Rice Burrough's *Tarzan of the Apes*, starring Elmo Lincoln, was made in 1916 in the coastal wetlands here. Like the book, the film was hugely successful. The National Film Corporation called the silent epic "a mastodonic monopoly embracing all that the mind of man can possibly conceive, suggest, or imagine," "the most stupendous amazing film production in the world's history," and "the most remarkable ...splendid...strange work the world of motography ever conceived from the realm of fiction." The film was a great one, and is worth an hour (running time 61 minutes) on a hot afternoon in Morgan City. A second title, *Thunder Bay*, was shot in 1952 on one of the early offshore oil rigs and at a nearby shrimp dock. It stars

Elmo Lincoln as the first film Tarzan. (Burroughs Archives)

Jimmy Stewart, Joanne Dru, and Dan Dureyea. The Turn-of-the-Century House Visitors Center staff will cue up either video on request. The center is open weekdays from 9 a.m. to 5 p.m. (504) 380-4651.

The Great Wall Atchafalaya riverfront downtown.

Standing below the 21-foot tall "great wall" is a fine place to appreciate the awe with which man faces the floodwaters of the Atchafalaya River. Constructed by the Corps of Engineers, the walls in Morgan City and across the river in Berwick are designed to withstand a flood of truly unimaginable proportions. Morgan City lies directly below the Atchafalaya Basin floodway at the very mouth of the river. When the Corps channels water from the Mississippi River into the Atchafalaya to prevent flooding in New Orleans, those waters wind up lapping the walls here. Climb the steps that scale the wall at regular intervals and you are in for a real surprise. On the river side a number of businesses and most of a neighborhood were left to God's protection. Some houses sit in several feet of water each spring, and there are places where fishermen dock their boats and walk down ramps into their homes.

Despite the immensity of the flood-control project, engineers predict total devastation of the city on the day that the Mississippi River makes its anticipated jump and begins to course down the Atchafalaya. Steps and viewing stations are located at the downtown section of the wall near Brashear and Front Street.

Avoca Island Ferry

I am a sucker for ferries, often opting to wait in line for the chance to glide across a stream rather than drive over it, so it was natural to make the five-minute detour from the Morgan City Visitors Center to check this one out. The Avoca Island Ferry holds 4 to 6 vehicles and is propelled by a steel cable cranked through a pulley. The ferry crosses the intracoastal canal and drops passengers on the small, privately owned marsh island just south of the city. The west side of Avoca (where the ferry lands) is occupied by the owners and a private hunt club. On the east side at the end of a nine-mile dirt road, a handful of residents live in a muddy cluster of ramshackle homes and trailers. Through some mystifying political machinations, the public ferry (operated by St. Mary Police Jury) provides free service to the private island daily. The ferry runs every half hour except at lunch time. To get to the Avoca Ferry from U.S. 90, turn south onto Myrtle Street. Follow Myrtle past the old cemetery and across the railroad tracks. The road bends and ends at the ferry landing.

Spirit of Morgan City and Eternal Flame Brashear Ave.

This old shrimp boat and model oil rig were placed on the neutral ground of Brashear Avenue below the bridge to commemorate the city's twin industries. Ironically, about the time the oil industry in Louisiana crashed in the eighties, the "eternal" flame died.

Lighthouses of the Gulf Front St., Berwick.

This exhibit, which was slated for development along the west side of the Atchafalaya River in Berwick, seems to have stalled after the development of a five-page brochure and placement of one old lighthouse on the site. Ask for a status report at the Morgan City or Atchafalaya Visitors Centers. Berwick is directly across the Atchafalaya River from Morgan City.

Special Events

Louisiana Shrimp and Petroleum Festival Labor Day weekend

After the first offshore oil well started producing in 1947, the former Louisiana Shrimp Festival (the oldest chartered harvest festival in the state) was renamed the Shrimp and Petroleum Festival. The idea of a shrimp and petroleum fair calls to mind images of jumbo crustaceans steeping in vats of crude, but the two products are never actually mixed. The main events are a coronation of the court pageant, and a blessing of the shrimp fleet. These events are surrounded by a weekend of free outdoor music and carnival rides.

The fest opens at 9 A.M. on Saturday morning with food and craft booths and a carnival midway, all in the shadow of the Atchafalaya Bridge ramp. This is not a picturesque setting, but if you have ever been in Morgan City during a steamy September, you understand the value of any shadow or scrap of shade. Bands play in Lawrence Park (near the bridge) and the coronation is held that evening. Sunday begins with an 8:30 A.M. outdoor Mass in Lawrence Park. Behind a pulpit adorned with a cardboard oil rig and jumbo shrimp, the priest conducts Mass before leading the festival court and crowd in a procession to the river. At 10 A.M. the priest boards a large, decorated shrimp boat which cruises along the waterfront, where he blesses the docked fleet. This part of the ceremony is best seen from the top of the "great wall." Once the blessing is completed, food, music, and rides are again the order of the day. (504) 384-3343.

Attractions North of Morgan City

Route 70 is the "old road" between Morgan City and Baton Rouge. This highway intersects U.S. 90 (Brashear Avenue) just west of the Atchafalaya Bridge up ramp. The Atchafalaya Basin Levee forms a verdant wall on the west side of the road, occupied at places by grazing cattle and egrets. To the east lie lakes, bayous, and darkening swamp that were part of the Atchafalaya's natural flood plain before levees were constructed. This area is the province of professional and recreational freshwater fishermen, and poses a lovely contrast to the industrial coastal reaches of Morgan City. There are several places to access the wetlands on the north edge of town.

Brownell Memorial Park and Carillon Tower Rt. 70, Morgan City.

The Brownell Memorial Park is a 9.5-acre tract of swampy land on the banks of Lake Palourde just 5 minutes north of Morgan City. The park was donated by Mrs. Claire Horatio Brownell as a quiet, non-denominational retreat and place of contemplation. There is a short elevated trail that leads to a 106-foot-tall bell tower and a garden. The swamp is filled with cattails, palmettos, ferns, and flowering plants. The park is open Monday through Saturday from 9 A.M. to 5 P.M. The bells in the Carillon are rung (mechanically) on every half hour and hour. Admission is free.

*Lake End Park Rt. 70, Morgan City.

Since the late 1800s, this cypress-studded area on Lake Palourde has been a popular picnic and swimming site. Palourde is nearly 6 miles long and four miles across from north to south. Its sweet and cool waters provide the best swimming in all of Cajun Country. Thirty acres were donated to the park in the 1930s by the Morgan City Land Company, and it has since grown into a fully equipped recreation area with restrooms, showers, sheltered picnic pavilion, camping, and a small sandy beach. A 38-slip marina is being built next to the old boat ramp. On summer weekends, the beach is a popular gathering spot for families and local kids who turn up the music and get the barbecue pits smoking. The best time to wheel in is at the close of day or during mid-week. There is nothing like a quiet dip in the lake after a day touring in the Louisiana heat. If you have the gear, pitch a tent beneath the cypress trees and you can catch a morning swim before hitting the road again (*see* Lake End Park Campground in the Accommodations section of this chapter). Admission to the park is $2 per car for up to 4 people. (504) 380-4623.

Scully's Swamp Tours Rt. 70, Stephensville (3 mi. above Morgan City).

From a position at the edge of a wonderfully unspoiled region of lakes, swamps, and bayous, Captain Bob Scully is perfectly situated to offer one of the best swamp tours in the state. The swamp above Morgan City was once part of the natural drainage system of the Atchafalaya Basin, but was lopped off by new levees. The area is unscarred by the oil and gas industry and features a profusion of wildlife, sweet water, and fresh air. Scully was born and raised in the swampy area around Stephensville, where his grandfather was an original settler. He builds his own boats, fixes his own motors, and knows the smallest bayous and their histories by heart.

Daily tours are scheduled on a 49-passenger, covered pontoon barge, but the best trip is in Scully's small skiff. By skiff, Captain Bob can get you quickly to the largest cypress you are likely to see anywhere. Some of the trees on the skiff route are 200 to 400 years old. Back at the launch there is a bar and restaurant where you can relax in one of two dining rooms, and order the best seafood in the Morgan City area (*see* review below). A two-hour tour costs $20 each for two people, and $15 each for groups of 3 or more. Typically Scully goes out once in the morning and twice in the afternoon. Call first to verify rates, times, and availability of the small boat excursion. (504) 385-2388.

Food

Morgan City can claim to be "Shrimp Capital of the World," but its title is industrial, not culinary. There is not a single restaurant in Morgan City that I would drive out of the way to visit. In fact, there are few that I would bother to eat at unless I was mighty hungry. Presumably residents find enough good eats at home, and the constant flow of oil patch workers hasn't bolstered the restaurant scene. There is a wide selection of fast-food franchises, a couple of small sandwich shops, and some seafood places that specialize in frying.

Scully's Restaurant Seafood, $$. 3141 Rt. 70, Stephensville.

The best eats we got in Morgan City were not in town at all, but a few miles north at Scully's Swamp Tour Restaurant. Not only were our platters of fried food and gumbo substantial, but the place was a lot of fun. Try appetizer-size crabmeat and crawfish stew with the salad bar, or go for a bowl of shrimp and okra gumbo with potato salad. Scully's is open Monday through Saturday from 10:30 A.M. to 9 P.M. (504) 385-2388.

Music

Morgan City is not the place to go if you are looking for Cajun music, or any other expression of the Cajun people. It is dominated by industry, and the music of choice is Country.

Randy's Cajun/Country. Rt. 182, Berwick.

This is a big Texas-style Country music establishment that has Cajun bands on Sunday afternoon. The place seats several hundred, has a huge dance floor, three bars, and 4 pool tables. Old-timers work the dancefloor, while kids hang around the pool tables in front. "Cajun" bands (with a decidedly Country sound) play from 3 P.M. to 8 P.M. on Sunday, and Country cover bands play 7 nights a week from 9 P.M. until closing. (504) 385-2272.

Lodging

Motels and Hotels:

Acadian Inn 1924 U.S. 90 East, $22 double. (504) 384-5750.

Morgan City Motel 507 Roderick St., $24 to $35 double. (504) 384-6640.

Plantation Inn U.S. 90 West, (505 Universe), Bayou Vista. $37 to $43 double. (504) 395-4511.

Scottish Inn 1659 U.S. 90 East, $22 to $24 double. (504) 384-7593.

Twin City Motel 1985 U.S. 90 East, $25 double. (504) 384-1530.

Holiday Inn 520 Roderick St., $45 to $48 double. (504) 385-2200.

Camping:

*Lake End Park Campground Rt. 70 N.

This is a beautiful campground that combines proximity to the highway with a great natural setting, lake swimming, fishing, and full-service facilities. There are 135 camper spaces with complete hook-ups, and room for dozens of tents on the cypress-shaded lawn overlooking Lake Palourde. The best time to camp here is on weeknights in the fall or spring, when the grounds are quiet and the white sand beach is empty. My favorite meal in Morgan City was fresh shrimp grilled beside Lake Palourde during a camping trip. It costs around $10 for both tents and RVs. (504) 380-4623.

Camping at Lake End Park. (Courtesy of LA Office of Tourism)

Patterson

West of Morgan City, U.S. 90 begins its snake dance with Bayou Teche. In some places the bayou is nearly visible from the road, and in others it kinks as much as four miles north. The road which most closely follows these capricious bends is scenic Route 182. Located on two adjacent oxbow bends in Bayou Teche are the little old lumber towns of Bayou Vista and Patterson. For about thirty years at the turn of the century, Patterson boomed around the Red Cypress Company of Frank Williams, "Cypress King of the World." Few of the old mill towns of Louisiana bear reminders of the once booming trade. The companies came, got all the timber, and left. Patterson (population about 4500) might have been just another quiet bayou town, deserted by the lumber barons and living off the seafood industry, were it not for nine glorious years between 1928 and 1936, when it was home to the world-famous Wedell-Williams Air Service. Today the city is the site of a fantastic museum commemorating the pioneering work of Wedell Williams' engineers and its daredevil pilots (*see* review of museum below).

Atchafalaya Delta Visitors Center U.S. 90 (Main St.), Patterson.

Here you will find rest rooms and brochures for attractions throughout St. Mary Parish. The shaded lawn which slopes gently to Bayou Teche is a perfect spot for a picnic. The Visitors Center is 2 miles west of Morgan City on the Route 90 service road and is plainly visible from the highway, sitting beside Cajun Jack's Swamp Tours.

Attractions

*Wedell-Williams Memorial Aviation Museum Rt. 182, Patterson.

Harry Williams was mayor of Patterson in 1926 when speed pilot and contraband runner Jimmy Wedell landed his plane in a field on the outskirts of town. The two got together and a partnership was born that built the fastest aircraft of the day, supplying top long-distance and pylon racers. In an era when aircraft were just beginning to be used commercially, the Wedell-Williams Air Service secured air-mail contracts between New Orleans and Texas, and put wings under dozens of barnstorming daredevils. The pair loved speed. Williams reportedly raced one of his mechanics to the airport each morning, and Wedell became the first pilot to record a speed of 305 miles an hour. Much has been made of the early astronauts who had the "right stuff," but the individuals commemorated at the Wedell-Williams museum were test flying planes at a time when pre-flight test technology was virtually nonexistent.

It is not surprising that these men who lived in the air died there, but it was a crushing blow to the business in Patterson when their top pilot, top engineer, and main financier all died in crashes within two years. Before his death in an air crash at Patterson in 1934 (at age 34), Jimmy Wedell held more air speed records than any man. With Wedell, Wedell's brother Walter, and Harry Williams all dead, Mrs. Williams (a silent movie star who owned the Latter Library mansion in New Orleans) sold their lucrative airmail routes to fledgling Eastern Airlines. The parts of Wedell-Williams record-breaking aircraft were dumped into Bayou Teche.

Although the Wedell-Williams Museum is responsible for preserving and documenting all of Louisiana's aviation history, the real attractions here are the aircraft parts and displays regarding the operations of Wedell and Williams. The museum, located on the site of the famous air service, houses replicas and original craft manufactured by the team, along with pieces of #44, the famous speed record holder of 1933 (raised from the muddy bottom of Bayou Teche). A video is shown depicting the careers and antics of Wedell, Williams, and many of the pilots of the barnstorming era. An adjacent collection displays trophies and clippings documenting the achievements of these brave men. The museum is one of the hidden treasures of Cajun Country, and a must see whether you are an aviation buff or not. Admission is $2 for adults and 50 cents for kids. They are open Tuesday through Saturday from 10 A.M. to 4 P.M. Take Route 182, which branches north from U.S. 90 in Patterson, and look for the signs. (504) 395-7067.

Cajun Jack's Swamp Tours 112 Main St. (U.S. 90), Patterson.

Captain Jack takes groups by party barge (accommodates 25) into the lower reaches of the Atchafalaya Basin. This is a beautiful area, but the best parts of the tour are unreachable during low water. Jack can show you where the local cypress company had its camps and made its cuts, and where parts of the first Tarzan film were shot. Best of all, he offers a "sunset cruise" (5:30 P.M. to 8 P.M.) during the summer. This later trip is recommended, as the air is cooler and the water is less crowded with fishermen. Cajun Jack's is on U.S. 90 in Patterson, beside the Atchafalaya Delta Visitors Center. Call first to make sure tours are running. (504) 395-7420 (after 6 P.M. 384-6828).

Lodging

Lonely Oak Campground and Seaplane Tour Rt. 182, Bayou Vista.

This small, private campground is literally on the banks of the stream, affording a perfect view of the sunset over its wide waters. There are rafts and jonboats available for those who want to get into or onto the water, and chairs and picnic tables for folks who prefer to watch from the edge. Tenters can pitch their gear on the grassy banks, but will find only cold water in the showers. Fees are $10 for RV's and $7 for tent camping. Owner Charles Seal is a seaplane pilot, frequently called on to ferry people or gear between offshore oil platforms. It is amazing just to watch him take off and land on the bayou. For a bird's-eye view of the swamp and coast, air tours cost $80 for a half hour, and $150 for a full hour. Lonely Oak is located in the middle of the Bayou Vista oxbend of Bayou Teche, on Route 182. (504) 395-6765.

Kemper Williams Park U.S. 90, Patterson.

Kemper is a new 290-acre recreation and camping facility located off highway 90 and adjacent to the Lower Atchafalaya River near Patterson. The park has 5 baseball/softball fields, 6 lighted tennis courts, a picnic area with playgrounds, pavilion structures, and a golf driving range. An 18-hole golf course and canoe trail are under construction. There is an RV camping area with full hook-ups and a tent area with showers that are also scheduled for completion by late 1992. It costs $10.00 to camp and $2 for day use (up to 4 people). The park is across U.S. 90 from the Atchafalaya Delta Tourist Commission in Patterson. (504) 395-2298.

Calumet to Franklin

All but those in a hurry will want to get off U.S. 90 in Calumet and take Route 182 west. The 45-mile section of Route 182 between Calumet and New Iberia follows Bayou Teche closely and provides the best views of its waters, sugar mills, plantations, and small towns.

Centerville/Burns Point Turnoff

Don't blink or you may miss this former steamboat landing on the bayou. Centerville is the turnoff for Route 317 to Burns Point, a coastal recreation and camping area about 18 miles south (*see* description below). There are several (private) antebellum homes along the bayou in Centerville. Bocage on Route 182, 1 mile west

Cane truck on Main Street in Franklin. (Photo by Julie Posner)

of Centerville, is open by appointment only, Monday through Friday. (318) 828-0132.

Burns Point Recreation Area Camping and fishing. Rt. 317 South.

This coastal park is also known as Pointe Salé (French for Salt Point). From Route 182, Route 317 follows Bayou Salé 18 miles south along one of three arable ridges in St. Mary Parish. The road passes miles of sugarcane, and the Ellerslie Plantation (1839, private), before dead-ending at the Rabbit Island Texaco Plant, the site of an ancient Indian burial mound (not open to public). A mile before the end of the road you will see a sign and turnoff for Burns Point Recreation Area. The narrow shell road to the point emerges from a tangle of reeds onto a spit of grass and sand on Cote Blanche Bay.

The area is dotted with picnic tables, campsites, a shelter, and a boat ramp. Typical of Louisiana's coastal fringe, the beach is not beautiful for swimming, but is great for fishing. This was the site of an old fishing camp, and there are plenty of places to catch redfish and trout from the shore. If you are looking for camping away from the hubbub, you will find it in the waterside sites. Tent campers will appreciate the hot-water showers, but bemoan the lack of shade. Camping costs $7 for RV's, $5 for pop-ups, and $3 for tents and vans. There is a $1 entrance fee for day use. (318) 836-9784.

City of Franklin

A lasting impression of Lower Teche Country is the sight of huge cane trucks rumbling through the grand entrance to the town of Franklin, 25 miles west of Morgan City by way of U.S. 90. Known locally as the Great White Way, E. Main Street (Route 182) in Franklin is shaded by dual rows of oaks, split by a grassy neutral ground, and lined with a half-dozen Greek Revival plantation homes. Cast-iron street lamps adorn the neutral ground. The lamps, which have become a symbol of the city, have a branching top portion which may be rotated during the sugar harvest to prevent cane-laden trucks from smashing the round, glass globes.

The city grew westward in a linear fashion along the higher southern side of Bayou Teche. Heading in this direction down Main Street, you first pass antebellum homes, a turn-of-the-century commercial and railroad district, and then the new suburbs of West Franklin where Route 182 sports fast-food franchises and discount department stores. Park near the intersection of Willow and Main Street and you will be in position to walk to the Franklin Visitors Center and stroll the historic district.

As you might guess from its name, Franklin is a community with stronger Anglo than French roots. During the eighteenth century it was known as Carlin's Settlement. In 1800, Guinea Lewis arrived from Pennsylvania, donated property for a courthouse, and laid out a street plan. The city was renamed in honor of Benjamin Franklin. When St. Mary Parish was established in 1811, Franklin became the seat of government. Until the War Between the States, it functioned as an important interior port city, shipping its sugar harvest on the waters of Bayou Teche. The arrival of the railroad and lumber industry after the war prompted growth of the business district west of Willow Street. Today petroleum and carbon black are important industrial products, but sugar remains the main crop. During the fall, smoke drifts in from surrounding cane fields and the city resounds with the rumble of passing trucks which spill loose cane onto the otherwise tidy streets as they make their way to the old Sterling Sugar Mill (tours offered).

City of Franklin Visitors Center 323 Willow St.

Located just three blocks off Route 182, the visitors center is a small office where you can get a list of plantations open for tours and city brochures. Be sure to pick up the *Walking Tour Guide to the Franklin Historic District*. The Center is open Monday through Friday from 9 A.M. to 4:30 P.M. If the Center is closed you may get maps, brochures, and other tourist information from the Forest Inn (*see* directions under Accommodations). (318) 628-6323 or 1-800-962-6889.

Attractions

*Walking Tour of Franklin Historic District Main and Willow St.

The oak-shaded Main Street of Franklin will make you want to stop and abandon your vehicle even on the hottest South Louisiana days. It may even put you in mind to hook up a buggy and clatter about town. The Franklin Historic District was first listed on the National Register of Historic Places in 1982, and contains over 400 significant buildings. You won't find any buggies (although the street lamps still bear "No Hitching" signs), but the area is easily viewed on foot in less than an hour. The best place to start a tour is near the intersection of Willow and Main Street at the Visitors Center, where you may pick up a list of the important structures in the area. Even without the list, you can find grand homes and quaint turn-of-the-century cottages by walking a five-block area bounded by Main (on the north), Willow (on the west), Morris (on the east), and Second Street (on the south). For a look at the early twentieth-century businesses and residences of Railroad Town, walk the five-block area west of Willow Street between Second and Main.

Arlington Plantation 56 E. Main St. (Rt. 182).

This mansion just east of Franklin was built in the 1830s by the Carlin family, original settlers in Franklin. A circular driveway curves past flowering shrubs, live oaks, and formal gardens. The front and bayou sides of the house are graced with large, columned porticos, while smaller identical porticos adorn the sides. The house is lit by bronze and crystal chandeliers and decorated with period antiques. Arlington is open for viewing by appointment Tuesday through Saturday from 10 A.M. to 4 P.M. Admission is $4 for adults and $2 for students; children 12 and under are admitted free. (318) 828-2644.

Grevemberg House Sterling St. (Rt. 322).

The Grevemberg House is a Greek Revival home constructed in 1851, and the only house in Franklin open for walk-in tours (no appointment necessary). The house was nearly destroyed by fire in 1983 and has been thoroughly restored by the local chapter of the Louisiana Historic Landmark Society. The floors are original, but most of the details, like the painted "faux bois" cypress, wallpaper, and draperies, are meticulous reproductions. The house is furnished with period furniture. Its grounds are partially occupied by Franklin City Park. Traveling west on Main Street (Route 182), bear right on Sterling Road (Route 322) and Grevemberg is about a half mile ahead on the left. The house is open Thursday through Sunday from 10 A.M. to 4 P.M. Tours cost $3 for adults and $1.50 for children 12 and under. (318) 828-2092.

*Sterling Sugar Mill Rt. 322.

Sterling offers tours every Saturday morning during cane-cutting season. Take Route 182 west and bear right on Sterling Road. The mill is located just past the Grevemberg house. (318) 828-0620.

Annual Plantation Christmas Tour 1st or 2nd weekend in December.

Each December the city turns on its lights and opens 4 of its old homes for tours. There are musical presentations at local churches, evening candlelight tours of the homes and, of course, an appearance by St. Nick. A musical highlight in recent years has been the ringing of handbells at the Church of Assumption at 924 Main Street. There are the brilliant light displays along Main Street and the reflective waters of Bayou Teche. An $8 fee buys admission to all the homes and other events. For more information write to City of Franklin, Christmas Tour Information, P.O. Box 1143, Franklin, LA 70538. 1-800-962-6889.

Food

Charlie's Meat and Deli Cajun/Down Home, $. 1803 W. Main St.

Charlie's serves weighty plate lunches and sandwiches from their deli counter. Lunch specials change daily, but there is always a choice of two main dishes. Friday there are seafood plates, like shrimp stew with rice and gravy, potato salad, fried bread, and bread pudding. Weekday choices include meatloaf, chicken stew, and crab and shrimp etouffée. These are served with rice, cornbread or rice dressings, or potato salad. Charlie's Meat sells whole, deboned chickens stuffed with a variety of fillings. Toss one in the cooler and throw it on the smoker when you get home. Charlie's is located on Route 182 in the west end of Franklin. The deli and lunch counter are open from 11 A.M. to 2 P.M., Monday through Saturday. The meat market is open weekdays from 8 A.M. to 6 P.M., and Saturdays until 2 P.M. (318) 828-4169.

Forest Inn Restaurant Cajun/Creole, $$. W. Main St.

The Forest Inn is the most popular restaurant in the Lower Teche Region. The restaurant and motel have been a family-run business for thirty years and pride themselves on their own crawfish and gumbo recipes. Their crab and okra gumbo is thick and spicy, while the oyster and crab gumbo is light and flavored with a splash of sherry. A bowl of gumbo or rich crawfish bisque in a nutty gravy make a hearty meal by themselves. Best among the more complicated seafood preparations is the Forest Two Step—fresh fish stuffed with a crab mixture, seasoned Paul Prudhomme-style (hot), and topped with a butter and wine sauce. We began hearing about the Mississippi Mud Pie at the Forest when we were still 60 miles away in Houma. A thick butter crust packed with chopped pecans is topped with a sweet cream cheese filling, homemade chocolate pudding, whipped cream, and more crumbled pecans. At lunch, several meat, seafood, soup, and salad combos are available for under $7. The Forest Inn is located on Route 182 in the west end of town. They are open Monday through Saturday from 5:30 A.M. to 9:30 P.M. (318) 828-1810.

Iberia Street Cash Grocery Local Fave, $. 501 Iberia St.

A gas station attendant directed us to this country grocery for "the best hamburgers in town." I can't remember the sandwiches, but the Iberia Cash Grocery offers time-warp dining at its most primitive. The one-room country store has wood-plank floors, walls lined with household goods, and a corner with two powerline-spool tables and wooden benches. The place seemed to be most popular among the kids, who paused to study the "new" prices scrawled over the candy rack: "All 1-cent candy is now 2 cents. 5-cent candy is now 7 cents. 10-cent candy is now 15 cents. Big candy is 50 cents". There are quite a few items that have been around the store so long that they are no longer for sale, but are on display. While you are waiting for a motherly ham and cheese sandwich on cross-cut white bread or a griddled burger, check out the newspaper clippings on the wall: "Bomb Dropped," "Titanic Sinks," and "Lindburgh Killer Electrocuted." The grocery is open from Monday through Friday, from 8:15 A.M. to 6 P.M., and Saturday until noon. (318) 828-0392.

Lodging

Best Western Forest Motel Rt. 182 West, $34 to $44 double. (318) 828-1810.

Side Trips Between Franklin and Jeanerette

It is only 13 miles from Franklin to Jeanerette by way of U.S. 90 or the more scenic Route 182, but there are several short and scenic side trips along the way. Among the most interesting detours on the Lower Teche are two oxbow bends which wind through vast cane fields and sugar settlements. The first of these oxbows begins on the west end of Franklin, and is followed by Irish Bend Road (Route 322), named to honor Alexander Porter, a wealthy Irishman who settled there in the early 1800s. In the middle of the bend, Porter built the massive *Oaklawn Plantation* (open for tours). A second horseshoe bend in Bayou Teche begins in Baldwin, a few miles west from where Irish Bend Road rejoins Route 182. The second oxbow, known as Indian Bend, is an 8-mile kink followed by Route 326. This route passes through the *Chitimacha Indian Reservation* in Charenton. A third interesting side trip is not an oxbend at all, but a 20-mile detour through the cane fields and marsh southwest of Baldwin which terminates at the coastal community and state park at *Cypremort Point*.

Medric Martin Grocery Irish Bend Rd. (Rt. 322), West of Franklin.

Medric Martin has operated this rustic grocery, bar, and lounge

Medric Martin Grocery.

The Martin brothers/Medric Martin Grocery. (Photo by Julie Posner)

for nearly sixty years. As the cane industry became more mechanized, fewer and fewer customers remained along Irish Bend Road. Martin still mans the rough-hewn wooden counter and bar, but there isn't much to buy except cold drinks. His brother wanders in every day to keep him company, and the two can tell of very different days in sugar country. The now silent juke joint beside the store is testimony to the changing times. The Medric Martin Grocery is not only the best place to stop for a soda, it is the lone commercial establishment on Irish Bend Road. It is located 6 miles from Route 182 in Franklin and 2 miles east of Oaklawn Plantation.

*Oaklawn Manor Plantation Irish Bend Rd. (Rt. 322).

Oaklawn is a luxurious Greek Revival mansion constructed in 1837 by Irish immigrant U.S. Senator Alexander Porter. It took over three years to complete construction, using bricks made from Bayou Teche clay and local cypress. The house faces down an elegantly sloping, landscaped yard towards the bayou. An apiary, old dairy house, and Live oak grove are located on the estate's 35 sculpted acres.

The history of Oaklawn is one of wealth and romance. C. A. Barbour, a wealthy steamboat captain, passed the house in his trips piloting lumber boats on the bayou. In 1926, he bought and restored the crumbling structure, only to see it burn down just before completion! Unflagging, Barbour rebuilt it from the ground up. Although the reconstruction was done from drawings of the original, the house now has many features of Barbour's conception. Marble floors were installed using material from the old St. Louis Hotel in New Orleans. Tons of Italian marble, French glass, and other exotic materials were shipped up the bayou. The top two floors are closed to the public, but regular tours are conducted on the lavish first floor. Audubon followers can pause and view current owner Senator Foster's huge collection of Audubon prints and books. From Route 182 in Franklin, head west on Sterling Road, which becomes Irish Bend Road (Route 322). The entrance to Oaklawn is 8 miles from Franklin, and 3.5 miles from the junction with Route 182 in the west.

Chitimacha Indian Reservation Rt. 326, Charenton.

The Chitimacha are the only Indian tribe native to South Louisiana still living on a portion of their original territory. In 1925, their numbers decimated to fifty, a reservation was established and the Chitimacha became the first federally recognized tribe in Louisiana. Native customs and lore, as well as the Chitimacha

Oaklawn Plantation. (Courtesy of Oaklawn)

language, are virtually extinct. A handful of elderly women still weave split cane baskets, which are the crowning artistic achievement of the tribe. Until the sixties, these baskets, which are among the finest in the world, were widely available and inexpensive. Following visits by folklorists and writers, demand for the tightly woven (some double-weave varieties can hold water) buff, red, and black baskets soared. They may still be ordered for about $20 a square inch from tribal craftspeople, but there is a waiting list.

A *Visitors Center* housing the tribal offices and a display on the history and crafts of the tribe is located about 4 miles from Route 182 in the heart of the reservation. The museum portion is operated by the Jean Lafitte State Park Service. Here you can see photographs of past chiefs and tribal members, elaborate specimens of old and new split cane baskets, and other artifacts. The center also will provide a list of tribal craftspeople. Larger and more interesting than the display at the center is the private collection of artifacts and crafts of Faye Stouff. Mrs. Stouff is the wife of the last Chitimacha chief. Her collection of handcrafted beadwork, homemade baskets, and tribal mementos is amazing. Mrs. Stouff operates a gift shop beside her home, less than a mile from the Visitors Center. The Visitors Center is located in the middle of the Charenton oxbow, 4 miles from Route 182 in either direction. They are open Monday through Saturday from 8 A.M. to 4:30 P.M., and Sunday from 9 A.M. to 5 P.M.

With little money being generated by native crafts or on the small farms of the reservation, the Chitimacha opened the *Bayouland Bingo Hall* in the 1980s. Today hundreds of people visit the high-stakes bingo games, arriving by bus from around the state. The schedule is subject to change, but now features a $10,000 bingo on Wednesdays (7 P.M.) and a $50,000 session on Saturdays (4 P.M. to 10 P.M.). Occasionally there are bingo marathons from 4 P.M. to 5 A.M. during which $100,000 is given away. It is not cheap to buy into these games. A set of cards can cost between $10 and $100. The smoky spectacle takes place on Bobtown Road, just off Route 326 on the reservation. (318) 923-7284 or 1-800-284-4386.

Cypremort Point State Park Rt. 319, 20 miles southwest of Baldwin.

This is one of two places in Lower Teche Country where travelers can access public recreation facilities on the coast. The drive southwest from U.S. 90 crosses 20 miles of sparsely populated fields and open marsh. At Cypremort Point you will find a grocery, bait shop, restaurant (not recommended), and bar. Once nourished by fresh water, the area was named Cypremort (French

(Photo by Julie Posner)

for "dead cypress") after the cypress trees were killed by saltwater incursion.

Several miles before reaching the end-of-the-road community, you will pass Cypremort Point State Park. Most of the 185-acre park is covered with cordgrass, but there is a man-made beach on the shore of East Cote Blanche Bay. The sand reaches about four feet from shore before giving way to mud bottom, but the park is a popular spot for swimming, boating, and crabbing. Facilities include a boat launch, a covered pier for crabbing, picnic shelters with grills, and clean restrooms with outdoor showers. This is a wonderfully desolate spot, but be advised that shade is at a premium. Camping is not allowed inside the park; however, tent and car camping is condoned on the grassy right-of-way outside the park gates (bring bug spray and sun screen). The park is open from 7 A.M. to 10 P.M. Admission is $2 per car for up to 4 people. From U.S. 90, take Route 83 southwest about 12 miles. In the town of Louisa follow Route 319 south another 8 miles to Cypremort Point. (318) 867-4510.

Bayview Inn Restaurant & Bar Local Fave, $$. Rt. 319, Cypremort Point.

This is the only place to eat within 25 miles and it is located right on the water. After a hot and shadeless visit to Cypremort Point Park you may want to stop here just to get out of the sun! The food is mostly fried. Bayview is open Tuesday through Thursday from 11 A.M. to 8 P.M., and Friday and Saturday until 9 P.M. (closed Mondays). (504) 385-3502.

Jeanerette

Although Jeanerette is grouped for geographic reasons with the nearby Anglo communities of the Lower Teche, this city of 7000 has strong French roots. Names like Patout, Broussard, and LeJeune on turn-of-the-century businesses on Main Street are the first indicator that the town has a very different ethnic mix than Baldwin and Franklin to the south. Jeanerette is located on the bayou about 8 miles northwest of Baldwin, and ten miles southeast of New Iberia. The town got its name from John Jeanerette, who founded a community at the site and became its first postmaster in 1830. Cajuns as well as Creole French came to the region, along with a few Anglo planters. In 1870, the railroad arrived and Jeanerette bloomed as a marketplace and shipping point for cane and lumber products. Petroleum has supplanted

Sugar mill in Jeanerette. (Photo by Macon Fry)

lumber as a mainstay of the local economy, but the sugar industry owns the landscape. Visit Jeanerette in the fall and you will find the streets bordered by piles of spilled sugarcane, and the air rich with the scent of burning sugar fields.

Attractions

Albania Plantation Hwy. 182 East, Jeanerette.

Albania is listed as open for tours "by appointment." We called and stopped by on several occasions, but were unable to rouse anyone. The mansion was built in 1837 and is on grounds darkly shaded by moss-covered oaks. It is now the private residence of Mrs. Emily Bridges, who has reportedly furnished it lavishly with period furniture. One room is filled with Mrs. Bridges' antique doll collection. To arrange a tour try calling Mrs. Bridges at (318) 276-4816.

*Le Beau Petit Musée 500 E. Main St.

After spending years driving through cane country, it took a stop at "The Pretty Little Museum" to finally understand exactly what is involved in the planting, harvesting, and processing of sugarcane. In addition to a 25-panel display on "200 Years of the Louisiana Sugarcane Industry," the museum shows a twenty-minute video entitled *Sugarcane to Sugar,* produced by the USL Center for Louisiana Studies, which traces the production of sugar from seed to mill. Among artifacts on display are a collection of cypress patterns from Jeanerette's Moresi Foundry. These patterns were used in the 1800s as models in the creation of gears for sugar and rice mills and steamboats. There is a room filled with mounted swamp animals and sundry items pertaining to many facets of life on the Teche. Le Beau Petite Musée is open Monday through Friday from 8 A.M. to 5 P.M. Regular admission is $3, seniors $1.50, and students 50 cents. (318) 276-4408.

City Park Wormser St. at Bayou Teche.

Jeanerette's City Park is a good place to unpack a picnic beside the bayou. There is a covered pavilion and several barbecue pits. To get to the park, turn towards the bayou on Wormser (just west of LeJeune's Bakery).

*Justin's Observatory 125 E. Main St.

It's easy to miss the sign that announces Justin's Observatory, but it is almost impossible to miss the three-story silver-domed structure towering over a garage in the background. Justin's Observatory in Jeanerette is one of the most unusual diversions in

(Photo by Julie Posner)

Teche Country. It is owned and maintained by self-taught astronomer Justin Lerive, who built it in 1984 after a disabling accident ended his employment as a welder's foreman at the Port of Iberia. Lerive lives in the frame house next door, but spends most of his time in the garage/observatory poring over astronomy magazines and entertaining guests. A tour of the observatory begins with maps, letters, and equipment in the garage, much of which was donated by out-of-town visitors. The highlight is a trip up two flights of stairs to the dome where Lerive keeps his eight-inch Celestron telescope.

As he guides visitors through his observatory, it is plain that next to looking at stars, Lerive likes best to talk about them. Like any man that is determined to see farther than the rest, his true bent is towards the broad picture. A question about solar flare-ups led to talk of the sun, the solar system, and the creation of the galaxy. His explanation ended with the cosmic proclamation, "Everything starts out round."

Among other topics Lerive touched on were the possible lunar and solar influence on such natural disasters as Hurricane Hugo and the San Francisco earthquake. In a part of the country where scientists are generally occupied with such earthly concerns as squeezing oil out of the ground and keeping the Mississippi out of the Atchafalaya Basin and turtles out of shrimp nets, Lerive's perspectives are delightfully expansive. His advice: "People need to take some time and look at the sky." Justin's Observatory is located on Main Street (Route 182) just east of Jeanerette. (318) 276-6220.

Jeanerette Sugar Company 2302 West Main St.
St. Mary Sugar Co-op Rt. 182 and Rt. 318, West Jeanerette.

Tours are not offered at these mills, but their location on Route 182 makes them a good place to pull over and witness the general 24 hour-a-day hubbub of the fall harvest time. You will see more during the day but, at night, the glare of the factory and flickering of truck lights reflected in clouds of steam create a monstrous, bristling specter.

Food

*LeJeune's Bakery Local Fave. 1510 W. Main St.
Now in its third generation here, LeJeune's has been a Jeanerette landmark since 1884. There are few things tastier than a loaf of their crusty french bread, hot from the oven. Stop by the bakery on any weekday around 11:30 A.M. and you can buy a loaf before

it has a chance to move from the brick oven onto the cooling rack. The storefront is closed, so all business is transacted at the side entrance, where you can see the bakers at work. LeJeune's only makes two items—french bread and gingerbread "stageplanks." The stageplanks are my favorite, but must be eaten hot to be truly appreciated. These faintly sweet, breadlike cookie-cakes emerge from the oven on Tuesday and Thursday between 10:30 A.M. and 2 P.M. Plan your trip around this event, and whether you are buying french bread or gingerbread, be sure to have a little cream cheese or butter to spread on top. Before leaving, grab a couple of extra bread wrappers (suitable for framing) which sport the original LeJeune's logo and slogan, "The proof of the pudding is in the eating." You can also purchase the same graphics on a t-shirt. (318) 276-5690.

★Yellow Bowl Seafood, $$. Rt. 182, East Jeanerette.

This is the one restaurant in Lower Teche Country that I would drive out of my way to visit. Folks have been making the trip to the Yellow Bowl from as far away as Lafayette and Morgan City since Tony Roberts opened the restaurant in 1961. Since that time the restaurant's reputation has been built on rich seafood preparations, especially crawfish dishes. Tony's son, Neil, owns the place and runs the kitchen with the help of two cooks who have been there since it opened. You can still get all the dishes that Robert perfected thirty years ago—crawfish etouffée, crawfish bisque, and fried crawfish (a specialty which Neil claims was first served at the Yellow Bowl). The ultimate entree is Crawfish Rochelle. Two fat, medium-sized soft-shell crabs are sauteed and served on opposite ends of a platter covered with rice smothered in the Yellow Bowl's famous etouffée.

When crawfish are not in season, try the seafood gumbo, shrimp bisque, and lightly battered fried fish and oysters (chicken and beef entrees are also available). For dessert, go for the definitive Louisiana pecan pie. The Yellow Bowl has a casual atmosphere that probably hearkens back to its days as one of the premier dance halls on the Teche. During the fifties, acts like Happy Fats and Bobby Charles packed he dance floor that now is the larger of two dining rooms. The food and ambiance at the Yellow Bowl make for a meal you will want to linger over. Seafood po-boys are available, and lunch specials are offered on Thursday and Friday. The restaurant is located on the bayou side of Route 182, 3 miles east of Jeanerette. They are open for lunch Thursday and Friday from 11 A.M. to 1:30 P.M., and until 2:30 on Sunday.

Dinner hours are 5 P.M. to 9:30 P.M. on Thursday, and until 10 on Friday and Saturday. (318) 828-4806 or 276-5512.

Lodging

*Bed and Breakfast in Acadiana 2148½ W. Main St., Jeanerette. Not everybody in Teche Country lives in pillared and porticoed mansions. This Bed and Breakfast is a modern, one-room cottage behind the bayou-side brick rambler of owners Barbara and Warren Patout (pronounced pa-too). Accommodations include a full kitchen, carport, washer/dryer, and TV. The refrigerator is stocked with soft drinks, fruit juice, and the ingredients for a "fix your own" breakfast. This place is very private and has the casual feel of a beach house. Don't pass up a chance to enjoy a drink or bite to eat with the Patouts. Warren has the big easy laugh of a saloon keeper, and can recount stories of the Teche Country sugar industry. The Patouts have a canoe and guests are welcome to paddle up and down the dreamy bayou. The Patouts' is within easy paddling distance of 2 sugar mills, an antebellum plantation, and the Moresi Foundry. The cottage rents for $35 to $55 per night. The Bed and Breakfast is located on the bayou side of Route 182 (W. Main Street) in the west end of Jeanerette. Call (318) 276-5061 for reservations.

THE UPPER TECHE

Just below New Iberia, the eastern edge of the Upper Teche region, the bayou turns north and is followed by Route 31. The land becomes more moist and broad fields begin to give way to forest. Limbs of live oaks meet over the road in moss-draped archways. This region between the Cajun Prairie and the Atchafalaya Basin is a historical center of Cajun, French, and Creole culture. The earliest settlers were French who arrived in the early eighteenth century. In 1762 a Spanish military garrison was established at the Post de Atakapas (named for the Indians who once inhabited the region). The community which grew around the post went on to become St. Martinville, a hub of opulent Creole culture on the wild frontier. Most of the countryside was given to farming and ranching, but the city was the westernmost bastion of high culture on the continent.

When Cajuns began arriving on the Upper Teche in 1765, they were not always greeted warmly by the established Creole society. Shunning the high society of St. Martinville, these rural people

Byway in Upper Teche Country. (Courtesy of LA Department of Wildlife and Fisheries)

moved up the bayou, east towards the Atchafalaya, and west onto the prairie to set up their own farms and communities. While the rich Creole society has all but disappeared, Cajun culture remains strong. Drive up the bayou on Route 31 through towns like Breaux Bridge and Henderson and you will find Cajuns raising crawfish and continuing the traditional pursuits of fishing and farming. You will also find a plethora of Cajun and Zydeco dance halls, and restaurants serving dishes prepared with "wild" Basin crawfish.

New Iberia

New Iberia calls itself Queen City of the Teche, but this active trade and industrial center of 36,000 played second fiddle to its older and more established neighbor, St. Martinville, during its first half century. The name "Iberia" was appointed by Spaniards and Canary Islanders who settled there and took up ranching in the late 1700s. Prosperity did not visit the community until the sugar industry and steamboats arrived in the 1820s. Wide and fertile fields around New Iberia, the discovery of salt on nearby Avery Island, and the cultivation of fiery peppers signaled the economic ascendance of the Queen City. After the War Between the States, New Iberia became the seat of government for newly formed Iberia Parish. With the discovery of oil and natural gas nearby and a connection with Gulf shipping lanes at the Port of Iberia, New Iberia boomed in the twentieth century.

Today, New Iberia is a busy city whose suburban fringe supports a collection of supermarkets, malls, and fast-food franchises. The historic downtown area is nestled on the banks of Bayou Teche at the intersection of Route 182 (Main Street) and Route 14 (Center Street), about 20 miles southwest of Lafayette. Here travelers can tour Shadows Plantation, walk to nearby restaurants, and spend the night in a Bed and Breakfast within throwing distance of the bayou. Just a short drive from downtown, the historic Konriko Rice Mill and Trappey's Hot Sauce Factory have visitors centers and tours. Although the downtown area may be easily toured in a couple of hours, there is enough food, music (on weekends), and interesting accommodations to make New Iberia a good choice for an overnight stop. A side trip to the coastal wetlands about 15 miles below New Iberia leads to a land of hot peppers, sugar, salt, and two of the most famous gardens in the South.

Iberia Visitors Center 2690 Center St. (Rt. 14) at U.S. 90. Some pals visited this center and reported, "They were so

Shadows on the Teche. (Courtesy of LA Office of Tourism)

friendly, it was scary!" The tourist information center, housed in an Acadian-style home, has restroom facilities and plenty of information on city- and parish-wide attractions. They can help with everything from finding accommodations to arranging a plantation or swamp tour. You can pick up parish and town maps, and a guide for a downtown New Iberia walking tour. The center is open daily from 8 A.M. to 5 P.M. (318) 365-1540.

Attractions

Downtown Walking Tour
In the heart of the city, Route 182 splits into two one-way roads, with Main Street carrying westbound traffic and St. Peter Street eastbound. The Downtown Walking Tour (map available from Visitors Center) covers a twelve-block area centered at the intersection of Main Street and Center Street (Route 14). Park at this juncture and visit Shadows on the Teche Plantation before walking east through the shady old residential district with its mix of antebellum, Victorian, and steamboat gothic homes. Then stroll west a couple of blocks on Route 182 to New Iberia's turn-of-the-century business strip. Here you will find some great lunch spots among old storefronts facing the Teche. There is a public parking lot beside Bouligny Plaza.

★Shadows on the Teche 117 E. Main St. at Weeks St.
After visiting Shadows, writer Henry Miller scribed a note to his friend Weeks Hall, "I expect to be back and write a book here—the book of camelias and hallucinations." The rich family history of this mansion and the beauty of its grounds provide a dreamy, soft-focus view of the genteel life that flourished along Bayou Teche for more than a century. Shadows was built in 1834 by wealthy sugar planter David Weeks. More than 250,000 bricks were molded of clay from the banks of the bayou to construct the 18″-thick walls and lower floor of the mansion. Most striking to those unfamiliar with the antebellum homes of Louisiana are the exterior stairways, which connect wide first- and second-floor galleries. These stairs are the only way to move between the two main floors of the house. Inside there are no hallways or closets. Rooms are furnished with fine Empire and Federal antiques.

At one time, Shadows was the center of five sugar plantations and its grounds stretched from present-day U.S. 90 to the silent waters of the Teche. After Northern troops occupied it during the War Between the States, the house fell into disrepair. In the 1920s, William Weeks Hall, great-grandson of the original builder, restored Shadows and became the fourth successive generation of the family to inhabit the house. Weeks Hall entertained intellectuals and celebrities from around the country. Many of these were invited to sign an upstairs parlor door. This door, now covered with scrawled messages from Henry Miller, Tex Ritter, and Elias Kazan, is on display on the first floor, near the gift shop. Many visitors concur with the observations of Kazan, who scribbled, "The most beautiful house I've seen in all (the) South." Hall left the house to the National Trust for Historic Preservation, which now operates tours daily from 9 A.M. to 4:30 P.M. Tours cost $5 for adults, $4 for seniors, and $3 for children. The grounds, including a planned garden and sloping lawn beside the Teche, are open for free. (318) 369-6446.

Statue of Hadrian Corner of Weeks and St. Peter streets.

This is not what you would call an organic attraction in New Iberia, but it is a singular work of art by any standard. Hadrian ruled the Roman Empire from A.D. 117 to 138. This work, sculpted in A.D. 130, is the only full-length statue of Hadrian in the United States. Brought to England from Italy in the nineteenth century, the statue was purchased by Iberia Savings and Loan in 1961 and is now on display in a glassed-in viewing area outside the bank.

Bouligny Plaza Main St. between Iberia and French streets.

This sun-drenched plaza on the banks of Bayou Teche has restroom facilities, a gazebo, and a large parking area within walking distance of downtown attractions and restaurants. The plaza is the location of a historical marker and bust of Lt. Col. Francisco Bouligny, who brought several hundred Spanish settlers to the site of present-day New Iberia in 1779 and is generally credited as the town founder.

Surrounding Attractions

*Trappey's Fine Foods, Inc. 900 East Main St.

Anyone interested in the unique food of South Louisiana should tour the region's two big hot sauce manufacturing plants. If you can only visit one, the tour at Trappey's gets my vote. It is a sinus-opening experience that covers the history, production, packaging, and eating of Trappey's products. Start in the Trappey's store (part of the original factory), where you can sample the huge line of hot sauces, pickled peppers, and okra that made the company famous, and get a cup of beans or gumbo from their tasting kitchen. You can sit down and dose your food with one of ten pepper sauces, including the searing original Pepper Sauce. Each sauce is graded by heat factor, so you may season to suit your own combustion ratio. Many of the sauces, pickles, and canned goods are unavailable outside of Acadiana. The entire line is for sale here, including such brightly labeled products as Ron Guidry's (a local hero) Louisiana Lightning, Chef Magic Garlic Pepper, and Red Devil hot sauces. Tabasco peppers were brought to Louisiana from Mexico in the mid-1800s. Trappey's was founded in 1898 by blacksmith-turned-planter B. F. Trappey, who opened the New Iberia plant in 1929. The factory now includes 216 pickling vats where tons of peppers, pickles, and okra are soaked in brine. The vat area, with its cypress beams, brick walls, and iron cooking baskets, is in use and on tour. Six million pounds of peppers are ground to mash and aged in oak casks each year. After aging for several years, the mash is mixed with vinegar and salt and bottled. Workers wearing masks for protection from powerful pepper vapors sort pickles and fill 200 bottles of sauce per minute. While on tour, be sure not to call Trappey's sauce "Tabasco," a name patented by the nearby McIlhenny Company. Trappey's is a short drive east of the historic district on Route 182. The store is open Monday through Saturday from 9 A.M. to 4:30 P.M. Tours are offered Monday through Friday at 9 A.M., 9:45 A.M., 10:30 A.M., 1 P.M., 1:45 P.M. and 2:30 P.M. The last tour on Friday is at 1 P.M. (no tours on Saturday). Admission is $1.50, children under 12 are 50 cents. (318) 365-8281.

Konriko Rice Mill and Store 309 Ann St.

Founded in 1912 by Phillip Conrad (the company name is a phonetic contraction of Conrad Rice Company), this is one of the oldest continually operating mills in the state and the sole manufacturer of unique Wild Pecan Rice. Tours originate at the Konriko Store (housed in the old mill office) and begin with a twenty-minute video which tells more about the history of the region than the rice industry. Your guide will show samples of rice with the husk attached, milled, and polished. After the video you are invited into the mill to see bagging and packaging operations. You may want to skip the tour and browse around the store, where you can sample the daily rice dish, served from a steaming crock pot, and look at a large selection of books on local topics. There are postcards and regional food products for sale. I recommend getting a couple of boxes of Konriko's Wild Pecan Rice, which cooks firm and has a rich, nutty flavor. The store is open Monday through Saturday, from 9 A.M. to 5 P.M. (free of charge). Tours are scheduled at 10 A.M., 11 A.M., 1 P.M., 2 P.M., and 3 P.M. The

Bunk Johnson's grave. (Photo by Julie Posner)

tour costs $2.75 for adults and $1.25 for children. To get to the store from Route 182, head south on Ann Street. (318) 367-6163, 1-800-737-5667, or 1-800-552-3245 (out of state).

Rosary House 699 E. St. Peter St. at Ann St.

Cajun Country is also Catholic Country, and this is the place to find candles, rosaries, religious medallions, trinkets, and hundreds of other religious items at close-out prices. The Rosary House was established in 1946 and has materials to suit all tastes and budgets. Rosary prices range from 15 cents to $200, while other items are priced from 5 cents to $2000. The store is located a few blocks from the Konriko Rice Mill at the corner of St. Peter and Ann streets. They are open Monday through Friday from 8 A.M. to 5 P.M.

Bunk Johnson's Grave Corner of French St. and Dale St.

Many legendary performers of the early jazz era have roots in Cajun Country. Foremost among these was William Geary ("Bunk") Johnson, a black trumpet player who reportedly taught Louis ("Satchmo") Armstrong how to play. Johnson was born to former slaves in New Orleans in 1879. For thirty years he played with famous jazz groups like Buddy Bolden's band. Bunk faded into obscurity in the early 1900s and settled in New Iberia, where he taught music in the public schools, worked at Shadows as a yard man, labored at the Konriko Rice Mill, and drove a cane truck. He enjoyed a brief return to the limelight when a jazz writer contacted Weeks Hall looking for him. Hall told the writer to "look in the Harlem Grill (a local hangout), but he will probably be incoherent." Bunk Johnson died in New Iberia in 1949 and was buried in this small cemetery. Enter the French Street gate and follow the path into the cemetery about thirty yards. The grave of Willie ("Bunk") Johnson is three rows over to your right.

City Park Parkview Dr., north bank of Bayou Teche.

We can't all enjoy mint juleps on arbor-covered verandas beside the bayou, but anyone can partake of the beauty of the Teche at this serene park. Whether you are making a picnic out of a plate lunch from Victor's or Theriot's (*see* food section) or wetting a fishing line, this is probably the most relaxing spot on the water. To get to the park, head west on Route 182 from Route 14. Cross the bayou at Bridge Street (here you will see the *Mount Carmel Convent*, built in 1830). Turn right on Davis Street, left on Pollard, and right again on Parkview Drive.

Farmers Market City Park, Sugarcane Festival Pavilion.

One more reason to visit City Park on the Teche is to get the best local produce. The market is open Wednesday and Saturday from 7 A.M. to 10 A.M. See directions for City Park.

Eating crawfish at the Guiding Star. (Photo by Julie Posner)

Justine Antebellum Home Rt. 86 (Loreauville Rd.) 4 mi. from New Iberia.

This antebellum home (1822) is a convenient stop on the way to the Basin town of Loreauville. The house has a Victorian facade, added in the 1890s, and was moved to this site in the sixties. Justine is known for its fine collection of antebellum furniture, Louisiana antiques, and primitive pieces. To get to Justine, cross the bayou on Route 87 and turn right on Route 86. The mansion is 4 miles from New Iberia on Route 86 (Loreauville Road). Tours are available by appointment and cost $3. (318) 364-0973.

Avery Island, Tabasco Factory, Jungle Gardens and Salt Dome
Located about thirty minutes south of New Iberia on Route 329. See South of New Iberia section.

*Jefferson Island, Live Oak Gardens, House and Boat Tour
Located about thirty minutes southwest of New Iberia off Route 14. See South of New Iberia section.

Special Events

*Louisiana Sugarcane Festival last weekend in September.

Creole Festival last weekend in April.

Recreation

*Lake Fausse State Park See St. Martinville Recreation section.
Boat rentals, picnic area, hiking trails, fishing dock, and camping in swamp setting.

*Airboat Tours, Inc. See Loreauville.

Food

Boiling Point Boiled Seafood, $$. U.S. 90, 4 miles east of New Iberia.

What's in a name? In this case the name tells the whole story. Boiled crawfish and crabs are all anybody bothers to order at this diminutive seafood joint. The handwashing sinks in a corner of the dining area and a long line outside the door on weekends during Lent are the marks of a classic boiled seafood haven. Crawfish are large and well seasoned throughout spring and early summer. Other months try the large, spicy, blue crabs. The

Boiling Point is open Monday through Friday from 10 A.M. to 10 P.M., and Saturday and Sunday from 3:30 P.M. to 10 P.M. The Boiling Point is located about 4 miles west of Route 14 on U.S. 90. (318) 365-7596.

*Danna's Bakery Local Fave/Bakery. 317 Hopkins Street, New Iberia.

This is the spot to stock up on sweets for a morning brunch or afternoon dessert in City Park or nearby Avery Island. You won't find fancy pastries here, just moist pecan macaroons, fresh blackberry tarts, and luscious sweet dough pies. I can't leave Danna's without a bag full of thumbprint cookies and nut bars. This bakery is a few blocks off the beaten path, but has been attracting customers from all over New Iberia since 1921. To get to Danna's take Route 182 west past the old commercial district and turn left on Hopkins Street. Danna's is open Tuesday through Saturday from 5 A.M. to 5:30 P.M., and Sunday until noon. (318) 364-7341.

*Guiding Star Rt. 90, west of New Iberia.

The Guiding Star has the biggest and cleanest crawfish east of Lafayette, and the best seasoning anywhere! Owner and boil chef Ralph Schaubert seasons his water with Tabasco mash, purchased in casks from the McIlhenny hot sauce company in New Iberia. Cayenne and salt are added for what may be the perfect blend of strong and hot flavors. Schaubert uses only select rice field crawfish. The tail meat pulls easily from the shell and the heads are laden with golden fat. The Guiding Star had a reputation as a "wild place" during their thirty years at their former location over on Route 14, where the parking lot was literally paved with beer-bottle caps. The new restaurant is not what you would call "wild" (the mayor of Erath was dining there with his family on my last visit), but it is definitely rustic. There are a couple of pool tables in a side room, but everything else is vintage boiling point decor, from the handwashing sinks in the dining area to the wooden tables covered with newspaper.

Crawfish are the big attraction from January to May. After May, huge "sweetwater" crabs from Lake Fausse arrive. These are blue crabs like those popular in New Orleans and the Chesapeake Bay, but they come from freshwater lakes and are incredibly large! The same pepper mash seasoning is thrown into the pot, and the seasonings would probably be enough to cook these crustaceans without boiling. The Guiding Star is open 7 days a week from 3 P.M. to 10 P.M. They are located in a small cinderblock building on Route 90, about 3 miles west of Route 14 in New Iberia (beside the Country Truck Stop). (318) 365-9113.

*Lagniappe Too Local Fave, $. 204 E. Main St.

This downtown lunch house (easy walking distance from the famous Shadows on the Teche plantation house) would be too cute if the food weren't so good. "Lagniappe" is a South Louisiana word for "a little something extra." In the case of Lagniappe Too, that "little something extra" is the attention that goes into every dish. Everything is made from scratch, including croutons on the soups, the dressing on the salads, and the two or three flavors of ice cream. Elaine Landry, who owns the restaurant and manages the kitchen, has lived in Chicago and Virginia and is not hung up on a strictly Cajun or Creole menu. The chicken salad is made with olives, eggs, and pecans. Soup choices include eggplant (a golden cream with small bits of eggplant), fantastic crab and corn, and a very light chicken andouille gumbo. For dessert I recommend getting both the bread pudding *and* the homemade ice cream! The bread pudding is almost as fluffy as its meringue topping, and the ice cream is the texture of just-whipped cream. Lagniappe Too also serves breakfast on weekdays. Try coffee and the Cajun-Style Biscuits with pecans and cane syrup for a genuine South Louisiana eye opener. Lagniappe Too is open Monday through Friday from 8 A.M. to 2 P.M. (318) 365-9419.

Theriot's Grocery and Meat Market Cajun/Down Home, $. 330 Julia St.

Theriot's serves the best traditional plate lunch fare in New Iberia from a window in the back of a country-style grocery. Daily specials include roast pork and beef, meatloaf, and baked chicken with a choice of 3 veggies and dessert. Seafood is served on Fridays. There is also a choice of sandwiches and fresh boudin or cracklins. Plunk down less than $3 for a plate here and take it over to City Park for a lunch on the bayou. Theriot's is located on Julia (a pretty side street two blocks west of Center Street) at the corner of Pershing. Lunch is served from 10:30 A.M. to 1 P.M. on weekdays. (318) 369-3871.

Victor's Cafeteria Local Fave, $. 109 W. Main St.

With the average age in America creeping upward, cafeterias are unlikely to die, but the small independent ones like Victor's have all but disappeared. Victor's is a plate food haven with cafeteria-style service. By far the most popular items are stuffed bell peppers with white beans (usually served on Thursdays) and the homemade chicken pot pies. These pies (available in meat and crawfish flavors) are served in individual pie pans and have a flaky top crust with forked edges. Chicken pies are usually served Thursday, but if you order one forty-five minutes in advance, they can prepare it any day. Victor's is the lunch spot of choice with the older crowd. It is easy walking distance from Shadows on the Teche plantation house. They are open Monday through Saturday from 6 A.M. to 2 P.M. (318) 369-9924 or 367-2882.

Music

New Iberia is not known for its music scene, but the area has three big dance halls and a couple of lounges where you can hear Cajun, Zydeco, Swamp Pop, and some of the most popular entertainers in Country music.

Club La Lou Country. Rt. 14, south of U.S. 90.

There are few places where you can see big-name country music performers like Vern Gosdin, Billy Joe Royal, and Jo-El Sonnier in such an intimate environment. There are even fewer places where these guys play for packed dance floors. Club La Lou was the premier dance hall south of New Iberia during the fifties, when local and regional acts were headliners. Today it has reopened as a country music venue where folks would still rather take a partner for a spin around the dance floor than sit dumbfounded around tables. Owner Wilbert LeBlanc did little to change the place when he reopened it. Windows in the shape of martini glasses still adorn the front doors, the facade is still flat with curved glass-brick corners, and the dance floor is still the center of attention. Best of all, the cost of seeing celebrity talent is usually around $10, a fraction of what it would cost for a concert at some cavernous sports arena in a big city. If you are a country music lover, you owe it to yourself to find out who is playing at La Lou. Head 2 miles south on Route 14 from U.S. 90. (318) 369-7020.

Foxtrot Lounge (Scottish Inn) Country/Swamp Pop. U.S. 90.

This is your classic South Louisiana lounge scene. Middle-aged folks dance to Country and Swamp Pop classics by competent local bands. Exit U.S. 90 at the Avery Island Exit. (318) 365-6711.

★Rainbeaux Club Cajun dance hall. 1373 Rt. 182 W.

For over thirty years the Rainbeaux (that's Cajun for rainbow) has been the destination of Cajun music lovers from all over Teche Country. They still have big Saturday evening French dances where older couples step close and fast, doing laps around a dance floor twice as large as a basketball court. Lending atmosphere are long strands of Christmas lights strung in a web across the ceiling. On Sundays things get going early, with local Country bands playing from 4:30 to 8:30. The Saturday Cajun dances begin at 8 P.M. and end at midnight. Admission is a dollar or two. From downtown New Iberia, head west on Route 182. The dance hall is on the bayou side of the highway on the far western outskirts of town. (318) 367-6731.

Lodging

Bed and Breakfasts:

★The Estorge-Norton House 446 East Main St.

Built entirely of cypress in the early 1900s by Edward Estorge, this three-story home overlooks the Old Spanish Trail and the spreading oaks around Shadows on the Teche. The first floor of the house was once an antique shop and is filled with a hodgepodge of old furniture. On the second floor there is a quiet reading room stocked with books and brochures, and four distinctively decorated rooms. Manager Charles Norton displays Southern hospitality and a great knowledge of the area while remaining an "invisible host" to those looking for privacy. He will show you around and give you a ride on the antique elevator (the first in New Iberia). In the morning, Norton serves a full breakfast in a sunny breakfast room. You can walk out the door, stroll the historic district, and get lunch at Lagniappe Too before driving down to Jefferson or Avery Island. Prices for a double (including breakfast) are $50 for a second-floor room with double bed and shared bath, and $55 with private bath. A two-room suite with a shared bath is $60. On the third floor is an apartment with one double bed and twin beds, kitchen, and private bath for $80. Call ahead to make arrangements. (318) 365-7603.

Interlude 2305 Loreauville Road (La. 86), northeast of New Iberia.

Interlude is the most unusual bed-and-breakfast I have ever visited. This 3-acre bayou-side estate was designed by present owner and architect, Margaret Fleming, as a thesis project in 1964. Entering Interlude is like stepping into a James Bond movie. The interior sports lavish sixties-style decor including intercoms, sunken rooms, ceilings open to the roof, and skylights. Guests are housed in a corner of the house with private entrances and sliding doors opening onto the pool and Bayou Teche. A

Continental breakfast consisting of fresh fruits, cheese, coffee, and juices is served in a mirrored dining area. The rate for double occupancy is $65. Interlude is about 15 minutes from downtown New Iberia on the Loreauville Road. From La. 182 (Main Street), head north across the bayou on Lewis Street. Go 1.2 miles and Lewis dead ends into Loreauville Road. Take a right on La. 86 (Loreauville Road) and continue for 2.6 miles and Interlude will be on the left. Call ahead to make arrangements. (318) 367-6704.

*La Maison Bed and Breakfast Rt. 83, 8 miles southwest of New Iberia.

If you want silence, seclusion, and privacy, look no further. Sixty acres of cane rustles outside the windows, and shade creeps slowly from one side of the porch to the other at this wonderful Acadian cottage near the farming community of Lydia. Actually "cottage" is too diminutive a term for this hacienda. The two-bedroom house has been modernized, and is furnished with a TV, washer and dryer, and fully equipped kitchen where you will find an icebox stocked with juices. Owners Eleanor and Ron Naquin live in a brick rambler next door and dispense a generous break-fast along with "insider" travel tips. Ron is a recreational shrimper and will often take guests (who cover gas expenses) for a short shrimping expedition on Vermilion Bay. The rate for double occupancy in one bedroom is $65. Double occupants using both bedrooms are charged $75. To get to La Maison, take U.S. 90 about 6.5 miles east from Route 14 in New Iberia. At mile marker 134 (which had been knocked over by a cane truck on our last visit) turn right onto Route 605. Route 605 turns Route 83. La Maison is two miles south of U.S. 90 on the left. Call first to make arrangements. (318) 364-2970.

Maison Marceline 442 East Main St.

Ernest Nereaux Jr., the owner of Maison Marceline, is an interior decorator and his tastes run towards the baroque. The guest room is co-joined by Nereaux's office and living quarters. The house was built in 1893 and has Victorian details, including pressed tin ceilings, but Nereaux has added such amenities as a jacuzzi in the guest room and a private gazebo by the rear garden. Whether it is to your taste or not, the renovation here was extensive. Nereaux offers house tours for $3 (9 A.M. to 4 P.M. daily). The cost of a room, including a full breakfast, is $80 double occupancy. No credit cards are accepted. Call in advance to make arrangements. (318) 364-5922.

Victorian Cottage (Perry House)

What this home lacks in privacy for its guests (entrance to the upstairs bedroom is through the family living room and kitchen), it makes up for in charm and hospitality. The current owners trace family roots back to plantation life in St. Francisville on her side, and the Poste des Attakapas on his. Accommodations are in a small upstairs room with four-poster bed and private bath. The house is located on historic East Main Street, just blocks from the Shadows plantation house and other walking tour attractions. Call first to make arrangements.

Motels and Hotels:

The Teche Motel 1830 East Main Street, $25 double. (318) 369-3756.

The Inn 924 East Admiral Doyle Drive, $35 to $39 double. (318) 367-3211.

Kajun Inn Motel 1506 Center Street, $24 to $29 double. (318) 367-3608.

Holiday Inn 2801 Center Street, $53 to $58 double. (318) 367-1201.

Best Western Motel 2700 Center Street, $43 double. (318) 364-3030.

Scottish Inn U.S. 90 East, $25 to $28 double. (318) 365-6711.

Camping:

Belmont Campground Rt. 31 and Rt. 86, 8 mi. north of New Iberia.

Belmont Campground is located on Bayou Teche in the heart of "Evangeline Country," halfway between historic St. Martinville and New Iberia. The campground has 200 sites on twenty-nine wooded acres. Swimming is permitted in the bayou and facilities include showers, full hookups, pay phones, and a pavilion. The fees are $10 for RV's and $8 for tents (two persons). To get to Belmont, take Route 31 north from New Iberia about 8 miles. The campground is located at the intersection of Route 31 and Route 86. (6 miles from St. Martinville). (318) 364-6020.

*Lake Fausse Pointe State Park See St. Martinville Recreation section.

Camping with full hook-ups and cabins, boat and canoe rentals, picnic area, hiking trails, and fishing dock in a swamp setting. This is a great recreational facility and is highly recommended.

Sher-Mac Campground Rt. 90 and Curtis St., New Iberia.

Sher-Mac has 160 camper sites, full RV hook-ups for $12.75, and partial hook-ups for $11.65. Showers and toilets are available for tent campers. (318) 364-4256

Pepper field at Avery Island. (Courtesy of LA Office of Tourism)

SOUTH OF NEW IBERIA
Avery Island

Avery Island's 2500 acres are a South Louisiana "feast of the senses," from the scent of thousands of blossoms to the searing heat of tabasco peppers and verdant vistas. Here you can visit the Jungle Gardens, Bird City egret sanctuary, and Tabasco hot sauce factory. The so-called island is not an island at all, but the largest of Louisiana's five major coastal salt domes. The 90'-high dome was caused by the upwelling of an immense subterranean plug of salt. French settlers called it Petite Anse (little cove) after the bayou which wraps around it. Around 1800, the island became the property of John Marsh, whose descendants, the Averys and McIlhennys, have lived there ever since. Five miles from the outskirts of New Iberia, Avery is visible as a wooded hill above the surrounding plain of marsh. The drive southwest on Avery Island Road carries visitors through floating marsh and cane and rice fields. The island is bordered on three sides by marsh, and on the fourth by cypress swamps thick with wildlife. Far to the south the marsh drops away to Vermilion Bay. From U.S. 90, exit on Route 14 north. Go a couple of blocks and turn right on Route 329, which doubles back under U.S. 90 to Avery Island. A $1 toll is charged to enter the island.

The Avery Island Salt Mine (No longer open for tours for insurance reasons. Thank the lawyers for that.)

The salt mine at the southeast edge of Avery Island is the longest-operating rock salt mine in the country, excavating a plug of salt estimated to be one-and-a-half times as large as Mount Everest. Fossil evidence indicates that during prehistoric times, man and mastodon alike congregated around saltwater springs here. It was not until 1790, when John Hayes stumbled upon a salt spring while hunting, that modern man began harvesting the island's salt. In 1862, J. M. Avery began enlarging one of the springs to facilitate evaporation mining when he discovered rock salt only thirteen feet below the surface! It was the first discovery of rock salt on the continent, and the resource was quickly put to use in provisioning Southern forces during the War Between the States.

During the first thirty-five years of operation, the mine suffered destruction by Northern troops, flooding, and transportation problems. In 1899, the International Salt Company began quarrying. They dug to a depth of 550 feet, employing teams of mules underground and rail lines above to ship the product to market.

After almost a century of operation, the International Salt Company has created a salt city 1000 feet deep and over a mile in diameter (some caverns have 100-foot-high ceilings), but has barely scraped a nick in the huge salt reserve. The industrial southeast end of the island is officially closed to visitors, but an inadvertent wrong turn down the road that runs between the Jungle Gardens Visitors Center and the Tabasco Factory will lead you into this fascinating area. Known as "the Tangle" for its web of roads once used by pepper field and factory workers and salt miners, the south end still sports the white frame structures that housed company employees, schools, and store.

Tabasco Pepper Sauce Factory (Tours offered)

Tabasco sauce may be the ultimate Cajun Country product. It is hot, it is the red color of boiled crawfish, and it is made with fresh Avery Island salt and peppers. The most famous hot sauce in the nation was patented by Edmund McIlhenny following the War Between the States. From a first batch of 150 bottles in 1868, it has become so popular that the trademarked name, Tabasco, is often used to refer to other products. Legend has it that the hot capsicum peppers used to make McIlhenny's sauce were brought to the area in the early 1800s by a soldier returning from the Tabasco region of Mexico. Today, the McIlhenny Company raises seedlings at Avery Island, and each August harvests adult peppers in Mexico, Columbia, and Honduras, as well as locally. Following company tradition, the field supervisor ensures that peppers are the correct color by comparing them to a *petit bâton rouge* (little red stick). The peppers are taken to the factory, mashed with Avery Island salt, and fermented for three years in oak barrels capped with salt. Finally the pepper mash is mixed with vinegar, stirred for a month, and strained for bottling.

The McIlhenny folks have a planned tour and visitors center that attracts thousands of visitors each year. The tour begins in a gallery which houses historic photographs and artifacts from the island. There is a 10-minute promotional video that shows people pouring on the Tabasco. The big disappointment is the factory tour, which is a walk down a glassed-in corridor with a view of the packaging area. At the end of the walkway, you wind up in the gift shop. There you can sample McIlhenny products and purchase a few unique items, like Tabasco C-rations from the Second World War, small vest-pocket-size bottles of the sauce to carry "in case of emergency," and dozens of products with the Tabasco/McIlhenny logo.

The pepper-scented production area is not part of the tour, but there is a way to get inside. Ask where you can purchase bags of the pepper mash, which is left after the sauce is strained. You will be directed to the adjacent brick factory where workers wander around fermenting casks of mash, oblivious to the choking fumes. The pepper mash is sold in bulk for use in red hots, Dentine gum, and as a seasoning for boiled seafood (*see* review of The Guiding Star Restaurant in New Iberia). The mash costs less than 50 cents a pound and a little bit goes a very long way in making sauce piquant. The price of a three-pound bag is worth the chance to get a whiff (whew!) of the factory itself. The Tabasco Factory is on the left after you pass the toll booth entering the island. Tour hours are Monday through Friday from 9 A.M. to 4 P.M., and Saturday from 9 A.M. to noon. Closed Sundays and holidays. Admission is free.

★Jungle Gardens (Open to public.)

In the early 1900s, Edward Avery McIlhenny put the wealth of several family enterprises, and his experience as an explorer, conservationist, and naturalist to work in developing the most exotic gardens in the South. The 200-acre compound surrounding his estate on Mayard Hill is a patchwork of hollows filled with flowering shrubs, bushes, lagoons, sunken fern gardens, and hilltop shrines. A fourteen-acre Live oak grove welcomes visitors with a canopy of shade that is perfect for picnics (snacks are sold at the visitors center, but you will have to bring your own lunch provisions).

The true beauty of the Jungle Gardens awaits those who walk the miles of secluded pathways. For the less energetic, a gravel road winds through the gardens with parking areas convenient to such notable attractions as the Buddha Shrine, Camelia Gardens, and Bird City. Watch for the island's deer as you go through.

The gardens at Avery Island are a kaleidoscope of native and imported plantings. They are not attended to on a frequent basis, but spread out naturally over the compound. McIlhenny brought in lotus and papyrus from the Upper Nile, hybrid grapefruits and finger bananas from China, and 64 varieties of bamboo, including a dense forest of 60-foot canes of Chinese Timber variety. The thousands of types of camelias and hundreds of azaleas are the main attraction here, painting the hillsides fantastic colors during late winter and early spring. There is always something in bloom. Camelias blossom from December through March. Azaleas and wild iris bloom from late February into April. Dogwoods begin to flower in April. By summer, water hyacinths, wisteria, and lilies are opening, followed by lotus and chrysanthemums. The Jungle Gardens and Bird City are open daily from 9 A.M. to 5 P.M.

Bird City egret rookery. (Courtesy of LA Office of Tourism)

Admission is $4.50 for adults and $3.50 for kids, and the cost covers both attractions. (318) 369-6243.

Bird City in Jungle Gardens

Located on the southeast edge of the Jungle Gardens is the largest egret colony in the United States. During the late 1800s, Avery Island was the last haven for these birds, which were prized by plume hunters for their showy "nuptial" feathers. When they disappeared from the island in 1892, E. A. McIlhenny searched out 7 young birds in the marsh and established this colony over a man-made lake on the eastern side of Mayard Hill. He built a nesting area of bamboo on pilings over the water and, in less than 25 years, nearly 20,000 egrets were nesting at the site each summer. The egrets and heron begin nesting each spring in February or March, and their young remain until the cold winds of winter send them south. Many other species of heron and smaller birds join the flocks of egrets and make the observation deck and grounds surrounding Bird City a prime destination for bird watchers. The Jungle Gardens and Bird City are open daily from 9 A.M. to 5 P.M. Admission is $4.50 for adults and $3.50 for kids, and the cost covers both attractions. (318) 369-6243.

*Jefferson Island

Like Avery Island six miles to the east, Jefferson is not actually an island but a large hill caused by the protrusion of an underground salt dome. Also like Avery, Jefferson Island is the site of some of the grandest public gardens in the state. What sets Jefferson apart as an attraction is the presence of 1300-acre Lake Peignur, site of a major industrial/geologic disaster in 1980. Boat tours of the catastrophe site, lake, and surrounding region are offered as part of the admission price. Jefferson gets its name from actor Joseph Jefferson, famous for his stage role as Rip Van Winkle. Jefferson, who purchased the island in 1865, used it as a winter retreat and constructed a grand Victorian mansion before selling out to John Bayless in the early 1900s. It was the late John Bayless, Jr., who began planting bright formal gardens inspired by those of E. A. McIlhenny on Avery Island. After hiring gardeners from England to help plant and landscape 20 acres with camelias, azaleas, hibiscus, and flower gardens, Bayless set 700 acres of the estate aside as a public attraction.

Gardens, House, and Boat Tour

Visitors to Jefferson Island are welcomed at the gift shop, where there is a 15-minute video depicting the history of the island, the gardens, and the story of the Lake Peignur disaster. There is also a cafe with a view of the grounds and lake. From the visitors center you may wander the gardens and oak-covered lawns before touring the ornate Joseph Jefferson house. The house has many elaborate cypress details, but most memorable are the vistas from high-backed rockers on the front porch, and the rooftop lookout, which provides a view of Avery Island 6 miles to the east. Perhaps the most interesting part of the Jefferson Island experience is the 40-minute boat tour (departing every hour) across Lake Peignur and up the Delcambre Canal to a commercial shrimp boat landing. The boat is a comfortable party barge with sun awning, and the views from the water are cool even on the hottest summer days. It is on this tour that you are likely to get the best accounting of the Lake Peignur salt dome disaster.

Disaster

There are other gardens, other historic homes, and other boat tours, but Jefferson Island lays sole claim to one of the most extraordinary geophysical events to strike South Louisiana in modern times. On November 20, 1980, Texaco Platform #20 was drilling for oil in the waters of Lake Peignur, a couple of hundred yards from the island. Sometime in the early morning hours, the drill pipe became jammed. A short time later the platform began to tilt precariously. Moments after being evacuated, the rig slipped beneath the water surface. At about the same time, miners working 1300 feet down in the Jefferson Island salt mine (which extended below the lake) noticed muddy water rising in the chamber floor. An alarm was sounded and the mine elevators began working nonstop to pull miners to the surface. The last of the miners arrived above ground to witness a startling event.

The oil rig had apparently punctured the mine and water was rapidly draining from the lake, forming a massive whirlpool as it poured into the underground caverns. Eleven barges disappeared into the maelstrom and two recreational fishermen abandoned their skiff and crawled through the mud to safety. A tugboat crew in the Delcambre Canal found the powerful craft being hauled backwards towards the lake and jumped ashore to watch it get sucked down! The spinning water collapsed surrounding banks, stealing fifty acres, five greenhouses, and a conservatory from John Bayless, Jr.'s estate.

Bayless watched and videotaped from the roof of his brick home as the floor of the lake collapsed, sending 3½ billion gallons of water roaring into the mine below. Within seven hours the lake

Lake Peignur goes down the drain. (Courtesy of Live Oak Gardens Foundation)

was empty. Local fishermen watched stunned as the Delcambre Canal, normally an outlet flowing into the Gulf, reversed its direction and, over the next two days, refilled the empty basin. Most of the barges bobbed back up to the surface, and no lives were lost in the event. Today the chimneys and columns of Bayless' brick home stand in the edge of the now deepwater lake. Jefferson Island is open daily from 9 A.M. to 5 P.M. (until 4 in winter). Admission includes the garden, house and boat tour, and costs $7.50 for adults, $6.50 for seniors, and $4 for children. To get to Jefferson Island from New Iberia, take Route 14 6 miles south from U.S. 90. Turn west onto Rip Van Winkle Dr. (318) 367-3485.

Loreauville (North of New Iberia)

Few outsiders make it around the tight, 20-mile oxbow bend in Bayou Teche, north of New Iberia, to find this village of about 900. Most travelers between New Iberia and St. Martinville shave 14 miles off the trip by taking Route 182 west and cutting off the Loureauville bend. Those who take the extra few minutes can stop for lunch at a Cajun cafe on the bayou, see the Indian mound in downtown Loreauville, and visit the grave of the town's most famous resident, Clifton Chenier, the King of Zydeco. Plan in advance and you can take an airboat tour of the breathtaking Lake Fausse region, or take in a show at Clifton's Club, a huge Zydeco dance hall owned by the musician's widow.

Indian Mound Main St. (Rt. 86), Loreauville.

At one time a village museum with forty historic structures and thousands of artifacts was open at this site. Upon the death of the proprietor, the buildings were auctioned off, but the mound remains. In fact, it is the only hill for miles around. North of the small downtown section of Loreauville on Main Street (Route 86), look for the mound in a grassy field, three houses above Bonin Street.

Patio Restaurant Seafood, $-$$. Main St. (Rt. 86), Loreauville.

How many other towns with a population under 1000 and a location designed to thwart drive-through visitors sport an ambitious seafood restaurant? Half the fun of eating here is in finding good food off the beaten path. I must admit I *have* had better seafood, but seldom enjoyed it more than in this bright cafe. The salad bar and homemade bread pudding make for a great lunch on a hot day (especially after a swamp tour with nearby Airboats,

Inc.). The Patio is open for lunch every day from 11 A.M. to 2 P.M. Dinner is served Tuesday through Saturday from 5 P.M. to 9 P.M. (318) 229-8281.

Clifton Chenier's Grave Landry Rd., Loreauville.

Zydeco fans who want to visit the unmarked grave of Clifton Chenier and the sprawling Clifton's Club Zydeco dance hall, will find both less than 5 miles off Route 86 in the flat alluvial prairie outside Loreauville. Take Route 86 into Loreauville. Just past the Patio Restaurant, turn west onto La. 3242 (a sign says "To Lake Dauterive"). Go 1.3 miles and take a left onto Landry Road. The cemetery is 1.5 miles down St. Landry. Take the second entrance. Go midway down and next to the drive on the right is the unmarked grave of Clifton Chenier. It is parallel to the Veret and Broussard graves.

Clifton's Club Zydeco dance hall. Croche Lane, Loreauville.

This is not one of those Zydeco halls where you walk in, are recognized as an outsider, and asked if you are "from the film crew." The folks at Clifton's Club, including his widow, Margaret Chenier, whom I found sitting at a table in the back, seemed genuinely surprised that any outsider had found the secluded dance hall. The welcome was warm anyway, and the music by Edward Brown and His Zydeco House Rockers was downright hot. It is a tribute to the strength of the music that Clifton helped popularize that a huge dance hall (seats 700 and has two bars) in such a remote location can draw big crowds for bi-monthly dances and trail rides. The music schedule here is quite unpredictable and not widely advertised, so you will have to call in advance to find out who is playing and when. To get to Clifton's Club, follow the same directions as those for his grave. Continue a half mile beyond the cemetery and turn left onto Croche Lane (Parish Road 409). Go 1 mile and the club is on the right. (318) 229-6036 or 367-9912.

*Airboats, Inc. Loreauville.

If I had to pick one swamp tour to go on based on natural beauty, profusion of wildlife, and great guide service, this would be it. Airboats, Inc. has two big advantages over most other swamp tours. They access the grandest cypress swamp in Cajun Country, and their fast, air-driven craft can negotiate narrow passageways and barely wet sloughs that are favorite hangouts for a multitude of wild animals. The tour takes you to the pristine swamp around Lake Fausse (once part of the Atchafalaya Basin). Here you will see ancient stands of cypress and miles of water

Airboat swamp tour. (Courtesy of Airboats, Inc.)

hyacinths (in the spring) and American lotus (in the late summer). Tours are conducted by Lon Prioux and his family. These guys grew up in the area, building the first airboats in the Basin and hunting ducks. Their love of the swamp is apparent in each enthusiastic comment and bit of lore. Plan the trip for early morning or late evening, when the sun is low and mist is hanging over the Marshfield Boat Ramp. When Prioux brings your craft quietly to rest in a field of lotus that reaches to the horizon in all directions, take a deep breath of the oxygen exhaled by the surrounding forest.

The airboats can only accommodate 5-6 passengers, so this tour is private and a bit more expensive than some others (unless you have a group or can join one), but the wild trip is worth every penny. Hour-long tours cost $10 a person, with a minimum charge of $50. Two-hour tours cost a bit more. Tours are offered daily. Call ahead to set up a time. Tours leave from the Marshfield Boat Ramp. From U.S. 90 in New Iberia take Lewis Street 4 miles to Route 86 (Loreauville Road). Turn right on Route 86 and travel 5 miles. Turn right on Black Line Road for one mile. Turn right again on the Marshfield Road and take it until it ends at the boat launch. For those spending a day or staying overnight at Lake Fausse Pointe State Park (*see* St. Martinville section for description), Airboats, Inc. offers pick-up and drop-off service from the park boat launch! Call (318) 229-4457.

New Iberia to St. Martinville

Between New Iberia and St. Martinville, Bayou Teche turns almost due north. Route 31 parallels the stream as it cuts through the alluvial valley between the Vermilion River and the Atchafalaya Basin. Route 182 (the Old Spanish Trail), which had followed the bayou to this point, veers northwest to Lafayette.

St. Martinville

St. Martinville, the seat of government for St. Martin Parish, is located 17 miles southeast of Lafayette and 10 miles north of New Iberia, at the intersection of Route 96 and Route 31. Nowhere is Teche Country's spirit of quiet reflection more hauntingly exuded than in the once grand village of St. Martinville. Established as a military post in 1714, the town was settled by French expatriates, wealthy planters who fled a slave revolt in Santa Domingo, Spanish soldiers, and members of the French aristocracy who escaped the revolution in that country. When the first Cajuns arrived around

St. Martin Square. (Photo by Julie Posner)

Evangeline Oak. (Photo by Julie Posner)

1765, they found a bustling Creole city centered around the Spanish military garrison, Poste de Atakapas. It is ironic that St. Martinville has become a veritable Cajun shrine whose "secular saint," Evangeline, has drawn tourists for most of a century. Few of the Cajuns who made the arduous journey from New Orleans to St. Martinville elected to stay there. When it was incorporated in 1817, the city, nicknamed Petit Paris, was a center of high culture and a resort for Creole families from New Orleans.

During the mid-1800s nearby New Iberia began to usurp St. Martinville as a steamboat port and trade center. Today there are few vestiges of the high life left in St. Martinville. Most visitors come to the former Creole capital to see such Cajun landmarks as the Evangeline Shrine, Evangeline Oak, and Evangeline State Commemorative Area. The old St. Martin Square, which occupies the center of town, has traded its gala balls and opera for a strip of bars and the overall feeling of the place is one of faded grandeur. The busiest nightlife is now in the black section of Main Street, where a couple of clubs feature Zydeco and disco-style dances, and the smell of barbecue is the harbinger of a busy Saturday night. Unless you are interested in spending the night at the Old Castillo Hotel Bed and Breakfast, St. Martinville is easily seen in a couple of hours on the way to New Iberia, Breaux Bridge, or Lafayette.

Attractions

St. Martin Square Rt. 31 and Rt. 96.

The spiritual and social center of St. Martinville is historic St. Martin Square, dominated by *St. Martin de Tours Catholic Church*. Around the square are a number of popular tourist attractions including the *Evangeline Oak, Petit Paris Museum, Old Castillo Hotel*, and *Evangeline Statue*. Bordering the square on the side facing the church is a row of turn-of-the-century shops and half a dozen taverns with balustraded galleries. I find these aging commercial establishments and their French-speaking clientele to be more interesting than the tourist industry that has grown around the Evangeline story. I usually spend more time in Thibodaux's Restaurant or one of the bars than chasing ghosts around the Evangeline Oak.

St. Martin de Tours Catholic Church 100 S. Main St.

Although the church was established in 1765 (one of the oldest churches in Louisiana), the current cement-covered brick building was built in 1832. Two wings extend from either side of the main chapel, one of which houses an 1870s replica of the famous

French Grotto of Lourdes, which is surrounded by the votive candles of supplicants. The church is open to walk-in visitors who observe a reasonable decorum.

Petit Paris Museum 103 S. Main St.

The dollar admission to the Petit Paris museum could wind up being your worst entertainment investment in Cajun Country. That depends on whether you are interested in another exhibit of recent Mardi Gras costumes, out-of-date brochures, and trinkets for sale. Come to think of it, maybe it's worth it for a laugh. Tours of the square are also offered for a fee, but anyone with two feet and twenty minutes can do that on their own. The Petit Paris Museum is open seven days a week from 9:30 A.M. to 4:30 P.M. (318) 394-7334.

Evangeline Statue (outside St. Martin de Tours Church)

Nowhere is the replacement of actual history by romance more apparent in St. Martinville than at the side of St. Martin de Tours Church, where a bronze statue of Evangeline has been placed on the site of the former Poste des Attakapas cemetery. Some folks around town have grown so accustomed to hearing local retellings of the Evangeline story that they will swear that this statue actually marks her grave. In fact, the statue was donated to the city by silent film star Delores Del Rio, who played the part of Evangeline in the 1929 movie filmed in St. Martinville.

Evangeline Oak Evangeline Blvd. at the bayou.

Not only has the St. Martinville Tourist Commission declared that the Evangeline Oak is the primary tourist attraction in town, they have also declared it the "most famous tree in America," an incredible feat for a tree that has never been poisoned or had anyone hung from it. It is located behind the town square beside Bayou Teche. Legend has it that townspeople stood in the shade of this tree greeting Acadian exiles who landed at the spot. There are a few blasphemers who point out that this is not actually the first "Evangeline Oak," and that others have been destroyed by various natural causes. Even these skeptics refuse to doubt loudly that there was an original tree where Gabrielle probably waited many days for his lost love to arrive. The current Evangeline Oak has had so many visitors posing for photographs beside its trunk that it is suffering from soil compaction. A park with a raised walkway around the tree and along the bayou is planned.

Guys under the Oak

Unless old age finally catches up with these ranconteurs, or the bayou rages up and washes them away, you can count on finding

Max Greig and the Romero brothers parked on chairs in the shade of the Evangeline Oak. Nothing reflects the pace of life in sleepy St. Martinville better than the fact that these old men, swapping stories by Bayou Teche, are one of the main attractions and most predictable events in town! Max Greig is the unofficial town historian, and his colorful account of the Acadians in St. Martinville is on sale at gift shops throughout the area. In the best St. Martinville tradition, these guys effortlessly blend fact and fancy as they describe life on the Teche. If you are lucky, the Romero brothers will pull out the accordion for an impromptu bayou-side serenade.

La Place D'Evangeline (Old Castillo Hotel), 220 Evangeline Blvd.

Constructed as a residence and trading post in 1792, this brick structure beside the Evangeline Oak is the oldest building in St. Martinville. It operated as the elegant Castillo Hotel until purchased by the Convent of the Sisters of Mercy in 1899. The Sisters of Mercy ran the only girls' school in St. Martinville there for 87 years. Since 1987, the newly named Place D'Evangeline has reopened as a Bed and Breakfast, reviving the tradition of hospitality and classy accommodations it maintained during its days as a hotel (*see* Lodging section below). (318) 394-4010.

Maison DuChamp Visitors Center Main St. and Evangeline Blvd.

This stuccoed cypress home beside St. Martin Square was built by Eugene DuChamp De Chastaignier around 1876. Today it is supposed to be operating as a visitors center, but I have yet to find it open. The posted hours are Monday through Friday from 9 A.M. to noon, and 1 P.M. to 3 P.M. If you find the Maison DuChamp closed, you may get information on attractions in St. Martinville at the Place De Evangeline/Old Castillo Hotel or Gateway Visitors Center in Lafayette.

St. Martin Parish Courthouse 400 S. Main St.

This Greek Revival structure, 4 blocks south of the square, was built by slave labor about 1859. It is made of brick coated with cement and has 4 large Ionic columns. Historians can access an extensive collection of French and Spanish documents from the Attakapas District dating back to the 1730s which are kept on file here.

*Longfellow Evangeline State Commemorative Area 1200 N. Main St.

How strong was the spirit of Evangeline? It was strong enough for the normally prosaic state park service to make the 157-acre Longfellow State Commemorative Area the first state park in

Louisiana in 1934. Locals claim that the house here was the property of Louis Arceneaux, the real-life counterpart of Long-fellow's Gabrielle. Despite its poetic name and local legends sur-rounding the park, the Longfellow Evangeline Area has a mu-seum and visitors center with the most clearly presented factual information available on the Acadian settlements in Canada and South Louisiana. Especially instructive are a series of maps depicting where and when Acadian settlements were begun, and tracing their subsequent movements. There are displays of tools, artifacts, and handcrafted items from the colonial period, including items from both Acadian and Creole households.

The site was originally a *vacherie*, as the Cajuns called their ranches. In the early 1800s, the land was purchased by wealthy Creole planter Charles Olivier du Clozel, who built the raised Creole plantation home that is now open for tours. Typical of the way legend has colored "fact" around St. Martinville, this house, with its distinctive Creole features, is commonly known as the "Acadian House." Unlike mansions built by Anglo planters in the mid-1800s, it is of simple Creole design, raised off the ground, with the first floor constructed of brick and second-story walls of *bousillage* (a mud and moss mixture). An attendant at the house will show you around and clear up any rumors you picked up from the old men on St. Martin Square. Most local visitors ignore the museum and house in favor of the recreational facilities. There are pavilions and grills (on the bayou), a boat launch, restrooms, and a crafts shop. The park is located on Route 31 (Main Street) about 2 miles from St. Martin Square. It is open from 9 A.M. to 5 P.M. daily. The house is open until 4:30 P.M. Admission is $2 a car for up to four people. (318) 394-3754, or 394-4284.

Way of the Cross

Along a 9-mile stretch of Route 96, northeast of St. Martinville, you will notice small birdhouse-size boxes posted on trees beside the road. Each box bears a Station of the Cross. On religious holidays folks walk and drive the length of the route placing candles at each station.

Oak and Pine Alley Route 96, 3 miles north of St. Martinville.

Wealthy sugar planter Charles Durand planted a 2-mile-long drive of alternating oak and pine trees here. Durand married off two of his daughters in a single glorious ceremony shortly before the War Between the States. Legend (a ubiquitous word around these parts) has it that, in an unmatched show of wealth, the trees along the drive were sown with spiders which spun webs through their limbs. On the morning of the wedding, Durand dusted these webs with gold and silver dust, creating a sparkling passageway for the wedding procession. The plantation was burned during the war, the mill collapsed, and the spiders failed to thrive, but a mile of Pine and Oak Alley remains. When entering the alley you may notice a wooden figurine nailed to the first of the huge oaks. This is one of the Stations of the Cross found at regular intervals along Highway 96.

St. Martinville to Breaux Bridge

Above St. Martinville the dry and arable land on either side of the bayou narrows. Off the beaten path of east/west traffic, the succession of small communities along the stream thins out and the landscape is dominated by groves of Live oaks. The only town along this 14-mile stretch of Rt. 31 is the small, predominantly black Creole community of Parks, where you will find the Double D Cotton Club, one of the most down-home Zydeco dance halls in Cajun Country (*see* Breaux Bridge music listings for a description).

Recreation

*Lake Fausse Pointe State Park Atchafalaya Basin Levee Rd.

Lake Fausse Pointe State Park is one of the newest and finest state parks in the South and a rare spot to experience the swamp on foot. The park occupies 6,000 acres immediately adjacent to the West Atchafalaya Basin levee (about 18 miles southeast of St. Martinville and 45 minutes southeast of Lafayette). Before the twentieth century the Basin stretched westward to the banks of Bayou Teche. New levees built by the U.S. Corps of Engineers following the disastrous flood of 1927 reclaimed this section of the swamp and the adjacent lakes from the Basin. Lake Fausse is home to one of the oldest cypress groves in Cajun Country. The park includes a multitude of day-use facilities, including about 5 miles of hiking trails through jungle-like forest, picnic and recreation areas on a bayou leading to Lake Fausse, a grocery store, bait shop, and paddleboat and canoe rentals. The paddleboats and canoes cost $30 a day, $20 a half day, $6 an hour, and $4 for half an hour.

On weekends during the summer, the park is abuzz with fishermen and recreational boaters. In the evening, day-use folks head home and those staying over can enjoy the perfect solitude of the swamp, catch a catfish off the dock, and take it back to cook while the birds and bugs set to singing. The park has dozens of campsites with full hook-ups, laundry facilities, and a super-clean shower and rest station. There are eight modern cabins with screened porches overlooking the bayou. Accommodating up to six persons, each is furnished with air conditioning, kitchens with cooking and eating utensils, linens, towels, and private baths. The alligators and snakes are generally friendly, but bring plenty of bug dope to fight ravenous mosquitoes and horseflies. Cabins cost $50 a night. RV and tent camping is $12 a night. Admission to the park is $2 per car for four people. Take Route 96 east from St. Martinville. Turn right on Route 679, then left on Route 3083. Route 3083 will end at the Atchafalaya Levee Road. Turn right on the Levee Road. The park is open during the summer from 7 A.M. to 10 P.M. Winter hours are 8 A.M. to 7 P.M. (318) 229-4764.

Camping Tip

Although the camp store has most necessities, overnighters are advised to stock up at nearby St. Martinville or New Iberia, since it will seem like a long, dark drive at night to get back to a full-service store or grocery. You can get live or already boiled seafood in these towns to eat in the evening. For fresh local produce, you can stop at Sue's Vegetables, a mile west of the Atchafalaya levee road on Route 3083.

Food

Despite its reputation as a bastion of Cajun and Creole culture, St. Martinville is not a great place to eat. You are best off planning a visit between meals in nearby New Iberia, Broussard, Henderson, or Lafayette.

*Danna's Bakery Local Fave/Bakery. 207 E. Bridge Street.

Danna's' original location opened in New Iberia in 1921. They serve the same great cookies and pies here. Get a few to eat on the banks of the Teche, to take for a snack at Lake Fausse Pointe Park, or just to hold off the hungries on the road. Moist pecan macaroons, nut bars, thumbprint cookies, and sweet dough pies are recommended. Danna's is open Tuesday through Sunday from 5:30 A.M. to 5:30 P.M. Closed Mondays. (318) 394-3889.

Thibodeaux's Cafe Cajun/Downhome, $. 116 S. Main (St. Martin Square).

Thibodeaux's looks like it should be great. It is in an old storefront on St. Martin Square, facing the St. Martin de Tours Church. This tiny cafe fills up with locals conversing in French at breakfast and lunch. Unfortunately the food, which is standard grill and plate-lunch fare, just doesn't stack up to the ambiance. The coffee and conversation can't be beat, though. Thibodeaux's is open Monday through Saturday from 6 A.M. to 4 P.M. (318) 394-9268.

Music

As with food, there is a notable dearth of music establishments in St. Martinville. The busiest scene is the black nightclub district on South Main Street. Those staying in the St. Martinville area may want to drive up the bayou to Breaux Bridge and Henderson, or over to Lafayette to find more nightlife.

Podnuh's Various/dance hall. Rt. 96 in Cade.

There is no telling whom you might find playing at Podnuh's (for all you Yankees, that's Southspeak for "partner"). Some weekends there are Zydeco bands, other times there are Swamp Pop reviews, Cajun, or Country music. On special occasions, soul greats like Percy Sledge or Clarence Carter have played. Typically the music is Country or Swamp Pop, and the crowd is older. The basketball-court-size dance floor gets packed with folks two-stepping, waltzing, doing the freeze and, on more than one occasion, dancing the "Paul Jones." The "Paul Jones" finds all the women forming a tight circle in the middle, and the men a larger circle around them. The circles spin in opposite directions like musical chairs until the music stops and you grab the partner in front of you. (318) 394-9082.

Tee's Connection Zydeco dance hall. 704 South Main St.

Tee's alternates Disco and Zydeco on weekends. (318) 394-3870.

Lodging

Bed and Breakfast:

★Old Castillo Hotel 220 Evangeline Blvd.

Whether you have dreams of Evangeline or nightmares of a schoolmistress grabbing you by the ear, the history of the Old Castillo coats its rooms like chalk dust. This was a colonial trading post, a hotel, and for most of the last century a Catholic school for girls. The first floor is now occupied by La Place D'Evangeline Restaurant. Five former classrooms on the second floor are crisply decorated overnight accommodations furnished with turn-of-the-century antiques.

Like the weary travelers who disembarked from steamboat or

stage coach at the adjacent landing, you check in at the restaurant on the first floor, then climb steps to the seclusion of your room. On the bayou side, one can open a window and get a wake-up call from ducks quacking by the bayou. Breakfast of *pain perdu* or *beignets* is served beneath walls bearing class photographs of girls who suffered through history lessons in the very room you slept in. The restaurant (not recommended) is open Sunday through Thursday from 8 A.M. to 9 P.M. and until 10 P.M. on Friday and Saturday. Rooms offering views of the bayou and the Evangeline Oak run $35 to $75 for two or more people. (318) 394-4010.

Evangeline Oak Corner Bed and Breakfast. 215 Evangeline Blvd.

Located within throwing distance of the Evangeline Oak and Bayou Teche, this Victorian home offers a funky alternative to the gleaming accommodations across the street at the Old Castillo Hotel. The five rooms are sparsely furnished with a hodgepodge of antiques and are rather musty, but you can't beat the location or view from the porch. I liked owner Hazel Robicheaux's testimony to the comfort of her rooms, "My beds are just like sleeping on the floor!" I could never completely explain the price listing here, which varies with the room, the number of people, and number of beds used. A double with separate entry and full private bath is about $40-$45. Some rooms may be opened onto each other for family use. (318) 394-7675 or 264-9115 (Monday through Friday).

Motels:

Beno's Motel and Steakhouse 101 Clover Hill Rd. (Rt. 31), $31-$36 double. (318) 394-5523.

Camping:

Harry Smith Lodge RV Park Rt. 96 near U.S. 90.

Harry Smith has huge facilities to accommodate RV rallies. They have 300 full hook-ups, 600 partial, two complete bath houses, and a 330'-by-30' covered pavilion. They are located in the quiet rural community of Cade, two miles east of U.S. 90. $12.50 for hook-ups. (318) 837-6286.

Lake Fausse Pointe State Park 18 miles southeast of St. Martinville.

One of the premier camping and recreational facilities in the state, the park has cabins and tent spaces. See description under Recreation for details.

Breaux Bridge

Breaux Bridge is the Cajun Capital of Teche Country and, by declaration of the state legislature, *La Capitale Mondiale des Ecrevisses* (the Crawfish Capital of the World). The city rests on the banks of the bayou near the intersection of Route 31 and Interstate 10, about 8 miles east of Lafayette and 13 miles north of St. Martinville. Originally known as La Pointe, Breaux Bridge was settled by Cajuns who took up ranching and hunting on the high ground west of the bayou in the late 1700s. By the 1800s, the village was made up almost entirely of Cajuns.

There are several accounts of how Breaux Bridge got its name. One holds that it was in honor of Agricole Breaux, the builder of an early bridge at the site. Others claim that the town was named for large landholder Firmin Breaux. Regardless, a long succession of wooden and steel bridges have spanned the Teche at Breaux Bridge, including one which was torched by Southern troops as they fled the advancing Northern army.

Through much of its history Breaux Bridge has been known as a wild place. In the mid-1800s, it was the site of several vigilante lynchings, and during the early days of Prohibition was notoriously "wet." Main Street was lined with saloons, speakeasys, and a large cockpit, earning the city the nickname "Little Mexico." The basic character of Main Street in this village of 6500 has changed little since the turn of the century. It still sports a plethora of taverns and card rooms like Liz's Lounge, The Crawfish Swamp, Teche Liquor, and Tina's Bar. During the annual Crawfish Festival (*see* description in this chapter), the raucous days are relived as beer flows in the streets and Cajuns congregate to celebrate their favorite crustacean. The city claims that the restaurant at the Hebert Hotel (no longer standing) was the first eatery to serve crawfish preparations, bragging that Herbert Hoover ate crawfish there in 1927 when he was sent by President Coolidge to survey damage wrought by the great flood.

It is a testimony to the unregenerate Cajun character of Breaux Bridge that the city resisted the Anglo influx of the oil boom when the nearby Anse La Butte field brought in one of the first producing wells in the state. The phone book is still packed with a handful of Cajun surnames like Breaux, Patin, Angelle, Thibodeaux, and Melancon. In fact, there are so many people of the same name that the city directory at one time accepted listings by nicknames like Tee Bob and Boo Boo to clear up the confusion!

The Breaux Bridge area has been a hotbed of Cajun and

Interstate 10 heading west from Breaux Bridge. (Photo by Greg Guirard)

Zydeco music for decades. With the arrival of the interstate highway in the 1970s, the town became a leader in the Cajun Renaissance, opening the most famous Cajun restaurant and dance hall in the state, Mulate's (*see* description in music section).

Tourist Information

The Chamber of Commerce 111 Rees St.

There is no official visitors center in Breaux Bridge, but we found a map of the city and a "Tourguide of Breaux Bridge" at the city Chamber of Commerce office. The Chamber is located about a half mile south of I-10 on Rees Street (Route 328) in the Huval Insurance Company Building. Heading south, the sign is on the right but the building is on the left. (318) 332-5406.

Archie's Trophy Shop 519 E. Bridge St.

A sport trophy shop is an odd place to find tourist information, but Archie's stocks three excellent booklets on the region, the city, and their history. Two of these, *First Facts* and *Devastation and Beauty*, are written by city historian Kenneth Delcambre. The prose is rough, but the information and photographs are excellent. *First Facts* is a city history, while *Devastation and Beauty* is the story of the great flood of 1927 (more incredible photos). A third book is a narrative history of Breaux Bridge written in college thesis form. The books are $3. Archie's is open Monday through Friday from 8 A.M. to 5 P.M. and Saturday until noon. (318) 332-3023.

Attractions

Downtown Breaux Bridge

Despite its reputation as a bastion of Cajun culture, Breaux Bridge is definitely not a tourist town. The old downtown district, which runs for half a dozen blocks on either side of the bayou at Bridge Street, and as many blocks north and south on Main Street (Route 31), is a quiet area of old shops, houses, and bars. Most of the existing structures were built in the late 1800s and early 1900s, and many are either closed or for sale. Among the interesting establishments are *Broussard's Hardware Store* (1922) at the corner of Main Street and Bridge Road and the *Kidder Building* (1909) across the street, which once functioned as a tavern, dance hall, and cockpit. The *O. Badon House* (1869) on East Bridge Street, ½ block off of Main, is one of the few Acadian-style homes remaining in town.

Crawfish race. (Courtesy of LA Office of Tourism)

Mulate's. (Photo by Julie Posner)

Breaux Bridge Oaks On Corner of Berard Fas St. and Courthouse St.

A vigilante committee of 200 men reportedly lynched two outlaws on these oaks in 1882. The trees are now registered with the Live Oak Society.

Crawfish Festival First full weekend in May.

This may not be the most traditional, but is the most Cajun of South Louisiana's hundreds of fairs and festivals. It celebrates a critter that has not only touched every life in the small towns of Upper Teche Country, but has become a symbol of the culture itself. Since Breaux Bridge was declared the Crawfish Capital of the World during the centennial celebration in 1959, this blowout has been an annual tradition. Today the main event attracts up to 200,000 celebrants to nearby Parc Hardy, where contestants compete in events like crawfish races, crawfish eating (the record is over 33 pounds in an hour!), and a crawfish parachute jump. While family events, carnival rides, and live music are underway at the park, the true bacchanalia occurs downtown. Along Main Street, the Downtown Merchants Association sponsors bandstands and food booths and sells copious quantities of beer. Traditional Cajun hard rock bands play in bars, while the street music varies from Country to Cajun Metal bands like Sneaux. Tons of crawfish are boiled and folks pull wagons loaded with cases of brew to wash them down. (318) 332-6655.

Rt. 94, Lafayette to Breaux Bridge

Many people visit Breaux Bridge as a side trip from Lafayette. Before there was an interstate, Route 94 was the main road between the Hub City and its rustic neighbor, Breaux Bridge. The 8-mile stretch of road is still called "Lafayette Highway" by folks in Breaux Bridge, and "Old Breaux Bridge Highway" by those in Lafayette. One and a half miles from Lafayette the road suddenly drops down the long, steep incline that was once the western bank of the Teche Basin. During the great flood of 1927, the combined flows of the Mississippi and Atchafalaya rivers formed a nearly unbroken sheet of water between this ridge and the state capital, 50 miles away in Baton Rouge. Evacuees from Breaux Bridge, Atchafalaya, and Pelba were brought by boat to this point for transportation to tent cities.

Food

Bayou Boudin and Cracklin 100 Mills Ave. (Rt. 94) on the bayou.

They may not be the "Cracklin King Of Louisiana" as claimed, but Bayou Boudin is a delightful and convenient pit stop for folks passing by on the interstate, or taking scenic Route 94 into Lafayette. In an authentic Acadian cabin right on the banks of Bayou Teche, these folks serve up ready-to-eat boudin, boudin balls (floured and fried), and spicy crawfish boudin. They also have cracklins and hog's head cheese. My favorites are the Sunday Barbecue and Pork Fricassee dinners. You can grab a cold drink from the case and sit at one of the picnic tables overlooking the Teche. Bayou Boudin is open from 7 A.M. to 6 P.M. daily. (318) 332-6158.

Mulate's Cajun/Seafood, dine & dance, $$ to $$$. 325 Mills Ave. (Rt. 94).

For most of fifty years, Mulate's has been a restaurant and dance hall, but it was not until Kerry Boutte took over the place in 1980 that it became "the world's most famous Cajun restaurant." The formula for success was simple: bring in the best young Cajun bands, serve good food, and don't monkey with the warm ambiance of the old place. Mulate's' (named for the original owner) walls are covered with paintings by "Zydeco" artist Francis Pavvy, and photos of visiting celebrities. A dance floor runs through the heart of the restaurant. The food is way above average for a "dance and dine" establishment, with a few unique items like Zydeco salad, a mixture of fresh snap beans, greens, grilled fish, and quail eggs with blue cheese dressing. Most folks order standard regional fare such as boiled crawfish, crawfish etouffée, and seafood gumbo. The gumbo is my pick. It has a dark roux flavored with stock, to which seafood is added at the last minute.

If the food at Mulate's is above average, the music can be sensational. Boutte established his reputation by bringing in up-and-coming bands like Zachary Richard and Beausoleil. These groups went on to stardom and the restaurant now features talented house bands like Don Montoucet's Wandering Aces. You can count on hearing authentic music in an authentic setting here daily, at both lunch and dinner. The great thing about Mulate's is that it manages to be a tourist attraction without being a tourist trap. Despite the film crews, celebrities, and tour buses that roll in, Mulate's remains a genuine good-timin' place where locals gladly share the dance floor with tourists (and don't mind offering a few dance instructions, either). Mulate's is open daily from 7 A.M. to 10:30 P.M., and from 11 to 11 on Sundays. Locally (318) 332-4648, in-state 1-800-634-9880, or out of state 1-800-42-CAJUN.

Poche's Meat Market and Restaurant Cajun/Down home, $. Rt. 31 North.

Poche's meats and lunches are mighty good for a place with billboards on the interstate. You can get everything from a bag of cracklins and pound of boudin to go, to sweet dough pies and plate lunches at this modern stop-and-shop. I usually stop for a few cracklins and a beer and to check the price of peeled crawfish meat (often on sale). Boiled crawfish are $8 for three and a half pounds and etouffée is $6, but everything else is under $5. From Breaux Bridge, continue north of town about 2 miles on Route 31 (under the interstate). From Interstate 10, take Exit 109 north (Route 328). Go two miles and turn left on Poche Bridge Road. The restaurant is just over the bridge at the intersection with Route 31. They are open daily from 5:30 A.M. to 9 P.M. Lunch is served from 11 A.M. to 2 P.M., dinner from 5:30 to 8. (318) 332-2108.

Music

Breaux Bridge is a Cajun and Zydeco bar-hopper's paradise. In most other places there are one or two dance halls that stand out as special places. The Breaux Bridge area has at least five that I would highly recommend, and probably as many more that I haven't even found yet!

Mulate's Cajun dance hall/Restaurant. 325 Mills Ave. (Rt. 94).

See description under Food section above.

Harry's Club Cajun dance hall. 519 Parkway Dr.

Harry's is a gathering spot for the older generation of Cajun music lovers. It is a big old hall with a large dance floor that empties at the end of each song and is packed again as soon as the next one starts. The first Sunday of every month the band gets started around 8. Occasionally Swamp-Pop or Country-Cajun bands play on Saturday evenings. To get to Harry's from Route 31 (Main Street) in Breaux Bridge, cross the bayou on Bridge Street and turn left on Rees. Just south of I-10 turn right on Parkway Dr. From I-10 take the Breaux Bridge Exit 109 south. Go a couple of blocks and turn left on Parkway Road. (318) 332-9515.

*Kaiser's Place Cajun dance hall. Rt. 94, 1 mile west of Breaux Bridge.

Of all the dance halls in the Breaux Bridge area, I favor this little wood-frame joint just west of town. You won't find any tour buses or kids doing the latest steps here, just a hardcore honky-tonk crowd. The music is Cajun, but is usually played in the swinging country style popularized in the forties. The dress code is casual, with cowboy boots the only recurrent fashion. Those determined to go to Mulate's for dinner should catch a dance there and then stop by this decidedly non-tourist spot on the way back to Lafayette. If you are bar-hopping, the $2 cover won't slow you down too badly. The Friday night show lasts from about 8 P.M. to 10 P.M. Saturday morning at 10 A.M. there is a Cajun jam session. The big traditional dance is Sunday evening at 6. (318) 332-1167.

*La Poussiere 1301 Grand Point Road (Rt. 347 East).

Looking for a Cajun Saturday night? This is the real thing. For over thirty years, Walter Mouton and the Scott Playboys have been playing the Saturday night dance at this wide and low dance hall on the outskirts of Breaux Bridge. Unlike the young couples who twine like pretzels on the dance floors at popular "dine & dance" joints, the older crowd here dances light and close. Even the fast songs are danced chest-to-chest with amazing grace. Admission is only a couple of bucks, and the music starts early, so you can check out La Poussiere on the way to one of the neighboring Zydeco halls. There is a Cajun dance every Saturday night from 8:30 P.M. until it ends. (318) 332-1721.

Caffery's Alexander Ranch Zin Zin Rd. Au Large (East of Breaux Bridge).

Talk about an obscure location! Half the people I asked in Breaux Bridge had never heard of the little Creole community about 6 miles southeast of town, much less Zin Zin Road. This club is worth hunting down. The dance hall is a huge screened patio with overhead fans for cooling. Dances are held on an irregular basis, so call in advance to find out what is going on. Actually, you may want to go out and see the place during the day. It is a beautiful drive and you can stop by the trailer next door and get a music schedule from Mrs. Caffery. A mark of this community's isolation is the super-rare Elvis Sun 45 I found at a little junk shop on Zin Zin Road (where it was being used as "money" by kids "playing store"). From I-10 go south at exit 109 (Rees Road) to Bridge Road. Take a left onto Bridge Road and go 1.4 miles. Take a right onto Doyle Melancon Road (Route 347). Go 1.7 miles on Doyle Melancon. At Zin Zin Road take a left. Go 2 miles on Zin Zin (the road curves to the left). Caffery's Ranch is on the left on the corner of Zin Zin Road and Latiolais Loop Road. (318) 332-5415.

Dipsey Doodle Club Zydeco dance hall. Zin Zin Road, Au Large.

There are still plenty of obscure places to be uncovered in Cajun Country, and this is one of them! Although the folks at Caffery's said that it was in "the blue building just down the road," I never found it. Good luck. No phone.

*Double D Cotton Club Zydeco dance hall. St. Louis Rd., Parks.

Also known as **Dauphine's Tuxedo Club**, this is a very funky dance hall "way out in the country." Parks is a small Creole farming community that grew just south of Ruth Plantation on the eastern bank of Bayou Teche (about 7 miles south of Breaux Bridge). Between the bayou and Route 347 (which follows the eastern bank) are rows of one- and two-room homes. According to Zydeco authority and DJ Herbert Wiltz, in the fifties and sixties Parks had a couple of clubs and used to get some of the major acts on the Chitlin' Circuit. This is surprising when you consider how rural the area is, but it all makes sense when you see the cars lining up for a Saturday night dance at Dauphine's. People from scattered farms between the bayou and the basin drive for miles to get down at the Double D. From Breaux Bridge, take Route 31 south 5 miles to the town of Parks. At the *T* in the road turn left and cross the bayou on Route 350. Turn right onto Route 347 and go .3 miles. Turn left on St. Louis Street (beside the large green church) and the club is a few blocks down on the left. (318) 394-9616 (club) or 845-4880 (home).

Henderson

Henderson has the fortune (or misfortune) to be the first exit on Interstate 10 on the western side of the wide Atchafalaya Throughway. The town is located on the edge of the Atchafalaya Basin about 5 miles east of Breaux Bridge (12 miles from Lafayette). It is not surprising that most people who drive past see Henderson as a town of billboards, restaurants and service stations. In fact, the town has two other distinct areas, the old "line village," which stretches east from near the Interstate to the Atchafalaya Basin Levee, and a strip of Basin-side restaurants and recreational facilities which stretches 7 miles south along the Atchafalaya Basin Levee Road. The latter is a great place to rent a canoe or small motorboat for a self-guided spin through the Henderson Swamp, or (for the less adventurous) to get onto one of the large tour boats that chugs through the area.

Henderson landed on the state map in 1971, when they incor-

Double D Cotton Club dance hall. (Photo by Julie Posner)

Refugees from the flood of 1927. (Courtesy of Lafayette Courthouse Archives)

porated and elected a mayor. The nucleus of the town, however, was born of disaster almost half a century earlier. Until the thirties, the site was little more than wide, moist fields pressed against the low levees of the Atchafalaya Basin. In 1927, the Mississippi and Atchafalaya Rivers raged above their banks and destroyed the homes of those living in the interior Basin villages of Pelba, Atchafalaya, and Bayou Chene (as well as hundreds of other communities throughout the Mississippi Valley). Flood waters pounded the levee system and broke through just south of present-day Henderson, at what became known as the Cypremort Crevasse. From this and other levee faults, the water rushed into neighboring towns, reaching twelve feet in nearby Breaux Bridge. Evacuees lived in makeshift tent cities in Lafayette. Months later, when the water finally subsided, former residents of the basin moved their houses by barge to new communities like Henderson, Catahoula, and Coteau Homes, which sprung up on the dry side of the new levee system.

For forty years after the flood, Henderson (then called Lenora) remained isolated on the edge of the Basin. Residents engaged in their former pursuits, operating apiaries, boat building, fishing, and net making. Following the development of the first planned crawfish pond in 1959, the fields around Henderson were devoted to this new and lucrative industry. The town grew slowly in a line from its nucleus near the Atchafalaya Basin levee westward. When the difficult Atchafalaya Throughway portion of the interstate was completed in the seventies (using the hard labor of many Henderson residents who had once lived within its banks), Henderson was at last linked with Baton Rouge and New Orleans. The town's crawfish harvest quickly found its way to the new restaurants which sprang up to feed hungry travelers and the town found its way onto the map. There is plenty of good food near the Interstate in Henderson, but the most interesting experiences await those who make the 10-minute drive to the restaurants, swamp tours, and boat rental facilities along the Levee Road.

Attractions

Atchafalaya Basin Levee Road

The entire Atchafalaya Basin is surrounded by flood-protection levees. Along the base and the crest of these levees are narrow gravel and shell roads used by farmers, fishermen, and levee inspection crews. Nowhere is there more convenient access from

Henderson swamp tour. (Courtesy of LA Office of Tourism)

the interstate to the swamps of the Basin than at the Levee Road in Henderson. Just ten minutes from the highway, the Levee Road provides opportunities to visit the swamp by canoe, motorboat or large tour barge. Driving south past McGee's Landing, the old flood-damaged levee is visible inside the new one, as is the huge gap of the Cypremort Crevasse. Those looking for a drink or a meal with a view of the swamp have a couple of good choices in the two-mile stretch of Levee Road immediately south of I-10. The road atop the levee is occasionally posted with "no trespassing" signs, but in the 7-mile stretch between Henderson and the Butte La Rose Bridge (*see* Butte La Rose below), vehicles generally ignore these postings and operate with impunity. From the top of the embankment, you can look east at the sparkling waters of Henderson Lake and the houseboats along its shores. On the west, the clover-covered levee slopes down to Bayou Amy.

To get to the levee road you must first get off the interstate in Henderson at Exit 115. One block south of the highway turn left on Route 352. This route carries you 7 miles east through the old "line village" before ending at a stream known locally as Bayou Amy, which is actually the borrow pit from which the Corps of Engineers removed dirt to create the new levee system. Cross Bayou Amy and turn right atop the levee to access the recreational facilities and vistas of the Levee Road (listed below).

Food

*Crawfish Town USA Exit 115 (Rt. 686), one mile north of I-10.
For a place that was built with tourists in mind and seats 400, I was surprised by how good the crawfish were here. I was even more surprised by some of the other seafood preparations. This is a huge place that does large-volume business, but the gumbo and jambalaya are as good as those served at many of the small mom-and-pop places off the beaten path. They welcome crowds arriving by tour bus, but the vast majority of patrons are discriminating locals who can appreciate a gumbo in which the seafood is added at the last moment and cooked to firm perfection. The restaurant has become a gathering spot for state politicos from Baton Rouge, who are allowed to put up a poster on the wall if they stop by for dinner.

Crawfish and crabs are the main attraction. They are clean and perfectly seasoned. I recommend getting the extra hot, which are not very spicy by Cajun standards. If you like your food hot-hot, just let the waitress know and the kitchen can accommodate your fiery whims. At peak hours, Crawfish Town USA is a perfectly noisy place to go with a gang of pals, or a big family group that likes to whoop it up and make a mess. After gorging on boiled seafood, you can wash at sinks located right in the dining room. Mosey over to the bar while waiting for the food and check out a jukebox packed with Cajun, Swamp-Pop, and Zydeco obscurities. Call ahead to see if Crawfish Town is running one of their weeknight "all you can eat" specials. They are open seven days a week from 11 A.M. to 10 P.M. (318) 667-6148.

Pat's Fisherman's Wharf Restaurant Rt. 352 and Levee Rd.

Pat's is the oldest and most famous seafood restaurant in Henderson. I sampled all of the seafood dishes and the highlight was a "camp-style" etouffée, which was a simple saute of crawfish tails and large chunks of onion and bell pepper in butter. A lot of people were ordering Pat's latest special, which is a plate of jambalaya, crawfish pie, and filé gumbo for around $12. Half the fun of eating at Pat's is the casual atmosphere (plastic tablecloths and porch seating) and bayou-side location. There could hardly be a more lovely place to dine than the porch at Pat's, which overlooks Bayou Amy. In the evenings, you will need a can of bug spray on your table to ward off marauding mosquitoes. My advice is to grab a window seat, order a beer, and select one of Pat's crawfish dishes (other than boiled). Pat's is open daily, 10 A.M. to 11 P.M. Off of I-10 take exit 115 south. Make the first left on Route 352. Pat's is at the end of the road, across the bridge, between Bayou Amy and the Basin levee. (318) 228-7110.

Robin's Seafood, $$. Rt. 352.

Robin's is one of Henderson's oldest and most popular seafood restaurants. Crawfish preparations are the focus of the menu, and the crowning achievement of the kitchen is a superb crawfish bisque. This thin but richly-flavored soup is the color of brazil nuts and is spiked with thinly sliced green onions. At the bottom of each bowl, soaking up the dark broth, are crawfish heads stuffed with seasonings, bread crumbs, and chopped tail meat. Nearly everything at Robin's is made on the premises, including some absolutely delicious desserts. Wherever you eat in the area, Robin's should be your dessert stop. There are four flavors of homemade ice cream, of which I highly recommend the smooth, rich, Belgian chocolate. The bread pudding is made with French bread and is lightly browned in places for a delightful combination of chewy and soft parts. It is topped with a sharp lemon sauce. Robin's is a bit less expensive than nearby competitors, but still puts linen and real butter on the tables. To get to Robin's from I-10, take exit #115 south at Henderson and turn left on Route 352. Robin's is a few miles down on the left. They are open daily from 11 A.M. to 10 P.M. (318) 228-7594.

McGee's Atchafalaya Cafe Seafood & swamp tours, $$. Levee Rd.

Built on stilts beside McGee's Landing Swamp Tours, this restaurant has big windows and open-deck seating with a panoramic view of the Atchafalaya Basin. McGee's serves a broad variety of Cajun food, including such exotica as fried alligator, frogleg etouffée, turtle soup, catfish *courtbouillon*, and crawfish *maque choux*. For those with less adventuresome tastebuds, there is a selection of po-boys for under $5, as well as fried food and standard Cajun fare. With such a huge selection, the preparations here are less than perfect, but the menu, like everything else in this rustic cafe, is a lot of fun. Even if you are not hungry, there is no arguing the pleasure of a window seat and cold drink here after a tour of Henderson Swamp (*see* swamp tour reviews under Recreation, below). Take Exit 115 south off I-10. Turn left on Route 352. At the levee, turn right on the Levee Road. Follow the McGee's signs. (318) 228-7555.

Webster's Meat Market Boudin. Rt. 347, Cecilia (north of Henderson).

Boudin is so ubiquitous around these parts that you will find billboards on the highway advertising it. Webster's does not have a billboard. I found this place on a tip from Pat Huval at Pat's Seafood Restaurant, and am mighty grateful. Theirs is some of the best boudin east of Lafayette. The building that houses the time-worn meat market was once Webster's Dance Hall, a jumping joint that once featured big names like Jimmy C. Newman and Happy Fats. For the past 25 years, the old wood dance floor has turned to supporting meat cases, racks of Evangeline Maid Bread, and snack cakes. If you are on the trail of the "best boudin," you will want to give Webster's a try. From I-10, take Exit 115 at Henderson and head north about 1 mile on Route 347. Webster's is open Monday through Saturday from 7 A.M. to 5 P.M. and Sunday until 12:30 P.M.

Music

Pat's Seafood Restaurant Cajun dine and dance. Levee Rd., Henderson.

Pat's has Cajun bands on the patio every Sunday afternoon. Enjoy music with a view of Bayou Amy. Pat's is located at the

McGee's Atchafalaya Cafe and launch. (Photo by Julie Posner)

corner of Route 352 and the Levee Road (*see* food section for exact directions). (318) 228-7110.

Angelle's Atchafalaya Basin Bar Cajun dance. Levee Rd., Henderson.

Angelle's usually has dances in their Basin-side bar a couple of weekends a month. Call for information. To get to Angelle's, just take the Levee Road from Henderson (*see* Recreation section for exact directions). (318) 228-8567, 667-6135.

McGee's Atchafalaya Cafe Cajun dine and dance. Levee Rd., Henderson.

This cafe overlooking the Atchafalaya Basin has some tasty Cajun food (*see* food section) and Cajun dancing every weekend. You don't have to buy dinner, but can just get a cold drink and enjoy the music and incomparable view of the swamp. Sundays you can enjoy a complete Cajun experience with a swamp tour, seafood dinner, and dance. Bands play from 8 P.M. to 10 P.M. on Friday and Saturday, and from 1 P.M. to 3 P.M. on Sunday. To get to McGee's, just take the Levee Road from Henderson (for exact directions see listings in the food and recreation sections). The kitchen stays open from 11 A.M. to 10 P.M. daily. (318) 228-7555.

Frenchman's Wilderness Campground Family Cajun dance. Butte La Rose.

Admission is free and you can bring your own beverages to the Saturday night fais do do at this beautiful Butte La Rose campground. The dances are real family affairs, and most of the campers are people from around the area who come to enjoy the music they love in a pastoral setting. Saturday dances start at 8 P.M. To get to the campground take I-10 east from Henderson to the Butte La Rose exit. The campground is just south of the interstate. (318) 228-2616.

Friendly Lounge Zydeco dance hall. Rt. 31, Cecilia.

This building looks like it only needs a good strong wind to fall down, but it withstands the pounding of dancing feet a couple of times a month. Call first to find out if, and when, there is a dance. From I-10, exit north at Henderson on Route 347. In the town of Cecilia (about 2 miles north), take the 355 bridge over Bayou Teche, and head south on Route 31. From Breaux Bridge, you may simply head north on Route 31. The Friendly Lounge is about 2 miles south of the bridge. (318) 667-8543.

Davis Lounge Zydeco dance hall. Rt. 31, Cecilia.

Like the Friendly Lounge, Davis has a very irregular schedule of dances and trail rides, and occasionally they have a soul DJ.

Call first to get the scoop. Davis Lounge is located 1 mile south of the Friendly Lounge on Route 31.

Recreation

The biggest recreational attraction in Henderson is obviously the Atchafalaya Basin Swamp. Whether you rent a boat, bring your own, or go on one of the commercial tours, any visitor to the area should see this watery region. Two of the biggest swamp tours in the state depart from Henderson; both accommodate tour-bus customers on their large pontoon boats. These operators have the advantage of being only fifteen minutes off the interstate. Although this part of the Basin is lovely during the high water of spring, its accessibility makes it one of the most heavily trafficked areas. When the water goes down in the fall, you can see the cypress stumps left behind by a thoughtless lumber industry, and abandoned oil pipelines. Folks forging out on their own in a canoe or on an airboat can avoid these somewhat disturbing sights.

★Wiltz Landing: Boat/Canoe Rentals and Bait Levee Road.

This is the only canoe and boat rental operator on the Basin. Canoes are a great value at $12 a day, while jonboats with 6-horsepower motors go for $30 (includes $3 of gas). There is a $1-per-day charge for paddles and life preservers. Neither the canoes nor the jonboats go fast, but some of the most beautiful scenery in the area is within 10 minutes of the launch. Pack a lunch and get bait and directions at the landing and you can spend a day to yourself in Henderson Swamp. Wiltz Landing #1 is less than a mile south of the Bayou Amy Bridge in Henderson. Wiltz #2 is about 1.3 miles from the bridge. (318) 228-7880.

Cajun Airboat Tours Wiltz Landing #2, Levee Road.

Captain Kirk Guidry and his *Cajun Enterprise* (a Florida-built airboat with a Corvette engine) can get you into shallow swamps where even a canoe can't pass. More important, it can traverse the clots of water hyacinths that block entrances to some of the most beautiful cypress stands in the Upper Basin. Kirk will go where you want to go, show you what you want to see, and stop wherever you want. He's proud of his small, airplane-prop-powered craft and will spin it up on dry land at the drop of a comment. While this boat can really get up and go, the most enjoyable moments of our tour were quiet ones, like when Kirk edged through a stand of cypress and cut the engine in an acre-wide "field" of floating water hyacinths, or pulled up next to a duck blind claimed by a beaver family. Rates are subject to change, since these craft consume huge amounts of fuel, but are around $10 a person at a minimum of $30 per trip. The boat only holds four. Cajun Airboat Tours operates out of Wiltz Landing #2, but you will have to call ahead to make an appointment. (318) 228-7670 or 228-7670.

Angelle's Atchafalaya Swamp Tours Whiskey River Landing, Levee Rd.

Angelle's is one of the two big tour companies accessing the Henderson Swamp in big, covered, party-barge-style boats. The Angelles are descendants of a family that once lived in the Basin town of Pelba. In fact, Murphy Angelle, born in 1910 and the oldest former resident of the village, can often be found hanging around the landing. The business is family-run and the Angelles treat tourists to tales of the old life in the Basin and the destruction wrought by the oil, gas, and lumber industries. The tour offers a good view of this desecration, as well as a "down under" view of the Atchafalaya Basin I-10 twin spans. Angelle's is popular with tour-bus operators so there is almost always a group to join. On slow days they will still go out for a minimum of $25. Follow the signs to Whiskey River Landing, which is the third exit on the Levee Road, 1.7 miles from the Bayou Amy Bridge. Tours cost $7 for adults and $4 for children. Boats depart at 10 A.M., 1 P.M., 3 P.M., and 5 P.M. (318) 667-6135 or 228-8567.

McGee's Atchafalaya Basin Swamp Tours McGee's Landing, Levee Road.

McGee's is one of two tour companies operating large, covered pontoon boats in the Henderson Swamp. The Allemand family has been running a boat landing at this site for over forty years, and from the youngest to the oldest, they know the swamp by heart. This slow, 2-hour cruise covers a four-to five-mile radius from the launch, basically the same ground as the other local operators. You will pass under the I-10 spans, see oil and gas pipelines and platforms, and camp boats of part-time basin-dwellers. There is a lot of recreational boat traffic in this part of the Basin, but guides communicate by walkie-talkie to inform one another of where wildlife sightings are occurring, so you usually will see a good variety of animals. Be sure to get a drink or dinner at McGee's Landing Restaurant when you get back to the dock. Follow the signs to McGee's Landing, which is the fourth exit on the Levee Road, 2 miles below the Bayou Amy Bridge. Tours cost $8.50 for adults and $5 for kids. Boats leave at 10 A.M., 1 P.M., 3 P.M., and 5 P.M. (318) 228-2384, 228-8519, or 228-7555 (cafe).

*Errol Verret Swamp Tour Levee Road.

Errol Verret is best known to Cajun music fans as an accordion builder and member of Beausoleil, but in the self-sufficient tradition of Henderson area residents, he now spends most of his time as a carpenter and boat builder. In his free time, Verret takes visitors on highly personalized Basin tours in his homemade, 18' aluminum skiff. The Verret tour specializes in wildlife exploration. He will leave from any landing along the Basin Levee Road and take you as deep in the swamp as you like. These tours cost a little more than the big party barges out of Henderson (they are comparable to an airboat tour in cost), but the additional bucks are worth getting off the beaten path. Because Verret has a lot of irons in the fire, you will want to call well in advance to schedule a trip. One big advantage of this personalized service is the opportunity to view the Basin during cooler morning and evening hours. He can meet you and depart from any landing on the Levee Road. The cost of a tour will depend on where you go, and how long you go out, but runs about $25 an hour plus gas. Four or more people will find this a bargain. (318) 394-7145.

Lodging

Basin Houseboat Rentals Henderson.

Lloyd Dekerlegand. 1 big, 1 small. Equipped. (318) 754-7570.

Lake Fausse Pointe Park Campground Levee Rd., Catahoula.

See St. Martinville chapter for information on this fine recreational area about 30 miles south of Henderson on the Levee Road.

Butte La Rose Campgrounds and Camp Rental

See Butte La Rose (below) for additional accommodations in the Henderson area.

Butte La Rose

Located several miles west of Henderson on a patch of high ground beside the Atchafalaya River (actually inside of the Basin levees) is the town of Butte La Rose. This was the site of a fort during the War Between the States, but is now covered with camps occupied by Lafayette weekenders and a few hardy full-timers. The strip of land has a couple of quiet campgrounds, a cabin for rent, and offers a scenic loop route off of Interstate 10. Just take the Butte La Rose exit (about 20 minutes east of Lafayette) and head south on Route 105. Route 105 becomes Route 3177 and turns westward to join the Atchafalaya Basin Levee below Henderson. It is about 8 miles from the interstate to the Levee Road. To complete the loop just drive north about 7 miles on the Levee Road to Route 352, which will take you back to I-10 at the Henderson exit.

Uncle Dick Davis Park Butte La Rose, near Levee Rd.

This postage-stamp-size campground sits between the road and a small bayou, less than 2 miles from the Butte La Rose Bridge at the Atchafalaya Basin Levee. The campground usually has a couple of long-term RV campers hooked up. There is no shower or dumping station (free RV dumping facilities are available at the Butte La Rose interstate exit). Overnight rates are $5 with electric hook-up. Tent camping is $3. There is a clean restroom.

Frenchman's Wilderness Campground Butte La Rose, just off I-10.

Frenchman's Wilderness bustles to the sound of live Cajun music in the pavilion every Saturday at 8 P.M. Most of the camper/dancers are not out-of-state visitors, but folks from around the area who come to cook out, enjoy the fresh air of the Basin, and hear Cajun music in a family setting. The campground is on a large verdant site just south of I-10 at the Butte La Rose exit. They have all the amenities, including a small swimming pool and clean showers. Rates for tents with partial hook-ups are $10; full hook-ups are $11.50. (318) 228-2616.

*Cajun Vacation Camp Butte La Rose.

This fully equipped three-bedroom, two-bath luxury camp in lovely Butte La Rose gives you a chance to vacation Cajun style. In fact, most of the folks who stay at the bayouside camp are from nearby Lafayette. There is a small pier and deck to fish from, and a back porch overlooking the bayou with a swing, picnic table, and barbecue pit. Inside, the place is loaded. You will find ceiling fans, a fireplace, television, and a totally equipped kitchen (including appliances, pans, and eating utensils). There is a king-size bed, a double bed, two twin beds, and a queen-size sleeper sofa. All you need to bring is your own linens, towels, and food. Butte La Rose is only half an hour from Lafayette and Lake Fausse Pointe State Park (*see* St. Martinville section). Although the camp does not have a phone, there is a pay phone at nearby Doucet's Grocery. The Cajun Vacation Camp is not cheap, but it's a great value for a small group or family that wants to really kick back in Cajun Country. Reservations are recommended but not required. For information and detailed directions contact Suzanne S. Seidel, 2223 Robley Dr., Maurice, Louisiana 70555. (318) 981-6750 or 984-1574.

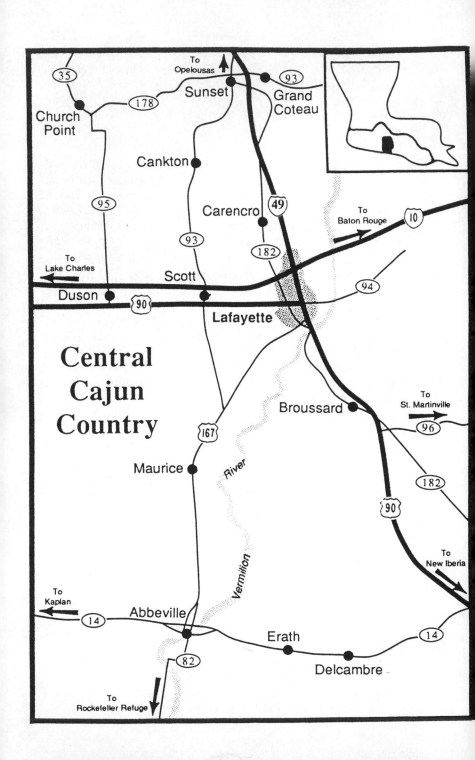

13

Central Cajun Country

Central Cajun Country is not a distinct geographic region but the name we've chosen to describe the hub city of Lafayette and the surrounding area. It includes farm hamlets that have become bedroom communities for Lafayette like Broussard and Scott, the Prairie outposts of Cankton and Church Point, and the lovely village of Abbeville to the south. The area was settled predominantly by Cajuns and remains a great place to seek out Cajun and Creole food and music. As it is the cosmopolitan crossroads of Cajun Country, most visitors will spend some time in the Lafayette vicinity. It is important when reading this chapter to remember that its boundaries were established for reading convenience and that there are many attractions covered in other regions such as Teche Country, Cajun Heartland, and Western Cajun Country that are within 20 minutes of Lafayette and Central Cajun Country.

LAFAYETTE

Known as the Hub City and Cajun Capital of South Louisiana, Lafayette (metro area population about 150,000) is the largest city in Cajun Country. It rests on the banks of Bayou Vermilion, with one foot beside the wild Atchafalaya Basin and the other on the rural Cajun Prairie. It is the seat of the Lafayette Parish government and a major world oil center, housing the offices of Louisiana's offshore petroleum industry. It is also the home of the University of Southwestern Louisiana (USL), whose students make up 20 percent of the population. Motorists entering town by interstate are heralded by a plethora of billboards, but behind the superhighway and suburban veneer you find small neighborhoods, great restaurants, and lively dance halls. Lafayette is remarkably safe and clean and has an attractive old downtown area that has managed to keep its shops open while avoiding cute remodeling.

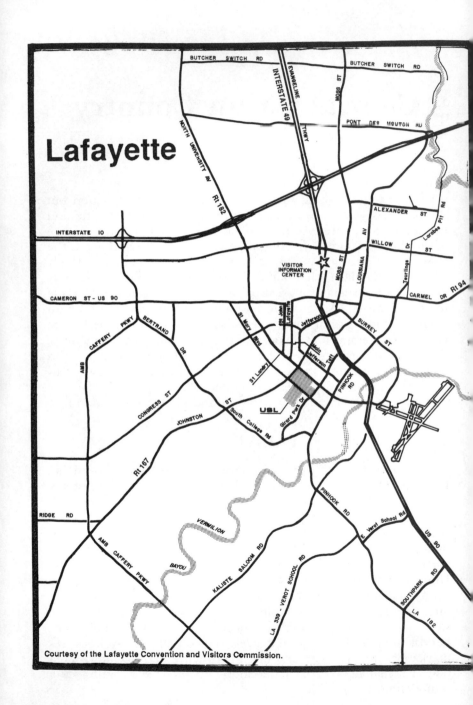

Lafayette

Courtesy of the Lafayette Convention and Visitors Commission.

Situated at the intersection of Louisiana's main north-south (Intrastate 49) and east-west (Interstate 10) highways, Lafayette is two hours from New Orleans and within ninety minutes of most major attractions in Cajun Country. Its central location and wide variety of accommodations (more than the rest of Cajun Country combined) make it a great place to stay while exploring the Cajun hinterlands. Within the city you can become better acquainted with the Cajun people and their culture by visiting the Cajun Cultural Center (operated by Jean Lafitte National Park), two Cajun historical theme parks and museums, and the Louisiana room at the USL library. Each spring the Festival International and colorful blooms along the Azalea and Camelia trails draw thousands of visitors to the Hub City. The biggest event in Acadiana takes place in the fall, when Lafayette hosts the Festivals Acadiens, a free four-day celebration of Cajun music, food, and crafts.

History

First Settlement: The first permanent white settlers in the area that is now Lafayette were Acadians. These pioneers attempted to settle along Bayou Teche near St. Martinville in the 1760s. Following conflicts with the aristocratic European Creole community, they moved westward to the area of present-day Lafayette in the 1770s. They settled just above the intersection of Bayou Tortue and the Vermilion River (generally called "the Vermilion River" to the south of the city and "Bayou Vermilion" to the north), where they established small ranches and farms. By 1812, a dispute had arisen between an Acadian, Jean Mouton, who had acquired much land in the area, and Anglo speculator John Reeves. Both were determined to establish the official town site on their holdings. Mouton got his way by donating the land on which a church and courthouse square were erected. In 1836, the town was granted a charter and named Vermilionville.

War Between the States: In the twenty years prior to the War Between the States, Vermilionville prospered. The Vermilion River was opened to steamboat navigation, giving the area a direct link to markets in Brashear (Morgan City). Rice became the main crop and the city was on its way to becoming a hub of commerce and culture by 1850.

While Lafayette grew peacefully, things were not so placid on the surrounding prairie. With local police diverted by the fear of slave rebellions, outlaws terrorized the surrounding countryside. In 1859, vigilante committees were conscripted to stem the tide of

Downtown Lafayette about 1930. (Courtesy of Lafayette County Archives)

lawlessness. Bands of armed men rode out of Lafayette, Broussard, and other nearby towns. Historian Carl Brasseaux described this vigilante movement as "unsurpassed in the history of the antebellum South." The movement rapidly outgrew the crime problem and became a tool for punishment and expulsion of those believed to be "undesirable." Although Louisiana's great war hero, General Alfred Mouton of Lafayette, was a Cajun, few of the local populace were slave holders and most had more heart for fighting outlaws than Yankees. Large numbers of Cajun conscripts deserted or surrendered to Union forces during the several Northern occupations of Lafayette.

Rebuilding: In 1880, the Louisiana and Texas Railroad arrived in Lafayette and by 1883, the line was complete to San Francisco. The following year Vermilionville became Lafayette. Commerce and public education experienced significant growth and the city began to attract a large number of educated and upwardly mobile Cajuns. The discovery of oil in Anse La Butte (near present-day Breaux Bridge) and the bringing in of the Cankton and Bosco fields in the early 1900s fostered the location of oil interests in the city. South Louisiana Industrial Institute (now the University of Southwest Louisiana) opened in 1920 and Lafayette became the educational center for all of Cajun South Louisiana.

Oil Boom: A new era in Lafayette began in 1952 when local businessman Maurice Heymann opened an office complex targeting Louisiana's nascent offshore oil industry. The complex of low-lying buildings, known as the Heymann Oil Center, became a mecca for the industry and, by 1959, it housed 250 companies. This growth touched off cataclysmic changes in the character of Lafayette. Between 1960 and 1970 the population grew from around 40,000 to 70,000, with only two percent of the residents earning a living by farming. Many of the newcomers were Protestant oilmen and their families. Other new residents were students at USL, which began to attract scholars from around the country to its computer and engineering programs. Oil growth between 1950 and 1980 and the corresponding growth of USL led to a flowering of fine and popular arts in Lafayette. The city became a veritable boom town.

Bust: The collapse of world oil prices in the 1980s caused economic ruin in Lafayette. Every sector of the local economy relied in some way on the influx of oil dollars. Small oil-related companies folded and others slashed operations and closed offices. Unemployment reached double digits as thousands of untrained and poorly educated oilfield workers lost jobs and hit the streets. By 1986, the rate of bank failures exceeded that of the Great Depression.

Some people around Lafayette reflect on the oil crash and joke, "All we really lost was a few Texans." While the city surely lost a lot more (in revenue terms at least), there is a sense that the eighties were a purge. Many old residents stayed and some of the jobless sought education in new fields or took up family professions abandoned decades before. Today the most rapidly growing industry in Lafayette is tourism. The national interest in food, music, and all things Cajun has boosted an economic recovery and brought a new awareness among locals of the region's uniqueness.

Getting There and Getting Around

Getting to Lafayette is easy, as the city is accessed by airlines, Greyhound-Trailways Bus, and AmTrak rail service. If you are driving, Lafayette is only three and a half hours from Houston, two hours from New Orleans, and an hour and a half from Alexandria by interstate. If you are not driving when you get to Lafayette, you will want a car once you arrive. There are a few points of interest, restaurants, and night spots within walking distance of downtown, but only with a car will you be able to appreciate the city's position as a geographic hub of Cajun Country.

The first thing you need in Lafayette is a good map. The streets are an inscrutable jumble. Like New Orleans, many streets radiate out from the river. On the south, these streets meet at improbable angles with those of the old downtown area laid out by Jean Mouton. On the north, the old downtown intersects with a grid pattern based on the railroad line. Superimposed on these are ancient routes like the Old Spanish Trail (U.S. 90) and Old Abbeville Highway (Route 167), as well as new interstates and subdivisions. Finally, it should be noted that some streets change names as they cross the Evangeline Throughway. To put it simply, Lafayette is the only city in which I have inadvertently driven in a complete circle!

Lafayette Attractions

Gateway Lafayette Visitors Center Rt. 167, Evangeline Throughway. Gateway Lafayette is a new park and visitors center located just southeast of Interstate 10 (exit 103) on the median of Route 167. Gateway has already met the criteria to become a viable tourist attraction, having accrued a temporary resident alligator and permanent alligator story. Just a few months after completion, a four-foot gator appeared in one of the Gateway ponds. It was assumed that the reptile had not wandered across three lanes of traffic to get to his resting spot, but that he had had some human help. After a couple days' work he was finally trapped and removed, but not before he depleted the duck population in the pond.

The Gateway is a clearinghouse for information on activities and attractions not only in Lafayette, but around most of the area. They have a knowledgeable and accommodating staff directing visitors to the various points of interest, whether they are trying to find out who is playing at the Friday afternoon street dances downtown or when the next cooking demonstration will be held at Vermilionville. Gateway is also a convenient place to pick up a copy of the *Times of Acadiana*, a weekly paper which features not only local news and commentary but an excellent entertainment and events calendar. Not the least of the services performed by the Gateway is orienting visitors to the mind-boggling and maze-like tangle of streets in the metro area. Detailed maps of Lafayette are available for a few bucks and a diagram of major roads is provided free of charge. The Gateway is open daily 9 A.M. to 5 P.M. If you have not already gotten a city map, buy one! 1-800-346-1958, (318) 232-3737, or in Canada 1-800-543-5340.

Downtown Lafayette

Just a mile south of the Gateway Visitors Center, Jefferson Street, the main street of downtown Lafayette, crosses the Evangeline Throughway (Route 167/90). Heading west from the Throughway, Jefferson Street sports a turn-of-the-century shopping district with numerous small shops, restaurants, and nightclubs. There is a City Newsstand, the FUN Novelty Store, Cajun Station Gift Shop (housed in an old filling station) and downtown's premier lunchroom, Dwyer's Cafe (*see* food section). Many of the older buildings are festooned with huge murals. Jefferson bisects a twelve-square-block area that is the historic and present center of the city and parish government. Among the public buildings of interest are the main branch of the public library, the Lafayette Museum, and the old courthouse. The best way to see this area is to park on the street in an adjacent neighborhood (free), or in one of the metered downtown lots and walk. Also, Parc Lafayette garage in the old downtown area (Polk and Jefferson streets) provides secure sheltered parking for $2.50 a day, or 50 cents an hour.

Downtown Alive Jefferson St. at Vermilion St.

This old-time street dance is held on Fridays from 5:30 to 8 P.M. during warm-weather months (April to June and September

Lafayette Hardware Building. (Photo by Macon Fry)

through November). Workers from downtown offices, students at nearby USL, and families from surrounding neighborhoods create a good-natured throng in the street; restaurants open their doors, and beer and hot dogs are sold on the sidewalk. The music varies from Zydeco to Cajun and Rock and Roll, usually performed by popular local groups. For information call (318) 268-5566.

Lafayette Museum/Jean Mouton House 1122 Lafayette St.

The Jean Mouton House was originally a two-room structure built by the Lafayette town founder in 1800 as a "Sunday house." He used the residence when visiting from his plantation in Carencro. One room of the old structure burned down. The remaining kitchen is an excellent example of early Acadian architecture, and is stocked with artifacts used by Acadian settlers. The original room is now attached to a house constructed by Mouton's son Alexandre, the first Democratic governor of Louisiana. Another three rooms were added in 1849, creating a Greek Revival facade and posing an interesting contrast of architecture between the three segments of the house. Inside the main house are eight rooms of period furnishings and artifacts of nineteenth-century life in Lafayette. There is an obligatory Mardi Gras room displaying costumes of recent royalty. Among interesting Civil War pieces is a double-framed newspaper printed on the reverse side of wallpaper, the only printing material available at the time. The Lafayette Museum is just a few blocks off Jefferson Street. It is open Tuesday through Saturday from 9 A.M. to 5 P.M. and Sunday from 3 P.M. to 5 P.M. Admission is $3. (318) 234-2208.

St. John's Cathedral, Oak Tree, and Cemetery 914 St. John Street.

St. John's is the seat of the Diocese of Lafayette. This huge Dutch Gothic structure with flying buttresses was built in 1916 to replace the old wooden edifice completed in 1822. Beside the cathedral stands the 500-year-old St. John's Cathedral Oak, a member of the Live Oak Society. The tree has a girth of over 28 feet and limb span of 145 feet. It is estimated that the largest branch weighs about seventy-two tons! Behind the church, explore St. John's Cemetery. Here, in above-ground tombs, lie the remains of town founder Jean Mouton, his wife Marie, their son General Alfred Mouton, and Cidalese Arceneaux. Arceneaux is believed by some to be the daughter of "Gabriel" of Longfellow's "Evangeline." St. John's Cathedral is located on the northwestern edge of downtown. (318) 232-1322.

Photographic History of Lafayette Courthouse at 800 Buchanan St.

The Clerk of the Court in Lafayette has collected over 2000 photographs of life in the Lafayette area over the last century.

Many are on display on the second floor of the Courthouse. There are photos of the downtown area, important buildings from the turn of the century, politicians like Dudley LeBlanc and Huey Long, and images of the great flood of 1927. Most of the photographs have been donated from private collections and have never been displayed before. The exhibit is housed in the Parish Clerk of Courts office, on the second floor of the Courthouse. It is free and open to the public weekdays between 8:30 A.M. and 4:30 P.M. (318) 233-0150.

Artists' Alliance 121 W. Vermilion.

The Artists' Alliance is a contemporary art center founded by area artists in 1985, and is located in the historic Lafayette Hardware Building (Lafayette's oldest standing commercial structure). The center is financed by national and state endowments, memberships, and donations. A gallery features both local and traveling exhibits, performance art, and dance. The Gallery is open Wednesday through Friday from 11 A.M. to 5 P.M. and Saturday 1 P.M. to 5 P.M. (318) 233-7518.

Maison du CODOFIL 217 W. Main St.

This building was occupied by the Bank of Lafayette in 1898. After stints as City Hall and a public library, it was restored in 1981 and became the home of the Council for Development of French in Louisiana. CODOFIL was founded by James Domengeaux in 1968 with the goal of promoting French in Louisiana. Domengeaux's motto was "Make French the atomic bomb of Louisiana." Although his objectives have not been fully realized, CODOFIL has contributed to the explosion of regional interest in preserving the culture, heritage, and language of French South Louisiana. (318) 265-5810.

Old City Hall/Le Centre International de Lafayette 735 Jefferson St.

This proud Deco building with stone mosaic floors once housed Lafayette City Hall. It is now home to the Centre International. Designed to help promote international economic interests, the Centre houses representatives from Belgium, Brussels, Montreal, and Quebec, as well as the offices of the Festival International de Louisiane. The Centre is located at the intersection of Lee and Jefferson, guarded by a statue of General Alfred Mouton. (318) 268-5474.

Food in Downtown

Dwyer's Cafe
Borden's Ice Cream
Cafe des Artistes

Cedar Deli
Louviere's

University and Oil Center Area Attractions

University of Southwestern Louisiana

USL is the second largest university in the state, with 16,000 students. Formerly known as Southwestern Louisiana Industrial Institute (SLII), it opened as a preparatory school in 1901. By 1920 it was operating as a four-year college and had become the educational center of Cajun Country. Construction on fifteen buildings began during the governorship of Huey Long, so the school has a distinctly Art Deco look, contrasting with its oak-shaded streets and walkways. The campus, located just south of the old downtown area, is relatively small and easy to walk. On the south edge, it is bounded by Girard Park, on the east by the low-lying buildings of the Oil Center, and to the west (across Johnston Street) is a neighborhood known as "The Saints" (because many streets are named for saints). The Saints and the area around Girard Park are the best places to look for parking. USL has French and Folklore programs active in the study of Cajun and Creole culture. The center of activity is the student complex surrounding Cypress Lake on Hebrard Boulevard between St. Mary Boulevard and University Avenue. The Student Union overlooking the lake has a bookstore and small cafe, and the adjacent Guillory Hall has a bowling alley and pool tables. (318) 231-6940.

Elderhostel Program at USL

I had never heard of Elderhostel until I began traveling extensively in Cajun Country. It seemed like everyplace I went (even the Cajun Mardi Gras celebration in tiny Church Point and the Saturday morning radio show at Dup's Lounge in Eunice) I kept running into small groups of senior citizens having a blast! I talked to a few and discovered that they were participants in the University of Southwest Louisiana's Elderhostel Program. Elderhostel is a program operating at universities throughout the world offering senior citizens an opportunity to expand their horizons through intellectual, recreational, and social activity, as well as travel. The program, which was initiated in 1975, offers a week of activities, classes, room and board, and local transportation at participating institutions for the incredible price of around $275.

Usually held the next-to-last week in September, three classes are offered on Cajun and Creole food, music, and crafts. Attendance is required at one class a day. Classes are taught by leaders in the field from the USL French, Louisiana Studies, and Folklife programs. The best part of the program are participatory food and music events. Hosts guide hostelers to places on the Cajun Prairie that elude even diligent travelers. For the cost of this program folks would be hard pressed to find as much good food, good music, and good company on their own. The program is timed to end just as the Festivals Acadiens (*see* description below) is beginning. Many hostelers linger in the area for these festivities. Hostelers must be sixty years or older (but may bring a companion fifty or over). Lodging in Lafayette is provided in a nearby hotel with shuttle service to campus twice a day. Meals are taken in the campus cafe, but there are several planned opportunities to enjoy great regional food in the countryside. For more information on the Elderhostel Program at USL call (318) 231-6344, or contact the national office at ELDERHOSTEL, P.O. Box 1959, Dept. TN, Wakefield, MA 01880-5959.

Cypress Lake Hebrard Blvd. between St. Mary's Blvd. and University Ave.

Cypress Lake is the best-known landmark on the USL campus. Shaded by feathery cypress branches hung with Spanish moss, the lake is home to crawfish, fish, turtles, frogs, and reportedly several alligators. The lake was originally a dry cypress grove and was the scene of USL commencements until World War II, when it was flooded for use as a reserve water supply. It now darkly reflects the facade of the new Student Union building.

University Art Museum Fletcher Hall, E. Lewis and Girard Park Circle.

The University Art Museum occupies two buildings on opposite sides of Girard Park. The permanent collection is housed in the USL Foundation Building, a replica Greek Revival-style mansion at 101 Girard Park Dr. on the corner of East St. Mary Boulevard. Works in the permanent collection are shown on an annually rotating basis. The main draws to the museum are the contemporary, decorative, and special interest exhibits at the new museum in Fletcher Hall. A recent exhibit featured works by Auguste Rodin. For exhibit information call (318) 231-5326. The museums are open Monday through Friday from 9 A.M. to 4 P.M. Fletcher

Hall is also open on Sundays from 2 to 5. Both are free except for special shows. (318) 231-5326.

USL's Dupre Library St. Mary Blvd. at Hebrard.

Even if you are not planning on using the research facilities, stop by and check the changing exhibits in the library lobby. One recent exhibit displayed old newspaper articles and photographs of Louisiana hurricanes. Inside, the walls are decorated with large photographic images of early life in Cajun Country. The *Jefferson Caffery Louisiana Room* houses materials of all types pertaining to Louisiana. It is one of the best sources of information on subjects relating to Cajun and Creole culture, the oil industry, local history, and genealogy. The collection includes books, magazines, government documents, maps, newspapers, and more. Specific topics may be referenced in vertical files of newspaper clippings and pamphlets.

Adjacent to the Louisiana Room are the offices of the *USL Press* and Center for Louisiana Studies, which publishes and sells a number of books relevant to the history, customs, and people of Acadiana. The library is open Monday through Thursday from 7:30 A.M. to 11 P.M., Friday until 6 P.M., Saturday from 10 A.M. to 6 P.M., and Sunday from 2 P.M. until 11 P.M. Hours change for the summer sessions. (318)231-6039 or 231-6025.

Girard Park St. Mary Blvd. and Girard Park Circle.

One of the loveliest city parks in Lafayette, Girard Park, with its spreading oaks and small streams, is a great place for a walk or picnic. It is the site of the music stage during the Festivals Acadiens. The park faces St. Marys Boulevard and is encircled by Girard Park Drive. It is flanked on two sides by the USL campus and lies just a few blocks from the Heymann Oil Center complex. At the back of the park is the Lafayette Natural History Museum and Planetarium.

Lafayette Natural History Museum & Planetarium 637 Girard Park Dr.

This small but modern museum features changing exhibits which interpret the region and explore the environment. The exhibits are fascinating for adults and kids will enjoy several "hands on" displays in the Discovery Room. Recent exhibits have been "Our Gulf Of Mexico: Handle With Care" and "Louisiana Creoles of Color." The museum has a planetarium with programs every Monday and Tuesday followed by an opportunity to gaze through the eight-inch telescope. The museum also operates the Acadiana Nature Center (*see* Metropolitan Area Attractions). They are open Monday through Friday from 9 A.M. to 5 P.M. (until 9

Cypress Lake at USL. (Photo by Julie Posner)

P.M. on Tuesday), and Saturday and Sunday from 1 P.M. to 5 P.M. Admission is free. (318) 268-5544.

Heymann Oil Center

Hardly a tourist attraction, this 16-square-block area near the USL campus is, however, worth a gawk if you are sightseeing on campus or on your way to the nearby Hub City Diner (*see* Food section). It is the center for Louisiana's offshore oil industry and a cornerstone of the local economy. Businessman Maurice Heymann converted his nursery to oil company office space in the early fifties. By 1959 the Center was home to over 250 companies. Hundreds more followed only to abandon town during the collapse of oil prices in the eighties. One expects big and tall buildings from oil companies, so the most surprising thing about this office park is that it has maintained its low-to-the-ground fifties aura. The main drags through the Oil Center are Heymann Boulevard, Coolidge, and Oil Center Drive, which intersect St. Mary Boulevard east of campus.

Food In University/Oil Center Areas

Hub City Diner	**Deano's Pizza**
Cafe Vermilionville	**Judice Inn**
Cafe de Lafayette (Student Union, USL)	

Lafayette Metro Area Attractions

Charles Mouton Plantation 338 N. Sterling.

The Charles Mouton Plantation was built in about 1820 and has been the property of Dr. Sterling Mudd (for whom the surrounding Sterling Grove historic district and adjacent Mudd Avenue were named) and Charles Mouton, nephew of town founder Alexandre Mouton. Present owners Coerte and Marjorie Voorhies renovated the Acadian-style home to closely resemble its original configuration. The Voorhies are local historians and their tour of the house is filled with anecdotes and insights into the building and its previous owners. Among the many Louisiana French and American antique furnishings is an Acadian cypress loom and spinning wheel. The Voorhies also operate a bed-and-breakfast, the Bois des Chenes Inn, in the carriagehouse at the rear of the plantation house (*See* Accommodations section). The plantation is on Sterling Street, two blocks east of the Evangeline Throughway.

Tours are given from 10 A.M. to 5 P.M. Tuesday through Sunday. Call in advance. Tours cost $5 per person. (318) 233-7816.

Acadian Cultural Center Surrey St. at Beaver Park.

This is the headquarters of the Jean Lafitte National Park Acadian Unit and the biggest of three projected Cultural Centers in Acadiana. This unit, scheduled to open in the fall of 1992, will house museum exhibits pertaining to the spectrum of Cajun cultures, from wetland to prairie. There will also be exhibits pertaining to the immigration and dispersal of Cajun families throughout the region. A major documentary film telling the story of the Acadians' expulsion from Nova Scotia is being made in Canada, France, and Louisiana. This film will be shown in a 200-seat theater. 1-800-346-1958, (318) 232-3737, or in Canada 1-800-543-5340.

Vermilionville

Vermilionville, the newest of Lafayette's two Cajun theme parks, is set on twenty-two acres between the Vermilion River and the Lafayette Airport. It is a condensed version of an early Acadian town, with replications of a Creole plantation home, overseer's cottage, cotton gin, chapel, schoolhouse, blacksmith shop, and more. The park is a "living history attraction." Host employees are costumed in period clothing and engage in continuous demonstrations and explanations of Acadian life and crafts. Demonstrations by visiting artisans can be excellent. Lectures, storytelling, and music by popular Cajun performers is scheduled each day in the performance center. You can grab a "Cajun Burger" or another Cajun fast-food item from one of the Vermilionville vendors and carry it into the hall.

A cooking school offers short demonstrations of Cajun and Creole cooking methods followed by a tasting session. If you want a full meal, *La Cuisine de Maman* restaurant serves traditional Cajun fare at an all-you-can-eat buffet for under $7. The food is good and unpretentious, but you can do better at Norbert's Cafe or the Depot Restaurant in nearby Broussard (*See* Restaurant section). Festivals and special events such as Cajun weddings, *Courir du Mardi Gras* (a horseback procession through a community), and boucheries are frequently staged. Allow about two hours to see everything (a little more if there is a performance or special event to see). Call first to see what events are taking place and who is performing. Admission is $8 for adults, $6.50 for seniors, and $5 for students. Children under 6 are admitted free. You may leave the grounds and return the same day for no additional charge. Vermilionville is open from 9 A.M. to 5 P.M.

Monday through Thursday, and until 9 P.M. Friday through Sunday. Take exit 103 A from I-10. Go southeast on the Evangeline Throughway for four miles. Turn left onto Surrey Street by the Lafayette Regional Airport. Vermilionville is at 1600 Surrey Street, across from the airport. (318) 233-4077, or 1-800-99-BAYOU.

Acadian Village 200 Greenleaf Road.

Like Vermilionville, Acadian Village is a historical theme park modeled on a condensed nineteenth-century Cajun town. A mark of the authenticity of the village is its use in dozens of films depicting the life of early Acadian immigrants. All but three of the dozen buildings at the Village are restored and correctly furnished period homes that were moved to the site by truck. There is a special event, festival, or demonstration at the park nearly every weekend but, unlike Vermilionville, it is not a "living museum." Unless you are there on a special occasion, there will not be a costumed host or vendors hawking Cajun food.

Acadian Village has several excellent permanent exhibits, including the home of Dudley LeBlanc. A senator, author, and spokesman for the Cajun people, LeBlanc was a hero in South Louisiana. To the rest of the country, his fame lay in the invention and mass marketing of the vitamin tonic Hadacol (12 percent alcohol). The house is packed with memorabilia from the life and times of the man known affectionately as "Couzan Dud." There are displays on Cajun music and a Doctor's Museum that is an authentic restoration of a late 1800s doctor's office. Although there is no food or beverage concession at Acadian Village, the lawn and pavilion are open for picnics and barbecues. Bring your own food and beer. A no-frills campground offers convenient access to overnight visitors (*See* Accommodations section). Call for a special events schedule. The Village is a project of the Lafayette Association for Retarded Citizens. Proceeds go towards the ARC and maintaining the park. Admission is $4 for adults, $3 for seniors, and $1.50 for children 6-14 years old. From I-10 take the Ambassador Caffery exit south four miles. Go right on Ridge Road. Travel 1.5 miles and turn left onto W. Broussard Road. The park is a half mile further down on the left. They are open from 10 A.M. to 5 P.M. daily. (318) 981-2364.

Acadian Village or Vermilionville?

Both Acadian Village and Vermilionville stage demonstrations and reenactments of the activities of early Acadian settlers. Unlike Acadian Village, however, Vermilionville is a park at which host employees dress in the attire of Acadian settlers and operate

Acadian Village. (Courtesy of LA Office of Tourism)

Canray Fontenot and Dewey Balfa at Festivals Acadiens.
(Courtesy of LA Office of Tourism)

demonstrations daily. Vermilionville also has food concessions. Acadian Village is more laid back, with many well-designed exhibits in an environment that encourages one to slip back to the 1800s and enjoy the park at their own pace. Acadian Village, with its bilingual brochures and guides, is very popular with French-speaking visitors. Cost may also be a concern if you are traveling in a group. Vermilionville costs about $3.50 more per person.

Azalea Trail

The Azalea Trail is a 20-mile, self-guided city driving tour that passes some of the lovely manicured lawns and ornamental stands of azaleas for which Lafayette is famous. The azaleas usually bloom sometime between mid-March and mid-April. A map of the tour and up-to-date information on what is blooming are available from the Gateway Visitors Center or Chamber of Commerce. 800-346-1958, (318) 232-3737, or in Canada 800-543-5340.

Acadiana Park, Nature Station, Trail and Campground (*see* recreation section)

Evangeline Downs Racetrack (*see* recreation section)

Festivals

Lafayette is the site of dozens of celebrations, conventions, and special events, but two of its festivals, Festival International and Festivals Acadiens, rank among the best in the country.

★Festivals Acadiens 3rd week of September.

The Festivals Acadiens is a celebration of regional music, food, and crafts that attracts over 100,000 visitors. The event is actually a combination of six festivals which usually begin in the middle of the week with the Culinary Classic and culminate with food, crafts, and plenty of free Cajun and Zydeco music in Girard Park on the weekend. In addition to the main festivals, there is an extended Downtown Alive street dance on Friday, and lots of music in the city's night clubs. If you enjoy the New Orleans Jazz and Heritage Festival but are fed up with tow trucks, crowds, a shortage of toilets, and lines at food booths, visit the Festivals Acadiens and breathe a sigh of relief. Shuttle service (50 cents) is available every 15 minutes to Girard Park from a free lot at the Cajundome. For up-to-date information, contact the Lafayette Convention and Visitors Commission, P.O. Box 52066, Lafayette, La. 70505. (318) 232-3808, 1-800-346-1958, or in Canada 1-800-543-5304.

The *Culinary Classic* is a two-day event beginning mid-week just before the weekend Festival de Musique Acadien. A *Pre-*

Classic Seminar, in which nationally renowned chefs offer cooking demonstrations followed by a buffet lunch ($15), kicks things off. The *Culinary Classic* food extravaganza is held the following night in the Cajundome. This is a major social event and a major feed. Local chefs compete for medals in nine categories, with awards presented to the top three dishes in each category. Guests are encouraged to sample all of the creations of these great chefs. The Culinary Classic costs serious bucks ($50), but offers some serious eating for the thousand or so who attend. Proceeds go to local charities.

Festival de Musique Acadien is one of the two major weekend events (along with the Louisiana Native Crafts Festival), running from about 10 A.M. to 6 P.M. on Saturday and Sunday. I would highly recommend this event to any fan of South Louisiana music. It is a free concert that takes place on a stage erected near St. Mary Boulevard in the picturebook setting of Girard Park. Dozens of the best new and traditional Cajun and Zydeco musicians appear in an unending stream, providing 16 hours of great outdoor listening and dancing. Overcrowding has not been a problem, as folks spread out blankets and lawn chairs on the grass while others join the dancing in front of the bandstand. In the shade of spreading oaks there are plenty of beer trucks, food booths from local restaurants, and porto-lets. The festival crowd includes plenty of families and elderly attendees and is orderly (even the USL students!). Golf carts provide transportation for the physically impaired to the nearby *Native Crafts Festival*.

The *Louisiana Native Crafts Festival*, just a short walk from the music and food area of the *Festival de Musique Acadien*, remains the best-kept secret of Festivals Acadiens. For a three-dollar admission one can see demonstrations of alligator skinning, decoy carving, net and trap making, and many other regional crafts. Representatives of Louisiana's Indian tribes demonstrate the weaving of native cane, rush, and pine-needle baskets. There is a pavilion which features instructional seminars, musical demonstrations, and appearances by storytellers and humorists. Best of all are the food booths! My favorite is an exhibit called "How Men Cook." In South Louisiana, "men cooking" does not mean burgers on the grill; at this booth you will find the whole range of regional cuisine with an emphasis on wild game and pot food. Demonstrations, free samples, Cajun humor, and advice are generously dispensed. Among the other food exhibits are a *cochon de lait* (roast pig) and cracklin' pot, each offering samples of the finished product.

*Festival International de la Louisiane 3rd week of April.

Billed as the biggest Francophone Festival in America, the Festival International is a cultural baptism into the food, music, film, and crafts of French-speaking nations and communities from around the world. Over 400 artists from Africa, Canada, the Caribbean, Europe, and the Americas join regional South Louisiana musicians on bandstands scattered through historic downtown Lafayette. Aside from local heros like Zydeco star Boozoo Chavis, crowds have been dazzled by the rhythms and dancing of the Drummers of Burundi, and the Jamaican calypso band The Jolly Boys. There are hundreds of performances, dozens of art and craft exhibitions, and activities for kids. The whole thing is one big, free, and orderly street fair. Stages are located far enough apart so there is no bleed-over or overcrowding. Even the lines at food booths move quickly. For more information, contact Festival International de la Louisiane, P.O. Box 4008, Lafayette, LA 70502. (318) 232-8086, 1-800-346-1958 (Visitors Center), or 1-800-543-5304 (in Canada).

Zydeco Extravaganza Last weekend in May.

Held the last weekend in May (the Sunday before Memorial Day) at Blackham Coliseum, this is the biggest event on the Zydeco calendar in Lafayette. Twelve hours of continuous Zydeco music featuring South Louisiana's best bands can be heard. I prefer the outdoor settings of Festival International and Festivals Acadiens to the cavernous Coliseum, but there is no arguing with the great talent and low price tag for this event. Admission is only $5 for adults and $2 for children. For more information call (318) 234-9695 or the Visitors Center at 1-800-346-1958.

Acadian Village Cajun Heritage and Music Festival 2nd weekend in October.

Like all the special events at Acadian Village, this festival is geared towards families. The Heritage Festival covers all aspects of Cajun life and sometimes includes representatives of other cultural groups of South Louisiana such as Houma and Coushatta Indians, and Creoles of color. The main focus of course is on things Cajun. Cajun humorists, storytellers, and musicians perform and there are Cajun food booths. For directions to the facility see the review of Acadian Village above. (318) 984-6110.

Lafayette Mardi Gras Late winter, early spring (dates vary).

Downtown: Lafayette lays claim to the second largest (behind New Orleans) celebration of Mardi Gras in the nation. Most of the parades wind down Jefferson Street downtown. Here there is a small-town carnival atmosphere. The biggest parades are the Krewe of Bonaparte at 6 P.M. on the Saturday before Mardi Gras, the Queen's Parade at 6 P.M. on the Monday before Mardi Gras, and the King's parade at 9 A.M. on Mardi Gras. For the Queen's Parade, families and students arrive early to enjoy amusements, rides, and food booths. The celebration in Lafayette is not quite as protracted as that of the Crescent City and offers a respite from the crush of huge crowds. Consult the index for information on the traditional *Courir du Mardi Gras* celebrations held in small towns of the surrounding Prairie. For up-to-date information contact the Tourist Commission at (318) 232-3808 or 1-800-346-1958.

Acadian Village Courir du Mardi Gras: Acadian Village has held an enactment of the traditional *Courir du Mardi Gras* on the Saturday before Mardi Gras since 1982. For the regular $4 admission you can wander through the theme park, see the demonstration, hear a full day of music, and get some regional eats at food booths. When the festivities wind down at the village, you will still have time to head downtown and catch the Queen's Parade. For more information call (318) 981-2364.

Vermilionville Courir du Mardi Gras: In their first Mardi Gras festival, Vermilionville hosted an enactment of the *Courir du Mardi Gras* two weeks before Fat Tuesday and had another celebration the Sunday before Mardi Gras. The usual admission of $8 for adults is charged. For more information call (318) 233-4077 or 1-800-99-BAYOU.

Shopping

Cajun Station 900 Jefferson St.

Housed in an old filling station in old downtown, this is an unusual gift and craft shop. You will find a wide selection of cook books and travel books, Louisiana spices, t-shirts sporting logos like "Cajun By Osmosis" and "Louisiana Wetlands," and a few recordings by regional artists. My favorite items are the locally made "Cajun Zydecos" (pickled hot peppers) and "Zydeco Beans" (hot pickled snap beans). You can also purchase the popular "upside down" pickles. They are open Monday through Friday from 9 A.M. to 5:30 P.M. and Saturday until 3 P.M. (318) 235-5238.

Cajun Country Store 211 N.E. Evangeline Throughway.

The Country Store is located on the Evangeline Throughway just south of the Gateway Visitors Center. You can purchase everything from Cajun dance videos to books, postcards, and novelty souvenirs here. They also have a large mail-order catalogue. The store is open seven days a week from 10 A.M. to 3 P.M. (318) 233-7977.

Fun Shop 310 Jefferson.

This gag palace (directly across from Dwyer's Cafe) is a hilarious place to stop when you are walking in downtown Lafayette. They are a mask and novelty retailer with a big selection. The Fun Shop is open Monday through Friday from 9 A.M. to 5 P.M. and Saturday from 1 P.M. to 3 P.M.

Fruit World 6404 Johnston.

If you are planning a picnic or a South Louisiana food basket to take home, Fruit World is a good stop. You can purchase a big variety of locally grown produce like mirlitons and okra or Pure Cajun Brand preserves like pepper jelly, pickled mirliton, jalapeños, and muscadine jelly. Fruit World is about 2 miles south of Ambassador Caffery Parkway. They are open daily from 8 A.M. to 6 P.M. (318) 988-3038.

Gateway Antiques 200 Northgate Drive.

Gateway offers antique and collectible items from buttons to backbars and everything in between. They are located behind Northgate Mall, just off the Evangeline Throughway (Route 167). (318) 235-4989.

Heartland Antiques 201 S.W. Evangeline Throughway.

Heartland sells Louisiana collectibles like armoires, trunks, furniture, and glassware. They are open Monday through Saturday from 10 A.M. to 5 P.M. (318) 232-2861.

Old Magic Antique and Jewelry 117 S.W. Evangeline Throughway.

Old Magic sells fine antiques and small collectibles such as jewelry, gemstones, coins, and watches. They are open Monday through Saturday from 10 A.M. to 5 P.M. (318) 264-1089.

Ole Fashion Things 402 S.W. Evangeline Thruway at 7th Street.

This shop specializes in larger pieces such as American antique furniture, architectural antiques, fireplace mantels, and fancy plumbing fixtures. They are open Tuesday through Saturday from 10 A.M. to 6 P.M. (318) 234-4800.

Ruins and Relics 802 Jefferson.

R & R is located conveniently on the downtown walking tour, near Old City Hall and the Cajun Station Gift Shop. They sell a wide array of antiques and collectibles. They are open Tuesday through Saturday from 10 A.M. to 5 P.M. (318) 233-9163.

Borden's. (Photo by Derick Moore)

The Real Superstore 3141 Johnston St. (Rt. 167)

This massive chain grocery is the cheapest place to pick up locally made canned foodstuffs and dry goods. They have a huge selection of hot sauces, regionally packaged rice, sugar, pickled okra, and other South Louisiana goodies for a fraction of what you would pay at a gift shop. For meat and fish items to take home, you are better off at a small specialty market. The Real Superstore is open Sunday through Thursday from 7 A.M. to 10 P.M. and until midnight Friday and Saturday. (318) 989-0086.

Food in the Downtown Area

★Borden's Ice Cream Local Fave/Dessert, $. 1103 Jefferson.

This is the kind of old-fashioned ice cream parlor that would set any child nagging his or her dad relentlessly. The facade is Art Deco, with glass bricks and stucco supporting a neon BORDEN'S sign. Inside, at a counter facing a row of booths, are the most wonderful counter ladies since the school lunchroom. Of course, that is just trimmings; the main event is the ice cream, which is available in a host of flavors and combinations. Borden's specializes in the really gooey stuff like splits and sundaes made with fruit toppings and wet nuts (in syrup). What knocks me out are the ice cream drinks. Here, at last, is a place where people know the difference between a shake, a float, a soda, and a freeze and serve definitive versions of each! Try the "Flip" (sherbert blended with carbonated water and milk) to cool off a hot day. There is no place better than Borden's to fight the South Louisiana heat. Located just off Jefferson Street on Johnston in downtown Lafayette, Borden's is within walking distance of downtown attractions. They are open daily from 11 A.M. to 10 P.M. (318) 235-9291.

★Dwyer's Cafe Cajun/Down Home, $. 323 Jefferson St.

The most popular lunch counter in Lafayette is busy proving that Main Street, U.S.A. is still alive. Dwyer's has been a fixture on Jefferson Street in downtown Lafayette for over sixty years and is an essential part of any walking tour of the old commercial district. That's the son of the original owner and cook wearing the tall chef's hat and greeting everybody from behind the serving counter. Dwyer's has good breakfasts (five omelets under $2) and the best coffee in the city. The coffee doesn't have a chance to get burnt on the hot plate because the morning crowd keeps the pot flowing. At lunchtime, ceiling fans stir air which is thick with the smell of pot roasts, gravies, and stewed chicken. The service is cafeteria style and by noon there is a fifteen-minute wait for plates

that are heaped with rice and cornbread dressings, mashed potatoes and vegetables. A full meal is under $4. Dwyer's is just a few
blocks off the Evangeline Throughway (Route 167). They are
open Monday through Friday from 4 A.M. to 4 P.M. and Saturday
until 2 P.M. (318) 235-9364.

Louviere's Cajun/Down Home, $. Jefferson and Lamar St.

You are unlikely to find a more hearty, hefty, or downright
Cajun meal than the working man's lunch at Louviere's. The
selection varies from day to day but the essence of the menu is a
choice of four or five stews (crawfish, shrimp, fish courtbouillon,
and beef and/or pork), served with a choice of two veggies for $3.
There are better plate lunches in Acadiana, but hardly a better
value. The rough little dining area is worth a visit in itself.
Adorning the walls are alligator and crawfish stencils, a hang-
man's noose, and "Jim Bowie's Gun." The latter is a huge musket
with the accompanying historical note: "Fought at the Alamo,
shooting from such a distance it took three days for the enemy to
fall." Louviere's is a few blocks down from downtown. They are
open for lunch only, from 10 A.M. to 2 P.M. weekdays. (318)
235-6258.

Papa Cue's Barbecue Local Fave, $. 224 South Pierce.

There is little likelihood that Papa Cue will be in the same
location when you read this, but he will be somewhere in Lafayette
and if you are a barbecue lover you must find him! Papa Cue has
had at least three "permanent" locations in the past ten years.
Papa uses lots of smoke, long cooking over low heat, and an
incendiary sauce of his own concoction. He brags, "Barbecue
contests? That is one thing I have never lost. We have the best ribs
since Adam!" One taste of his pork and beef ribs or chicken and
you will agree. Papa Cue's Barbecue is presently located one and a
half blocks off Cameron near downtown. They are usually open
on weekdays from 11 A.M. to 2 P.M. Try calling ahead. If you
don't find him there, ask around town, or look for him on the
street in front of Lafayette Motors downtown around 11 P.M. on
weekends. (318) 237-3664.

Food in the University and Oil Center

Cafe de Lafayette Cajun/Down Home. USL Student Union, Hebrard
Blvd.

A good plate lunch can be had right on campus at USL. For
under $5 you can choose among staples like red beans, cabbage,
and fried chicken. The cafe is located on the second floor of the

Student Union by the Cypress Lake. They are open Monday through Friday from 11:30 A.M. to 1:30 P.M.

★Cafe Vermilionville Cajun/Creole, $$$. 1304 W. Pinhook Rd.

This restaurant, in the colonial Vermilion Inn, is a great spot to splurge on a meal that combines Cajun, Creole, and French cooking with the freshest local ingredients. The menu varies daily, but some unique dishes that frequently appear are swordfish maque choux, snapper andouille, and the award-winning Kahlua grilled shrimp. Common throughout is a reliance on light but flavorful sauces, ultrafresh ingredients, and top-quality seafood. In the spicy crawfish bisque, the crawfish were huge, and the corn and crab soup was thick with select lump crabmeat. Cafe Vermilionville has the richest, thickest, and most pungent soups in Cajun Country. The smoked turkey and andouille gumbo is simply paradisiacal. My favorite light meal is the Soups Three, a selection of demitasse servings of any three soups (not always on the menu but available upon request) and a garden salad. Dinners with appetizer or dessert are about $20-$25. Lunches are $10-$15. Cafe Vermilionville is open Monday through Friday from 11 A.M. to 10 P.M., Saturday from 6 P.M. to 10 P.M., and Sunday until 2 P.M. (jazz brunch). Reservations are recommended. (318) 237-0100.

Dean-O's Pizza Local Fave, $-$$. 305 Bertrand Dr.

When I die let it be at the hands of a Cajun Executioner! Sooner or later someone was bound to come up with a "Cajun pizza." If your idea of Cajun is spicy, try the Cajun Executioner. This aptly named pie will show no mercy, pounding the innards with a combination of hot sausage, jalapeños, fresh onions and bell peppers, shrimp, and pepperoni. There are several good pizzas in the sub-atomic heat category, the best of which are the fresh seafood pies. The Marie LeBeau is topped with piles of fresh lump blue crabmeat (seasoned but not hot). The Seafood Seizure combines shrimp, scallops, and broccoli sauteed to perfection and may include crabmeat. These pies resemble pizza only in general shape and construction. Sit in a booth and enjoy vendo-vision (for a quarter) on the table TV screen. Small (10″) pies are about $7, medium (12″) are big enough to feed three and cost about $12. Dean-O's is one block north of Johnston (Route 167), near the Cajundome. They are open Monday through Saturday from 11 A.M. to 11 P.M. (until 1 A.M. on weekends), and Sunday from 4 P.M. (318) 233-5446.

★Hub City Diner Local Fave/$-$$. 1412 South College.

Just before opening his new fifties-style (I am talking olde-tyme) eatery in 1990, owner George Graham described the menu as being, "diner fare with Louisiana flair." The Diner is one of the only places you can get home-style Louisiana cooking at breakfast, dinner, and late at night. The menu offers such standard diner fare as meatloaf and gravy, chicken-fried steak, and vegetable plates, as well as local items like Catfish Louisiana (topped with shrimp etouffée) and Pain Perdu Po-boy (French toast stuffed with sliced ham and topped with Steen's cane syrup—don't knock it 'til you've tried it). Breakfast specials include the Hub City Special Omelet (with tasso, shrimp, and ro-tel tomato) and banana-pecan waffles. Breakfast costs $3-$6, lunch and dinner are $5-$10 (no single item is over $7). There is a full-service soda fountain in front with vintage appliances. The Diner is open Monday through Saturday from 6 A.M. to 10 P.M. (midnight on Friday and Saturday) and 11 A.M. to 9 P.M. on Sunday. (318) 235-5683.

*Judice Inn Local Fave, $. 3134 Johnston (Rt. 167).

This tiny hamburger stand has been operated by the Judice family since 1947 when kids used to drop by for a bag of burgers to take into the drive-in theater across the street. The theater is gone, but you can still get curb service on weekends by pulling up and honking your horn! I doubt if anything significant has changed at the Judice Inn in the last forty years except maybe the addition of air conditioning which, along with the beers and soft drinks (Cokes served in 6-oz. bottles), ranks as the coldest in town. If you don't like burgers, you are outta luck here. The menu has hamburgers, cheeseburgers, potato chips (in small bags from a rack behind the counter), cold drinks, and beer. That's it. These burgers are not the thick gourmet variety, but tasty irregular-shaped patties served with mustard sauce on a toasted bun. There are candy bars and mints for dessert, but to complete an authentic 1950s dining experience, you will want to top off the tank at Borden's Ice Cream parlor (*see* review in downtown section). The Judice Inn is open Monday through Saturday from 10 A.M. to 10 P.M. (318) 984-5614.

Food in the Metro Area

*A B Henderson Gator Cove Boiled Seafood, $$. U.S. 90 E.

Gator Cove has the best boiled crawfish in Lafayette and some of the biggest I have ever eaten. They are pond raised, clean, and filled with bright yellow fat as sweet as creamery butter. This is not a tourist joint, so the crawfish are seasoned for the local palate (plenty hot). They are boiled with cayenne and salt, then dusted with pepper after cooking. A heaping serving of 3½ pounds goes for about $9. At the peak of crawfish season, they serve as many as 10,000 pounds a week! Crabs and shrimp are also available.

Although the Cove is primarily a "boiling point," they have a menu of fried seafood and a few pot dishes. Visit on Friday and Saturday night when all the fried shrimp or catfish you can eat is $10. You are likely to run into the local softball team downing brews and gobbling seafood. If you have a couple of whippersnappers that don't eat seafood, they can order BBQ, burgers, or pizza (with seafood toppings) from Henderson's Barbeque Lodge. Henderson's is open daily, 11 A.M. to 10 P.M. From Lafayette, go east on U.S. 90. The Cove is just past the airport on the north access road behind Henderson's BBQ Lodge. (318) 264-1374.

Blair House Restaurant Cajun/Creole, $$-$$$. 1316 Surrey St.

Since opening in 1950, Blair House has won accolades in *Travel and Leisure* and *Gourmet* magazines. I like a place that stakes at least part of its fame on homemade bread. Jim and Janet Blair serve up small, slightly yeasty white loaves with each meal. The main focus of the menu is local seafood. From the dozen or so seafood preparations on the regular menu, my favorite was the fried stuffed catfish topped with mouseline sauce ($13). It was wonderfully light and had a filling that melded perfectly with the fish. Salads are simple and fresh. The house dressing is a creamy ranch with a hint of garlic and chives. At lunch, the adjacent Blair House Cafe serves delicious soups (try the alligator and sausage gumbo), salads, and po-boys for a good bit less than the restaurant. Blair House is just around the corner from Vermilionville. They are open Monday through Friday from 11 A.M. to 10 P.M. and Saturday from 5 P.M. to 10 P.M. (318) 234-0357.

★Charley G's Seafood Grill Local Fave, $$$ dinner & $$ lunch. 3809 Ambassador Caffery Parkway.

A meal at Charley G's is healthy enough that it won't stop your heart and homey enough that it will warm your soul. A basket of fresh bread accompanied by a bowl of olive oil seasoned with rosemary (for dipping) is the first sign that a meal here is an experience to savor. Get started with the "Sampler" of Cajun sausage (made in-house), bay shrimp, and soft-shell crawfish, or try the grilled Creole tomato slice (hot) topped with feta cheese (cool) and roasted peppers in olive oil (warm). Plenty of people just share an appetizer, duck and andouille gumbo, or superb Southern Caesar Salad over a drink in the lounge. Others come after a show to indulge in the best desserts in the city. A complete dinner is a full night of entertainment. The casual dining room offers a view of the grill, where flames leap as catfish and soft-shells are gently turned. Charley G's accommodates shameless eaters with just-made crab cakes in thickened bechamel sauce, soft-shell crab topped with lump crabmeat and meunière sauce, and smoked fried gulf shrimp. The menu is simply glorious! They are open for lunch (specials for under $10) Monday through Friday from 11 A.M. to 2 P.M. Dinner hours are Monday through Saturday from 5:30 P.M. to 10 P.M. (11 P.M. on weekends). (318) 981-0108

★Creole Lunch House Cajun/Down Home, $. 713 12th Street.

The specialty at the Creole Lunch House is chef/owner Merline Herbert's patented stuffed bread. A rich filling of Creole sausage, meat, cheese, and peppers (optional) are wrapped in homemade French bread dough and baked to a crusty perfection. Take a friend so you can split some bread and have room for Herbert's soulful specialties like baked chicken (stuffed with spices and herbs) served with dirty rice. Herbert also fixes a mouth-watering plate of black-eyed peas served with sweet cornbread. They are seasoned to warm the palate and put a sweat on the forehead. Equally spicy is the Sausage Creole, which comes in a sauce piquante over rice, accompanied by a corn muffin.

Herbert opened her first shop in a wood-frame house at 713 12th Street in 1985, when she retired from her job as a public school principal. If they had put her in the cafeteria, no one would have wanted to graduate. At the 12th Street location, you can eat in the tiny six-table dining area or on an outdoor patio. If you want supper or a Saturday meal, you will have to visit the new Northgate Mall shop which leers across the shopping promenade at the General Nutrition Center. Health-conscious folks can stop and pick up some vitamins and wheat germ before shoveling down some fried pork chops, dirty rice, and stuffed bread. The mall is just off I-10 (exit 103) on the Evangeline Throughway (across from the Gateway Visitors Center). The Northgate Mall shop is open Monday through Saturday, 11 A.M. to 7:30 P.M. The 12th Street shop (a couple of blocks east of the Evangeline Throughway) is open Monday through Friday from 10:30 A.M. to 2 P.M. (318) 232-9929.

★The Depot Restaurant Cajun/Down Home, $. 809 Cameron St., Broussard.

"Depot" is an appropriate name for a place that downloads meals of such train- or truckload proportions. Between the copious quantities of home-cooked food and relaxed country atmosphere, a lunch at the Depot can make time stand still. Rene and Valerie Balser and Rene's mom, Shirley, team up in the kitchen to prepare such simple and savory fare as meatloaf and gravy, fried catfish, hamburger steak, and crawfish fettucine. If you are lucky they will be serving Dad's Pork Barbecue (pit cooked) or marinated Chicken Catalina.

The buffet generally includes three entrees, four or five vegetables, and several desserts. Double-dark chocolate cake with soft-serve ice cream and barely sweet bread pudding are wondrous. The buffet alone costs $5; with the sparse but fresh salad bar add 50 cents, with a choice of hearty soups or gumbo, add $1. The Depot is located in a wood-frame structure in Broussard, about 2 miles southeast of Lafayette. They are open Monday through Friday from 11 A.M. to 2 P.M. (318) 837-3663.

Meche's Donuts Pastries. 200 E. Willow or 1017 E. University.

Meche's is the local doughnut chain. If you are looking for a quick breakfast, you can get the goodies hot every morning here. (318) 232-3782 or 235-2617.

*Norbert's Cajun/Down Home, $. U.S. 90 and Ave. C, Broussard.

This little lunch counter is the oldest restaurant in Broussard and serves the best plate lunches and barbecue east of Lafayette. John Norbert and his wife, Lillie Mae, turn out definitive Creole dishes like crawfish stew, real "dirty" dirty rice, and tasty chicken or crawfish pies. They have a selection of three or four meats and five veggies (pick two) each day. Monday the special is chicken fricassee and red beans, Friday's special usually includes fried catfish and crab jambalaya. I recommend the Thursday barbeque plate. Pork ribs are slow-cooked over a smoky fire until crusty on the outside and tender within. They are served with a moderately hot oniony barbeque sauce, creamy potato salad, dirty rice, and hot-hot corn. Norbert's chicken and crawfish pies, available daily, are his pride. It is a joy to sit at the counter and watch the Norberts turn out their lunches, and to hear them talking in rich Creole accents. Lunch plates cost about $4. Norbert's faces U.S. 90 in Broussard, a few minutes southeast of Lafayette. They are open from 10:30 A.M. to 2 on weekdays. (318) 837-6704.

Prejean's Restaurant Seafood, Dance & Dine, $$-$$$. I-49 Service Rd.

Prejean's is popular among locals and tourists for their fried seafood dishes and platters, but I liked the steak and bread pudding best. The main attraction here is not on the menu at all—it's the live Cajun music and dancing. Unlike some of the other dance and dine places, the dance floor seldom seems dominated by semi-professional folk dancers. There is usually a good mix of families, children, novices, and enthusiasts stepping out. Prejean's gets some excellent bands. Look for accordionist Blackie Forestier or Gervais Matte and The Branch Playboys for a really good show. To get to Prejean's from I-10, take exit 103 B (I-49/167) north. Prejean's is on the service road on the right-hand side just before the Evangeline Downs Racetrack exit They are open Monday through Friday from 11 A.M. to 10 P.M., and Saturday and Sunday in the evenings. Music at Prejean's is every weekday evening from 7:30 P.M. to 9:30 P.M. and weekends 7 P.M. to 11 P.M. (318) 896-3247.

*Prudhomme's Cajun Cafe Cajun/Creole, $-$$. 4676 N.E. Evangeline Throughway, Carencro.

If I had to recommend one restaurant in the Lafayette area for lunch or dinner, Prudhomme's would be it. I have driven up from New Orleans just to eat here. The restaurant gets its name from proprietress Enola Prudhomme, sister of the state's most famous chef. Enola's son, "Sonny," runs the kitchen and turns out many Prudhomme family favorites, like blackened foods, etouffée, and eggplant pirogues. The eggplant pirogue is an incredible production. It is a crisply fried eggplant canoe stuffed with crawfish and shrimp and smothered in a buttery cheese sauce with a couple of large fried shrimp garnishing the top! Enola has a new low-cal Cajun Cookbook, and serves several items which she describes as "low octane," but the highlights here are rich preparations of local ingredients like tasso, fresh rabbit, and crawfish. Most dinners are under $13 and include vegetable, salad (with homemade dressings), dessert and, best of all, a homemade bread tray! Jalapeño cheese bread, white loaves, and spice muffins arrive fresh from the oven. Only margarine is provided, so I recommend the homemade sour cream salad dressing as a spread.

Prudhomme's lunch specials are even more unbelievable than their dinners. Chef Sonny has won dozens of medals for seafood preparations, but proudly exclaims, "I was a welder. Give me a good round steak with potato salad. That's Cajun cooking. I got to have that blue plate." The blue plates here include a sensational garlic pork roast with cornbread dressing and sweet potatoes. I recommend the oyster po-boy (not listed on the dinner menu, but available). A freshly baked loaf of French bread is hollowed out, brushed inside with oyster mayonnaise, and stuffed with perfectly fried oysters (under $4).

Why would anyone drive here from New Orleans to eat? Consider this: in the time you wait in line at K-Paul's you can probably drive to Enola's cafe and be seated. The food will blow you away and you can spend the money you saved to hear some live music, get a motel room, and return to Prudhomme's at 11 A.M. the next morning for lunch! Prudhomme's is about fifteen minutes north of Lafayette on the I-49 Service Road, just south of the Route 182 Carencro exit. They are open Tuesday through Saturday from 11 A.M. to 10 P.M. and Sunday until 2:30 P.M. (318) 896-7964.

Randol's Seafood Restaurant Seafood, Dine & Dance, $$-$$$. 2320 Kaliste Saloom Rd.

Frank Randol claims to have earned a "Master's in Crabology." He steams his seafood "Chesapeake Bay-style," rather than boiling it. The result is a firmer, more succulent meat. A lot of folks get "Barbecued Crabs," which are actually battered and deep-fried hardcrabs basted in barbecue sauce! I can't report that this dish is a delicacy but locals like it and it is messy enough to be a lot of fun. I prefer the steamed crabs and the seafood and sausage gumbo. About 30 percent of the clientele is tourists (many arrive by bus) who come to hear Cajun bands and dance. Some of the dancers are good enough to put on quite a show. Bands play from 8 P.M. to 10 every night. Randol's is located at the far south end of town. From I-10, take Ambassador Caffery Parkway south (exit 100) about 5 miles to Kaliste Saloom Road. Turn left on Kaliste Saloom and look for Randol's on the left. They are open Monday through Friday from 11 A.M. to 2 P.M. and daily from 5 P.M. to 10 P.M. (318) 981-7080 or 1-800-YO-CAJUN.

*Vive la Différence Cajun/Creole, $$$. 101 East Second St., Broussard.

Ken Koval, the owner and chef at *Vive la Différence* (or "*Vive*," as it is affectionately called by its loyal patrons), is one of the most creative chefs on the Lafayette scene. His menu is small and handcrafted daily. It offers a four-course dinner, which includes an appetizer or mouthwatering soup, crisp salad, main course (meat, fowl, or fish selection) and dessert, for a set price of around $22. Koval gets all the little things right, like the complimentary herb butter and blue cheese puree with crackers that arrived before one meal and the homemade English biscuits that came with another. The entrees, which display a rich blend of Creole and Mediterranean cooking, include Fillet of Snapper Nicole (gently flavored with parmesan cheese and mustard). Desserts such as hand-churned ice cream are prepared on the premises.

Vive la Différence is housed in a turn-of-the-century home with a wraparound porch now enclosed in glass. The porch and five interior rooms with 16-foot ceilings offer a relaxed and romantic atmosphere for a fine meal. *Vive* is open 6 P.M. to 11 P.M. Tuesday through Saturday, and 11 A.M. to 3 P.M. on Sundays. (318) 837-2937.

Poupart's Local Fave, Bakery. 1902 Pinhook Rd.

Poupart's is your best bet for breakfast pastries, specialty cookies, and fresh french bread. The baked goods are not quite what you would find in fine cafes in New Orleans' French Quarter, but they are a lot less expensive and far above your standard commercial bakery fare. Chocolate peanut bars, brioche triangles, and filled croissants are about 50 cents each. They have a couple of tables but most of their business is "to go." Poupart's is located on Pinhook near Kaliste Saloom Road. They are open Tuesday through Saturday from 7 A.M. to 6:30 P.M. and Sunday from 7 A.M. to 4 P.M. (318) 232-7921.

Meat Markets

LeBouef's Meat Market Red boudin/plate lunches. 3450 W. Pinhook.

This is one of the few places that still makes *boudin rouge* (not a product for the squeamish). The sausage has a rich flavor like bone marrow and a dark red color from the fresh calf's blood. I found the texture a bit dry and actually preferred their regular links. LeBouef's has daily plate lunches to go, and on Sunday they always serve a barbecue plate with sausage, pork ribs, steak, or chicken right from the pit (under $4). They are open daily from 7 A.M. to 9 P.M. (318) 989-9065.

★Bruce's U-Need-A-Butcher Cracklins. 713 Surrey Rd.

Bruce's makes a variety of popular meat products, including a very good (hot-hot) boudin. Their specialty, however, is cracklins, cooked fresh each morning. They are just the right size and have just the right amount of meat on the skin for texture and flavor. They are also highly seasoned with salt and pepper while still hot. The best time to get these is when they come smoking out of the pot at 9 A.M. each morning. They also have jars of their seasoning for sale. The U-Need-A Butcher is at 713 Surrey Street, just a couple of blocks off the Evangeline Throughway. They are open Monday through Friday from 7:30 A.M. to 5:30 P.M. (318) 234-1787.

Comeaux's Grocery Meat Market/boudin. 1000 Lamar or 2807 Kaliste Saloom Rd.

Comeaux's is perhaps the most popular boudin maker in Lafayette. To my taste, the links are a bit heavy on the giblets (especially liver), but that is obviously the local preference. I like their hog's head cheese better. Comeaux's is open from 7 A.M. TO 6 P.M. Monday through Friday, and until 5 P.M. on Saturday. (318) 234-6109 and 988-0516.

Veron's Grocery Meat Market. 4303 Johnston.

Veron's is a small grocery with quite a few specialty foods. It is a good place to stock up on the flavorful Ellis Stansel's Popcorn Rice. They also sell spicy stuffed pork chops to take home and toss under the broiler. Veron's is open daily from 8 A.M. to 7 P.M. (318) 984-6328.

Lafayette Music

While Lafayette attracts a variety of popular artists to its arenas and clubs, its most exciting sound is the indigenous music played nightly in bars, lounges, restaurants, and dance halls. Within the metropolitan area you will find Cajun, Swamp Pop, and Zydeco. For an up-to-date listing of who is playing, pick up a copy of the *Times of Acadiana* (available for free at the Gateway Visitors Center). Many people use Lafayette as a central base to explore musical hideaways in surrounding towns or to visit the famous Mulate's in Breaux Bridge. Be sure to consult the music chapter in this book to get information on nearby night spots.

Zydeco:

El Sido's Zydeco dance hall. 1523 Martin Luther King Dr.

The great thing about El Sido's is that you can pretty much count on them to have a dance every Friday and Saturday and some Sundays. El Sido's (better known as Sido's or just Sid's) also enjoys a location only about a mile from downtown and a mile off I-10. Although it is relatively new, Sido's has the important things right, like a big dance floor and plenty of tables. It is a family-run business. Proprietor Sid Williams owns a grocery and lives nearby; on most Fridays, his brother Nathan performs with The Zydeco Cha Chas (one of the hottest young Zydeco bands) while Nathan's wife works the door. On Saturdays, Sid brings in the biggest names in Zydeco, like Rockin' Sidney, John Delafose, Lynn August, and Zydeco Force. The music usually starts around 10 P.M. If you get there early, walk across the street to Sid's One Stop and grab a cold drink and a bag of cracklins or link of boudin. To get to Sido's from I-10 take exit 103A (Evangeline Throughway) south. About a mile down make a right on Willow Street. Turn right again on St. Antoine. El Sido's is at the corner of Martin Luther King Drive. (318) 235-0647 or 237-1959.

*Hamilton's Zydeco dance hall. 1808 Verot School Rd.

William Hamilton hosts dances a couple of weekends a month at this venerable old dance hall opened by his father, Adam Hamilton, in the twenties. Do not miss a dance at Hamilton's! In the style of many of the old country dance halls (and this was way out in the country when it was built), Hamilton's is an aging, wood-frame building in front of the family home. When I passed by recently, Mr. Hamilton, who has managed the hall for the last twenty-eight years, was out back tending some of his livestock. The crowd here is mainly black Creoles but Mr. Hamilton has hired a few local bands like the Blue Runners, so it is not unusual to find a few USL students on the dance floor. Hamilton's is on the southernmost edge of the city limits, where cattle outnumber buildings. From I-10, take the Evangeline Throughway south to Pinhook Road (Route 182). Go right on Pinhook. About three miles down take a right on Verot School Road. Hamilton's is on the right between Ambassador Caffery Parkway and Pinhook Road. (318) 984-5583 (home).

Gayon's Zydeco Zydeco lounge. 1919 Breaux Bridge Hwy. (Rt. 94).

Alex "Gayon" Williams told me it would be easy to find his lounge, as it was "right behind the Bypass." It was easy to find once I figured out that "the bypass" is not a road but a little gas n' grocery, and Gayon's is literally "behind it." Zydeco dances are a hit and miss proposition here. They usually have bands a couple of weekends each month, but they have gone months with just a soul/disco format. This place has more of a lounge feel than a dance hall. There is a pool table by the bar. From I-10, take exit 103A (Evangeline Throughway) south. Make a left on Louisiana Avenue, followed shortly by a right onto Carmel Drive (better known as Old Breaux Bridge Highway). Gayon's is "behind the Bypass." (318) 237-4645.

Cajun Music:

Prejean's Dine & dance. 3480 Rt. 167/I-49, north of Lafayette.

This family-style seafood restaurant gets a lot of locals as well as tourists by featuring live Cajun music and dancing seven nights a week. The music is better than the food (although they do have tasty steaks). I usually settle for coffee and bread pudding (served with Jack Daniels sauce) or just get a couple of beers and an appetizer. The music schedule varies, but look for Blackie Forestier or Gervais Matte and The Branch Playboys for a really good show. There is no admission. If the restaurant is busy, you will want to order dinner. The bands play for tips. Bands play from 7:30 P.M. to 9:30 on weekdays and until 11 P.M. on weekends. To get to Prejean's from I-10, take exit 103 B (I-49/167) north. Prejean's is on the service road on the right-hand side just before the Evangeline Downs Racetrack. (318) 896-3247.

Randol's Dine & dance. 2320 Kaliste Saloom Rd.

Since 1985 Frank Randol has been serving up Cajun music along with his fresh steamed seafood (*see* restaurant review section). According to Randol, the restaurant does about 30 percent tourist business, but most of the folks on the dance floor seem to be hard-core Cajun dance enthusiasts. In fact, novices may find the Cajun *Saturday Night Fever* pace on the dance floor a bit intimidating. Randol's uses a simple formula of ultrafresh seafood and top-flight performers, like Paul Daigle, Kermit Venable, and Blackie Forestier, to keep the crowds returning. Live music is featured seven nights a week, starting at 8 P.M. Randol's is located at the far south end of town. From I-10, take Ambassador Caffery Parkway south (exit 100) about 5 miles to Kaliste Saloom Road. Turn left on Kaliste Saloom and look for Randol's on the left. (318) 981-7080.

Downtown Club Scene:

*Grant Street Dancehall Mixed bag. 1113 W. Grant St.

Grant Street is Lafayette's premier night club for R&B, roots music, rock and roll, and the most popular Zydeco and Cajun bands. If you are familiar with the New Orleans club scene, Grant Street is a more down-home version of the famous Tipitina's. It is located beside the Southern Pacific Railroad in an old brick warehouse. Grant Street has expansive wood floors, wooden beams, and no noticeable cooling or heating system. Nobody notices the temperature when the good times get rolling here. In the winter the crowd of students, professionals, and assorted locals is too busy making their own heat to worry about radiators. In the summer there is plenty of cold beer. Considering it is located right downtown, Grant Street Dancehall can be surprisingly hard to find. From I-10 take exit 103A (Evangeline Throughway) south to Jefferson Street. Go right on Jefferson. Do not go under the railroad overpass, but stay to the right. The dance hall is two blocks off of the Evangeline Throughway at the corner of Jefferson and Grant Streets. (318) 237-8513.

Antler's 555 Jefferson St. Downtown.

Popular local bands and college-oriented rock and roll. (318) 234-8877.

D. L. Menard at Prejean's Restaurant. (Photo by Macon Fry)

Boadi's 209 Jefferson St. Downtown.

Popular local bands and college-oriented rock and roll. (318) 234-3911.

Poets 119 James Comeaux St., near Pinhook Rd. and Kaliste Saloom Rd.

Popular local bands and college-oriented rock and roll. (318) 235-2355.

Country Dance Halls:

Cowboy's (Denim and Diamonds) Ambassador Caffery N.

This place is like a smaller version of Gilley's, an urban cowboy's delight. It has a huge dance floor, an army of pool tables, and two bars. The walls are decorated with western-wear ads and ceiling fans stir the smoke about. Cowboy's features popular local country bands (most of whom play the top hits of the day) and occasional appearances by Cajun hotshots like Roddy Romero (the teenage accordion master) and Wayne Toups. Some people around town still refer to Cowboy's as Denim and Diamonds. It is located just north of I-10 at the Ambassador Caffery exit (exit 100). (318) 232-3232.

*Yellow Rose 6880 Johnston.

Yellow Rose is Lafayette's premier country music venue and a great place to see some of the most popular country performers in the nation. Conway Twitty, Vern Gosdin, Joe Stampley, Billy Joe Royal, and dozens of other top stars play in this modest-size dance hall. For half of what it would cost to see these artists play in big arenas in most cities, you can get right down in front and dance at the Yellow Rose. During the week Jeff Dugan or another local band plays hits from off the country charts. Yellow Rose is located on Johnston Street (Route 167) on the southwest edge of town. From I-10 take the Ambassador Caffery exit south to Johnston/ Route 167. Go right on Johnston. The Rose is open Wednesday through Saturday 7 P.M. to 2 A.M. (318) 989-9702

Lounges:

When it comes to music, the term "lounge" has got a pejorative connotation. It conjures up images of has-beens or never-were types doing Elvis and Tom Jones imitations in Reno. The lounge scene in Lafayette is something else entirely. For the dozens of accomplished session men and singers who have worked in the recording studios of Cajun Country, Lafayette is a Mecca. It is a place where R&B, Swamp Pop, and Rock and Roll grooves are still

Tommy McLain at Yesterday's Lounge. (Photo by Macon Fry)

appreciated and where fine musicians can make a living playing the music they love. Artists like Warren Storm, Tommy McLain, Willie T, T. K. Hulin, and Little Bob draw faithful followings nightly. The crowds on the Lafayette lounge scene are generally middle-age folks who love to dance.

Teal's Holiday Inn Holidome, south of I-10 on the Evangeline Throughway.

Teal's is a typical hotel lounge that often features not-so-typical talent. Swamp Pop legend T. K. Hulin is likely to be appearing here. Holiday Inn. (318) 233-6815.

Top End 2842 Evangeline Throughway.

The Top End Lounge is a weird-looking adobe building on the I-49 service road just north of I-10. For several years the house band has been tenor sax man extraordinaire Willie T. and his band The Heat. There are happy-hour food specials like free jambalaya or crawfish. (318) 233-4525.

*Yesterday's Four Seasons Motel, 4855 West Congress St.

Yesterday's has had a number of locations, but has kept an all-star stage band in each incarnation. Among the stars that have been part of the Yesterday's show are Warren Storm, Tommy McLain, Lynn August, Willie T., and Clint West. Warren Storm and Willie T. play Tuesday through Saturday from 9 P.M. to 2 A.M. There is Cajun music at 3:30 on Sundays and other bands on Sunday and Monday night. Ladies drink free on Wednesdays, and Thursday night there is a free supper. (318) 989-2421.

Special Events:

Downtown Alive!

Jefferson Street in Downtown Lafayette is the scene of a free street dance every Friday from 5:30 until 8 P.M. during warm-weather months (April to June and September through November). This is a great way to begin a weekend of music and food in Cajun Country. For information call (318) 268-5566.

Spring Zydeco Festival Kingfish Beach/Lake Martin.

Mother's Day has always been a special occasion in the Zydeco community. Since 1989 local radio station KJCB has sponsored this blowout on the Lafayette city limits. Take Route 94 (the Old Breaux Bridge Highway) east to Lake Martin Road. Turn right on Lake Martin Road and follow the signs. The show starts at 9 A.M. and lasts until 10 P.M. Tickets are $5 in advance and $7 at the gate.

Lafayette Recreation

Evangeline Downs I-49, 2 miles north of Lafayette.

"Il Sont Partis!" (And they're off!) is the cry that marks the raising of the gate at Evangeline Downs. Horse racing and wagering are two time-honored traditions in Cajun South Louisiana. Eddie Delahoussaye (a two time Kentucky Derby winner), Randy Romero, and Ray Sibille are just a few of the great jockeys who have ridden at Evangeline Downs. (Aside from being home to great jockeys, Evangeline Downs has been the residence of a number of alligators over the years. These reptiles make their home on the moist infield, occasionally wandering onto the track or into the parking lot.)

All it takes to join the excitement and tradition at Evangeline Downs is $1 to park and $1 general admission (outdoor bleacher seating). Food and drink are available inside. Folks with kids park close to the fence and watch the races over tailgate picnics. If you want to sit in the climate-controlled grandstands, it costs an extra $2 for a seat or table. No minors are allowed. From I-10, head north on I-49. The season runs from late April through early September. Races are run Friday and Saturday with a post time of 7:15 P.M. Sunday post time is 1:15 P.M. and Monday's is 6:45 P.M. (318) 896-7223 or 1-800-256-1234.

Acadiana Park Nature Station, Hiking Trail, and Campground E. Alexander St.

Acadiana Park is a 120-acre facility on the northeast edge of town with picnic tables, tennis courts, a beautiful city campground (*see* Accommodations), and 3.5 miles of nature trails. The trails wind through bottomland forest in a thirty-four-acre area that abuts the Vermilion River. A three-story nature station has interpretive exhibits on flora, fauna, and geography of the region. Naturalists are available to answer questions and give guided tours (call in advance for a guide).

In South Louisiana high ground is at a premium, so there are not many undeveloped places to put on your walking shoes, unwind, and work off all the calories. The Acadiana Nature Station is one of those places, a natural jewel in Lafayette. From Route 167 (Evangeline Throughway), go north on Louisiana Avenue to Alexander Street. Turn right on Alexander and look for signs to the nature center. The Nature Station is open Monday through Friday from 9 A.M. to 5 P.M., and Saturday and Sunday from 11 A.M. to 3 P.M. Trails are open from sunrise to sunset. (318) 261-8348.

Acadiana Park and Nature Station. (Photo by Philip Gould)

Pack & Paddle 601 E. Pinhook.

Whether it is bicycling, canoeing, or hiking, the one-stop information center and equipment store in all of Cajun Country is Pack and Paddle. The staff here, including owner Joan Williams, has hiked or biked just about every byway in Acadiana. They are generous in sharing advice on routes and itineraries for local excursions. You can purchase detailed maps to roads, trails, and waterways in the area, as well as any type of gadget an outdoorsman could want. For longer trips in the region, Ms. Williams has published a biking guide, *Back-Road Tours of French Louisiana*, that will be a big help to the two-wheel enthusiast. Pack and Paddle sponsors day trips on weekends and overnight bike excursions throughout the year (fees charged). P&P has bicycles for $15 a day and $55 a week. Tents, sleeping bags, and panniers are rented also. Canoes are sold but not rented. (318) 232-5854.

Crepe Myrtle/Wilderness Trail

This 26-mile route is a pleasant day trip by bike or short drive by car. It leaves from the northern suburbs of Lafayette and after a few turns joins Wilderness Trail Road. The Wilderness Trail portion of the circuit follows the upper reaches of the Vermilion River through shady wooded areas, green pastures of horse country and past the homesite of Louis Arceneaux (believed by many to be the real-life fiancé of Longfellow's Evangeline). The route was officially dubbed The Crepe Myrtle Trail in 1990 for the many plantings along its course. Bikers will find flat terrain, little traffic, and arrows painted on the pavement at most turns.

Guided Tour Services

I would suggest that anyone who has time and a vehicle explore Cajun Country on their own, but there are a number of step-on tour operators in the Lafayette area who will accommodate families and small groups. Some of these make an effort to get you to less obvious attractions and out-of-the-way eateries.

Acadiana To Go: Mary Wright specializes in step-on guide service, but may be able to accommodate smaller groups. (318) 981-3918.

Allen's Cajun Experience Tours: Allen Simone has a small bus he uses to shuttle clients. Mr. Simone is a noted (bilingual) Cajun humorist and storyteller who appears on radio shows as Nonc Allen (Uncle Allen), so you can expect more than a litany of mundane facts. Call for rates and information. (318) 543-8000 or 235-8000.

Cajun Tours de Lafayette: Offered through Provost Adventures in Broussard, this tour service offers set 3½-hour expeditions in the morning and afternoon for about $17 per person. (318) 837-2831.

Allons A Lafayette, Inc.: This service specializes in step-on guides. For $30 an hour (minimum of 3 hours), they will provide a guide and car to show you around. (318) 269-9607.

Cajun Country Tours: Cajun Country Tours offers shuttles and guides between local hotels and tourist attractions in the area. Their prices vary from $11 for a Vermilionville excursion, to $35 for a trip to New Iberia. Packages with accommodations are extra (including an opportunity to stay on a houseboat in the Atchafalaya Basin). (318) 235-8000.

Lodging

Hotels and Motels:

Budget Western Inn of America 2111 N.W. Evangeline Thwy., $23 to $28 double. (318) 235-4591.

Days Inn 1620 N. University at I-10, $43 double. (318) 237-8880.

Holiday Inn Holidome 2032 N.E. Evangeline Thrwy, $63 to $70 double. (318) 233-6815, 1-800-942-4868.

Holiday Inn North 2716 N.E. Evangeline Thruway, $51 double. (318) 233-0003.

Hotel Acadiana 1801 W. Pinhook Road, $53 double. (318) 233-8120, 1-800-826-8386.

Lafayette Center Travelodge 1101 W. Pinhook Rd., $32 double. (318) 234-7402.

Lafayette Hilton and Towers 1521 W. Pinhook Rd., $65 to $70 double. (318) 235-6111.

Lafayette Inn 2615 Cameron St., $16 to $22 double. (318) 235-9442.

La Quinta Motor Inn 2100 N.E. Evangeline Thrwy., $54 to $60 double. (318) 233-5610.

Motel 6 2724 N.E. Evangeline Thrwy, $26 double. (318) 233-2055.

Plantation House Motor Inn 2800 N.E. Frontage Rd., $27 double. (318) 232-7285.

Quality Inn 1605 N. University Ave., $40 double. (318) 232-6131.

Ramada Inn Airport 2501 S.E. Evangeline Thrwy., $49 double. (318) 234-8521.

Red Roof Inn 1718 N. University Ave., $35 to $39 double. (318) 233-3339.

Starlite Motor Inn 2207 N.W. Evangeline Thrwy., $22 double. (318) 232-0070.

Super 8 Motel 2224 N.E. Evangeline Thrwy., $32 double. (318) 232-8826.

Travelodge Executive Plaza 120 E. Kaliste Saloom Road, $40 double. (318) 235-5500.

Travelodge North 1801 N.W. Evangeline Thrwy., $41 double. (318) 234-7402.

Bed and Breakfast:

Bed and Breakfast options in the city of Lafayette are limited. There are several B&B's within half an hour of the city in New Iberia, St. Martinville, Washington, and Sunset (consult index for information on these).

A la Bonne Veillée Guest House Rt. 339, (Verot School Rd.)

You get an authentically restored, 1840s Louisiana-French-style cottage on thirty rural acres all to yourself at this B&B fifteen minutes south of Lafayette. The cottage has two bedrooms, a full bath, kitchen, living room, two working fireplaces, central air and heat, television and phone. Rates are $85 for single occupancy, and $100 double. Special rates are available for families. (318) 937-5495.

Bois des Chênes Inn 338 N. Sterling St.

Coerte and Marjorie Voorhies operate this B&B in the turn-of-the-century carriagehouse behind their own home, the Charles Mouton Plantation (1820). The carriagehouse has many modern amenities and is disconnected from the main plantation, affording guests plenty of privacy. Rates start at $65 and include a full breakfast and tour of the plantation house. The Bois des Chênes Inn is located in the Sterling Grove historic district, just two blocks east of the Evangeline Throughway and a short drive from downtown attractions. (318) 233-7816.

Mouton Manor 310 Sidney Martin Rd.

Although the Evangeline Downs Race Track and Moss Street shopping malls are a half mile away, looking from the upper gallery of Mouton Manor it is easy to imagine nothing but fields stretching for miles. The plantation grounds are a quiet retreat on Lafayette's suburban north side. Mouton Manor was constructed in 1806 and its rooms are furnished with comfortable antiques. The house is shared with the owners but is large enough to feel reasonably private. Upstairs rooms with private bath and private access to the gallery start at $55; downstairs rooms start at $65. A nice breakfast is included. (318) 237-6996.

Old Castillo Hotel/La Place d'Evangeline See St. Martinville (Upper Teche Country). (318) 394-4010.

Chrétien Point Plantation Bed and Breakfast See Sunset (North of Lafayette). (318) 662-5876.

Campgrounds:

Acadiana Park Campground 1201 E. Alexander.

Located adjacent to the Acadiana Nature Trail Park. $6 full hook-ups, shower and restrooms available (*see* Acadiana Nature Station for directions). (318) 234-3838.

Acadian Village Campground 200 Greenleaf Dr.

Located in an open gravel lot, these sites with complete hook-ups are geared toward RV's. Campers pay $8 a night and get a reduced rate to the village. (318) 981-2489.

KOA Camping Right off I-10 at the Scott exit.

$18.50 for full hook-ups, $14.50 for a tent space. (318) 235-2739.

Maxie's Mobile Valley and Overnight Camping U.S. 90 East (6 miles east of Lafayette).

$10.55 full hook-ups. (318) 837-6200.

Frenchman's Wilderness Camp Ground (See Butte LaRose/ Henderson in Upper Teche section). (318) 228-2616.

NORTH OF LAFAYETTE

If you are planning on visiting Evangeline Downs or the fantastic Prudhomme's Cajun Cafe, which are just east of I-49, you will want to take the interstate north. For a scenic drive and a look at the small towns of Carencro and Sunset, or the horse country south of Opelousas, try driving Route 182 (University Boulevard) out of town.

Carencro

Just above the funky suburbs of North Lafayette, 7 miles outside the city limits, is the town of Carencro. This small Prairie town was first settled by ranchers in the mid-1800s. In 1874, land for a church was donated and for a short while the community was known as St. Pierre. Despite the arrival of the railroad in 1880 and the growth of Lafayette, this bedroom community of the Hub City is barely a stop in the road for travelers on the old route to Opelousas. There is still a large cattle auction barn right on the main highway. Hungry motorists on Route 182 can stop for a tasty plate lunch at Lloyd's Cafe, a rustic place with the best dirty rice anywhere, or travel a couple of blocks west on St. Peter Street for a first-class Cajun meal at Paul's Pirogue.

Lloyd's Cafe Cajun/Down Home, $. Rt. 182.

Lloyd's goes beyond quaint to truly rustic. Their sign is badly faded, exposing another one that advertises "Tiny's Place," but locals know this is the spot for a hot plate lunch. The wood-frame building shelters six wooden tables and a counter, behind which you will find a rack of hankies, Tom's Snacks, and a box of moon pies (dessert). Daily lunch specials cost $4, but the meal of choice is the Sunday dinner. You get a choice of barbecued chicken or pork steak with yams, beans, and rice dressing for $5. The barbecue is coated with a sweet and hot onion sauce and is highly recommended. Sometimes I just order a soft drink and a heaping plate of the moist dirty rice, which has just the right proportion of giblets and seasoning (it is only available on Sundays). On weekdays Lloyd's opens at 5 A.M. for breakfast. Lunch is served daily from 10:30 A.M. to 1:30 P.M. (318) 896-8812.

Paul's Pirogue Cajun/Seafood, $$. 209 E. Peter St.

Paul's Pirogue has excellent versions of all the typical Cajun stews and soups, good boiled crawfish, and seafood platters, plus a few items you will not find anyplace else! This is the only restaurant that I know of serving the traditional Gumbo Z'herbes, or "Green Gumbo." This gumbo is made with greens, onions, and tasso and thickened with bits of potato and beans rather than roux. Gumbo z'herbes is a Creole dish that was often served during Lent. Legend has it that for each variety of greens used, the cook would make a new friend. I don't know how many different greens Chef Angelle threw in, but he won me over with this sharp, hot soup. The shrimp and crab etouffe%e was also fabulous. It is a mild stew with no roux, but plenty of butter to thicken. Paul's is famous for its Cajun Mayonnaise, which is spiked with cayenne pepper and is a great accompaniment for anything consumable! Jars may be purchased to take home. For dessert try the Gateau Sirup, or syrup cake, with a scoop of ice cream. This is a warm spice cake sweetened with Steen's cane syrup and filled with pecans. Paul's Pirogue is open seven days a week from 5 P.M. to 10 P.M. (Friday and Saturday until 11 P.M.). (318) 896-3788.

What Time Is It? Bakery and Sandwich Shop 217 E. St. Peter St.

If your idea of breakfast is hot doughnuts or beignets, this is the spot. They are located just off Route 182 beside Paul's Pirogue. They are open from 6 A.M. to 7 P.M. Tuesday through Sunday. (318) 896-5310.

Grand Coteau

About 3 miles north of Carencro, Route 182 crosses Interstate 49. Five miles farther north, just above the spot where Route 182 crosses back over to the west side of the interstate, lies the single most idyllic and tranquil village in Cajun Country. This community of 1100 residents is nestled along a sweeping ridge that formed a western bank of the Mississippi River centuries ago (the name *Coteau* means "ridge" in French).

Grand Coteau is home to St. Charles Jesuit College and the lovely Academy and Convent of the Sacred Heart, the oldest school west of the Mississippi and site of the only miracle to occur in the United States (as certified by the Vatican). The room where this miracle transpired is now a shrine open to the public and well worth a visit. Many of the homes within a block or so of the main street are on the historic register. There are superb examples of early Acadian architecture, Creole cottages, and turn-of-the-century wood-frame commercial buildings like Belleman's Grocery.

Academy of the Sacred Heart

For a quiet walk and contemplative moment amongst stately oaks, visit the Academy of the Sacred Heart. Hundreds of Catholics visit the Academy and the convent of the Sisters of the Sacred Heart on retreats each year. The prestigious private school was founded in 1821 and had an initial class of eight students. The pillared and balustraded academy is open to the public. Just drive around back to the visitors' parking area beside the stables. A tour of the oldest structure and museum documenting the history of the school is available for a fee. There is no charge to visit the Mary Wilson shrine.

The miracle which took place at the academy in 1866 has been described as the "most dramatic event in American Catholic Church history." Without ruining the excitement of learning the full story of the miracle firsthand, here are the basics: In 1866, a young postulant at the convent named Mary Wilson became deathly ill. After struggling with the illness, she said novenas to John Berchmans. Berchmans appeared to her twice in visions at her death bed and Wilson was immediately cured (she went on to die eight months later; her grave may be seen in the Sacred Heart Cemetery). This confirmed miracle led to the canonization of Berchmans as a saint. The shrine is in the very room where the visions occurred. You can view exhibits in this shrine/chapel while listening to a short taped account of the whole event.

Tours are offered Monday through Friday from 10 A.M. to 3 P.M., Saturday and Sunday from 1 P.M. to 4 P.M. The fee for adults is $5, for seniors $3. From I-49, take the Grand Coteau/Sunset exit. Turn onto Route 93 towards Grand Coteau. Route 93 becomes Main Street. When you reach the traffic light, turn left onto Church Street. This road will take you to the Academy. (318) 662-5275.

Sunset

Sunset is a sleepy town of 2600 just a couple of miles west of Grand Coteau on Route 182. The village was originally called Sibilleville after a local planter who introduced yams to the region. After the War Between the States, when the people of nearby Grand Coteau refused to allow the railroad to pass through their town, prominent planter Napoleon Robin (for whom Sunset's main street is named) gave the company the right-of-way across his property. With the arrival of rails, the town grew and changed its name to Sunset. This is horse-breeding and racing country. Until a few years ago there was a well-known "bush track" (as the small, dirt horse racing tracks of Cajun Country are known) just south of town. Gambling is a popular pastime and the town is home to the Sunset Game Club cockfighting pit.

Attractions

Romain Castille Home 254 Budd St.

This Victorian-style two-story cottage was built in 1902 and is now the home of Senator and Mrs. Armand Brinkhaus. Mrs. Brinkhaus offers tours of the home when she has time and sells sharp and sweet homemade jellies from the old train caboose in the back yard. My favorites are the garlic, basil, and pepper jellies. (318) 662-5401.

Chrétien Point Plantation

Built in the early 1830s, Chrétien Point is the oldest Greek Revival plantation house in Louisiana. It was the center of a 10,000-acre cotton plantation which was the site of armed conflict during the War Between the States. It has 12-foot-high ceilings, large windows for cross ventilation, and six fireplaces on interior walls with imported French-Empire-style mantels. Following the war, Chrétien Point fell into disrepair. Some rooms were used to store hay, while livestock roamed freely through others. The present owners have restored the manor and live there. They offer tours and bed-and-breakfast accommodations. Tours are scheduled daily from 10 A.M. to 5 P.M. The last tour starts at 4. The fee is $5 for adults and $2.50 for children. To get to Chrétien Point, turn off Route 182 just northwest of Sunset onto Route 93 south. Go 3.8 miles until you hit the Bristol/Bosco Road (Route 356). Turn right, go one block, and turn right again. Chrétien Point is one mile down on the left. (318) 662-5876.

Chrétien Point Plantation Bed and Breakfast

This B&B offers accommodations of rural gentility. There are 3 rooms for rent in the main plantation house, ranging from $110 to $125, and an upper suite available for $500 (double occupancy). Room prices include a tour of the house, complimentary bottle of wine, use of the tennis court and pool, and plantation breakfast. All of the rooms are on tour, so check-in time is 5 P.M. and check-out is at 9 A.M. Directions to the plantation are provided above. Call in advance to make arrangements. (318) 662-5876.

Sunset Game Club Rt. 182, north of Sunset.

This cockpit has been labeled by local fight fans as "the Madison Square Garden of cockfighting." The pit is located on Route 182 just north of town. They are open January through June and have tournaments about once a month.

Food

Dugas Cafe Cajun/Down Home, $. Rt. 182, Sunset.

With its Art Deco facade, I keep expecting to walk into Dugas Cafe and find Earl Long pontificating from a stool at the lunch counter. Old Uncle Earl would sure appreciate the sign reading "No personal checks cashed; we have a supply from last year." Mrs. Dugas runs the kitchen and counter as she has for the past thirty years. She fixes a different lunch special each day and turns out a top-notch Cajun meatloaf redolent of garlic, green peppers, and onions. (Mrs. Dugas had this to say about her seasoning: "We love garlic, grow it in our garden, and cook with it a lot.") Heaped on the side are mounds of rice and smothered potatoes swimming in gravy. The plate lunches come with a simple cobbler with biscuit crust for $4. You can't miss Dugas'; it is the green-and-white building beside the railroad tracks in the center of Sunset. They serve lunch from 10:30 A.M. until 2 P.M. on weekdays. (318) 662-9208.

*Rowena's Grocery and Meat Market Specialty: Boudin. Rt. 182.

Since Enola Prudhomme told me about Rowena's boudin, I haven't passed by Sunset without stopping for a moist and meaty link. This is some spicy, hot boudin. You can see the red and black peppers in these sausages, and the skins sweat red bullets of steam. But it is not the heat that makes this boudin so great—it is the perfect mixture of rice and pork. There is no preponderance of giblets inside and the pork is just fatty enough to keep the whole thing moist. The boudin balls, which are deep fried with no batter, are also good.

Manager Kenneth Burleigh joked that today's boudin and cracklins just aren't as good as those that used to be cooked outdoors; "A little dust fell in it and gave it that taste." But his product is one of the best. In regards to the Prairie andouille, which is made with "guts stuffed in guts," Burleigh explained, "Once you get past the smell it's real good!" Rowena's is on Route 182 just west of Sunset. They are open daily from 7 A.M. to 8 P.M. (318) 662-5630.

WEST OF LAFAYETTE

The primary east-west routes through Lafayette are Interstate 10 and U.S. 90, the Old Spanish Trail. Unless you are in a big hurry you should definitely plan on taking U.S. 90, which roughly parallels the interstate to the south and passes through half a dozen tidy old railroad towns before reaching the western outpost of Lake Charles. If you blink you may not realize that you left Lafayette when you arrive in the hamlets of Scott and Duson. Just a short drive north of U.S. 90, however, are the deeply traditional French Acadian towns of Church Point and Cankton, each with its own attractions.

Scott

Scott is only about three miles from the Lafayette city limits. You probably will not realize you are in another town, unless you turn right on St. Mary and drive past the cluster of old buildings around the railroad tracks one block north of the highway. Here you will find the infamous Scott Bar and Grill, and the converted saloon that houses a studio/gallery of Cajun artist Floyd Sonnier's drawings. Drive just six miles north of the interstate on Route 93 and you will come to Cankton, the site of now closed Jay's Cockpit, once one of the most notorious cock-fighting locations in the state. Across the highway at Cormier's Cock Pit you can still catch a fight several nights a week.

Floyd Sonnier's Beau Cajun Art Gallery 1012 St. Mary St.

Noted Cajun artist Floyd Sonnier has a gallery and studio in this classic old-west saloon. The saloon was built beside the recently completed railroad tracks in 1902 by a Mr. Borque, who coined the phrase "Scott: where the west begins." The phrase has been co-opted by the Scott Bar, which sits across the tracks, but many of the old interior fixtures remain. An old stand-up bar with foot rails and no stools supports boxes of Sonnier's prints. In one corner you will see an original gaming table from the saloon. This was a rough and tumble place in its day and attracted a good number of farmers and oil workers. Respectable ladies would not have entered. Today everyone is welcome to browse through Sonnier's work, which is primarily pen-and-ink drawings depicting scenes of rural Cajun life and the countryside. The gallery is located two blocks north of U.S. 90, on the corner of St. Mary and Delhomme streets. It is open weekdays from 10 A.M. to 5 P.M. and Saturday, 10 A.M. to 4 P.M. (318) 237-7104.

Food

Scott Bar and Grill Local Fave, $.

This is the humble spot where the sign proclaims, "Where the west begins and friends meet." It is not much of an eatery, but it is plenty popular with the local blue-collar crowd, who purchase bags of greasy-spoon hamburgers ($1.50) or cheeseburgers ($1.80). The grill is on one side and the old bar and jukebox on the other. You can't see the bar from Route 90, but it is just a block north of the highway at the corner of St. Mary and Cayret streets. They are open from 9 A.M. to 11 P.M. every day but Sundays. (318) 235-9363.

Darby's Meat Market U.S. 90, Scott.

Darby's fixes a classic Lafayette-style boudin with plenty of liver and giblets mixed with the rice and a medium dose of pepper. Their cracklins are very meaty and they claim to have the "best fresh-ground meat and sausage in town." Darby's has been satisfying Scott and Lafayette customers for twenty-seven years. They are located on the north side of U.S. 90 in Scott. Darby's is open

Cormier's Cock Pit.

Jay's Cockpit. (Photo by Julie Posner)

from 7 A.M. to 7 P.M., except Sundays, when they close at noon. (318) 235-5452.

★Best Stop Meat Market. Rt. 93, 1 mile north of I-10.

Even though I am not partial to the more liver-flavored boudin found in these parts, this is one of the "best stops" around. The heat factor is moderate and they get the seasonings and moistness just right. For something different try the non-traditional smoked boudin. The Best Stop is a great place to pack a cooler of meats to take home. Their tasso (available in turkey for non-beef eaters) and smoked sausages are excellent and you will want to get a small bag of extra-spicy cracklins to gobble in the car. The Best Stop is exactly one mile north of Interstate 10 at the Scott/Cankton exit (Route 93). From U.S. 90, just head north on Route 93 and look on the left after you cross I-10. The Best Stop is open 6 days a week from 6 A.M. to 8 P.M., and Sundays until 6 P.M. (318) 233-5805.

Music

Country Corner Lounge Country or Cajun music. U.S. 90 & Rt. 724.

Originally this lounge was called Shawn's, and featured live Cajun music. The format seems to have changed to country along with the name. Bands play on Friday and Saturday from 9 P.M. to 1 A.M. and Sunday from 6 P.M. to 10 P.M. The Country Corner is located between Scott and Duson on U.S. 90.

Cankton

Cankton is nothing more than a small crossroads on the Cajun Prairie six miles north of Interstate 10 on Route 93, but it has developed a bit of notoriety for its two (now one) cockpits.

Jay's Cockpit Rt. 93, north from I-10.

The best known of Cankton's two cockpits is now closed and hunkering in disrepair. The faded raw wood sides of the building and wagon wheels beside the door inspire images of wild and woolly nights of music, dance, and the crowing of razor-heeled game birds. Jay's got some big-name bands in the sixties and seventies, including the western swing outfit Asleep At The Wheel. Couples would drift between the dance floor, the bar, and the cockpit out back.

Cormier's Cock Pit Rt. 93, 6 miles north of I-10.

Raymond Cormier is not only the operator of one of the largest cockpits in the Lafayette area, but also an ambassador for the sport. Unlike many pits which require memberships and season tickets, Cormier welcomes anyone who obeys the house rules against fighting and cameras in the pits, and is willing to pay the $6 to $10 entrance fee.

Cormier's is a place that will confirm some of your images of a cockpit, while dashing others. As you would perhaps expect, the joint is a little rough around the edges. A dimly-lit bar up front has a pool table, a country jukebox, and a bandstand where Raymond's daughter, Sheryl Cormier, used to play accordion. There is plenty of cigarette smoke, beer, and private wagering.

The pit itself is a well-lit, air-conditioned, and relatively clean (though primitive) little indoor stadium. On a fight night, you will find more couples flirting than guys duking it out. In fact, I have never seen any people fighting here. The crowd is about 40 percent couples, 40 percent cockfighters or breeders, and 20 percent men and women who come for some serious wagering. Cockfighting is surely not for everyone, but if you make up your mind to go see a cockfight, this is a safe, hospitable (though cockers are naturally suspicious of casual visitors), and comfortable place to do it. Head north from I-10 at Scott about 6 miles and look on the right. The bar is open most nights. Fights are held frequently between November and July. For more on cockfighting, refer to the index.

Duson

Duson is a town of 1400 that is 8 miles outside the Hub City, at the western edge of the Lafayette region. C. C. Duson was a real-estate agent of Scots-Irish extraction who worked for the railroad and was responsible for establishing numerous towns across the Cajun Prairie around the turn of the century. The main street in Duson is Avenue A, which crosses U.S. 90 and intersects Route 95 just south of I-10. You know you are out in the countryside when the local video store sells "Tasso on Buns." The main reason you are likely to get off the road here is to see the Saturday night dance at Harold's bar and eat crawfish at Thibodeaux's Restaurant across the street.

Thibodeaux's Cajun/Seafood. 207 North A St.

This is a full-service Cajun restaurant with very good boiled crawfish in season. The rest of the menu is hit and miss, but includes everything from catfish courtbouillon to pizza and chili dogs. They are open 7 days a week from 6 A.M. to 11 P.M. and on Friday and Saturday they are open 24 hours. (318) 873-3840.

Harold's Cajun Lounge/Dance Hall. North A St.

Directly across from Thibodeaux's, Harold's is a funky little bar, dance hall, and pool room. There is a Cajun band every Saturday at 8:30 P.M. For the past few years local entertainer Bill Pellcrin has provided the music. (318) 873-8932.

Shawn's Country Music/Lounge. U.S. 90 at North A St.

Shawn's has country bands every Sunday from 6 P.M. to 10 P.M. The first Sunday of each month, from 1 P.M. to 5 P.M., they serve free barbeque and cap it off with a Cajun or country band in the evening. (318) 873-4313.

Church Point

Church Point is about thirty minutes from Lafayette and 16 miles north of I-10 and Duson on Route 95. The town was originally known as Plaquemine Point; like many communities in South Louisiana, it bore the name of the closest body of water which, in this case, was Plaquemine Brule. Jesuits from Grand Coteau built a church here in the early 1800s and the settlement became known as Church Point. Although the town remained a small Prairie outpost through the War Between the States, it was a prominent gathering place for surrounding farmers on Sundays. With a population of 4500, Church Point is now a neat turn-of-the-century village and bastion of Cajun French culture and language. Among its famous sons are accordionists Iry Lejeune and Shirley and Alphee Bergeron. The town is the site of an annual *Courir du Mardi Gras* celebration and a springtime Buggy Festival. It is also the location of the bustling Sound Center music store and recording studio.

Sound Center 329 Main St. Church Point.

The Sound Center is home to Lanor Records and recording studio. Owner Lee Lavergne founded Lanor back in 1960 and is still recording and selling R & B, Soul, Cajun, Zydeco and Swamp Pop from the small store that adjoins his studio and home. He also has a good selection of records from the other regional labels, including some old stock that you won't find anywhere else. Lee works at the counter and can tell you about local recording artists like the great Iry Lejeune and Shirley Bergeron, while you preview the 45s you pick out on a record player in the showroom. If

Lee Lavergne at the Sound Center. (Photo by Macon Fry)

one of Lee's Lanor Recording artists, like Link Davis Jr. or Charles Mann, is in the studio, you may get a chance to meet the musicians themselves.

Among the treasures record collectors flock to the Sound Center for are "The Evil Dope," an anti-drug rap by Phil Phillips (famous for "Sea Of Love"), and tapes by South Louisiana Swamp Pop legend Charles Mann, who gave Lee his biggest hit with "Red Red Wine" back in the mid-sixties. Rockabilly fans keep buying the wild "Hot Hot Lips" by Ralph Prescott. Lee has kept nearly all of his old Lanor recordings in print but some of the more recent ones are worth checking out, too. For Zydeco, try the hysterical "She Kept Chewing Gum" by Donald Jacob, a song about a guy who's uptight because his woman won't spit out the double-bubble while they're making love (dedicated to "all you gum-chewing people out there"). Among the best new Lanor Cajun recordings is a tape by accordionist Donald Thibodeaux, who is the house musician at the Saturday morning broadcasts from Fred's Lounge. The Sound Center is open Monday through Saturday from 10 A.M. to 5 P.M. A mail-order list of Lee Lavergne's Lanor recordings is also available. (318) 684-2176.

Church Point Courir du Mardi Gras

The *Courir du Mardi Gras* is run early in Church Point, allowing participants and onlookers to enjoy Mamou's festivities (or New Orleans) on Tuesday. This is a super event for anyone interested in Cajun culture, food, and music. It is a heck of a party, too!

The whole family will be comfortable at the festivities here. Things can get a bit lively late in the day when everyone is tanked up and the riders have returned, but for the most part the Church Point run is a fascinating alternative to the crowded and boisterous celebration in Mamou.

All the participants mask and gather at 7 A.M., outside the Saddle Tramp Riders Club at 1036 E. Abbey. The Cajun band on the sound truck cranks up around 8, as horseback riders mill about the rodeo arena and other revelers board the flatbed trucks that will carry them to farms around the region. By 8:30 the procession is on its way. Once the riders have left, a couple of huge pots of gumbo are set to simmer and ladies of the community begin to arrive at the Saddle Tramp meeting hall with all manner of local goodies right from their home kitchens! A couple of radio stations broadcast from the hall over primitive remote kits, while everyone browses around and waits for the band to arrive.

The dance and food at the Saddle Tramp generally come

Mardi Gras riders, Church Point. (Courtesy of LA Office of Tourism)

together around 11 A.M. Admission is a paltry $2 and is good for the whole day. The food here is some of the best I have had at a small-town festival anywhere. Heaping bowls of gumbo are about $3 and the tasty home-baked sweets are almost free. As the day wears on the dance floor gets more crowded, but there is no crush. Everyone seems to know there are plenty of good times and good food to go around. At two o'clock, most folks leave the hall and line Main Street to watch the tired but jubilant (and drunk) riders return. The dance resumes when the procession arrives back at the Saddle Tramp with the playing of the traditional "Mardi Gras Song." (318) 684-5693.

Buggy Festival First weekend in June.

Considerably smaller in scope than the *Courir du Mardi Gras* celebration is the Church Point Buggy Festival. Old horsedrawn carriages restored by owners around the Prairie clop through town. There are carnival rides, Cajun food and music, and a parade on Sunday. For more information contact Jean Murphy at 810 S. Broadway, Church Point, Louisiana 70525. (318) 684-2739.

SOUTH OF LAFAYETTE

The road heading south from Lafayette Johnston Street (Route 167) is called the Old Abbeville Highway. This road follows the Vermilion River 15 miles down to the historic village of Abbeville, where it intersects Route 82, the Hug the Coast Highway. Once past the congested oil suburbs of Southside Lafayette, Route 167 passes quickly through the rice fields and cattle country of Vermilion Parish. You will see handsome riverside homes, small cabins, and lush fields.

Maurice

The first town heading south out of Lafayette on Johnston Street (Route 167) is Maurice. This little village of 550 is hardly a stop in the road (unless you catch a red light at the only traffic signal between Lafayette and Abbeville), but a couple of great food landmarks make it a worthy destination.

*Hebert's Specialty Meats Stuffed & Deboned Chickens. Rt. 167.

Lafayette is the southernmost outpost of Louisiana's "smoke belt." By the time you hit Maurice, just 12 miles south, you are in the province of fresh meats and stuffed fowl. Typical of the area,

Hebert's (which serves Lafayette's finest restaurants) sells only fresh meat—no boudin or smoked products. Here you will find lean pork, turkey or mixed sausage, marinated pork, seasoned ribs, and rolled round steak (all for under $2.50 a pound!). Hebert's specialty is the stuffed rabbit and chicken. Chickens are whole, deboned birds (a feat you will not want to try at home) stuffed with cornbread, shrimp & rice, or plain rice dressing. All of the dressings are superbly prepared. These birds are fantastic when slow cooked on the backyard grill or in the oven. I can't visit the Lafayette area without picking up a couple to bring home to roast on the Weber. Each bird will feed four or five and costs $8. Hebert's is open Monday through Saturday from 7:30 A.M. to 6:30 P.M. and Sundays until noon. (318) 893-5062.

*Soop's Restaurant Cajun/Down Home $-$$. Rt. 167.

Adjacent to the meat market run by their father and brother, Rachel Hebert and her six sisters prepare some of the tastiest Cajun food you will find anywhere. Lunch is my favorite meal here, as it often offers a chance to sample the stuffed chicken prepared fresh daily in the meat market next door. Lunch plates at Soop's include vegetables and two or three starches and rarely exceed $4. At dinner Soop's provides a rare opportunity to try game dishes like fried rabbit, chicken-fried quail, and the mouth-watering quail and sausage gumbo. All of the soups at Soop's are delicious. The crawfish bisque may be the best I have eaten and the seafood gumbo is laden with fresh crabmeat. Boiled crawfish here also deserve special mention. The mudbugs are perfectly cooked with a straightforward seasoning, and are a real value at $6.50 for 4 pounds. Soop's is open Monday through Thursday from 9 A.M. to 9 P.M., and Friday and Saturday until 10 P.M. They are located on Route 167, just fifteen minutes from Lafayette. (318) 893-2462.

Abbeville

Abbeville is a lovely village of 13,000 residents on the banks of the Vermilion River, just half an hour south of Lafayette and the same distance west of New Iberia. It is the seat of Vermilion Parish and center of the state's biggest cattle-producing region. In true South Louisiana style, however, the city's greatest reputation is culinary. Abbeville is home to two of the finest oyster bars anywhere, and a wonderfully rustic seafood patio. The town is noted for its two quaint downtown squares, which give it a distinctly Old World charm. The squares and historic center of Abbeville were laid out by the French priest Antoine Desire Megret, who founded the village and named it after his home in France in 1843. While Abbeville is beautiful year round, the best time to visit is in the fall and early winter when the city's famous oyster bars are open and the smoke from Steen's Syrup Mill flavors the air around St. Mary Magdalen and Courthouse Squares. It is a great first or last stop when driving the scenic Hug the Coast Highway (Route 82), which begins just south of town. Abbeville is small enough to see in less than a couple of hours, but it will take many return visits to sample all of the good food.

Abbeville Tourist Information Center 7507 Veterans Memorial Dr. (Route 14 Bypass).

Stop here to view the small exhibit of artifacts and photographs of parish life around the turn of the century. The center provides public restrooms, a parish map, and a street guide/walking tour to attractions in the old downtown area. The Visitors Center is staffed by volunteers and its hours are irregular. They are usually open Monday through Friday from 9:30 A.M. to 4 P.M. (318) 893-4264.

Attractions

Walking Tour of the Old Town Center
A map of downtown Abbeville attractions is available at the Visitors Center but is hardly necessary, as the area covers only about eight square blocks along the banks of the Vermilion River. Without any stops at the town's fine eateries, Abbeville may be toured on foot in forty-five minutes. Park near the Steen Syrup Mill (built in 1910) and stroll north around St. Mary Magdalen Square and Courthouse Square, which are surrounded by turn-of-the-century storefronts. A portrait of town founder Antoine Megret hangs in the courthouse. If you are lucky enough to arrive before ten, go straight to the Crescent Lunch Counter for some mouthwatering biscuits and jam. Walk south along the river to see the old cemetery and rice mills.

Steen's Syrup Mill 119 North Main St.
There used to be hundreds of syrup mills in Cajun Country. Many families made their own syrup at home by boiling the crushed cane from their fields. Today Steen's is the biggest remaining syrup mill and its strong but sweet product is a favorite topping for biscuits, corn bread, pancakes, and pain perdue (french toast)

Downtown Abbeville. (Courtesy of LA Office of Tourism)

throughout the region. The mill began operations in 1910 when a hard freeze threatened to destroy C. S. Steen's sugar crop before he could get it to the local refinery. He built the makeshift mill to save the crop. The mill has remained in the Steen family for the past seventy-five years and until recently offered plant tours. You can't get inside to see the operations up close anymore because you might slip, fall, and sue for a godzillion dollars, but during the fall huge trucks of cane can be seen unloading and the aroma of simmering sugar fills the air. Steen's is located just behind St. Mary Magdalen Square and Church Street.

Riviana Rice Mill Rue du Bas and 1st St.

Walk about five blocks south of the Steen's Mill on Main Street and, at Railroad Avenue, you will see the huge Riviana, Water Maid, and Mahatma Rice Mills. In late summer and early fall, trucks full of rice unload here and clouds of chaff rise from the refinery. Riviana was founded in the late 1800s and claims to be the "oldest existing mill in the state."

Godchaux Park S. Main St.

This little park is a good place for a picnic and to let the young 'uns unwind. There is playground equipment and benches. A sign on the grounds warns, "Prohibited: Gathering of persons which by nature, character, or size may forseeably disturb others." I assume that translates, "no hell-raisin'." The park is within walking distance of the downtown area on Main Street, about two blocks past the railroad tracks.

Food

I grew up near the Chesapeake Bay, have lived ten years in New Orleans, and have eaten East Coast and Gulf oysters. I still put the ones at Black's and the neighboring Dupuy's in a class by themselves. They arrive fresh daily from the wetlands between Vermilion and Grand Isle. Folks used to eating at New Orleans oyster bars may be disappointed that the oysters are not opened before their eyes at the bar, but all apprehension will fade when the tray arrives. These babies are so firm, so cold, and so clear they will send oyster lovers to nirvana. They are also perfectly shucked, with never a nick or speck of mud on the oyster meat, which sits in a brimming shell of unspilled oyster juice (or liquor, as it is called by oyster heads). I am not trying to be diplomatic, but both these places are great! Oyster fanatics may want to eat at both just to say they have eaten at the TWO best oyster bars in the world!

(Photo by Julie Posey)

*Dupuy's Seafood/Oysters $-$$. 108 S. Main St.

Dupuy's has been an Abbeville tradition for over a hundred years. Ninety-six years ago Joseph Dupuy sold shucked oysters in this same location on the banks of Bayou Vermilion for ten cents a dozen; the price dipped to five cents a dozen during the Second World War. The bivalves here are still an amazing inflation buster at $4 per salty dozen. I challenge anyone to find more perfect and more perfectly shucked oysters. They are served in a tiny, no-frills dining room on ice-laden trays with all the condiments. The room sports a wall of awards won by its famous oyster shuckers and a collection of newspaper clippings about the restaurant that date back to the early 1900s. Oysters are a cold-weather dish and the perfect accompaniment is a hearty bowl of Dupuy's delicious gumbo or oyster stew. Seafood po-boys are available for $4 and dinners for $5 to $10. Dupuy's always opens on the new moon in late August and closes in May. They are on the right after you cross the Vermilion Bridge, catty-corner to the church. Dupuy's is open Monday through Saturday from 11 A.M. to 9 P.M. Closed May through August. (318) 893-2336.

*Black's Oyster Bar Seafood/Oysters, $-$$. 319 Pere Megret St.

Black's is the newcomer on Abbeville's oyster scene, having only been around twenty-three years, but don't be surprised to see lines on Friday and Saturday nights. You can order any number of well-prepared seafood dishes (and even a burger or steak for the timid), but folks travel miles to eat the incredible bivalves! They arrive at your table or at the bar on a tray of ice with condiments for mixing your own cocktail sauce. They are so lovely that you may devour half a dozen before remembering to season them. A dozen of these epic morsels is only $3.75. If you are shy about raw seafood, Black's serves a knockout Chesapeake-style oyster chowder. Finely minced onion and celery are sauteed 'til limp, then the oysters, "oyster liquor," and milk are added and cooked just until the edges of each oyster begin to ruffle. Try Black's delicious fried seafood loaves for around $4. Spicy "Zydeco beans" (hot pickled snap beans) are served as a condiment on the bar and in the tasty Cajun Bloody Marys. Black's is a brick building with large windows overlooking St. Mary Magdalen Church. They are open Monday through Thursday from 10 A.M. until 9:30 P.M., and until 10 P.M. on Friday and Saturday. They are closed on Sundays and in the months May through August.

*Bertrand's Riverfront Restaurant Seafood/Cjun $$. 503 W. Port St.

Like town founder Antoine Megret, David Bertrand studied the priesthood before returning to his hometown of Abbeville. Now he preaches the gospel of great food. Grab a seat by the window overlooking the Vermilion River Bridge and start off with one of Bertrand's Bloody Marys. The mix for this drink (sold bottled at the register) includes horseradish, molasses, and plenty of pepper. The traditional celery stick is replaced by a hot pickled string bean. After the drink you will be ready for Bertrand's soups, salads, and appetizers (which make a meal by themselves). The house crab soup is made with a curry base and the gumbos are thick and rich with seafood stock and oyster liquor. Forego raw oysters in favor of "grilled" ones, which are actually pan fried in peanut oil until the thin crumb crust is gently toasted. Salads are attractive and come with a choice of artichoke vinaigrette, creamy cracked pepper, or spicy ranch dressings. French bread is baked daily on the premises. For dinner, pick from a selection of grilled fish and chicken entrees. Lunch is served Tuesday through Friday and Sunday, 11 A.M. to 2 P.M. Dinner hours are Monday through Thursday from 5:30 P.M. to 9:30 P.M. and Friday and Saturday until 10 P.M. Bertrand's is beside the Vermilion River Bridge in downtown Abbeville. (318) 898-0270.

Bertrand's Charity Street Local Fave, $. 400 Charity St.

Tired of fast-food franchises supplanting down-home eateries? Visit this former Kentucky Fried Chicken outlet turned blue-collar diner. If you are getting an early start on the day, Charity Street is the only place to get a good cup of coffee in Abbeville at 5 A.M. You can get two eggs with toast and bacon for a couple of bucks. Add a few cents for homemade biscuits. Three-egg omelets are under $3, unless you opt for the deluxe crawfish etouffée omelet for $3.75. This is just the meal to fortify before a full day on the Hug the Coast Highway or at nearby Live Oak Gardens. Bertrand's diner is located just east of Courthouse Square. They are open Monday through Saturday from 5 A.M. to 9:30 P.M. and Sunday until 1:30 P.M. (318) 898-9008.

★Hebert's Meat Market Specialty: Red boudin. Lafitte Rd.

Typical of the meat markets south of Lafayette, Hebert's specializes in fresh meat. One of the unusual items made here is Plantin, a well-seasoned pork sausage wrapped in a very thin veil of fat. According to Hebert, Plantin is often grilled, as it holds together well over the flame and bastes itself. Hebert's also sells both *Paunce* (stuffed calf stomach) and *Chaudin*, which is similar but made with pork stomach. Hebert's is one of few places I have found that carry the blood sausage, *boudin rouge*. This ready-to-eat delight is made with pork blood, giving the filling a more moist texture than beef blood. To get to Hebert's, turn north off of the Route 14 Bypass onto Route 338 (Lafitte Road) and look for the meat market about a mile down on the left. Hebert's is open Monday through Friday from 7 A.M. to 6 P.M., and Saturday until Noon. (318) 893-5688.

★Richard's Seafood Patio Boiled Seafood, $$. Rt. 355 S.

This is a classic boiling point. "Patio" is an oft-used term to describe the more rustic of South Louisiana's boiled seafood joints, and in this case, it is an appropriate one. The low-lying wood-frame structure with unadorned white wood walls, cement floors, and plastic-covered tables has all the ambiance of a front porch during a noisy family reunion. You won't find any tour buses down here, just folks from all over coastal Cajun Country who have come to sample the large, spicy crawfish. Getting to Richard's is half the fun, as it means driving down a narrow road along the lower reaches of the Vermilion River. Some diners arrive by boat and dock right in front of the restaurant. In typical boiling point fashion, the crawfish arrive piled on beer trays in steaming 3½-pound heaps, and the beer flows liberally.

Richard's is open (seasonally—mid-November through mid-June) seven days a week from 5 P.M. to 10:30 P.M. From Lafayette take Route 167 south. Follow the signs towards Route 14 business. Turn right on Route 335 before crossing the Vermilion River Bridge (S. Henry Street) and look for Richard's about 3 miles down on the right.

Music

★Levy's Place Zydeco dance hall. Lafitte Rd. (Rt. 338 N.)

Stumbling across a place like Levy's drove home the fact that it would be nearly impossible to compile a complete guide to the dance halls of Cajun Country. I was looking for Hebert's Meat Market on a Saturday afternoon when I saw the line of cars and heard the sound of an accordion coming from this white clapboard hall. I never made it to Hebert's that day, but got to sample their pork at what turned out to be a big *boucherie* and Zydeco dance. Ms. Lernest Levy greeted friends and neighbors while the rest of her family stirred the cracklins and roasted the pig. *Boucheries* are special events here, but at least once a month the Levys host a big Zydeco dance with a top-name band in the hall next to their house. Pool tables are pushed back and folks crowd the wood-plank floor at this wonderfully funky place. Call to see if there is a dance when you are in the area. From the Route 14

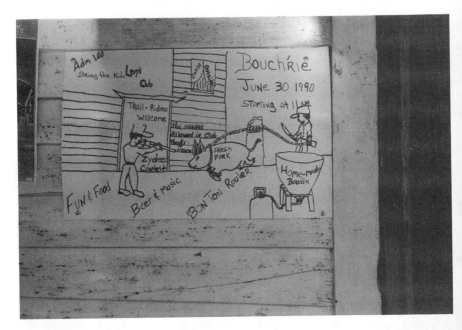

Levy's dance hall. (Photos by Macon Fry)

bypass (Veterans Memorial Drive) turn north onto Route 338 (Lafitte Road). Levy's is 2.5 miles ahead on the right. (318) 893-7834.

Vallot's Club Zydeco dance hall. 620 S. Miles St.

Vallot's is an old hall with a gritty feel. The neighborhood is a bit rough, but the music is excellent. East of Abbeville on Route 14 Business, turn south on Miles Street. Go five blocks and Vallot's is on the right (just past the railroad tracks). Call Thomas Vallot at (318) 893-9994 (club) or 898-1911 (home).

Ponderosa Lounge Zydeco dance hall. 811 Nugier Ave.

The Ponderosa is another Abbeville hall that is in a neighborhood that's a bit rough for the casual tourist, but the crowd here is older and more mellow than at Vallot's. In trying to find the place, people kept telling me, "It's over in the Sticks" or "cross tracks," two names often used to describe the neighborhood. The Ponderosa has been bringing the top names in Zydeco to Abbeville since 1980. Manager Black Collins says, "I don't allow no trouble-makin' youngsters. You gotta be twenty-one or over." Look for music here one weekend a month during the summer. Go hungry so you can try out the barbeque next door. Turn south off the Route 14 bypass between the Sonic and the Taco Bell, onto Alphonse Road. Take the first left onto Nugier Road. The Ponderosa is two blocks down. (318) 893-2376.

Festivals

French Market Festival First weekend in November. Downtown.

There are many carnival-type activities going on during the French Market Festival, but the main celebration is one of food. Among the unusual food events in past years were the preparation of a 5000-egg omelet (in a 12-foot skillet), and an appearance by the "Great Boudini." More prosaic, but with equally tasty results, are omelet-toss contests, guest chef demonstrations, and plenty of hot pancakes covered with Steen's Cane Syrup. The affair begins at about 9 A.M. each day. On Saturday, festivities run into the evening with a Cajun *fais do-do*. (318) 893-2491.

*Louisiana Cattle Festival First weekend in October.

Abbeville is the economic center of Vermilion, the state's most important cattle-raising parish, so this is a celebration with real regional roots. In addition to a street fair with carnival rides and candy apples, there is plenty of good Cajun food available in the street. On Friday and Saturday there are big Cajun dances. The main events are the Saturday morning cattle show and Sunday morning horse show. The horse show features rodeo events like barrel racing (in which riders guide their mounts at breakneck speed through a cloverleaf pattern of barrels) and reining. October is probably the best time to visit Abbeville. The syrup mill is flavoring the air and cold oysters are served at the local oyster bars. (318) 893-2491.

Recreation

★Clem's "Bush Track" Horse Racing N. Lafitte Rd. (Rt. 338 N.)
    Clem's is carrying on an almost lost tradition in Cajun Country. Before the opening of Evangeline Downs and Delta Downs in the sixties, horse racing was a popular pastime at informal "bush" tracks throughout Cajun Country. Many great Louisiana jockeys cut their teeth on the rugged bush circuit. The Sunday morning races at Clem's have been a family tradition for decades. There is a $2 admission and races are run from 8 A.M. to 2 P.M. every Sunday. Turn north off of the Route 14 bypass onto Route 338 (Lafitte Road). The track is across from Hebert's Meat Market, about a mile down on the right. (318) 893-8160.

Lodging

Heritage Motor Inn 2115 Charity St., $32 to $35 double. (318) 893-6420.

Sunbelt Lodge Motel 1903 Veterans Memorial Dr., $37 to $41 double. (318) 898-1453.

Coulee Kinney Campground Rt. 14 Business (Charity St.) West.
    This scruffy little park operated by the city offers no-frills camping at a low price. There are no bathrooms, toilets, or dumping stations. There are 52 sites with water and electric hook-ups. Camping costs $4 a night. Go west on Route 14 Business (Charity Street) .7 miles from the Bayou Vermilion Bridge (twenty feet beyond Fouche Road) and take a left onto a dirt road. A half mile down the unmarked dirt road you will see a sign for the campground. (318) 893-8550.

Erath

There is not very much to this town of 2,250 stretching about ten blocks along Route 14. Erath is, however, home to D. L.

Menard, Cajun music's biggest living star, and the site of a great old-time Cajun dance hall.

Attractions

D. L. Menard's Chair Factory Rt. 331 S.

D. L. (Doris Lee) Menard is Cajun music's biggest star and most distinctive voice. In the 1960s D. L. recorded "The Back Door," one of the great Cajun anthems of all time. It is not D.L.'s hit recordings, however, that have won him fans around the world. Menard's popularity is born of charisma and love of life that busts through every time he smiles (which is most of the time).

D. L. doesn't waste much time when he gets back from an international tour, getting right back to making chairs in the shop beside his home in Erath. Menard explains that he decided to build chairs one day when he needed something to sit on. He works alone stacking lumber, turning wood on the lathe, and constructing sturdy platform and ladder-back rockers and dining chairs. When I suggested listing the D. L. Menard Chair Factory in a "crafts" section of this book, he protested, "This is not a craft but a factory!" Whatever you call them, D. L.'s chairs are built with a care and precision that defies their price (around $40 for a platform rocker). The joy of stopping at D. L.'s factory to order a chair and chatting with the "Cajun Hank Williams" is worth much more than the price of a chair. Be sure and get D. L. to sign your chair. Contact D. L. before visiting by writing to him at Route 1, Box 9, Erath, Louisiana 70533, or stop by and visit the factory on Route 331, a couple of miles south of Erath.

Food

Big John's Seafood Patio Boiled Seafood, $$. Broadview Rd.

This is a neat place to eat if you are planning on catching music at one of Erath's nightspots and don't feel like driving over to Abbeville. Big John's is an old-style wood-frame boiling point located literally at the end of the road! The crawfish here are not the largest, but are clean and tender. They are open from January until June daily, from 5 to 10 P.M. Take Route 14 to Erath. Go north on Route 339. Make a left on Broadview and follow it to the end.

D. L. Menard, the "Cajun Hank Williams." (Photo by Julie Posner)

Smiley's Bayou Club. (Photo by Julie Posner)

Music

The Wild Wild West Rt. 339 just north of Rt. 14.

Things can get a bit "wild" at this small dance hall and bar, especially when "oldies" bands play on Friday and Saturday. A more reserved crowd shows up for Cajun music on Sundays from 6 P.M. to 10 P.M. (318) 937-4325.

★Smiley's Bayou Club Cajun dance hall. Rt. 14, Erath.

This is the club where Erath native D. L. Menard (the "Cajun Hank Williams") got his start playing guitar and singing with Badeaux and the Louisiana Aces. Smiley's has been around for more than fifty years and attracts a lot of old-timers to their Friday, Saturday, and Sunday afternoon dances. Behind a cinderblock front, Smiley's is all wood, from the dance floor to the tables, chairs, plank bar, and railing around the bandstand. Ceiling fans tick overhead while well-dressed older couples dominate the dance floor. It is free to get inside but costs $3 (for men) to dance. Pay the waitress the dance fee and she will staple a red ticket to your collar. The dance floor rules are explained on a sign over the band: "No one under 18 allowed. No shorts permitted. No same-sex dancing." There is a Cajun jam session on Fridays from 7:30 "until everyone has played," Cajun-country music on Saturdays from 9 P.M. to 1 A.M., and an old-time Cajun band on Sunday from 2 P.M. to 6 P.M. Smiley's is located in the business strip on Route 14 in the center of Erath.

Delcambre

Delcambre (pronounced "DEL-come") is French for "community of meadows." This village of 2000 located on Route 14 at the edge of Iberia Parish and Teche Country (twenty minutes west of New Iberia and forty-five minutes south of Lafayette), is home to one of the region's most productive shrimp fleets. The 200 shrimp boats docked beside the Delcambre Canal bring in over $14 million of shrimp annually. The shrimpers are honored and the shrimp fleet blessed each year at the August Shrimp Festival.

Attractions

Shrimp Boat Landing

For a pleasant break from driving, and a look at the Delcambre shrimp fleet from up close, stop at the covered picnic area and fisherman's wharf just south of Route 14.

Blessing of the Delcambre shrimp fleet. (Courtesy of LA Office of Tourism)

Shrimp Festival

The year 1990 was the 40th anniversary of the annual Delcambre Shrimp Festival. The four-day event, held in mid-August, is pretty typical of small-town fairs around the country, with carnival rides and carnival type food. On Friday night, the Shrimp Queen is coronated and a big French dance is held. The highlight comes on Sunday when the parish priest holds mass at the local community center before leading a procession to the dockside for the "Blessing of the Fleet" at 10:30 A.M. The priest boards a decorated shrimpboat, which carries him alongside the fleet in the harbor so that he may perform the rites. This is a colorful little festival, but the mid-August heat can be suffocating.

*Live Oak Gardens, Jefferson Island 15 minutes from Delcambre.

See South of New Iberia in the Teche Country chapter for complete details and directions.

Music

Smiley's Bon Ami (formerly The Red Carpet). Rt. 14.

Located on the moist meadow between Erath and Delcambre, this big dance hall seems to be at the very edge of civilization, but during their Saturday Country/Swamp-Pop dances and Sunday French dances, the parking lot is packed beyond imagination. I don't know where the people come from, but they love to get dressed up and go out to dance.

Lodging

Uncle U Campground Rt. 89 north of Delcambre.

This tiny private campground has electric hook-ups, but no showers or restrooms. A cottage is available for rent for $50. Uncle U is located 1 mile north of Route 14 on Route 89 (on the left). $7 per night, camp rental $50. Call Euda or Clite at (318) 685-4486.

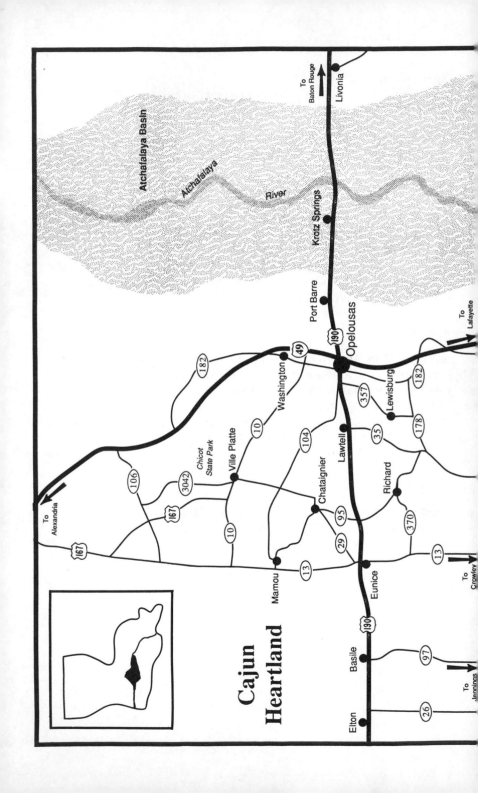

14

Cajun Heartland

If food and music are used as a cultural barometer, the area at the northern apex of Cajun Country has every right to the title "Cajun Cultural Heartland" bestowed upon it by folklorist Alan Lomax. One has only to visit an old dance hall like Borque's or Slim's Y-Ki-Ki, or pry his or her eyes open at the live early-morning radio broadcasts from Fred's or Dup's lounges, to appreciate how integral music is to life on the northern Prairie.

The Cajun Heartland is a roughly triangle-shaped region defined by the richness of its culture more than distinct geographic boundaries. It includes most of St. Landry and Evangeline Parish at the top of the Acadiana triangle, with U.S. 190 (the Acadiana Trail) forming its southern base. The land here reaches such heavenly elevations as sixty to seventy feet above sea level, but is generally flat. It rolls out in a majestic expanse of silver crawfish ponds and green rice and soybean fields, and is dotted with little railroad and cow towns.

The main east-west route through the region is U.S. 190, which begins in Port Allen just across the Mississippi River from Baton Rouge and enters Cajun Country at Bayou Gross Tete in Livonia. From Livonia the Trail carries travelers over the Morganza Spillway and Atchafalaya River into the historic town of Opelousas, where it intersects Interstate 49, the primary north-south highway in the state. Like the Old Spanish Trail to the south, this has been a major avenue of commerce and land transportation since the Indians used it as a footpath, but owes most of its character today to the Missouri Pacific rail line that was built along its course at the turn of the century.

BATON ROUGE TO OPELOUSAS

The portion of U.S. 190 which extends from Baton Rouge to Opelousas is the gateway to the Cajun Heartland. For over thirty

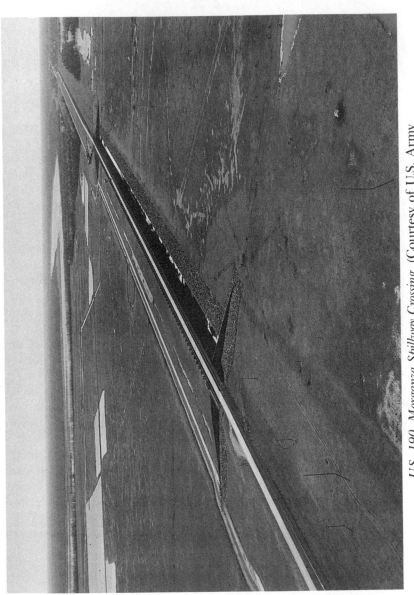

U.S. 190, Morganza Spillway Crossing. (Courtesy of U.S. Army Corps of Engineers)

years, until the Atchafalaya Throughway on Interstate 10 was completed in the 1970s, this was the main route for motorists traveling between Baton Rouge and Cajun Country. Were it not for dramatic elevated crossings at the Morganza and Atchafalaya floodways, this stretch of highway would resemble any number of old thoroughfares abandoned with the completion of interstate highways. There are lonely truckers' motels and Art-Deco-style white tile gas stations, many now being reclaimed by vines and brambles.

Livonia

Located 17 miles west of Baton Rouge on U.S. 190 on the banks of Bayou Grosse Tete (French for "big head") at the junction of Route 77, Livonia has a population of about 600 and one of the best eateries in the state! I often get off the Interstate and drive north on scenic Route 77 when traveling between Lafayette and New Orleans just so I can stop for a meal at Joe's.

*Joe's "Dreyfus Store" Restaurant Cajun/Creole, $ to $$. Rt. 77.
This eatery is the best reason to travel U.S. 190 between Baton Rouge and Cajun Country. People come from all over the state to sample the recipes Joe Major perfected while working as a chef at New Orleans' prestigious Petroleum Club. Major offers everything from fried fish and po-boys to stuffed quail and catfish etouffée for under $11. All of the entrees come with a potato, vegetable, and hot french bread. The fancier preparations are as good as anything served in New Orleans' high-priced eateries, but Chef Major shines on country dishes like turkey pot pie with flaky homemade crust and po-boys with home fries.

The menu changes daily, but always has a batch of regional favorites like roasted cornish game hen stuffed with cornbread dressing. Piquant corn and shrimp soup, oysters Bienville, and a slew of other appetizers are reverently prepared. I dream about Major's homemade white boudin smeared with pepper jelly. Top off the tank with sensual Creme Cafe Caramel, a custard topped with whipped cream and caramel sauce. Joe's is open Tuesday through Sunday from 11 A.M. to 2 P.M. for lunch and Tuesday through Saturday from 5 P.M. to 9 P.M. for dinner. They are .3 miles south of U.S. 190 on Route 77 in Livonia. From I-10 exit at Route 77 north. (504) 637-2625.

Morganza Spillway

Eight miles west of Livonia, U.S. 190 crosses the lower guide levee of the Morganza Spillway. The spillway is one of several mammoth water-control projects initiated by the Corps of Engineers following the disastrous flood of 1927. At U.S. 190 there is a five-mile-wide swath of farmland that abuts the Atchafalaya River levee on the southwest and the Mississippi River on the northeast. When the Mississippi threatens to exceed its banks, the Corps of Engineers opens floodgates at the Mississippi and allows the turbid river water to pour into the Atchafalaya Basin. Crossing the great expanses of cultivated land on the 5-mile-long overpass, imagine the scene in 1973 when the gates were opened and this verdant expanse was covered with a sheet of churning Mississippi River water. Continuing west on U.S. 190, the road crosses the Atchafalaya River Bridge (constructed by Huey Long in 1934) and drops down into the town of *Krotz Springs*, a small fishing village and notorious speed trap located squarely within the West Atchafalaya Spillway (consult the index for more information on the Atchafalaya and flood-control structures).

Port Barre

Twenty miles west of the Atchafalaya River and 4 miles east of Opelousas is the town of Port Barre (pronounced "Port Barry"). The town is best known as the "Birthplace of Bayou Teche," which springs from a brief confluence of Bayous Courtableau (cuh-tah-bluh) and Wauksha. Route 103 crosses U.S. 190 here, offering an opportunity to follow the bayou north to historic Washington (*see* index) or south through the old Creole settlement of Leonville and on to Breaux Bridge.

Birth of The Teche Park U.S. 190.

A historical marker and small picnic area on a bluff overlooking the black waters of the bayou are located on the north side of U.S. 190 on the east end of town.

Roy's Fine Foods Cajun/Down Home, $. U.S. 190.

Located on the strip in Port Barre, this place has the same neon-and-fifties facade that it sported when Route 190 was the fastest way to get from Lafayette to Baton Rouge. Although cook Wilson LeBlanc has only been at Roy's five years, he has plenty of experience serving customers on the Acadiana Trail. LeBlanc worked for thirty-eight years dishing up plate lunches at the popular Little Capitol truck stop (shaped like a miniature version of the phallic landmark in Baton Rouge) before it blew up in a natural gas explosion in 1986. Some daily specials include crawfish etouffée smothered in onion and thickened with butter, sausage Creole, and smothered sevin steak. Plate lunches come with corn bread, rice, dessert (mix-cake), and a choice of vegetables (corn *maque choux* and smothered cabbage are recommended). Roy's is open daily from 5 A.M. to 2 P.M., and 5 P.M. to 10 P.M.

Opelousas

Located twenty miles north of Lafayette and fifty-six miles west of Baton Rouge at the crossroads of Intrastate 49 and U.S. 190,

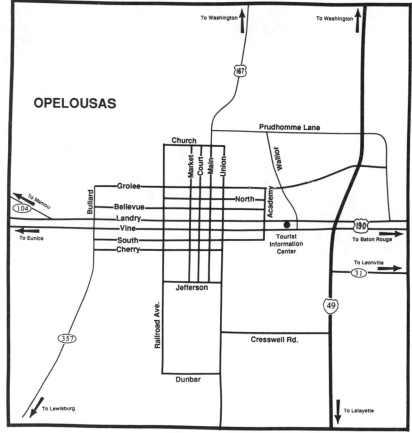

Opelousas. (St. Landry Tourist Commission)

Site of Clyde Barrow's last shave. (Photo by Julie Posner)

Opelousas (population 19,000) is the seat of St. Landry Parish, and the largest town and main economic center in the Cajun Heartland. Opelousas (pronounced op-uh-LOO-sus) calls itself the Yam Capital of Louisiana for the luscious golden-orange sweet potatoes grown in the surrounding fields. Each year there is a Yam Festival (or Yambilee, as it is called) featuring performances by Cajun and Zydeco bands and a local group called the Yamettes. Opelousas's biggest cultural attractions are its Zydeco dance halls. While most residents are descendents of the Acadians, the city is a cultural capital for the large Creole population of St. Landry Parish. It is the birthplace of the late Zydeco King, Clifton Chenier, and home to colorful Slim's Y Ki Ki, one of the best-known Zydeco dance halls in the state. It is also the ancestral home of world-famous chef Paul Prudhomme.

Opelousas, the third oldest city in Louisiana, is located on a bluff seventy-five feet above sea level (a veritable mountain in these parts!). Founded as a French trading post in 1720, it functioned as a marketplace for *courier des bois* (French traders and trappers). In 1769 a detachment of Spanish soldiers was stationed here to defend travelers between New Orleans and Nagidoches and the settlement became known as El Poste de Opelousas, deriving its name from the local Indian tribe. When the first Acadian immigrants arrived in the late eighteenth century the post was a burgeoning trade center where whiskey and guns were traded for furs and skins and three-fourths of the population spoke French. In 1803, when the Louisiana Purchase was transacted, Opelousas was named the seat of St. Landry Parish government and the town became a center for commerce in cotton, cattle, and later rice. A Methodist minister who moved to Opelousas from New Orleans complained in a letter dated 1803, "I have great difficulties in this country as there are no laws to suppress vice of any kind; so that the Sabbath is spent in frolicking and gambling."

Although no longer a wide-open frontier town, Opelousas still has its share of frolicking, with Saturday morning Cajun dances, Friday night Zydeco blowouts, and several fairs like the Yambilee Festival, St. Landry Parish Heritage Festival, and nearby Zydeco Festival, which features a full day of performances by all the top bands. It is the only town north of Lafayette in Acadiana with a variety of nice and budget-priced accommodations.

Attractions

The Jim Bowie Museum and Visitors Center U.S. 190 E., Opelousas. This tourist information center greets travelers on the east edge of town. The first thing you are likely to notice is the tottering farmhouse that once belonged to a "free woman of color" in Prairie Ronde. The house, now open to the public, is partially restored and its billowing sides and roller coaster floor resemble the fun house at an amusement park. Adjacent is an Acadian-style house which contains an information desk and the Jim Bowie Museum. At the information counter ask for the brochure which outlines a walking tour of historic Opelousas.

It is odd that this city, with its rich Spanish, French, Cajun, and distinctive Creole heritage, has claimed Jim Bowie as its favorite son, especially since it is unclear whether he actually spent much time there. Land records show members of the Bowie family arriving in the area in the early 1800s (when Bowie was not yet 10). There is a historical marker on Route 182 (Union Street) just south of town at the site where the Bowie family plantation stood. The collection of Bowie knives, artifacts, and news clippings housed in the Jim Bowie Museum gives an interesting glimpse of one of America's great frontier heroes. The Visitors Center and museum are open from 8 A.M. to 4 P.M. daily. (318) 948-6263 or 1-800-424-5442.

Historic District Walking Tour (Map available at Visitors Center).

U.S. 190, the main street in Opelousas, splits as it enters the city, with St. Landry Street becoming the primary westbound route and Vine Street handling eastbound traffic. There is plenty of free and inexpensive street parking in the downtown area near the courthouse, where the walking tour of historic Opelousas begins. Whether you walk or drive, this tour can be easily managed in less than two hours. Although there are many historic homes on the tour (none of which are presently open to the public), the highlights are the old commercial establishments and public buildings around Courthouse Square.

Across from the Deco-style *St. Landry Courthouse* is the *"New" Rexall Drug Store* (built about 1905), which still has racks of 1950s postcards of Opelousas street scenes for a dime, and a great selection of dust-covered vintage "Cool Ray" sunglasses.

Around the corner on St. Landry Street is the old *Shute Building* (vacant and for sale on my last visit), which housed the Star Barbershop. This is the site where Clyde Barrow, of the notorious outlaw gang Bonnie and Clyde, allegedly got his last shave (a close one?) before being gunned down two days later in an ambush on a dusty road in northern Louisiana's Bienville Parish.

Just a couple of blocks west of the Courthouse on Main Street is the *Firemen's Museum*. The museum occupies one of the bays in the old Opelousas Fire Hall. Here you will find a mule-drawn fire wagon, restored hook-and-ladder truck, and a roomful of antique firefighting paraphernalia. Don't wait for a guided tour; the two times I passed by, the collection was open but unattended. Located on the corner of Bellevue and Main and open daily.

No tour or even cursory visit to downtown Opelousas is complete without a stop at the *Palace Cafe* on the corner of St. Landry and Market. This cafe was founded over sixty years ago and is the oldest restaurant in Opelousas. The best reason for stopping at the Palace Cafe is not its history but the homemade shakes, onion rings, and blue-plate or sandwich specials (*see* review in Food section).

Michel Prudhomme Home 1152 Prudhomme Circle.

The Michel Prudhomme Home (formerly Ringrose Plantation) is not on the walking tour but is only a couple of miles from downtown. This is the oldest building in Opelousas, a French Colonial plantation built in the early nineteenth century by an ancestor of Louisiana's most famous chef, Paul Prudhomme. Some of the older residents of Opelousas can remember playing in the abandoned house as children and there are stories of buried cash being found by them on the plantation grounds. The home is now being managed by the Preservationists of Saint Landry Parish, who offer tours. Take Route 167 north from Landry (U.S. 190). Turn right on Prudhomme Street and left at Prudhomme Circle. Admission fee is $3, which goes towards maintenance and restoration efforts. (318) 942-2683.

Savoie's Sausage & Food Products, Inc. Rt. 742, southeast of Opelousas.

Savoie's has one of the best "plant tours" in Acadiana, provided of course that you are not shy about raw meat. The wood-frame Savoie's Grocery tells the story of Eula Savoie's entry into business back in 1949, but belies the size of the sausage, sauce, and seasoning factory out back. Mrs. Savoie guides visitors through the spice mixing room, roux-making area, and sausage-stuffing assembly line (which turns out over 10,000 pounds a day) before showing off the high-tech smokehouse. After the tour you can sit at an enameled table in the store and eat smoked sausage on a stick. It is important to go through with the sausage-eating part of the tour because seeing sausage made is a bit like falling off a motorcycle. If you are ever going to do it again it is a good idea to pick up and begin right away. Savoie's is open Monday through Saturday from 7 A.M. to 5 P.M. Tours can be arranged between 9 and 2 Monday through Friday, but the best time to get there is in the morning. To get to Savoie's, go east on U.S. 190 and turn right after crossing under I-49 onto Frontage Road. Go a couple of miles and turn left on Route 31. Go 1.5 miles to the fork and stay to the left onto Route 742. Savoie's is 3 miles farther. Call before stopping by for a tour. (318) 942-7241.

Tony Chachere's Creole Foods 533 North Lombard.

This small factory makes some of the state's most popular seasoning mixes and barbeque sauces. Tours are offered to individuals and groups who call in advance. There isn't a lot to see, but the smells range from delectable to sinus-opening and there is an opportunity to buy products from this respected Opelousas businessman and cook right off the assembly line. The factory is located near the downtown area at 533 North Lombard. Call in advance. (318) 948-4691.

Runyon Products, Inc. Rt. 357, south of Opelousas.

The most interesting factory tour for the musically inclined is the workshop for Santy Runyon's Runyon Products, Inc. Runyon is an acclaimed musical and technical genius who has been manufacturing mouthpieces for horns and woodwinds since the early forties. Art Pepper, Ernie Shaw, and Harry James are just a few of the luminaries who have endorsed his handiwork. Runyon's creations have enabled musicians to get previously unavailable tones and volume from their instruments. In addition to producing 8000 to 10,000 mouthpieces a month, octogenarian Runyon manufactures a slew of devices from neck straps to key raisers that help musicians get the most from their horns. The workshop at Runyon's is as amazing for its variety of custom-made machines that mold and cut plastics and metal as it is for its selection of specialized products. This cottage industry is a sax-man's dream. Runyon Products, Inc. is located on Highway 357 one half mile south of U.S. 190 on the right-hand side (leaving town). Call (318) 948-6252 to arrange for a visit.

Grand Coteau I-49, 10 miles south of Opelousas.

An idyllic village a few miles south of Opelousas. *See* Central Cajun Country chapter, North of Lafayette section.

Shopping

Antique Attic Judson Walsh exit, three miles south of Opelousas.

Festivals

*"Here's the Beef" Festival Late April. Yambilee Ag-Arena. U.S. 190.

A wall of smoke greets festival-goers at the door to the Yambilee Agricultural Arena. Somewhere behind the smoke a band is playing and people are dancing, but your sinuses will tell you right away that this is a barbeque blowout. You fans of mouthwatering red sauce, crusty ribs, and smoky-tender brisket will love this hoedown. The festival, sponsored by the St. Landry Cattlemen's Association, is only a couple of years old, but is shaping up to be a big event on the national barbeque calendar. No admission is charged, but beers and BBQ are sold at dozens of pits scattered across the dirt-floored arena. The festival grounds are directly behind the Opelousas Yamatorium, on U.S. 190 in the west end of town. Call the Chamber of Commerce to get an exact date for the festivities. (318) 942-2683.

Yambilee Festival Last weekend in October. Yamatorium. U.S. 90 W.

The Yambilee is the biggest and oldest harvest festival in St. Landry Parish. It features yam recipe and cooking contests, and plenty of typical carnival-type foods. Bands perform and there is an amusement midway outside the festival hall. (318) 942-2683.

*St. Landry Heritage Festival 2nd or 3rd week in May.

The St. Landry Heritage Festival is the kind of celebration that you can plan a whole trip around. The towns of Opelousas, Eunice, and Washington host dozens of events celebrating the food, muswhile dashing others. As you would perhaps expect, the joint is a little rough around the edges. A dimly-lit bar up front has a guest chefs at local restaurants. Thanks to native son Chef Paul Prudhomme, chefs from around the world come to share ideas with local cooks and to share their food with the general public. Ten bucks buys admission to an all-you-can-taste food sampling where local cooks and visiting chefs dish out their best stuff. Among the locals you will find skilled amateurs whipping up regional specialties that seldom find their way to restaurant tables.

During the weekend there is a dance in Opelousas and a number of old homes in Opelousas and Washington are open to public tours. Eunice hosts a Prairie Wildflower Festival with walking tours at various sites where scraps of virgin prairie still sport an abundance of wild blossoms. For information call 1-800-542-5442.

Food

Country Meat Block 1618 South Union (Rt. 182 south).

Whether you are looking for the best boudin in Opelousas, tasty plate lunches, or custom-cut meats, try Kelly Cormier's market. Cormier's boudin is made with large pieces of Boston butt pork, which has been marinated, cooked, and then mixed with rice. It is mildly seasoned with a good meaty flavor. Cormier makes his andouille sausage like people on the Prairie have been doing it for years, with chopped, smoked hog chitterlings (not the lean pork used around LaPlace). Cormier learned how to cut meat during thirteen years at a Church Point slaughterhouse, and he dispenses cooking tips that are worth even more than his steaks. The proof of his cooking advice is found next door at the Country Meatblock Diner, where plate lunches of barbecued beef are recommended on Thursday. If you need something to cool down the taste buds or settle down a pack of restless young 'uns, Kelly also has a snowball window! The meat market is open Monday through Friday from 7 A.M. to 5:30 P.M. and on Saturday from 8 A.M. to 1 P.M. From U.S. 190, head south on Union Street (Route 182) about 2 miles. (318) 948-4170.

*The Palace Cafe Local Fave, $ to $$. 167 W. Landry (U.S. 190).

This little diner built in 1954 is an essential stop on any visit to the Opelousas area, even if it's just to sit at the counter and down a cold milkshake created in an antique Hamilton Beach blender. After over sixty years in business, The Palace is the oldest restaurant in Opelousas and the hands-down favorite among the Courthouse Square crowd, who flock there for Pete Doucas' (Mr. Pete, as everyone calls him) fried chicken salad and homemade baklava. The salad is a cool combination of greens and tender chicken, well-tossed in a light mayonnaise dressing and served on an oval dinner plate. Order a side of thin and crisp onion rings with your salad. Try the smoked sausage with rice and gravy, or calf's liver smothered in onions. At lunch (the best time to eat here), these and a selection of sandwiches are served with a choice of three vegetables for under $5. Wednesday's special is well-seasoned roast pork with rice and gravy, cornbread and dressing, and candied yams. Some good! The Palace is located at the corner of Market and Landry. They are open Monday through Saturday from 6 A.M. to 9 P.M. On Sunday they open at 7 A.M. (318) 942-2142.

Soileau's Dinner Club Cajun/Creole, $$-$$$. 1620 North Main St.

Soileau's has been in business on North Main Street for over fifty years. The best bet here is to order simple dishes. That means try the huge fried fresh Gulf shrimp ($11 a dozen) and U.S. Choice steaks ($11-$16). Most entrees come with salad and a choice of potatoes. The favorite of locals, who call in orders by the dozen each day, is the stuffed Idaho baked potato, filled with smoked sausage and cheese. Avoid the stuffed and sauce-smothered fish. For lunch or an economical dinner, order the shrimp po-boy, packed with six of the same jumbo shrimp that come on the dinner plate ($6). To get there, head north on Route 167, which joins Main Street on the north edge of town. Soileau's is open Sunday through Thursday from 11 A.M. to 10 P.M. and on Friday and Saturday until 11 P.M. (318) 942-2985.

Toby's Cajun/Creole, $ (lunch) or $$ (dinner). Rt. 182 S., Opelousas.

An Opelousas landmark for thirty years, Toby's is located in the hilly horse country on the southern edge of town and has the ambience of a private country club. The first things to catch my eye on the lengthy menu were the Creole Baked Duck and Pot Roasted Quail served with rice dressing, green beans, and tossed salad. Skip the fish topped with combinations of shrimp, crabmeat, and just about everything else and try one of these more traditional dishes. My favorite meal is the Saturday barbeque plate of pork steak or chicken with slaw, dirty rice, and a roll. You can eat the barbeque there, get it to go, or take it into the lounge. There is also live music on Wednesday through Saturday nights (*see* music listings below). Toby's is 3.5 miles south of U.S. 190 on Old Sunset Highway (Route 182 south). They are open Monday through Saturday from 8 A.M. to midnight. (318) 948-7787.

Music

Opelousas and the surrounding area were a popular settling point for former slaves, free men of color, and other French-speaking black people during the late eighteenth and early nineteenth centuries. The present-day descendants of these early settlers, who call themselves Creoles, have made the region a veritable Mecca for Zydeco music enthusiasts. Not only is Opelousas the birthplace of Zydeco's best-known practitioner, the late Clifton Chenier, but the area is home to C.R.E.O.L.E., Inc. (an organization promoting Creole culture and music), the annual Zydeco Festival, and two of South Louisiana's most venerated old Zydeco dance halls. A short drive southwest to Lewisburg uncovers two fantastic old Cajun dance halls.

*Slim's Y-Ki-Ki Zydeco dance hall. Rt. 167 N.

Slim's has been one of the most popular Zydeco dance halls in the state for forty years, attracting the top bands and visitors from around the world. Slim (Arnold Gradney) opened the club back in 1947, and now runs it with the help of his son Tony. It is a place that puts out the welcome mat regardless of race or age. The dance floor, which cuts a wide swath between the bar and stage, is the center of attention. There is generally more competition for space on the floor than at tables, but it is wise to arrive by 9:30 or 10 if you want a seat. The choice seats are at the end of the club opposite the door, where the huge airplane propeller-size fans that cool the place manage to move a little air. Beer and liquor are available at the bar, but the most popular drink configuration is a pint bottle of liquor, a bowl of ice, and some set-ups. The crowd at Slim's tends to be older, well dressed, and regular, with many of the same couples showing up weekend after weekend. Slim's is on Route 167 (Main Street) in the north end of town. Dances are held most weekends on either Friday or Saturday. Admission is $4 to $6. (318) 942-9980.

*Richard's Club Zydeco dance hall. U.S. 190 W., Lawtell, La.

Richard's joins Slim's Y-Ki-Ki as a true landmark on the Zydeco circuit. This rugged old place has been in business over forty years. Prior to establishing itself as a Zydeco hall, it was a major stopping point on the Chitlin' Circuit, featuring some of the big names in R&B. Richard's has gotten a lot of publicity since two albums featuring Boozoo Chavis and John Delafose were recorded there in recent years. The ambience in the tattered wood-frame building is even more homey than Slim's and the crowd is a bit younger. They are used to plenty of visitors here; in fact, owner Kelvin Richard saw me jotting down notes on a recent visit and asked if I was with the "film crew" from England! Like Slim's, you will find some of the best names in Zydeco here. Richard's is actually located on U.S. 190 just west of Opelousas in Lawtell. Dances are held most weekends on Fridays and/or Saturdays. For information call Mr. Kelvin Richard at (318) 543-6596 (home).

Offshore Lounge Zydeco dance hall. Just off U.S. 190, Lawtell.

Popular Zydeco accordionist and bandleader Roy Carrier runs this smaller wood-frame dance hall and lives in the adjacent trailer, and his son Chubby is a frequent performer. There is a Zydeco jam every Thursday and dances on some weekends. This location is a bit tricky, especially when the hand-lettered sign that marks the turnoff from U.S. 190 has been blown over, but it is just off the highway. Heading west on U.S. 190 into Lawtell, go a half mile past the point where east- and westbound lanes split and make a right. This road is not marked, so check your odometer. Cross the railroad tracks and the red wood hall will appear in front of you. (318) 543-9996.

Toby's Little Lodge Lounge Cajun dance & dine. Rt. 182 S.

There is live Cajun music on Thursday nights at 9 P.M. Soul, Country and oldies bands play on Wednesday, Friday, and Saturday nights. Look for Little Bob and the Lollipops to be appearing one night a week. (318) 948-7787. You can find good eats at the neighboring Toby's Little Lodge Restaurant.

*Borque's Cajun dance hall. Lewisburg, La.

Drive 9 miles into the farm country south of Opelousas and on a narrow blacktop in the hamlet of Lewisburg you will find one of the most picturesque Cajun dance halls in Acadiana. Visiting Borque's is a bit like time travel. You won't find any tour buses in the tiny gravel parking lot, where the cry of a fiddle blends with the sounds of crickets and cicadas. You enter from a little wooden porch into the bar area, where there is a pool table and two card tables. The bar has two large windows and a door opening into the dance hall. In the old style, it is free to watch from the bar, but you will have to drop a dollar to get in and dance. The dance floor heaves as couples waltz and two-step to the puff of an accordion. Borque's has Cajun music every Saturday from 9 P.M. to 1 A.M. and every Sunday from 5 P.M. to 9 P.M. Go south towards Church Point on Route 357 (Old Lewisburg Road) for about 8 miles. At Weston's Grocery turn right onto Route 759. At the *T* in the road turn right. Borque's will be .2 miles farther, nestled among pine trees on the left (a total of .4 miles from Weston's Grocery). (318) 948-9904.

*Guidry's Friendly Lounge Cajun dance hall (Lewisburg, La.)

It is amazing that an isolated farm community can sustain a dance hall at all, but the incredible fact is that Lewisburg has two of the most down-home Cajun nightspots on the Prairie! Little more than spittin' distance from Borque's is the even funkier Friendly Lounge. A young crowd hangs out at the pool tables, foosball game, and bar in the front, where Country and Swamp Pop tunes blare from the jukebox. A dollar or two buys entrance to the dance hall in back, where old-timers smooch over beers and crowd the dance floor. If you are lucky, Donald Thibodeaux (best known for his Saturday morning performances at Fred's Lounge in Mamou) will be on the bandstand pumping the accordion and singing in French. Guidry's has Cajun music every Sunday from 5

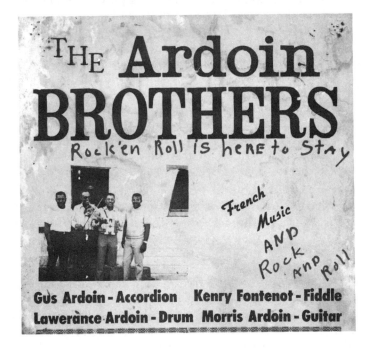

Posters from Slim's Y-Ki-Ki

P.M. to 9 P.M. To get to Guidry's follow the same directions as to Borque's. If you get to Borque's, you just passed Guidry's! (318) 942-9988.

*Zydeco Festival in Plaisance

This has become the main event on the Zydeco calendar. The best bands from across Acadiana perform on a stage set in the middle of the flowering Cajun Prairie between Opelousas and Ville Platte. Always held the Saturday before Labor Day, this festival runs from 11 A.M. to midnight with continuous music and food. Labor Day weekend in South Louisiana can be blisteringly hot, but the good times and copious quantities of beer and cold drinks wash all such earthly concerns away. Many of the bands appear at dance halls later in the evening, so you can plan on soaking up music and sun all day and eating at the Pig Stand in Ville Platte or the Palace Cafe in Opelousas before going out for another round. The Zydeco Festival is a non-profit event sponsored by the Southern Development Foundation in Opelousas. It takes place the Saturday before Labor Day at the Southern Development Farm on Route 167. To get there from Opelousas, take I-49 north to Rt 167. The festival site is on the right about 8 miles from I-49. For more information call Wilbert Guillory at (318) 942-2392.

Wilderness Campground Country/Swamp Pop. I-49 south of Opelousas.

Every other Saturday this wooded campground adjacent to I-49 has a band or DJ in their pavilion. Take I-49 south a few miles from Opelousas to Exit 15, then go south on the west Frontage Road about 1.5 miles. (For information on camping see Lodging listing below). (318) 662-5154.

Lodging

Hotel/Motel:

Cardinal Inn U.S. 190 west (2 miles), $21 to $30 double. (318) 942-5624.

Quality Inn 4501 I-49 south, $54 double. (318) 948-9500.

Town House Motel 343 W. Landry, $24 to $37 double. (318) 948-4488 or 942-7025.

Yambilee Courts Motel 1143 N. Main St., $22 to $28. (318) 942-9762.

Camping:

Acadiana Wilderness Campground I-49 South, Opelousas. Every other weekend there is dancing in the pavilion. Camping costs $12 for RVs, $10 for pop-ups, and $8 for tents. From Opelousas head south a couple of miles on I-49 and take exit 15, then go south on the west Frontage Road about 1.5 miles. (318) 662-5154.

Washington

Walking through the small steamboat town of Washington is a remarkable experience. Eighty percent of the town is on the National Historic Register, yet there is no sense of self-conscious reconstruction or preservation like one gets in Williamsburg, Virginia. There is no "old downtown area"; it is as if the entire place was just frozen in time somewhere around 1880. Washington is about six miles from Opelousas on Louisiana 10 and only five blocks off Intrastate 49 at exit 25 (about 40 minutes north of Lafayette). The town may be toured on foot in two and a half hours, but you may want to prolong your visit by planning a meal at the Steamboat Warehouse Restaurant or by planning a night at one of the several bed and breakfasts.

Situated on the banks over the River Opelousas, Washington is on hilly lands originally deeded to Jacque Courtableau, for whom the adjacent river was renamed Bayou Courtableau (pronounced "cuh-tah-bluh"). The land was subsequently granted to a "guardian of the Church," which began selling arpent (a bit less than an acre) lots in 1822. The settlement was called Church's Landing until it was incorporated in 1835 and renamed Washington. The first steamboat reportedly arrived in Washington in 1832 and the town rapidly grew into the largest steamboat port between New Orleans and St. Louis.

Washington is a place apart from the rest of Cajun South Louisiana. Settled by merchants and wealthy steamboat captains in greater numbers than Acadians, the bustling village had little in common with the tiny cow towns and pioneer settlements of the yawning Prairie. Tons of cotton, molasses, sugar, hides, and cattle were loaded at steamboat warehouses and exchanged for finished and manufactured goods unavailable on the frontier. There were operatic performances and all the vices associated with quantities of men and money.

With the arrival of the railroad in 1883, Washington's importance as a center of commerce declined. The last steamboat departed in 1900, leaving the town a veritable storybook land of antebellum and Victorian homes and plantations. Local merchants, Lafayette commuters, and retirees who call Washington home are proud of the village and enjoy life in a town where you still only have to dial the last four digits to get a neighbor on the phone.

Attractions

Washington is a place that just begs you to stop the car and take a walk. Many of the most beautiful old homes and businesses are located on a ten-block stretch of Main street and in a hilly corridor three or four blocks wide on either side. There is unlimited free parking.

Washington Museum and Tourist Center Corner of Main St. and Dejean.

This is a fine place to begin poking around. Here you can watch a short video on the town history, look through a roomful of books, artifacts, and clippings pertaining to the old steamboat days, and get a town map and tour guide brochure. The museum is open Monday through Friday from 10 A.M. to 3 P.M., and on Saturday and Sunday from 9 A.M. to 4 P.M. (closed for noon lunch hour daily). (318) 826-3626.

The Historic Washington Walking Tour

This hike includes nine antebellum homes that are open to the public (map available at Visitors Center). They are generally shown by the actual homeowners ($3 fee), who make time for guests if possible, so it is essential to call ahead (you can use the phone at the Visitors Center) to make an appointment. You won't need a reservation to walk the paths of Cedar Hill Cemetery or shop at the huge Old School Flea Market (*see* Shopping section below). You can begin the tour anywhere, but I recommend starting at the bayou on Main Street. Below are just a few of the highlights of the walking tour.

The Hinckley House 405 E. Dejean St.

This house is only a couple of blocks from the Visitors Center and is the one residence in Washington you should visit whether you are an old house buff or not. Built in the late 1700s by trading-post operator Asa Norton, the house has remained in the same family for nearly two centuries. It is constructed of cypress beams and molding joined by pegs and square nails. The plaster walls are bound with deer and cattle hair. Throughout the years each generation has brought in "new" treasures and furnishings

Last steamboat warehouse in Louisiana. (Photo by Julie Posner)

while preserving much of the old. Two of the more prominent family members were steamboat captains and there is an excellent array of steamboat memorabilia on display. Today the house is owned and shown by family historian Arthur Hinckley. (318) 826-3670.

Nicholson House of History Main St. and Vine.

If you are into spooks, call on Mrs. Nicholson; the dead come back to life as the lady of the house shows bloodstains in the attic, which once housed a Confederate hospital. The wounded who died were allegedly buried under the house, where Mrs. Nicholson points out a number of earthen mounds. If all this fails to get your imagination working, just ask Mrs. Nicholson if she has actually seen any ghosts. (318) 826-3670.

De la Morandiere St. John and Sittig St.

On a hill overlooking Bayou Courtableau and the steamboat warehouse is a two-story French Planter-style home built in 1830, with 5000 square feet of airy rooms. One of the most elegant Washington homes, De la Morandiere is not open for tours, but may be viewed from the adjacent streets. The present owners, Mr. and Mrs. Steve Johnson, operate a bed and breakfast for those who want to relax and enjoy the spacious grounds and perhaps dine at the adjacent Steamboat Warehouse Restaurant. (318) 826-3510.

Jack Womack's Steamboat Restaurant Bayou Courtableau at the bridge.

This is not just one of the best restaurants in St. Landry Parish; it is actually an old Steamboat Warehouse where goods were stored before export on one of the big paddlewheelers. Pass by for a drink at the bar, a listen at the jukebox, and a stroll along the dock (*see* review in Food section).

Magnolia Ridge Plantation Dejean and Prescott St.

This plantation house, built in the early 1800s, functioned as headquarters for Southern and Northern forces during the War Between the States. The house is not open for tours, but most of its extensive grounds are open during daylight hours. In addition to a small garden beside the house, there are miles of trails scaling the bluff beside Bayou Courtableau and a cypress swamp with a raised walkway. The trails are not well marked, and there are several points where signs steer visitors away from closed areas, but Magnolia Ridge is a pleasant one- to two-hour hike during the cool of morning or evening. To get to Magnolia Ridge from Main Street in Washington, turn north on Dejean Street (Route 103).

Go four blocks and make a right on Prescott. There is a parking lot on the left. The house is privately owned, and admission to the grounds is free.

Cedar Hill Cemetery Vine St. and Wilkins.

Cedar Hill is located at the western end of the walking tour. This cemetery gains an ethereal feel from its odd collection of sunken and overgrown graves and the avenue of moss-hung cedars running through the center.

Arlington Plantation Dejean St., 1.7 miles west of the Visitors Center.

Arlington (not close enough to be on the walking tour) was built in 1829 and is situated on a ridge overlooking the confluence of bayous Boeuf (pronounced "buff"), Cocodrie, and Courtableau. Folks showing old plantation homes enjoy counting things like the number of bricks used in construction, and Arlington racks up some impressive numbers. At 8000 square feet of floor space, it is the largest plantation in the area. It sports nine fireplaces, three staircases, and a forty-foot-long schoolroom upstairs. The home is currently owned by Mrs. Robert Olivier, who gives tours by appointment but can be pretty hard to get ahold of on the spur of the moment. (318) 826-3298.

Battle of Bayou Bourbeaux Reenactment Rt. 103, Washington.

History buffs interested in the War Between the States will want to visit this festival and battle reenactment, held annually in October. October is a cool time to visit Washington and check out the "battlefield" scene. There is a "period dance" on Saturday night, and food and beverages are provided through the weekend.

Participants dress in authentic military garb, fire real period cannons, skirmish, and are judged in several categories. Awards are presented in pistol and saber competition, for best-drilled unit, most authentic camp, pistol shoot, and best camp coffee. The actual battle reenactment occurs at 2 on Sunday. Heading north into Washington on Louisiana 10, just before Bayou Courtableau turn left onto Route 103 (Dejean Street). Go 1.5 miles and the battlefield will be on the right next to the bayou. Admission is $3 a day for adults and $1 for children under 12. Self-contained camper space is available for $25 a weekend. No ice chests are allowed. For current information write P.O. Box 751, Washington, 70589, or call (318) 826-5256 after 6 P.M.

Food

*Jack Womack's Steamboat Restaurant Cajun/Creole, $$ to $$$.
Main St.

The Steamboat Restaurant is housed in the only remaining
steamboat warehouse in South Louisiana, prompting owner Jack
Womack to bill it as Louisiana's "most unusual restaurant." Huge
cypress beams and raw wood dominate the decorating, while
spinning ceiling fans and a great jukebox keep the atmosphere
cozy. This is one of a few places where it pays to stretch out and
order some of those nouveau Cajun dishes like fish blanketed and
stuffed with seafood and sauces. The Catfish Palmetto, a fried fish
topped with crawfish, tasso, and almonds in a cream sauce, won
Chef Frankie Elder a gold medal for best seafood dish and is
highly recommended. A less high-falutin' specialty is Elder's seafood gumbo (dark and pungent), which arrives at the table accompanied by a freshly baked St. Landry Parish yam! This perfectly
wedded combination appears on kitchen tables throughout the
parish, but is sold only at the Steamboat Warehouse. An occasional daily special of note finds the famous yams served up with
succulent roast pork. Different desserts are prepared fresh each
day. I had to get two helpings of the buttery apple cobbler with
pecan crunch crust. (318) 826-7227.

Mark's Meat Market Rt. 10, south of Washington.

Mark's has some very hot and meaty boudin that is light on the
liver and easy on the rice for less than $2 a pound. They are
located between Washington and Opelousas on Route 10. Mark's
is open from 7 A.M. to 6 P.M. on Monday through Friday, and
from 7 A.M. to 5 P.M. on Saturday. (318) 942-3471.

Cajun Catfish Hole Seafood, $-$$. Rt. 10, south of Washington.

This is a newish family-style seafood restaurant with sandwiches,
steaks, and chicken dishes too. The meal of choice is the $7 daily
all-you-can-eat catfish special, which includes a choice of potato.
The Catfish Hole is located between Washington and Opelousas
on Route 10.

Music

Washington is NOT a music town. It is a quiet, mainly Anglo
community that shares little in the *joie de vivre* that inspires French
dances in Prairie communities half its size. However, it is only a
short drive to the dance halls of Opelousas and Lawtell.

Bell's Washington Campground Tavern Country/Oldies. By the bridge.

This raucous joint is not like anything you will find at your KOA-type campgrounds! Bell's features live Country and fifties music Friday and Saturday from 9 P.M. to 1 A.M. They are located by the bridge on the banks of Bayou Courtableau, just across from Washington. (318) 826 9987.

Shopping

Old Washington Antique School Mall Flea Market Vine and Church St.

Thirty dealers and 20,000 square feet of antiques, junk, and esoterica make this a fascinating place to buy or browse. You will find some real oddities and bargains here, the kind that would make antique dealers in New Orleans weep. The old, two-story, wood-frame school is within easy walking distance from the Washington Visitors Center. It is presently open every other weekend (the second and last) of each month. (318) 826-5252 or 826-9909.

Cajun Antique Flea Market 110 N. Main St.

This is another good place to find trash, treasures, bargains, and strange stuff on the walking tour. They are open Saturday and Sunday from 9 A.M. to 5 P.M.

The Acadian Connection 202 S. Main St.

Dot Mayer, who grew up at nearby Magnolia Ridge Plantation, operates this fine gift shop on the walking tour route. In addition to work by local craftsmen, Dot stocks a big collection of books and brochures on regional subjects (harkening back to her days as city librarian). Behind the shop is La Chaumière Bed and Breakfast (*see* Lodging section below). The Acadian Connection is open Thursday through Sunday from 1 P.M. to 4 P.M. (318) 826-3967.

Lodging

For a quiet and pampered getaway, Washington has four luxurious bed and breakfasts among its historic homes.

Camellia Cove 205 West Hill St.

Annie and Herman Bidstrup are the owners of this beautiful two-story house (circa 1825) situated on two acres of camellia- and crepe myrtle-covered grounds. When the Bidstrups bought the place in 1982, they found a lot of old papers and artifacts in the attic which have become part of the home's charm. Overnight guests can relax in large rocking chairs on the raised gallery and thumb through a book of before-and-after photographs of the Bidstrups' restoration. The house is conveniently located on the downtown walking tour. One room costs $65 and is totally furnished with period antiques and a huge bath. The other two rooms, which cost $55, use a bath in the hall. (318) 826-7749.

La Chaumière 216 S. Main Street.

Everyone who stays here has the same things to say: "What a great little place! What a great deal! I just couldn't believe how friendly Dot was!" Dot Mayer, the former head librarian of Opelousas, operates this quaint B & B in the small cottage built in the 1930s behind her own more modern home. The cottage has wood floors and a tin roof (perfect for rain storms!). It is decorated with antiques and homey artifacts like antique Mexican tin-paintings. Dot stocks the fridge so you can make your own breakfast, but the food is basic (white bread for toast, preserves, and orange juice). (Some friends who stayed there on their honeymoon were treated to a bottle of wine.) La Chaumière is a real bargain and is the only B & B in Washington that offers the privacy of accommodations not connected to the owner's house. Spring through fall, Dot rents the cottage for $40 per couple! The rate may be a little lower in the cold-weather months. La Chaumière is located right on the downtown walking tour. (318) 826-3967.

Homeplace

This elegant plantation was built in 1826 and is the home of Tom and Celeste Stephenson. The Stephensons rent two rooms upstairs which share a bath in the hall. One of the rooms has the walnut bed in which Tom and all his brothers were born. The Stephensons furnished the place with period antiques and offer guests a leisurely tour of the house and grounds. Mrs. Stephenson is quite a cook (I got to sample a few of her pies and cakes during the St. Landry Heritage Festival Tour of Homes), and she will whip up a full breakfast for you in the morning. Homeplace is located 4.5 miles east of Washington. Cost is $55 and $65 for two people. (318) 826-7558.

De la Morandiere St. John and Sittig St.

This is one of the huge and grand homes of Washington. It was built in 1830 by a descendant of one of the first settlers of Poste Des Opelousas, Etienne Robert De la Morandiere. Guests share the house with the present owners, Steve and Kandi Johnson, who bought and restored it in 1987. Both of the guest rooms have private baths and guests are welcome to use the parlor and unwind on the spacious upper or lower verandas. The house is furnished with antiques, including a huge tester bed dating from the 1830s in the downstairs bedroom. This room also features a private entrance through French doors onto the veranda. Both bedrooms have working fireplaces, so consider staying here if you are traveling in the cold-weather months. The cost per couple is $50 to $65. (318) 826-3510.

Bell's Washington Campground Main St., beside the bridge.

If you are the type who likes to stay at the Holiday Inn so you don't get any surprises, this is not for you. Most campgrounds have a general store; this one has a tavern! This scruffy little campground is right on the edge of Bayou Courtableau. Walk over the bridge and you are at the Steamboat Restaurant and Washington Visitors Center. There are picnic tables and shelters on the banks of the bayou. On Friday and Saturday nights Country and oldies bands often play in the tavern from 9 P.M. to 1 A.M. RV camping costs $10 a night and $25 a week. Tent camping is $6 a night. (318) 826-9987.

Eunice

Located about 20 miles west of Opelousas on U.S. 190, and forty-five minutes from Lafayette, Eunice is a hotbed of traditional Cajun music, food, and *joie de vivre*. Anyone interested in the folkways of Cajun Country must visit Eunice. The city (like several other towns in these parts) was founded by railroad man C. C. Duson. It is appropriate that Duson named the town after his wife, as Eunice is a place where folks hold firmly to family and church traditions. The weeks after the city's big *Courir du Mardi Gras* celebration are quiet, but as Lent nears its end on Good Friday, back yards bustle with extended families and friends boiling crawfish and frying fish on outdoor burners. Once Sunday Mass is over and Easter Eggs have been found, folks get back to their usual enjoyment of all the food and music the region offers.

Once known as Faquetique Community, Eunice rightfully bills itself as the Cajun Prairie Capital. It has the best accommodations on the northern Prairie, all the fast-food outlets and discount stores you could hope to find, and a location that allows quick access to the towns of Mamou and Ville Platte. It is the site of one of three Cajun Cultural Centers sponsored by the Jean Lafitte National Park and the location of the tremendously popular Cajun *Roundez Vous* live Saturday night broadcast.

Attractions

The Eunice Museum 220 C. C. Duson Dr. (Rt. 13).

Located in the old train depot at the site where C. C. Duson sold the first land parcels for the town, the Eunice Museum has a collection of artifacts and information disproportionate to its size. There are old photographs of the city and an exhibit of artifacts and information on Prairie life at the turn of the century. You can view free exhibits and videos on Cajun music, instruments, and Mardi Gras. From Route 190 turn south one block on Route 13 (C. C. Duson Drive). The museum is open Tuesday through Saturday from 8 A.M. to 5 P.M. (closed for lunch hour). (318) 457-2565.

Eunice Chamber and Information Center 220 C. C. Duson Dr. (Rt. 13).

Unlike the staff at many information centers, the folks here really know what is going on in the area in the way of food, music, and festivals. The center is located a couple of blocks from the Liberty Theater and Cajun Cultural Center beside the Eunice Museum. From U.S. 190 turn south one block on Route 13 (C. C. Duson Drive). The museum and Chamber are open Tuesday through Saturday from 8 A.M. to 5 P.M. (closed for lunch hour). (318) 457-6540.

Liberty Theater 2nd St. and Park Ave.

This grand old theater was constructed in 1924. Over the years it has been a vaudeville house, a first-run movie venue, and a dollar cinema before finding new life as home to the Saturday night broadcast of *Roundez Vous Des Cajuns* show (*see* Music listings below). While the Saturday show is not to be missed, the theater is an attraction in itself, donated to the city and restored by volunteers in the community. The 800-seat auditorium is frescoed with plaster ornaments and painted friezes.

*Acadian Cultural Center 250 W. Park Ave. at 3rd St.

One of three Acadian Cultural Centers under development by the National Park Service, the Eunice unit, which opened in the summer of 1991, focuses on the life and history of Prairie Cajuns. The center includes museum exhibits, a kitchen for cooking demonstrations, and a craft area where local artisans stage demonstrations. Several videos are shown continuously throughout the day in a comfortable theater. These include excellent documentaries on Cajun and Zydeco music, crawfish farming and, best of all, a feature on the highly unusual practice of "handfishing" called *Anything I Catch*. Time your visit for Saturday afternoon and

Liberty Theater. (Photo by Macon Fry)

see the *Roundez Vous des Cajuns* show at the neighboring Liberty Theater (*see* description in this chapter), or stop by on Sunday around 2 P.M. for the Cajun Jam Session. There are special events at the Cultural Center nearly every weekend, so call in advance to find out what is going on. The Center is open from 8 A.M. to 5 P.M. Sunday through Friday and until 8 P.M. on Saturdays. (318) 457-8499.

Cajun Prairie Restoration Project Martin Luther King, Jr., Dr. & Magnolia.

Driving across the miles of Cajun Prairie it is easy to forget that there was ever anything on this flat, moist table of earth but rice and soybean fields. A century ago the Prairie was quite a different place. C. C. Robin visited the Prairie in 1803 and wrote, "Crossing the wide prairie, strewn with flowers whose stems raise them to the height of the horse on which the traveler is riding." On a ten-acre site leased by the City of Eunice from the Union Pacific Railroad, botanists from L.S.U.E. and volunteers have begun to recreate a chunk of "natural" Prairie habitat. Seeds for the necessary native grasses and wildflowers were gathered from the scattered existing strips of virgin Prairie and along railroad right-of-ways. The seeds were then planted on tilled ground at this site. The result is a chunk of wild Prairie offering a seasonal panoply of colors similar to what Samuel Lockett saw in 1870 when he exclaimed, "I look upon the prairie as naturally the loveliest part of Louisiana." The refuge is located less than a mile north of U.S. 190.

Watley's Store N. St. Mary.

Mr. and Mrs. Watley regularly appear at the Jazz and Heritage Festival and at the Festivals Acadiens to display their traditional Acadian-style hide-covered ladder-back chairs. If you stop by their little store, you will find a number of the chairs for sale, a room full of used cypress boards, cypress benches and cupboards, and mattresses made of moss and corn shucks. In the spring, Mrs. Watley sometimes has fresh-picked blackberries and homemade blackberry pies for sale. To get to Watley's, turn north off of U.S. 190 onto St. Mary (just west of Perry Pete Ford). Go about two blocks and look on the right. If you cross the railroad tracks, you've gone too far. 318-457-5140.

Eunice City Park U.S. 190 W.

This public recreation area on the shores of a large, man-made lake is perfect for fishing, boating, or just picnicking in a sylvan setting. There are seven shelters with smokers and tables, public restrooms, and a small dock. To get to the park, head west on U.S. 190 2 miles from Route 13. The park is just past the country club on the north side of the road. The park closes at 10 P.M.

Shrine of Charlene Richard Rt. 1105 in Richard.

Charlene Richard has yet to be canonized by the Catholic Church, but if believers around the Prairie have their way, she will soon be recognized as the first Cajun saint. Thousands of South Louisiana Catholics make a pilgrimage each year to the grave of this girl who died of leukemia at age twelve in 1959. Her tomb, in a quiet cemetery in the town of Richard, is festooned with flowers, momentoes, and notes to Richard imploring her intercession in all manner of worldly problems. For more information you may contact the Friends of Charlene Association, P.O. Box 91623, Lafayette, 70509-1623. To visit the grave, just take Route 13 about 5 miles south from Eunice and turn left (east) on Route 370. Go 6 miles. The cemetery is behind St. Edward Church at the corner of Route 370 and Route 1105.

Festivals

*Crawfish Etouffée Cook-off Late March.

Well over a hundred amateur and restaurant cooking teams from around the area compete for bragging rights in this annual event. Even the mayor has had a booth the last couple of years. Samples are sold by each team. There is a Cajun dance pavilion and plenty of other entertainment.

*St. Landry Heritage Festival Second week in May. (*see* Opelousas listings.)

Eunice hosts a wildflower walk and several musical events each year as part of the larger St. Landry Heritage Festival.

*Mardi Gras

Eunice has the widest array of Mardi Gras activities to be found anywhere in South Louisiana. Unlike the raucous partying of Mamou and New Orleans, Mardi Gras in the Cajun Prairie Capital is a real family event. That isn't to say there is a shortage of beer, spicy food, and Cajun music. It's just that things don't get out of hand here. Many celebrants come from around the state for the three-day celebration, which includes historical and cultural presentations at the Acadian Cultural Center and a traditional Tuesday morning *Courir du Mardi Gras*. For more Mardi Gras information consult the index.

Saturday and Sunday before Mardi Gras

The weekend before Mardi Gras, Eunice is the site of two or three traditional Cajun and Zydeco dances. Held at St. Mathilda's Church and at the Liberty Theater, these events sometimes require that participants mask.

Monday before Mardi Gras

The day before Mardi Gras, the Liberty Theater and Cajun Cultural Center have living history presentations, displays, lectures, and slide shows regarding the Prairie *Courir du Mardi Gras* tradition. These activities begin early in the afternoon and last into the evening.

Fat Tuesday

On Mardi Gras, the revelry begins early. Riders in the *Courir du Mardi Gras* gather on horseback at the National Guard Armory at 8 A.M. The main public celebration takes place in front of the Liberty Theater and Courthouse, at the corner of Second and Walnut streets. There is a children's parade shortly after the riders depart, followed by performances by Cajun and Zydeco bands at a half dozen stages set up around the middle of town. Amidst the hubbub are vendors selling hot boiled crawfish, boudin, gumbo, and homemade sweets. The climax of the day's festivities is around 3 P.M., when a small parade snakes through town followed by the band of triumphant Mardi Gras riders returning from a day of plunder.

Music

★Roundez Vous des Cajuns Broadcast/dance. S. 2nd St. and Park Ave.

This is not only the biggest attraction in Eunice, but one of the premier weekly events in South Louisiana! Every Saturday night at 6, the old Liberty vaudeville theater plays host to the *Roundez Vous des Cajuns*, a two-hour show featuring Cajun and Zydeco bands, humorists, and cooks reciting their favorite recipes. During a recent show an elderly gentleman explained how to make soap. Many of the directions were in French, but I did make out the main ingredient—"First you need five pounds of fat!"

The show, broadcast live on KJJB (105.5 FM) and KEUN (1490 AM) in Eunice and KRVS (88.7 FM) in Lafayette, has been described as a Cajun cross between the Prairie Home Companion and the Grand Ol' Opry. In many ways it harkens back to the days when dances or *fais-do-do's* were held in private homes and halls. It is an event for the whole family and one place where you will hear more people speaking French than English. The emcee is Cajun folklorist Barry Jean Ancelet, who tempers his French patter with enough English to allow the Anglos to follow along. The show starts promptly at 6 P.M. and is over at 8, but it has become so popular that you may want to get there half an hour early to get a ticket and a good seat. Admission is $1. Cokes, popcorn, and sweet dough pies are sold at the concession counter. The Liberty Theater is located downtown at the corner of Second Street and Park Avenue, directly adjacent to the new Cultural Center. There is plenty of street parking and the City Hall lot is open for RV and bus parking during the show.

Gilton's Lounge Zydeco dance hall. U.S. 190 E. and Rt. 95.

Gilton's is the biggest Zydeco dance hall in the region and possibly in the state, with over 1500 seats. Not only is this place a bit cavernous, but the new just doesn't seem to wear off. Proprietor Gilton Lejeune has set about correcting these deficiencies by serving seafood on band nights and packing the place with the most popular names in Zydeco. Gilton's is located a block off U.S. 190 at the intersection of 190 and Route 95 just east of Eunice. Gilton's has Zydeco most Saturdays, but before you make a special trip, call his Zydeco hotline at 318-457-1241.

Savoy's Music Center Cajun jam session. E. Laurel (U.S. 190 E.).

This music store on Route 190 on the east side of Eunice houses the workshop of Cajun musician and accordion maker Marc Savoy. Savoy is an accomplished accordionist and intense preservationist of Cajun culture. On Saturday mornings he hosts a jam session in the store that often features his wife, Ann Allen Savoy, on guitar, and sometimes grows to include three accordions, fiddles, and triangles. This is an informal but regular gathering that generally gets underway by 10 A.M. There is no admission but no one will complain if you bring a six-pack of beer or a couple of pounds of boudin from Johnson's Grocery (*see* Food listings) to pass around. If you get there early, thumb through a copy of Ann Savoy's wonderful book, *Cajun Music: A Reflection of a People*, or ask if Marc is not too busy to show the shop where he produces diatonic accordions under his own "Acadian" brand. 318-457-9563.

*Dup's Lounge Cajun broadcast/dance. Rt. 13 N.

Dup's is easy to pick out on Saturday morning by the crowd of pickups and cars lining the blacktop on Route 13. Walk into Dup's at 9 A.M. and you will find the dance floor packed with couples two-stepping to a Cajun band. Formerly a feed store, Dup's is a rough-hewn place with a dozen tables casually scattered in the back and a jukebox by the stage. On Saturdays the disc jockey from KEUN in Eunice (1490 AM) has her ancient remote broadcasting gear set up near the stage. The ambiance is as homey as your neighbor's front porch.

Proprietor Berlin Carriere serves beers and passes the guest book at the old bar. When I asked Mr. Carriere why he called the Bar "Dup's," he explained that he only bought the place six years ago and didn't want to scare off the regulars by changing the name. Things obviously change slowly out here! Dup's gets a lot fewer tourists than the more popular Fred's in Mamou. A recent visitor from Texas commented in the guest register, "The people here seem to know we aren't from here, probably because we are the youngest in the crowd." That means they were under forty-five. The dance floor, dusted with fresh cornmeal, invites all to try some early-morning warm-up steps. There is no cover charge and the band frequently plays until 1 or 2 P.M., so Dup's is a great place to stop on your way to or from the more punctual show up the road at Fred's Lounge. Dup's is located on Route 13, just 4 miles north of Eunice. 318-457-9162.

Lakeview Campground Lounge Cajun dance hall. Rt. 13 N.

Yes, even the campgrounds in this part of the state have Cajun dances! Actually, a heck of a lot more people come to Lakeview for music on Saturdays than actually pitch a tent or park an RV there. Bands play every Saturday from 8 P.M. "until" in the small tavern that sits in the middle of this aging RV haven. It is a wonderful feeling to step out of this joint and hear the mingling of frog "rrribits" and muffled band. Admission is free for campers and $1 for non-campers. Lakeview is located just up the road from Dup's, about 4 miles north of Eunice on Route 13. 318-457-9263.

VFW Restaurant and Dance Hall Cajun dance hall. E. Laurel (U.S. 190).

This spot became so instantly popular when it opened in '89 that they are already contemplating an addition. Friday night you can hear Country and Swamp Pop music. Saturday there is a big Cajun dance. 318-457-1055.

Homer's Cajun dance hall. 555 E. Laurel (U.S. 190).

Homer's is a raucous little bar with Cajun dances every Friday night after the show at the Liberty Theater. 318-457-5922.

Jam session at Savoy's Music Center. (Photo by Raleigh Powell)

Dup's (a.k.a. Carriere's) Lounge. (Photo by Julie Posner)

Food

⋆Johnson's Grocery Meat Market (boudin). 700 E. Maple.

This is the high altar of boudin, the home of the golden link! Johnson's has been perfecting their boudin recipe since 1937 and has singlehandedly shattered the rule that states, "The best boudin is always no more than three miles away from home." Folks come all the way from Lake Charles to pick up enough of the spicy links to get them through the week. Back when Johnson's was only making boudin on Saturday, things got really crazy. In a day Joe Johnson would make, weigh, and sell up to 2000 pounds. The line for links, or "Rue Boudin," as it was called, would wind through the store and out the door.

There is still a strong Saturday morning boudin tradition, perhaps because it is the perfect breakfast before spending a morning dancing and imbibing at the Saturday Cajun broadcast at Fred's or Dup's Lounge. Nothing opens the blinkers like a hot cup of coffee (which you have to get elsewhere) or a cold can of beer and a hot-hot link of boudin. Johnson's boudin is notable for a lack of liver and other by-products, for its even-handed mixture of rice and pork, and for its fiery flavor. Joe Johnson has a wide variety of excellent regional specialties like tasso, garlic sausage, paunce, and fresh meats. The latest addition to his counter is chewy ropes of Cajun beef jerky. Meats can be shipped nationwide.

To get to Johnson's from U.S. 190, take Route 13 (called C. C. Duson Drive in town) south to Maple Street. Go east on Maple a few blocks. They are open Monday through Friday from 6 A.M. to 6 P.M. and Saturday from 5 A.M. to 5 P.M. 318-457-9314.

Allison's Hickory Pit Local fave, $. 501 W. Laurel (U.S. 190).

Linus Allison fixes some of the tastiest Ville Platte-style barbeque on this side of the Prairie. Pork steaks and ribs come soaked in an oniony sauce that is not exceedingly sweet or hot, just succulent. BBQ plates cost $6 or less. 318-457-9218.

Mama's Fried Chicken Cajun/Down Home, $. 1640 W. Laurel (U.S. 190).

This is a franchise for the regional Mama's Chicken chain, but it is also a small Cajun restaurant with an independent and creative cook. Lannie Degeyter took over the Mama's in Eunice ten years ago, after picking up cooking while working at Pat's in Henderson. From the beginning he has had an edge in the chicken market because his birds come in fresh every day from the poultry house next door. Lannie's recipe is well seasoned, but tame compared to Popeye's.

High altar of boudin. (Photo by Derick Moore)

It is not chicken, however, on which Lannie has built his reputation. The plaque over the door informs all that Mama's won the Crawfish Etouffée Cook-off in 1987. There are daily Cajun plate lunches like fried catfish with potato salad for under $4. The Sunday dinner is a highly seasoned pork roast that begins cooking on Saturday and is served with backbone stew, rice dressing, and potato salad for under $4. My favorite meal is a small etouffée and four chicken wings. Mama's is open Sunday through Wednesday from 10 A.M. to 9 P.M. and Thursday through Saturday until 10 P.M. 318-457-9978.

★Pelican Restaurant Cajun/Down Home, $. W. Laurel (U.S. 190).

The Sunday midday meal at the Pelican is reason enough to spend Saturday night in Eunice or to make the drive from anyplace as close as Lafayette. The key is to either get there early or to arrive between the Catholics, who start pouring into the tiny dining room after Mass at about 11:20, and the Baptists, who arrive closer to 12:30. I would say that this was real home cooking, but few people cook like this at home anymore. For a set price of $4.50, you get either baked duck, pork roast, beef roast, or pit-cooked barbeque (a choice of chicken, ribs, or pork steak) and a choice of three mouthwatering side orders like yams, black-eyed peas, and cornbread or rice dressings. Each dinner comes with complimentary ice tea or coffee, a chilled mustardy potato salad, and dessert. You will simply not find a better home-style meal anywhere! Plate lunches and suppers are offered throughout the week, but after the Sunday dinner, you may not need to eat again for seven days. The Pelican is open Sunday from 6 A.M. to 2 P.M., and Monday through Saturday until 10 P.M. 318-457-2323.

★Ruby's Cafe Cajun/Down Home, $. 221 W. Walnut.

Ruby's has been dishing out soul-satisfying plate lunches for over thirty years. No midday walk through the shady streets around the Cultural Center and Liberty Theater is complete without a stop here to sample the pork roast, redolent of garlic and covered in a dark gravy. The facade is worn, but inside Ruby's is a quaint restaurant with fifties-style diner-decor ambiance. From the pink-and-green walls to the formica counter and Mello-Joy clock over the kitchen, there is a distinct impression that Ms. Ruby hasn't changed things much.

There are some things no one wants to see change, and the food here is one of them. The fare is simple. Chicken fried steak, baked chicken, and the highly recommended pork roast are all served with three or four veggies. No one could explain why the huge "small plate" cost $2.95 and the truly enormous "large plate"

Mardi Gras street party in Mamou. (Courtesy of LA Office of Tourism)

cost only fifteen cents more, but don't order the large unless you are mighty hungry! Ruby's is open Monday through Saturday from 5 A.M. to 3 P.M., but they often begin to run out of popular items like the pork roast by 1:30. They are located right behind the Liberty Theater and Cultural Center. 318-457-2583.

Lodging

Motels:

Howard's Inn U.S. 190 East, $36 double. 318-457-2066.

La Parisienne Motel 1151 East Laurel (U.S. 190), $27 to $37. 318-457-4274.

Stone Motel U.S. 190 East, $27 to $34 double. 318-457-5211.

Camping:

Cajun Campground U.S. 190, 4.5 miles east of Eunice. $7 for tents and $11 for RV's. 318-457-5753.

Lakeview Campground Rt. 13, 4 miles north of Eunice. $10.50 for full hook-ups. Music every Saturday night at 8 P.M. in the pavilion. 318-457-9263.

Mamou

Mamou, with a population of 3,200, sits near the top and center of the Cajun Prairie, 10 miles north of Eunice on Route 13. Nearly a century after C. C. Duson printed handbills exclaiming "Go West, Young Man, Go West and Go to Mamou!", this little town still has the feel of the Old West about it. On Sixth Street, which is the main thoroughfare, businesses (mostly little bars) have the same flat, sun-bleached facades common to little cattle towns in Texas. Actually, the cattle industry long ago made way for cotton and then the rice and soybean fields that now surround the area. Few people come here to view the architecture anyway, unless it is to stay in the totally archaic Cazan Hotel. The main reason folks show up in Mamou is to see the famous Saturday morning Cajun Broadcast from tiny Fred's Lounge and to attend the city's huge *Courir du Mardi Gras* celebration.

Attractions

Holiday Lounge Rt. 13 at the Mamou turnoff.

The Holiday may be the most unusual bar in Southwest Louisiana. A couple of questions come to mind. What is a big lounge like this doing in a field 10 miles from the nearest sizable town, and why is there a life-size, full-length portrait of Governor Edwin Edwards over the door? The simple explanation to both questions is that the Holiday was for years the biggest gaming house on the Prairie. The bar and plush booths are wrapped in turquoise vinyl, while the walls are covered in a gaudy tropical print wallpaper. In one corner is a low stage, backed with mirrors, and in the rear are rooms which once entertained a sporting crowd. Folks around here are mainly proud of aging proprietor Tee-Ed Manual. They will tell you he has the "biggest house in town" and had "the first Cadillac around these parts." This is a great place to stop for a drink. If you are lucky you might catch Tee-Ed hanging around in his double-breasted suit and wide tie. He will be glad to tell you, around a fat, unlit cigar, about the good old days before jukeboxes replaced the slots. The Holiday stands in the middle of a grassy field beside the Mamou turnoff on the west side of Route 13.

Mamou Mardi Gras (Late winter)

Mamou was the first town to revive the *Courir du Mardi Gras* tradition, and their celebration is now the biggest in Cajun Country. The festivities begin with a street party on the Monday before Mardi Gras. All of the bars on 6th Street open their doors and the music, beer, and crowds flow freely. The big event is the Mardi Gras morning *Courir du Mardi Gras* ride. The participants gather on horseback downtown around 7 A.M. A noisy throng sees them off and proceeds to party in the street to the sounds of live Cajun bands until the riders return at 3 P.M. For more information on the *Courir du Mardi Gras* and Mardi Gras dates, see the "Special Events in Cajun Country" appendix.

Food

★Ortego's Meat Market (Tasso). South St. (Rt. 95).

When Leroy Ortego went into the meat business forty-four years ago, cotton was king in this region and no one had yet dreamed that crawfish could be a money crop. Leroy's kids run the place now, and they still do things the old way in this corner of the Prairie. They have their own cattle yard and they slaughter, smoke, and cut all the meats in the market. There is no concealed back room from which shrink-wrapped and pre-priced meats suddenly appear. Behind the low counter laden with smoked meats are two band saws and a table saw where the final cuts are made right before your eyes. Here the stainless steel, white tile, and styrofoam trays of urban meat counters give way to raw wood, cement, and brown paper. The fresh-cut meats are beautiful, but the specialties of the shop are smoked. Tasso is available in both beef and pork and is as good as any you will find. If you are in Mamou for the Saturday morning radio show at Fred's Lounge, be sure and stop at Ortego's first to stock up on tasso, as it closes early. Ortego's is one mile east of Route 13 on South Street (Route 95). They are open from 7 A.M. to 5 P.M. on weekdays and until noon on Saturday. (318) 468-3746.

Loretta's Cafe Cajun/Down Home (breakfasts), $. Sixth St.

There are only a couple of places to eat in Mamou. My choice is Loretta's, which opens at 5:30 so you can get a full breakfast before crossing the street and beering it up at the Saturday morning dance at Fred's Lounge. The breakfasts are simple and very inexpensive (biscuits are thirty cents). Loretta serves plate lunches with a choice of vegetables. Try the duck and sausage gumbo. Loretta's is on Sixth Street beside the Hotel Cazan and across from Fred's Lounge. They open at 5:30 A.M. (318) 468-4075.

Music

*Fred's Lounge Cajun Broadcast/Dance. Sixth St.

Farmers in jeans and boots, nattily dressed professionals from Eunice and Ville Platte, and Japanese tourists with camera bags can all be found imbibing and dancing at the most famous bar in Cajun Country at 9 o'clock any Saturday morning. You won't find tour buses parked outside Fred's; the place is scarcely big enough to hold the occupants of a half dozen mini vans. Inside it is decidedly rustic. A piece of twine wrapped around the band area is the only barrier between the musicians and folks hoisting cans of Falstaff. On weekends just before Mardi Gras and just after Lent, the crowd at Fred's is particularly exuberant, but Fred has signs to remind everyone of the two primary rules of the house: "No substitute musicians" and "No standing on the jukebox"! In his forty-four years hosting the live dance and radio broadcast, Fred Tate has seen film crews from England, France, Germany, and Japan crowd into his tiny bar. Fortunately, international fame has done little to change the humble bar or discourage the mostly local clientele from beginning their weekend there. Fred's is on Sixth Street in the middle of Mamou. Every Saturday the band plays from 9 A.M. to 1 P.M. You can tune in to the broadcast on KVPI radio, 1250 AM. (318) 468-5411.

Papa Paul. (Photo by Julie Posner)

Cazan Hotel. (Photo by Raleigh Powell)

*Papa Paul's Zydeco dance hall. Poinciana (Rt. 1160) and 2nd St.

You won't find a more down-home old dance hall than this one, or a fuller, more dependable schedule of top-notch Zydeco. Dances are held nearly every Friday, Saturday, and Sunday. Proprietor Papa Paul lives in a small house behind the hall, where chickens cackle beneath the floor and his ducks waddle around the marshy back yard. Papa Paul's barbeque, located adjacent to the club, gets smoking while the music gets hot and dancing gets frenzied.

Papa Paul has been living in Mamou all his life (76 years by most accounts) and has been operating the dance hall half of that time. He doesn't speak much English, but when he's not dancing, he greets visitors warmly at the bar. The raw wood-plank dance floor bounces to the contortions of dancers. There's a great Zydeco/Soul jukebox. Papa Paul's is located on the corner of Poinciana (Route 1160) and 2nd Street. Heading north on Route 13, go to the north edge of town and turn right on Route 1160; go a couple of blocks and Papa Paul's is on the right. (318) 468-5538 (home).

Lodging

*Cazan Hotel Sixth St.

This is not the kind of place where you get a mint on your pillow (you *do* get a pillow!), but it is a remarkable hotel nonetheless. The Cazan was originally built as a bank back in 1912 and became a hotel in 1946. A huge mahogany bar, built by a high-school shop instructor, was installed in the old lobby and a wall of slot machines were placed where the tellers' cages used to be. Upstairs a dozen rooms were remodeled for overnight guests. The slots are gone, but the beautiful thing about this place is that the rooms are basically as they were in 1946. Sure, window air-conditioning units have been added, but the screen doors on most rooms and transom windows hint at what the climate conditioning used to be like. The heaters are antique gas radiators that work like a charm once you figure out how to light them.

To say that the Cazan is showing its age would be a major understatement. Some of the rooms verge on shabby, but they are as clean and comfortable as they are primitive. For the more adventurous, this is the ultimate place to spend a Friday night. You can stop by Papa Paul's Zydeco Hall on Friday night and wake up Saturday morning to the strains of Cajun music from Fred's Lounge across the street. After the show at Fred's, be sure to hit the bar at the Cazan, where you can often find proprietor Mr.

Burke Perottie (pear-oh-tee) downing beers and telling jokes with his brother, Mayor Warren Perottie, and the local game warden. Check out the good selection of South Louisiana faves on the jukebox. A double with one bed is $20. Be sure to reserve in advance, as the dozen rooms fill up on some weekends. (318) 468-7187.

Ville Platte

Ville Platte, or "Flat Town," as it was aptly named by the early settlers, is located near the northernmost point of today's Cajun Country, about 20 miles northeast of Eunice and 25 miles northwest of Opelousas. This is the last stop for a northbound traveler looking for the sights, sounds, and flavors of real Cajun Country. Ville Platte has an important musical landmark in Floyd's Record Store, as well as the most popular little barbeque stand in South Louisiana. This is the place to stock up and chow down before or after exploring Chicot State Park and the State Arboretum north of town, where the terrain rises into piney-wood hill country and there is plenty of camping, hiking, and fishing to be done.

The area around Ville Platte was first settled in the late eighteenth century and the town was incorporated in 1858 on what was the main road from Opelousas to Alexandria. With fewer than a thousand residents, Ville Platte became the seat of government for the newly formed Evangeline Parish in 1910, but it was not until the discovery of oil nearby in the thirties that the city really began to grow. Despite its status as a parish seat, the pace of life in this upland Prairie town with a population of 9000 is decidedly slow. The most exciting event in Ville Platte is the annual Cotton Festival, held the second weekend of October.

Ville Platte Chamber of Commerce 306 West Main St.

You will not find much information here, but the people at the Chamber were able to give us a good Evangeline Parish map and brochures for Chicot Park and the Cotton Festival. (318) 363-1878.

Attractions

Floyd's Record Store 434 E. Main St.

Floyd Soileau (pronounced Swallow) is the biggest distributor of South Louisiana music anywhere. He is also one of the record men responsible for the rebirth of interest in Cajun and Zydeco music in the sixties and seventies. In the past twenty years, Soileau has released records by most of the important modern Cajun, Swamp-Pop, and Zydeco artists, including Dewey Balfa and the Balfa Brothers, Clifton Chenier, and Johnny Allan. As many as a third of the records on some jukeboxes in Cajun Country are on Soileau's Jin, Swallow, and Maison de Soul labels. His artists have performed in every place from American Bandstand to Carnegie Hall and the Newport Folk Festival.

Floyd's Record Store is a Mecca of sorts for fans of the region's music who know they will find whatever Swamp Pop, Zydeco, or Cajun recordings they are seeking here. He also has a huge stock of reissue and oldies 45s, as well as the latest hits. Want to hear a single before you buy it? Just ask, and they will slap one on the record player at the counter.

While you are in the neighborhood, walk down the street to the Pig Stand for lunch; you will probably see Floyd there. Floyd's is open 8 A.M. to 5 P.M., Monday through Saturday. (318) 363-2138.

*Snook's Bar and Cajun dance hall Rt. 190 W., Ville Platte.

This Cajun landmark has dances every weekend! (318) 363-0451.

Louisiana State Arboretum Rt. 3042 N.

The first State Arboretum in the nation is located 8 miles north of Ville Platte. There are hiking trails at the Louisiana Arboretum (and in nearby Chicot State Park) which are not only dry, but actually hilly! Some of the hills rise up from Lake Chicot at an incline of 30 percent. Two and a half miles of footpaths wind through the hilly 600-acre arboretum, crossing ravines on wooden bridges and scaling slopes in gentle cutbacks. The place is a majestic and peaceful domain of moss, hollow trees, gullys, and hills, inhabited by woodpeckers and deer. If you are looking for a quiet walk and find the trails at Chicot Park too congested, the Arboretum is a perfect getaway. No pets or picnicking are allowed on the grounds, so exercise your mutt and chow down at Chicot. The Arboretum is located on Route 3042 1.5 miles north of the Chicot State Park main entrance.

*Chicot State Park Rt. 3042 N.

Chicot, the largest of Louisiana's State Parks, was built in the 1930s on the rolling hills surrounding 2500-acre cypress-studded Lake Chicot, one of the most popular freshwater fishing spots in the region. It is the only park in Cajun Country where backcountry hiking and camping are available. Nearly 15 miles of trails skirt the lake and climb through the neighboring piney-wood hills. Numerous trailheads with parking areas allow easy access for those wanting to take a short walk or day or overnight trip. Other

Record man Floyd Soileau. (Photo by Julie Posner)

Chicot State Park. (Courtesy of LA Office of Tourism)

trails diverge to secluded backwoods camping areas with vistas of the lake. For overnight hikers, maps of the park and its trails, backcountry camping permits (50 cents), and park rules are available at the south entrance.

There are two entrances and main areas in Chicot Park, referred to as North Landing and South Landing. The south entrance, on Route 3042, offers access to 27 fully furnished vacation cabins (all you need to bring is soap, towels, and grub). Cabins have screened porches, heat and air-conditioning, equipped kitchens, and are located near the boat launch. There are also many campsites with full hook-ups within walking distance of the lake, several trailheads for hikers, a swimming pool (no swimming is permitted in the lake), and picnic areas with grills. This is by far the busiest section of Chicot.

The North Landing provides access to the best hiking and backcountry camping, over a hundred developed campsites adjacent to Lake Chicot, and a boat launch with fish-cleaning station and boat rentals. Access to the North Landing is possible from a road inside the park from the South landing or from Route 106. This is the quiet end of the park. You can sit by the dock, watch the alligators, and ignore the posted "no fishing" sign with impunity.

There are no concessions at Chicot, so you must buy your supplies and bait in Ville Platte. During the summer, April 1 to September 30, the park is open from 5 A.M. to 10 P.M. Other months the park is open from 7 A.M. to 7 P.M. Admission is $2 per vehicle with up to four people. Camping is $12 with hook-ups. To camp on the trails you must fill out a form and pay a fee of 50 cents per person. Cabins for four are $35, cabins for six are $45. Boat rentals are $8, with a $10 deposit. Chicot is located 6 miles north of Ville Platte on Route 3042. (318) 363-2403.

Crooked Creek Recreation Area Rt. 106 W.

Crooked Creek is a little campground on the shores of a 400-acre lake 12 miles west of Chicot State Park. On weekends the area is frequented by locals who come to swim at the sandy beach, use the picnic shelters (which include smokers as well as grills), and to fish. There are two boat ramps (well isolated from the public swimming area), and plenty of spots to fish from the shore or the new fishing pier. The 100 camping sites, which include full hook-ups, and the tent camping areas all have views of the lake. The park is open from 7 A.M. to 11 P.M. Day use is $1 per person. Camping is $10 for RVs and $7 for tents. From Ville Platte take Route 10 west about 8 miles, then turn north onto Route 13. Continue on Route 13 for another 7 miles to Route 106. Take a left onto Route 106 for 5 miles. For information and reservations call (318) 599-2661.

Jack Miller's Barbecue Sauce Factory 811 Humana Rd.

Ville Platte has a style of barbeque sauce all its own. It is medium hot and sweetened with whole bits of onions. There are a couple of people making this type of sauce in town (originally they started in business together, so the recipes are quite similar), but Jack Miller's is by far the most famous. To buy the sauce you will have to go to the grocery, but if you want to see it made just stop on by the plant on weekdays. To get to Jack Miller's small factory (located right beside his house), just head east on Route 10 (Main Street) from Floyd's Music. Turn right on Humana, beside Humana Hospital. Miller's is a half mile south of Route 10. They are open Monday through Friday, 7 A.M. to 4 P.M. (318) 363-1541.

Kary's Roux and Pig Stand Bar-B-Q Sauce Railroad Ave. and Rt. 10.

Kary's makes oniony barbeque sauce in the classic Ville Platte style. This sauce, packaged under the Pig Stand label, is brushed on all the barbeque served at the Pig Stand Restaurant on Route 10 in Ville Platte (*see* Food section). To get to Kary's, head west on Route 10 from Floyd's Music to Railroad Avenue. Turn left on Railroad and Kary's is one block south of Route 10. (318) 363-6100.

Cotton Festival 2nd weekend every October.

Cotton is no longer "king" in this area, but the festival goes on. The main event is a jousting competition known as *Tornoi de la Ville Platte*. Horseback riders in full regalia charge around a course spearing small steel rings suspended over the track. (318) 363-4521.

Food

Dupre's Grocery Meat Market. 102 W. Hickory.

For over twenty-one years Herbert Dupre has served the best cracklin's, boudin, and smoked meats in Ville Platte from his little market on Hickory Street. Dupre has stood the test of time by doing the messy and time-consuming work like stuffing his paunce and boudin and smoking his meats himself. He pays attention to local tastes and provides his clientele with such locally popular products as smoked ox tails for seasoning. Dupre credits the special flavor of his smoked meats to a blend of china ball and hickory wood. This is the place to stop whether you are looking for a steak or other fresh meat to take up to Chicot Park and grill, a cooler of smoked seasoning meat to take home, or just want a bag of crispy cracklin's and a beer to get you on down the road. Dupre's is located in south Ville Platte at 102 W. Hickory (just off Railroad Avenue). (318) 363-4186.

*Jungle Dinner Club Boiled Seafood/Local Fave, $$. W. Main St. (Rt. 10).

The Jungle has a variety of seafood as well as some spectacular steaks, but their specialty is the boiled crawfish. These are some of the most uniquely seasoned and hottest boiled crawfish anywhere. I worked my way up through the Mild, Hot, and Super Hot before attacking the final pinnacle of flame, the Extra Super Hot. These are not even on the menu, podnuh, and for good reason! Unless you have something to prove, or really want the Honorary Cajun Certificate that comes with eating an order of the E.S.H., don't get them. Manager Wendel Manuel simply warned, "Take out your contacts first!"

The real reason you should not get the extra super hot crawfish is so you can better appreciate the other seasonings, which seem to include a little sugar and vinegar. The water running off the crawfish was so tasty, I found myself mopping it up with the tail meat, potatoes, and corn. During the sixties, the Jungle was the most popular bandstand in the area, featuring acts like Fats Domino, Dale and Grace, and country star Ernest Tubb. They are open Sunday through Thursday from 5:30 P.M. to 11 P.M. and Friday and Saturday until 1 A.M. They are located on the west edge of town. (318) 636-9103.

▲Pig Stand Cajun/Down Home and Barbeque, $. 318 E. Main St. (Rt. 10).

It is fitting that the Pig Stand Restaurant sits at the geographic pinnacle of the Cajun cultural heartland, for you will not find a better example of solid and soulful Cajun cooking. For forty years Lester Daire has been tantalizing tastebuds with lunch specials like Turtle or Tasso Sauce Piquante, Smothered Sausage, and Chicken Stew. Of course, most folks come to this diner for the Pork Barbecue, either steak or ribs. Northern Cajun Country is well known for its smoked meats, but what sets the Pig Stand apart is the sauce, which is full of onion and garlic. Usually ribs, pork steak, or roast are included on the lunch menu with side orders of black-eyed peas, rice and gravy, rice dressing, and potato salad (enough starches?) for under $5. Often, items from the lunch menu are still available at the same price through the dinner hour. The Pig Stand is the only good late-night spot to eat north of Lafayette, with barbeque and breakfast available until 2 A.M. on

Friday and Saturday. The Stand is a block from Floyd's at 318 E. Main Street. They are open Tuesday through Thursday and Sunday from 6 A.M. to 11 P.M., and Friday and Saturday until 2 A.M. (318) 363-2883.

Lodging

Platte Motel W. Main St. (Rt. 10), $22 to $36 double. (318) 363-2148. Adjacent to Jungle dinner club.

Camping:

Crooked Creek Recreation Area
See description under Attractions section.

Chicot State Park
See description under Attractions section.

Basile

Basile is a community of about 2500 residents and one fine Prairie dance hall just 11 miles west of Eunice on U.S. 190, at the intersection of Route 97. The town was founded in 1905 and named for its first settler, Basile Fontenot. Fontenot is still a common name in the area, with the town's main landmark being Fontenot's Main Street Lounge dance hall (a few blocks north of U.S. 190). A couple of miles west on U.S. 190 is Bayou Nez Pique (French for "tattooed nose"), one of the major streams of the northern Prairie, named for a local tribe of Indians who practiced body art. Today Basile is barely a stop in the road, floating amidst flooded crawfish and rice fields.

*D.I.'s Cajun Restaurant Boiled Seafood/Dine & Dance. Rt. 97 S.
D.I.'s is a place that looks like God just tossed it out on the Prairie. It stands on a lonely piece of land amidst endless acres of crawfish ponds. Owner and boil chef D.I. Fruge was one of the first big crawfish farmers in the area and started boiling the crustaceans in his barn back in 1979. When folks began to catch on to how good his crawfish were, he moved the boiling pots from the barn to a lounge down the street and, finally, to the present location. This is a full-service restaurant with Cajun dances on Tuesdays, but the main attraction is the uniquely seasoned boiled crawfish. D.I. won't divulge the secret of his seasoning, but in addition to the usual cayenne and salt, his crawfish have an aromatic flavor that might be nutmeg or allspice. A popular side is

boiled potatoes, which are quartered, brushed with butter, and dusted with a faintly sweet pepper mixture. Other than these, stick with the crawfish here. D.I.'s is open Tuesday through Saturday from 5 P.M. until 10 P.M. There is a Cajun dance on Tuesday and Saturday nights at 8 P.M. From U.S. 190, go 9.5 miles south on Route 97. From I-10 go 10 miles north on Route 97. (318) 432-5141.

Music

*D.I.'s Restaurant Boiled Seafood/Dine & Dance. Rt. 97 S.

Every Tuesday night at 8 P.M., D.I.'s has a Cajun dance with music by one of the popular young groups of the area. Unlike some of the dine and dance Cajun restaurants in the Lafayette area, D.I.'s caters strictly to a local crowd. They have the only Tuesday night dance on the Prairie, so they manage to draw folks from the nearby towns of Eunice, Mamou, Elton, and Kinder. During crawfish season, the crowds get out of hand and you may have to wait in line if you arrive after 7 P.M. To get to D.I.'s, take U.S. 190 west from Eunice. In Basile head south on Route 97 about 9.5 miles. From Interstate 10 head north on Route 97. (318) 432-5141.

Ivy's Lounge Rt. 97, south of U.S. 190

Ivy's is an old wood-frame dance hall and bar that has gone through some weird changes. I have been there when a Cajun band was playing and also when a DJ was spinning contemporary rock while kids shot pool. On one recent visit a Cajun band played, but the main event of the night was a bear-wrestling contest between sets! (318) 432-5800.

Betty's Bearcat Lounge U.S. 190, West Basile.

The Bearcat Lounge no longer has music or dances on a regular basis, but this spot has seen hundreds of performances by locals like the late Nathan Abshire and Dewey Balfa. Today it is a rustic watering hole on the west end of Basile. To get to the Bearcat, take U.S 190 to the west end of Basile. It is about a quarter of a mile past the third caution light, on the right. (318) 432-8603.

Lodging

Fruge Park and Recreation Area and Campground Rt. 97 S., Basile.

This campground is far enough from U.S. 190 and I-10 that it is amazing anyone has ever found it. It is a cinch you won't find it

Old Elton Jail. (Photo by Julie Posner)

Coushatta baskets. (Photo by Macon Fry)

listed in any of the campground directories for the state. Although it is primitive (no running water when I visited), Fruge Park offers a great opportunity to pitch your tent on the sprawling South Louisiana Prairie. The campground is on a wooded tract beside a small lake with a little fishing pier. It is located in a region of thousands of acres of crawfish and rice fields and is the perfect place to camp after eating at D.I.'s. You will sleep to a cacophony of frogs and night noises (including the singing of mosquitoes). From U.S. 190 go south on Route 97 for 8.5 miles. Take a right onto Route 1123. Go 1 mile, and at the stop sign immediately past the cemetery, take a right. Go two blocks and the entrance is on the left. It costs $3 for a primitive site, $4 for a pop-up or tent with hook-ups, and $7 for RV's with a/c. (318) 432-6707.

Elton

The towns just seem to peter out as you head west on U.S. 190 and you might miss the village of Elton entirely were it not for the huge rice driers looming over the horizon. Actually, the Estherwood Rice Mill Tour is a good reason to put Elton on your itinerary. After a visit to the mill, you can get a plate lunch at Lurcy's and stop by the Coushatta Indian reservation just north of town. Elton is the westernmost stop on U.S. 190 in Cajun Country; from here the Acadiana trail blazes west through the pine barrens of Allen and Beauregard parishes before entering Texas.

The Old Jail U.S. 190, Elton.

This is one of those "tourist attractions" that is hard to understand. The jail is a two-room brick building about five yards off U.S. 190 in Elton. It is grown over with weeds. One side is used as a trash receptacle, while the array of bottles on the floor indicates the town drunks have spent a few nights in the other side (without the nuisance of having the doors locked behind them). To really appreciate the old jail I had to talk to Police Chief Roger LaFleur, whose brother was chief when it was still in use. LaFleur remembered nights when there were "twenty men in both cells." According to LaFleur, the new jail is "the most modern in the state. We even got bulletproof glass instead of bars. We just don't have any occasion to use it anymore." You can find Roger and his Cajun band, Roger's Raiders, playing at Lurcy's (his wife) restaurant on weekends.

Coushatta Tribe of Louisiana

The Coushatta or Koasati tribe was recognized by the federal government in 1971. Their reservation and tribal center is located just a few miles north of Elton. The Coushatta first entered documented history in the journals of DeSoto in the sixteenth century. The Coushattas were displaced, their towns destroyed, and they were exposed to many diseases. The tribe escaped mass removal operations under the leadership of a man named Red Shoes, who led the band to the lower reaches of the Red River in Louisiana.

Today the Coushatta, numbering about 300, live in the pine forests near Elton, where they remain a close-knit unit, still speaking their language and carrying on their traditional arts and crafts. Baskets woven by the Coushattas of long-leaf pine needles and corn husks are known for their decorative qualities and durability. Samples of the baskets and information on where to purchase them and on the craftsmen is available at the tribal offices and Visitors Center. From U.S. 190 on the west end of town, look for a green state sign pointing to the turnoff for the reservation. Take the first right past the Canal gas station. Go one block and turn left onto Martin Luther King Dr. Follow this for 3 miles. Take a left by the convenience store, go about a quarter of a mile, and the tribal center will be on the left. (318) 584-2261.

Estherwood Rice, Inc. U.S. 190, Elton.

There are several rice mills in South Louisiana that advertise tours, but nobody else will invite you into the milling area to watch the process. Estherwood was originally located in the southern Prairie town of the same name. David Bertrand and Tom Lejeune moved the family business to Elton when they took over from their parents in 1984. It is the only mill that processes the much-sought-after popcorn rice (so called because of the rich popcorn aroma that rises when cooking). It is also the only mill that still packs rice in ten- and twenty-pound cotton bags. The custom-made bags, printed with South Louisiana scenes and logos, have become a trademark of Estherwood milled rice.

When Tom and David moved to Elton the old cotton bag machine was the only packaging tool they had, so they began designing and printing their own bags. These bags have quickly become popular gift items. They now meet a specialized demand from individuals who request a particular logo printed on rice bags for party favors, Christmas presents, or to give out at family reunions. Estherwood is open year round, but the mill is busiest in the late summer through Christmas. While you are waiting for your tour, check out the wall covered with pictures of old rice farming scenes and display case of custom-printed bags. Before leaving you can buy one of the ten- or twenty-pound cotton bags of rice for $3 or $5, respectively. For the same price plus freight, they will mail rice anyplace in the states. Estherwood is open from 7 A.M. to 4 P.M., Monday through Friday, except on holidays. Visit during late summer to mid fall, Tuesdays through Thursdays, to see the plant in operation. (318) 584-2218.

Lurcy's Cajun Restaurant Cajun/Down Home, Dance & Dine, $. U.S. 190.

Lurcy and Roger LaFleur are die-hard Cajuns. After a career in the military, during which Roger won awards for "Best Military Dining Hall" and runner-up awards three times, they came back to live in Roger's hometown of Elton. Since 1985, Lurcy has been operating the cafe on Route 190 while Roger tends to duties as chief of police. Like military food, the eats here may be plain, but they will stick to your ribs. The most interesting items, like Smoked Chicken and Tasso Sauce Piquante over rice with two veggies, appear as lunch specials. My favorite dinner items are fried chicken and the chicken, okra, and tasso gumbo.

In addition to the good food, Lurcy has been pulling in big crowds for her Monday- and Friday-night Cajun jams. These are popular family gatherings and musicians travel from as far away as Lake Charles to bend the strings and squeeze the accordion. Lurcy's is open seven days a week from 7 A.M. to 10 P.M. and until 11 P.M. on Friday and Saturday. The Monday and Friday music starts at about 7 P.M. Lurcy's is located on U.S. 190 in the heart of Elton. (318) 584-5168.

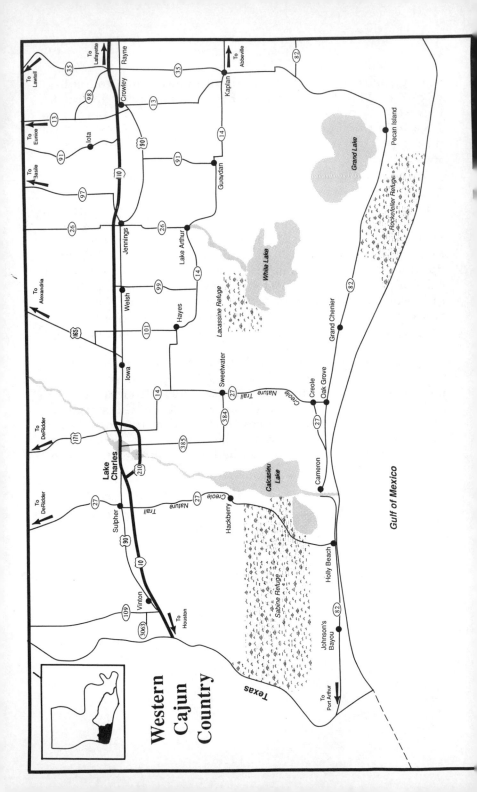

Western Cajun Country

15

Western
Cajun Country

Western Cajun Country is by far the largest of the six regions defined in this book. Stretching west from Lafayette and Abbeville for over a hundred miles, and up to sixty miles north from the Gulf of Mexico, most of the Western Region is sparsely settled marsh and prairie. The most dense settlement is in the towns along U.S. 90 and Interstate 10, paralleling the Southern Pacific Railroad where it cuts across the Cajun Prairie. Along this route and Route 14 to the south, rice fields dominate the landscape and towns are signaled by rice driers towering over the flat pan. The railroad arrived in this area in the early 1880s, before the first settlers and first roads. Anxious to populate the land around the new trunk line, the railroad recruited farmers from the Midwest to populate towns along the way. Rail stations were established approximately every five miles and many of these grew into the planned succession of communities that exists along U.S. 90 today. Anglo names and Victorian and turn-of-the-century architecture predominate in these charming farm villages.

To the south of U.S. 90, the prairie sinks to marshland and Cajun names abound along waterways that wind toward the Gulf. Route 14 roughly parallels U.S. 90 and forms a general demarcation between the drier prairie and permanently wet coastal regions. The coastal parishes of Vermilion and Cameron are two of the largest and most sparsely populated parishes in the state. Cameron encompasses over 1500 square miles of marsh, flooded prairie, and water, and has fewer than 10,000 residents. Many of the residents live on small, oak-covered ridges near the coast, called *cheniers*. Unfenced cattle graze in the marsh and residents make their livings fishing, trapping, and in the oil industry. Recently completed Route 82, also known as the Hug the Coast Highway, connects the communities in Southwest Louisiana's coastal fringe. This route is traveled by fishermen, birdwatchers, duck hunters, and those who seek recreation in the serene Sabine and Rockefeller Wildlife Refuges.

Most visitors will want to see the rice and rail communities along U.S. 90, so this chapter is organized primarily in an east-to-west continuum along this route, with side trips outlined to the towns immediately to the north and south. There are few opportunities to access the scenic Hug the Coast Highway (Route 82), except via Abbeville in the east and the Creole Nature Trail at Lake Charles in the west. The Creole Nature Trail and Hug the Coast Highway (highly recommended for those who have a little extra time and enjoy wildlife watching) are described at the end of this chapter.

THE RICE BELT

Rayne

This mill and rail town of 10,000 residents, 16 miles west of Lafayette, is known (by legislative decree) as The Frog Capital of the World. Since the many rice-field canals that provided choice habitats for the croaking amphibians have been enclosed, the city has adopted a second title—"The Mural City." The feed stores, old warehouses, and store fronts that greet travelers on U.S. 90 are festooned with a dozen murals depicting frogs fishing, frogs dancing, and frogs playing Cajun music. Route 35 crosses U.S. 90 in Rayne, which is the midpoint between Lawtell (22 miles to the north) and Kaplan (20 miles to the south). The first and third weekends of each month, Rayne's two flea markets open to throngs of bargain hunters from around the Prairie.

Attractions

Rayne Antique Flea Market 411 E. Texas Avenue (U.S. 90 East).
Among the treasures I have found at the Rayne Flea Market are stacks of Cajun recordings from the forties, an "official" 1931 *Guide to the State of Louisiana*, and bunches of old postcards. There is just no telling what you will find, but it is a sure bet that it will cost a lot less than at the antique shops in New Orleans. The flea market encompasses 22,000 square feet in a 100-year-old warehouse right beside the railroad tracks and U.S. 90. They are open the first and third weekends each month from 9 A.M. to 5 P.M. If you miss the Rayne market dates, it is just a short drive to

Washington (*see* Cajun Heartland section), where the Old School Flea Market is open on the second and last weekends of the month. From I-10 take exit #87 and go south fifteen blocks to the railroad tracks. The flea market is located on U.S. 90 on the eastern edge of town. (318) 334-9983 or 334-9520.

Antiques and Collectibles 113 Louisiana.

The newer of Rayne's two flea markets has antiques for collectors and plenty of stuff for junk hounds, too. Like the Rayne Flea Market, Antiques and Collectibles is open the first and third weekend each month, from 9 A.M. to 6 P.M. They are located in the Old Mervine Kahn Building in downtown Rayne. From I-10 take exit 87. Go south fifteen blocks and left onto Louisiana, just before the railroad tracks. (318) 783-4657.

Pettijean Crawfish Farm Rt. 98 north.

During crawfish season this farm tries to accommodate small groups of visitors. Call first. (318) 334-4369.

Food

Michael's and Sun's Local Fave, $ (lunch)-$$ (dinner). U.S. 90.

Michael's and Sun's draws a crowd with their workingman's lunch buffet. Four and a half dollars buys all the down-home grub you could hope to eat. At dinner time on weekends, folks usually go for Sun's unique Crawfish Fried Rice. This dish is a gigantic pile of rice, stir-fried vegetables, and about half a pound of extra-large crawfish tails. Michael's and Sun's is open Monday through Thursday from 7 A.M. to 3:30 P.M., Friday and Saturday until 10 P.M., and Sunday, 11 A.M. to 2 P.M. (318) 334-5539.

*Hawk's Boiled Seafood, $$. Rt. 1110 (north of Rayne).

Hawk Arceneaux serves the largest crawfish ever offered for human consumption. However, it's not the size that most distinguishes the crawfish here; it's the sweet flavor. Hawk describes the secret to his crawfish in one word: "purging." Most restaurants wash the mud off the outside of their crawfish. A few add salt to the wash water, to clean the inside. Only Hawk Arceneaux goes through a 24-hour freshwater purging process. Behind his restaurant are freshwater holding tanks from which his chefs dip and boil up to 1500 pounds a night. Some people don't like the fact that most of the seasoning here is sprinkled on the outside. Others complain that the craws are actually *too* clean and they miss that "swampy" flavor. To me, these are the ultimate.

Half the fun of going to Hawk's is getting there. Although they

The Mural City and Frog Capital. (Photo by Ed Neham)

Rayne Frog Festival. (Courtesy of LA Office of Tourism)

are only about 7 miles from Rayne, their location is wildly inscrutable. I recommend going there when there is still a little sunlight left, so you can find the place and avoid the crowds that have somehow discovered this great eatery. When it is raining, the road into Hawk's is covered with thousands of frogs, exiting flooded roadside ditches for the perils of life on the road. Hawk's is open Wednesday to Saturday from 5 P.M. to 10 P.M. (seasonally—mid-November to mid-June).

From I-10, take the Rayne exit. Go north about 50 yards and make a left on Route 98. There are some sharp turns, so make sure you stay on Route 98. Go about 6.5 miles and make a right onto tiny Parish Road 2-7. This is a dirt road marked by a small Hawk's sign. Go .8 miles and Hawk's will be on the left. If you are going to Hawk's from U.S. 190, take Route 367 in Eunice and head south 11.7 miles. Turn right on Route 1110. Go 1.6 miles and turn left on the small Parish road marked with a Hawk's sign. (318) 788-3266.

Lodging

Acadian Oaks Campground Rt. 98 N.

This small campground is convenient to I-10 but just far enough off the highway to provide peaceful camping. Tent sites and RV spaces with full hook-ups cost $10 a night. Exit at Route 35 north. Make an immediate left on Route 98. The campground is about a mile north of I-10. (318) 334-9955.

Special Events

Rayne Frog Festival First weekend in September.

The Frog Festival has been listed as one of the "Top Ten Festivals in the Nation." They surely have the best frogleg etouffée and fried froglegs of any festival I've attended. Featured events include Cajun and Zydeco music, frog eating, jumping, and racing contests, and the coronation of a "Frog Queen" (I guess that beats being named the "Boudin Queen" or "Swine Queen"). There are carnival rides and food booths open throughout the day on Saturday and Sunday. The Frog Festival Midway is located in W. J. "Bill" Gossen Park. Take the Rayne exit from I-10 and head south on Boulevard. Turn right on Oak Street and you will find the park.

Downtown Crowley. (Photo by Julie Posner)

Rice Museum. (Photo by Julie Posner)

Kaplan

Located 17 miles south of Rayne at the intersection of Route 35 and Route 14, Kaplan is a tiny rice and cattle town of 5000 which grew around a rail spur established in 1901. Five years later the town began to celebrate a distinctly non-American festival, Bastille Day. The celebration is still the biggest event in town (aside from the rice harvest), and perhaps the oldest festival in Cajun Country. During most of the year, the only excitement is stirred up by games of bourré at one of the town's several card bars, like Tina's Western Frontier Lounge or Lefty's.

Bastille Day July.

The Bastille Day celebration is held to commemorate the storming of the French prison, the Bastille, in 1789. Mr. Eleaza, one of Kaplan's early settlers, came directly from France and established the fair to honor the birthday of French Independence. (318) 643-2400.

Vermilion Parish Fair 2nd weekend in October.

Crowley

Crowley, with 16,000 residents, is perhaps the archetypal Cajun Prairie rice and rail town. The seat of Acadia Parish, it is one of the major population centers between Lafayette (24 miles to the east) and Lake Charles. The old historic district has a distinctly Anglo feel, resembling the kind of town a model train hobbyist constructs at his favorite rail crossing. It is a city of beautiful Victorian homes and shaded streets. The streets emanate out in a neat grid from the railroad, with Parkerson (Route 13), the main route, bisecting the town. Crowley is the official Rice Capital of Louisiana and home to a dozen or more rice mills and driers. Befitting its location at the center of Louisiana's rice country, the city's best-known attractions are the Rice Museum, the Rice Research Station, and the annual Rice Festival. Local businesses have joined in the boosterism and the town now sports a Rice City Liquor, Rice City Exxon, Rice City Television Sales, and Rice Hotel. The most notable non-rice business in town is the Modern Music Center, where record man Jay Miller opened his pioneering recording studio in 1949. A new suburban Crowley has grown in the swath between U.S. 90 and I-10 at the intersection of Route 13. Here you will find such technological advances as fast food, shopping malls, and multi-screen movie theaters.

Crowley Visitors Center/Chamber of Commerce 114 E. 1st St.

Located in the old Missouri Pacific Passenger Depot at the foot of Parkerson Street, the Crowley Chamber of Commerce is a good first stop for visitors. The Visitors Center has parish and city maps, public restrooms, and a wide selection of brochures for regional attractions. There is also a printed itinerary for a walking tour of the historic district available upon request. You can leave your vehicle in the lot and begin your tour of the nearby rice mills and residential and business districts at the Center. They are open Monday through Friday from 9 A.M. to 4:30 P.M. (318) 788-0177.

Attractions

The Walking Tour

The walking tour of historic Crowley begins at the Visitors Center and takes about an hour. Most of Crowley's dazzling turn-of-the-century homes are located in a two- or three-block swath along the east side of Parkerson Avenue, the old Main Street. Walk six blocks north through this residential area, then return to Parkerson Avenue at the courthouse. Before heading back to the Visitors Center, try walking two blocks north of the Courthouse to sample the homemade tamales at the Rice City Liquor Store. Return to your car by way of Parkerson Street and you will pass rows of narrow old storefronts. Nestled among these shops is the Modern Music Store, home to the oldest continuously operated recording studio in Louisiana.

Modern Music Center and Master-Trak Studios 413 N. Parkerson.

There is nothing modern about the storefront that greets visitors to this South Louisiana music Mecca. Old instruments hang from the ceiling, and dust covers racks of vintage 45-rpm records. Jay Miller became the first record man in Cajun Country in 1946 and has been recording and selling South Louisiana music here since 1949. Clifton Chenier, Rusty and Doug Kershaw, Jimmy "C" Newman, and Cajun superstar Wayne Toups are just a few of the legendary musicians who have recorded here and whose records may still be purchased in the store. If you are lucky enough to catch Jay Miller holding forth at the cash register, get him to bend your ear about the good old days, or about his latest "sure to be a hit" record. Miller doesn't have a lot of his old material in print, but he does have a number of excellent albums and forty-fives recorded in the last ten to fifteen years, including records by Buckwheat Zydeco, Fernest Arceneaux, and Wayne Toups. Modern Music is open Monday through Friday from 8:30

A.M. to 5 P.M. and on Saturday from 8 A.M. to noon. (318) 783-1601.

Rice Museum U.S. 90 west.

The Rice Museum is located just west of Crowley on U.S. 90 in a small frame house. The exhibits here were mostly designed when the museum opened in the early sixties. Some of the displays have become museum pieces in their own right! The artifacts include a wooden model of a rice mill, old photographs of Crowley, and relics of past Rice Festivals. The old Oil Room exhibit is precious, as is the miniature working model of a rice mill. Just ask the curator and she will dump some unhulled rice in the hopper and flip the switch. Particularly interesting was a chunk of "climatron," a building material composed of rice hulls, chaff, and cement, which was actually used to build a couple of local houses in the fifties. If you like your museums with a down-home flair, this one is for you. The museum has opened and closed several times in the last few years. If they are still in business, you will find them open March through November. They operate Wednesday through Friday from 10 A.M. to 3 P.M. Admission is $1.50 for adults, $1 for children, and includes a free "Have A Rice Day" souvenir. From the intersection of Parkerson and U.S. 90, head west on U.S. 90 for 1.5 miles and the Rice Museum will be on the right. (318) 788-0177 (Chamber), 783-6842 (Museum).

Rice Research Station of the LSU Agricultural Center Rt. 1111 N.

The Rice Station sports some of the most verdant acreage anywhere. There are no planned tours, but the research staff welcomes curious visitors and will take a few minutes to explain their work and answer questions about rice cultivation. From Crowley, head east on U.S. 90. Just east of town, turn left on Route 1111. After crossing over I-10, go three blocks and take a right. This road will pass through plots of land with experimental patches of rice before ending at the Rice Station headquarters. (318) 788-7531.

Rice Mill Row Mill St.

The biggest concentration of rice mills and driers in South Louisiana is located on Mill Street at the foot of Parkerson Avenue in Crowley. The tall buildings are the driers, in which hot air is pumped through the fresh product. In the late summer, this area is enveloped in a cloud of rice dust as trucks are weighed and unload their harvest into huge hoppers.

Crowley Flea Market 210 E. 1st. St.

This flea market, located in a rail depot just one block west of the Visitors Center, provides good picking for junk hounds, collectors, and antique buffs. The Crowley Flea Market is open the first and third weekend each month from 9 A.M. to 5 P.M. (318) 783-3944.

Food

Belizaire's Cajun Restaurant Dine & Dance, $$. 2307 N. Parkerson Ave.

Belizaire's does a respectable job with their fried seafood, and has live Cajun music and dancing Wednesday through Saturday starting at 8 P.M., and Sundays at 4 P.M. Their clean and spacious interior and easy access off the Interstate make them a popular stop for tourists. They are located one block south of I-10 on Route 13. Belizaire's is open Monday through Thursday from 11 A.M. to 10 P.M., Friday and Saturday until midnight, and Sunday from 11 A.M. to 8 P.M. (318) 788-2501.

Elliott Brothers Meat Market. 1217 E. 8th St.

Here's the best boudin and cracklin's on the lower Prairie. As you would expect, there is a healthy amount of local rice in these sausages, but it is well complemented with lean meat which has not been shredded beyond recognition. Mike Elliott took thirty pounds of his boudin to a show in Missouri, where it was universally avoided, leaving him to grouse, "They don't know how to cook rice—or eat it, either. They don't even eat gravy on it, just butter." The Elliott brothers have no problem selling their spicy product in Crowley, where they produce over 1000 pounds a week. The Elliots' store is at U.S. 90 and 8th Street, in the southeast end of town. They are open Monday through Friday from 8 A.M. to 5:30 P.M., and Saturday from 7 A.M. to 12:30 P.M. (318) 783-2704.

Frosto Local Fave, $. E. 3rd and North G Ave.

The Frosto has been a Crowley institution for over forty years. This vintage burger stand and dairy bar turns out typical fast food. I like their Frosties, which are nothing more than soda pop and ice cream thrown together in a blender (a sure way to cool off from your downtown walking tour, and an excellent accompaniment for the tamales from Rice City Liquor). (318) 783-0917.

Rice City Liquor Store Local Fave, $. 630 N. Parkerson

Folks from out West have been heard to comment that Louisiana tamales are a roll of grits stuffed with meat, but one whiff of the red sauce wafting from the back room and you will be ordering a dozen instead of six. Pat Istre's family has been running Rice City Liquor since the forties, when liquor was sold only in package stores, but has been surviving since the sixties primarily on the popularity of their homemade tamales. They are open Monday through Friday from 8 A.M. to 6 P.M., and Saturday from 10 A.M. to 4 P.M. They make the tamales fresh daily, and usually run out by 5 P.M. (318) 783-9856.

Special Events

The Rice Festival 1st or 2nd weekend in October.

Inaugurated in 1937, the Rice Festival is Louisiana's oldest harvest festival. The festival includes the crowning of the Rice Queen, and a parade with guest appearances by other festival queens from around the state. The main attraction is the street party that unfolds in the old downtown district of Parkerson Street on Saturday and Sunday. There are food booths (selling typical carnival-style food), and live Cajun bands play on an outdoor bandstand. (318) 788-0177.

*Iota Courir du Mardi Gras Exit #72, Egan (5 miles west of Crowley).

Iota is a farm community about 14 miles northwest of Crowley that has preserved many aspects of the traditional Courir du Mardi Gras that have disappeared elsewhere. Most of the riders wear the traditional painted screen masks. Upon reentering town at the end of the ride they are often showered with money. On Mardi Gras day the riders depart about 7 A.M. While they are visiting farms around the countryside, the town holds a folk craft, food, and music festival downtown. There is dancing and street food. Before the riders return, the children of Iota command the raised dance floor, where they sing the Mardi Gras song and dance. After the performance, they are showered with change from the crowd and a general melee ensues as they chase coins about the stage. This event harkens back to the days when a *"petite Mardi Gras"* was held on Mondays, and children would visit neighbors on foot in a simulation of the adults' *Courir du Mardi Gras*. The riders return to Iota around 2 o'clock, so it is possible to catch the happenings here and drive over to enjoy the culmination of their Mardi Gras.

Music

Belizaire's

This is one of half a dozen or so (the number is growing rapidly) family restaurants that feature live Cajun music and

Iota Mardi Gras. (Photo by Julie Posner)

dancing on a regular basis. While it lacks the charm of some of the older traditional dance halls, kids are allowed inside, so it is a great place to bring the family. Belizaire's has music on Wednesdays and Thursdays, when many of the older clubs and halls are quiet. Cajun bands play Wednesday through Saturday at 8 P.M. and on Sunday at 4 P.M. See directions above. (318) 788-2501.

Lodging

*Rice Hotel 125 3rd St.

This 84-year-old hulk is one of the few old downtown motels in South Louisiana that has not yielded to the wrecking ball. The Rice Hotel is far from grand, but it is meticulously clean and infinitely charming, from the antique "Petticoat Junction"-style switchboard to the rooms with their aging but comfortable furnishings and ceiling fans. There are no televisions in the rooms, but the one in the lobby is a popular evening gathering place. At other times, the TV runs because the lady at the desk says, "It gets too darn quiet in here." Unfortunately you can't stay here during the Rice Festival. All three floors are reserved for the kings, queens, and chaperones. It is $21 for a double with one bed, and $32 for a double with two beds. The hotel is located a block west of Parkerson, on 3rd Street. (318) 783-6471.

Crowley Inn Rt. 13 N., $38 double. (318) 788-0970.

Cajun Haven Campground I-10 exit #72, Egan (8 miles west of Crowley). If you are looking for camping spaces literally beside the interstate, this is your spot. $10 full hook-ups. (318) 783-2853.

Trail's End Campground I-10 exit #72, Egan (8 miles west of Crowley).

This is a miniature RV resort, with full hook-ups, pull-through sites, a small swimming pool, tennis courts, ice, bathhouse, and a playground. In season, you can pick your own peaches, blackberries, blueberries, and muscadine grapes. Camping is $11.50 a night. Exit #72, and south 1.5 miles. (318) 783-9810 or 234-2738.

Gueydan

Gueydan (pronounced GAY-don) is a farming community of about 1,600 on Route 14, 11 miles south of U.S. 90. From Crowley you will need to drive west on U.S. 90 about 8 miles to Midland, and catch Route 91 south. The city has been proclaimed the Duck Capital of America for the thousands of ducks that forage in nearby rice fields and winter in the marsh, which stretches south 30 miles to the Gulf of Mexico. For most of a century the Gueydan area has been a prime destination for duck hunters, many of whom own or lease camps in the southern marshes. Each year they celebrate the plentiful waterfowl in the Labor Day weekend Duck Festival. The best reason for a cursory traveler to stop here is to pick up a stock of the locally grown Ellis Stansel's Popcorn Rice at the local feed store.

Gueydan Duck Festival Labor Day Weekend.

There has been talk of moving this festival to a cooler time of year, so call first to determine the actual date of the celebration. Historically the festival was timed to coincide with the opening of the hunting season. Saturday and Sunday activities include a cooking contest, live music, and food booths. The festival is held in the Duck Festival Park on the east end of town. (318) 536-6780.

Gueydan Hunting Directory

Published by the Gueydan Chamber of Commerce, this pamphlet details outfitters, day hunts, camp operators, and leases in the Gueydan area. Information is provided on rules and regulations, and a number of local recipes are included for good measure. To get a copy of this brochure, write to the Gueydan Chamber of Commerce at P.O. Box 562, Gueydan, LA 70542. (318) 536-6330.

Boatner & Linscombe Feed Store (Popcorn Rice) 300 1st St.

A stop here will give you more than a taste of local color and accents. Boatner is the main outlet for the fabulous Ellis Stansel's Popcorn Rice, as well as feed, seed, fertilizer, garden supplies, and livestock remedies. The popcorn rice, unavailable at major supermarkets, has a rich flavor and firm texture. A ten-pound bag costs $8, and five pounds goes for $4.50. The bags are made of cotton and are printed with the Stansel logo. Boatner Feed Store is on Route 14 West at 1st Street. They are open Monday through Friday from 7 A.M. to 5 P.M. and Saturday until noon. (318) 536-6751 or 536-6385.

To order Ellis Stansel's Popcorn Rice directly from Mr. Stansel, write: P.O. Box 206, Gueydan, LA 70542.

Jennings

Jennings is the seat of Jefferson Davis Parish. Like the other rice and cattle towns that grew along the Old Spanish Trail, this city, halfway between Lafayette and Lake Charles, boomed with the arrival of the railroad. S. L. Cary, a land agent for the Southern Pacific Railway, published tracts that drew Anglo and German settlers to the area from throughout the Midwest in the 1880s. Unlike some of the other towns, however, Jennings experienced a second spectacular economic boom in the early 1900s when oil was discovered at the Evangeline Field, just north of town. This was the first "bringing in" of an oil well in Louisiana, and it touched off an influx of merchants, speculators, and vice in the formerly conservative community. Perhaps sensing that oil was too prosaic to attract tourists, the city changed their motto (by legislative decree!) in 1979 from "The Cradle of Louisiana Oil" to "The Boudin Capital of the Universe." Like Crowley, this city of 12,500 is characterized by a quaint Victorian residential district clustered around a crumbling old commercial strip. Modern suburbs extend between the historic town center and the interstate to the north.

Attractions

Jefferson Davis Parish Tourist Center/Chateau des Cocodries I-10 exit 64 north.

The Jeff Davis Tourist Center is located right beside the interstate in the Louisiana Oil and Gas Park. Here you will find public restrooms, city and parish maps, brochures, and a helpful staff. After getting your fill of tourist brochures, you can mosey over to one of the state's more unusual roadside attractions. Interstate 10 passes thousands of acres of natural alligator habitat. For those who do not have time to look for an alligator in the wild, the *Chateau des Cocodries* has the state's only captive gator within easy interstate access (a dubious distinction for the poor reptile). The *Chateau* is a small cement and cinderblock cell/viewing area directly adjacent to the Tourist Center. The center is open Monday through Friday from 9 A.M. to 4 P.M., Saturday from noon to 4:30 P.M., and some Sundays. The *Chateau des Cocodries* is open seven days a week, 8 A.M. to 5 P.M. (318) 824-9533.

Oil and Gas Park I-10 exit 64 north.

The Louisiana Oil and Gas Park was built to commemorate the first producing oil well in the state of Louisiana, which was brought in at the Evangeline Field, a few miles north. In 1901, Jules Clement, a rice farmer and rancher, noticed bubbles coming from one of his flooded fields. Inspired by the huge Spindletop gusher struck earlier that year in Texas, he stuck a stovepipe into the ground over the bubbles. When he tossed a match into the

Early oil well. (Courtesy of Lafayette Courthouse Archives)

pipe, the bubbles ignited and the oil rush was on. With the help of the men who financed the Spindletop well, the Jules Clement Well #1 was brought in a few months later, producing over 7000 barrels a day. I haven't noticed any bubbles coming out of the pond at the Louisiana Oil and Gas Park, but I saw some kids pulling in fish hand over fist. The park is open during daylight hours daily. In addition to the pond, Visitors Center, and alligator, it has a replica of the state's first oil well and picnic tables with a view of the interstate.

Attractions

Walking Tour
There is no "official" walking tour of Jennings, but anyone exploring Western Cajun Country should take half an hour or so and stroll Main Street between U.S. 90 and the railroad. In this nine-block stretch, most of the store fronts are just as they were eighty years ago, with only a few details fading. Most of the stores were built during the oil boom and many have facades dated 1901 or 1902. Some stores, like *Ardoin's Crescent Drugs*, have maintained their original identity. Ardoin's is nothing less than a living museum, its windows filled with old medicine bottles and its shelves bearing yellowed "department" signs.

Anchoring Main Street is the newly reopened **Jennings Cinema* (432 N. Main Street, (318) 824-8813), an Art-Deco-style theater of the type that once stood on Main Streets around America. The Deco details on the front are in great condition. Interior walls are decorated with two-tone hourglass lamps. First-run movies are shown at a bargain price and the air conditioning blows cold. To see the historic residential district, you can walk back to your car by way of Cary Street, which parallels Main one block to the west.

Zigler Museum 411 Clara St.
The Zigler Museum was created in 1963 by the late Mrs. Ruth B. Zigler, who established a museum trust and donated the property, which had been the Zigler family home since 1908. The museum houses a small but high-quality collection of work by European masters. Most impressive is its Audubon collection, and the gallery of works by Louisiana artists. The Central Gallery displays a new exhibit each month. From I-10 take exit 64 south 1 mile and take a left onto Clara Street. If you are walking the old downtown area, the museum is just four blocks west of Main Street. It is open Tuesday through Saturday from 9 A.M. to 5 P.M.

and Sunday from 1 P.M. to 5 P.M. Admission is by donation. (318) 824-0114.

Food

★Boudin King Cajun/Down Home, $. 906 Division St.

Although there is a certain novelty to a restaurant whose reputation is built on boudin and which serves the steaming links at a drive-up window, Boudin King has some stuff on the menu that is a heck of a lot better than their sausage. Try instead the perfectly seasoned fried chicken and crispy homemade onion rings. For a real surprise check out the chicken and sausage gumbo. Never mind the styrofoam bowl; this is some of the best gumbo around! For about $5 you can get a meal to remember— two pieces of chicken, a small gumbo, and a small order of onion rings. From I-10, go south on Route 26 for 2 miles to the light at Division Street. Take a right onto Division and the Boudin King is four blocks up on the right. They are open Monday through Saturday from 8 A.M. to 9 P.M. (318) 824-6593.

Lodging

Sundown Inn Rt. 26 North. $25 double. (318) 824-7041.

Travelodge Evangeline Rd. $36 double. (318) 824-6550.

Holiday Inn Rt. 26 North. $45 double. (318) 824-5280.

Lacassine Loop Tour (South of Jennings)

Some of the most beautiful wetlands in Western Cajun Country can be seen by driving a 50-mile loop south of Interstate 10 between Jennings and Lacassine. This loop passes by the former resort and lumber town of Lake Arthur, the marshes of the Lacassine Wildlife Refuge, and the idyllic swamp at the ancient Lorrain Bridge over Bayou Lacassine. The complete loop may be a bit lengthy for travelers just passing through (allow about 2½ hours), but is a worthwhile destination for folks making a day trip from Lafayette. Those who want to linger in the area will find modern accommodations available in Jennings, and four camp-grounds on the scenic loop with waterside sites. The Lacassine Loop is comprised of an 11-mile segment of Route 26 (between Jennings and Lake Arthur) on the east; the southern leg is a 20-mile chunk of Route 14, between Lake Arthur and Hayes. The loop is completed by taking Route 101 8 miles north, rejoining Route 90 in the town of Lacassine. You will need to figure additional miles and time to access the several attractions along the way.

Lake Arthur

Lake Arthur, 11 miles south of Jennings at the intersection of Route 26 and Route 14, is one of the loveliest villages in Western Cajun Country. From its spreading oaks covered with Spanish moss to its cypress-studded waterfront and grand homes overlooking the lake, the town has a distinctively slow, shady South Louisiana ambiance. Lake Arthur was originally conceived as a resort community in the late 1800s. The town was developed on the banks of Lake Arthur, a wide basin fed by the Mermentau River. No sooner was it laid out than two mills opened and lumbering became the primary industry. Franklin D. Roosevelt was among the celebrities who regularly visited the town, stayed at its grand hotel, and enjoyed hunting in the surrounding wetlands (before he was stricken with polio). Today the former resort is a slumbering village. Its hotel has been torn down and an oak-shaded park with man-made beach now occupies the downtown waterfront.

Lake Arthur Park Lakefront, downtown.

The former site of Lake Arthur's grand hotel is now occupied by a beautiful little lakeside park. There is a man-made beach and a pier with diving platform, but to cool off you may have to simply enjoy the breezes off the water and shaded picnic pavilions. Ricefield pollution has kept the beach closed to swimming for most of the last two summers. To determine if the beach is open, call Lake Arthur City Hall at (318) 774-2211. The park is open from 7 A.M. to 9 P.M. during the summer season.

Music

Lake Arthur VFW Post Cajun Dance. 3rd St.

Typically, the best Cajun music in Western Cajun Country is found at VFWs and community or church halls. The Lake Arthur VFW has been holding Saturday night dances for over fifteen years. They now have bands on Saturday at 8 P.M. and on Sundays at 2 P.M. Admission is $2. Take Route 14 to the east side of town and turn north on Third Street. The VFW is a mile up, on the right. (318) 774-2946.

Food

Nott's Corner Restaurant 639 Arthur Ave.

Nott's is an old country-style restaurant with a super-relaxed atmosphere. Their walls are decorated with historical photographs of the Lake Arthur area. The food is as good as any you will find on Route 14 (that is not saying a lot). Try their po-boys, or boiled and fried seafood. Nott's is open daily from 7 A.M. to 9 P.M. (318) 774-2332.

Lodging

Lakeview RV Park Rt. 26, 1 mile north of Lake Arthur.

Eighteen RV spaces with complete hook-ups. The campground is about a mile north of Lake Arthur on Route 26. (318) 774-2694 or 774-2695.

Rt. 14 West

Lacassine National Wildlife Refuge Rt. 3056.

The Lacassine National Wildlife Refuge encompasses 31,776 acres of freshwater marsh. The Refuge is administered by the United States Fish and Wildlife Service and is designed to protect wetlands wildlife and habitat. Most visitors to the refuge (which is largely inaccessible except by boat) are birdwatchers and fishermen. The list of birds sighted at Lacassine contains over 230 species.

There is no boat launch in the refuge, but two commercial launches (*see* listing below) provide access to the 16,000-acre Lacassine Pool and surrounding bayous. Visitors arriving by car can stop at the refuge office, pick up a brochure on Lacassine, and walk a short pier into an adjacent bog. Lacassine is open to the general public from March 15 until October 15. The refuge office and visitor contact station are located on the Mermentau River about 11 miles from Lake Arthur. Take Route 14 west from Lake Arthur for 7 miles. Turn south onto Route 3056 (Lowry Road). The refuge offices are 4 miles south. Office hours are from 7 A.M. to 3:30 P.M. weekdays. (318) 774-5923.

*Myers' Landing Campground and Boat Launch Rt. 3056

Myers' is a country campground that appeals to fishermen, birdwatchers, and other outdoorsmen. Campsites are situated right on the banks of the Mermentau River. The camp store sells bait, fishing supplies, gas, and camping gear. They also stock "essential" groceries like weenies, marshmallows, and beer. Myer's is a special place, from their store, which has a picnic table overlooking the river and sells bait on credit, to the thickly shaded grounds. The restroom is clean, but there are no showers. Full hook-ups are $10 a night; tent spaces are $5. The boat launch costs $2. Myer's is located a couple of miles from the Lacassine Refuge. Take Route 14 for 11 miles west from Lake Arthur. Turn south on Route 3056. About 3 miles down you'll see signs on the left for Myers' Landing. (318) 774-9992 or 774-2338.

Gary's Landing and Campground Rt. 3056.

Gary's is a rough launch and campground on the edge of the Lacassine Refuge. Sites, equipped with water and electric hook-ups, cost $10 a night. To get to Gary's, follow the same directions as to the Lacassine Refuge. About half a mile before the refuge entrance, bear left and follow the signs to Gary's Landing at the end of the road.

Harris Seafood Restaurant Dine and Dance, $$. Rt. 14 W., Hayes.

I don't know where they come from, but huge crowds rendezvous at this restaurant/dance hall every Wednesday and Saturday night. In fact, you can forget getting a seat in the dance hall area unless you call in advance for reservations, or get there before 6. Harris has the formula for success pared down to the Cajun essentials: fresh boiled and fried seafood served in a no-frills (cement floor) dining room, and a great big dance floor. We visited three times in 1990-1991, and on each visit found another addition underway! By far the most popular items on the menu are the fried seafood platter, boiled crawfish, and crabs ($11 a dozen). Cajun and country bands play on Wednesday and Saturday, from 7:30 P.M. to 11 P.M. Harris is located on Route 14, just west of the Route 101 intersection. They are 20 miles west of Lake Arthur and 8 miles south of U.S. 90 in Lacassine. Harris is open Tuesday through Saturday, from 11 A.M. to about 11 P.M. and Sunday from 5 P.M. to 10 P.M. Closed Monday. (318) 622-3582.

*Lorrain Bridge and Campground Lorrain Rd. (North of Hayes).

A two mile detour east from Route 101 takes travelers to an enchanted corner of Cajun Country. In the late 1800s, the community of Lorrain flourished at the juncture of Bayou Lacassine and Bayou Chene. The waterways carried schooners laden with lumber and rice through the marshes and into the Gulf. A small buggy bridge was built over the bayous just below their convergence. That bridge was destroyed and a new, all-wooden one built in 1920. This is the bridge that is still standing (barely!) and carrying very occasional traffic today. With the arrival of the

Lorrain Bridge. (Photo by Janet C. Doucet)

railroad, the bayous lost much of their importance as commercial thoroughfares, and Lorrain became a virtual ghost town. There is almost nothing left of the town today except a cemetery. The once-busy Lacassine Bayou crossing is silently reflected in the murky waters of the forking streams. A rare pickup rattles by, shaking the old wooden bridge for all it's worth before disappearing in the cypress-and-oak forest.

The Lorrain Bridge Campground is one of the wonderful "undiscovered" spots we turned up in our travels. This tiny campground nestles against the west bank and cypress swamp of Bayou Lacassine, directly beside the old bridge. There is a gentle rise in the bank here and trails of Spanish moss hang down to tent level. At the water's edge there is a small wooden deck, perfect for fishing or picnics, and a slope graded for backing a boat trailer down. The bayous are lovely at this juncture and the current slow, so if you have a canoe, this is a primo spot for embarking on a paddle trip. To get to the Lorrain Bridge from the juncture at Route 14, head north on Route 101 two miles and turn east on Lorrain Road (Lorrain Road is 6 miles south of U.S. 90). Go 1.5 miles and turn right at the *T* in the road. In another mile you will cross the Lorrain Bridge.

Lorrain Bridge to U.S. 90

From the Lorrain Bridge you may return to U.S. 90 by way of Route 101 north, or you may continue east across the Lorrain Bridge. This is a twisting route that covers some wildly rural area, much of which is forested with cypress. After crossing the bridge, the road alternates from blacktop to gravel for 6 miles before dumping you onto Route 99, 7 miles south of U.S. 90 at Welsh.

Jennings to Lake Charles on U.S. 90

It is thirty miles from Jennings to Lake Charles by way of U.S. 90 or I-10. There is not much to see or do in the small rail towns of Roanoke, Welsh, Lacassine, and Iowa, which crop up at 4- to 7-mile intervals along the way. If you do not have time to take the Lacassine Loop Tour, you may want to get on the interstate and blaze through this stretch.

John Blank Sportsman's Park (Pool and Campground). Main St., Welsh.

RV and tent camping costs $4. The campground is located two blocks south of U.S. 90 on Main Street. (318) 734-2231.

Lake Charles

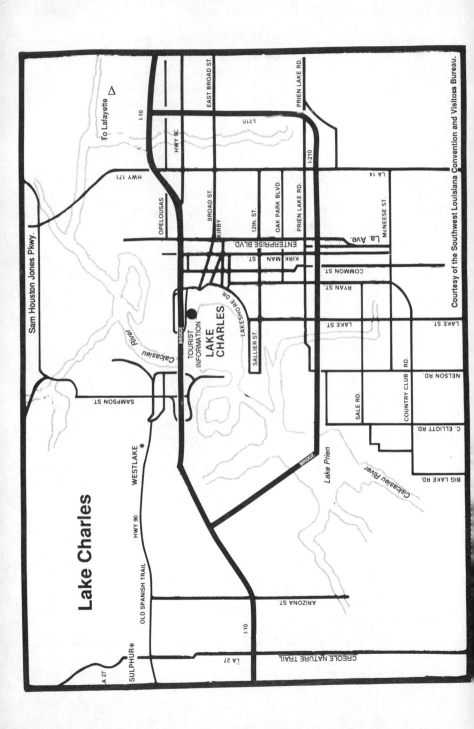

Courtesy of the Southwest Louisiana Convention and Visitors Bureau.

Lacassine

In Lacassine (17 miles west of Jennings), Rt. 101 heads south 8 miles to the Lorrain Bridge and Lacassine Wildlife Refuge on Rt. 14. (*see* Lacassine Scenic Loop Tour.)

Lake Charles

Lake Charles rests on the east bank of the Calcasieu River, 70 miles west of Lafayette. The seat of Calcasieu (Indian for "crying eagle") Parish, it is one of the two major population centers in Cajun Country, with 75,000 residents. In this western outpost, the people, scenery, and way of life have more in common with neighboring Texas than with the rest of South Louisiana. Cowboy attire is common, and most residents find employment in the Port of Lake Charles, at nearby chemical plants, or in the oil industry. It is an area where restaurants are more likely to serve a good plate of barbequed ribs than etouffée, and where the music of choice is Country, not Cajun.

Until 1821, Lake Charles was the last secure settlement in southwest Louisiana, as the lands to the west of the Calcasieu River were alternately claimed by Spain and Mexico. The city and adjacent lake (which is actually a basin in the Calcasieu River) were named for Charles Sallier, who became one of the first settlers in the region in the 1780s. The town began as a stop on the Old Spanish Trail, and grew as a schooner port with excellent access to the Gulf of Mexico, 34 miles to the south. At the end of the War Between the States, Lake Charles had only 400 residents. With the arrival of the Southern Pacific Railway and deepening of Calcasieu Pass (the main Gulf outlet for the Port of Lake Charles), the population grew to 3000 by 1890. Like most of Cajun Country, lumbering was the main industry at the turn of the century, but it was replaced by oil and petrochemicals in the 1930s. Unlike other cities, however, Lake Charles held closer ties with its western neighbors than with Cajun Country and most goods were shipped to Galveston rather than New Orleans.

Lake Charles is still reeling from the crippling blow struck when oil prices collapsed in the 1980s, bringing double-digit unemployment to this industrial area. Motels, restaurants, and block after block of businesses in the downtown area (located on the Lakefront near the Calcasieu Bridge) remain boarded up. It has even been suggested that meter maids slip a dollar bill rather than a ticket under the wipers of cars parked illegally on downtown streets. The dire economy and concentration of chemical plants make the city's immediate environs hard to appreciate, but there are a few small restaurants and dance halls worth seeking out. Fans of regional music make the trip to Lake Charles to visit the legendary Eddie Shuler's Goldband Studios and record shop. Most people will want to use the city as a base for exploring the fantastic Creole Nature Trail and wetlands to the south.

Southwest Louisiana Visitors Center 1211 N. Lakeshore Dr.

In Lake Charles, the interstate is an elevated highway, so it is hard to decide where to jump off to look around. If you need orienting beyond the suggestions here, the Visitors Center has a helpful staff, parish and city maps, and a ton of brochures. Among the more interesting maps is one locating and listing the hundreds of chemical plants which adorn the banks of the Calcasieu River. I recommend that you pick up brochures to the Historic Charpentier District and the Creole Nature Trail (a must see!). The center is open Monday through Friday from 8 A.M. to 5 P.M., and Saturday and Sunday from 10:30 A.M. to 3:30 P.M. From I-10, exit at Lakeshore Drive (the last exit on the east side of the Calcasieu River Bridge). Lakeshore Drive will curve beneath the interstate. The Visitors Center is on the south side of I-10. (318) 436-9588 or 1-800-456-SWLA.

Attractions

Charpentier District Walking/Driving Tour

Much of the old downtown area in Lake Charles burned in the great fire of 1910, so homes and businesses vary from Victorian and turn-of-the-century to modern styles. The Charpentier (carpenter) District is a roughly six-square-block area just south of the interstate where one can view dozens of homes constructed between 1885 and 1920 (a tour map and brochure is available from the Visitors Center). At the time when most of these houses were built, there was no architect living in Lake Charles. Thus they bear unique touches scribed by the carpenters who created them. Spires, galleries, and oddly ballustraded porches abound. The area is bounded by Hodges Street on the west, Kirby on the south, Louisiana Avenue on the east, and Beldon on the north. From I-10 westbound, exit at Enterprise Boulevard. Travel south about eight blocks and turn right onto First Street. This will intersect Louisiana Avenue at the southeast edge of the district.

Fire and Water Driving Tour (Industrial loop).

For a startling look at the churning and burning petrochemical plants that glower across the lake at Lake Charles, cross Prien

Lake on the swooping Interstate 210 bridge and descend into the chemical corridor of Westlake industries. Upon intersecting I-10 on the west side, you may return to Lake Charles via the I-10 bridge over the Calcasieu River. It is recommended that you take this drive at night, when the natural gas flares, thousands of plant lights, and smoking stacks set the Calcasieu aglow like the river Styx. Hold your nose.

Lakeshore Drive
    The five-mile course of Lakeshore Drive, along the edge of Lake Charles and Lake Prien to the south, offers a view of some of the grandest homes in the city and a broad vista of the smoking stacks of Westlake industries. Catch Lakeshore Drive at the Visitors Center beside the Calcasieu Bridge and you will first drive past the comical North Beach recreation area (again, with a wonderful industrial view). Just south of the beach the road passes the Lake Charles Civic Center. At this point sport fishermen can often be seen pulling speckled trout from the basin. The rest of the drive is mainly past lakefront residences.

Imperial Calcasieu Museum 204 West Sallier.
    The Imperial Calcasieu Museum houses an extensive collection of books, documents, and artifacts relating to the history of the parish and Lake Charles. There is a library and reading room packed with documents and texts, a pharmacy exhibit, Victorian bedroom suite, and art gallery. Most interesting is the collection of materials on the War Between the States. Although I am not a war buff, I lost myself for an hour, reading letters and first-hand accounts of battlefield existence sent home from the front by local soldiers. The museum is located on property which originally belonged to the early settler Charles Sallier. Behind the building stands the 300-year-old Sallier Oak. To get to the museum from I-10, exit on Enterprise Boulevard. Head south to 12th Street. Take a right onto 12th Street, which turns into Sallier. The museum is located 12 blocks off Enterprise Boulevard, at the corner of Ethel Street. They are open Tuesday through Friday from 10 A.M. to 5 P.M., and Saturday and Sunday from 1 P.M. Admission is free, but donations are accepted. (318) 439-3797.

Children's Museum 809 Kirby St.
    The Children's Museum of Lake Charles is a place where kids can learn from participatory exhibits. There is an airplane simulation, a mock dentist's office, and several other vocational exploration booths. From I-10, go south on Enterprise Boulevard to Kirby Street. Turn right onto Kirby and look for the Children's

North Beach, Lake Charles. (Courtesy of LA Office of Tourism)

Museum a few blocks down on the right. The museum is open Tuesday through Sunday from 2 P.M. to 5 P.M. and Saturday 10 A.M. to 4 P.M. They are closed on major holidays, the last week of August, and first two weeks of September. Admission is $1. (318) 433-9420, 433-9421.

McNeese State University Ryan St. and McNeese St.

McNeese was founded as a two-year junior college in 1939. In 1940 it was named for John McNeese, who became the first state superintendent of schools in 1888. In 1950 it became a four-year state college. The nickname of the school's athletic teams is the Cowboys. McNeese hosts annual rodeo competitions.

Elderhostel Program at McNeese State University

Elderhostel is a program operating at universities throughout the world offering senior citizens an opportunity to expand their horizons through intellectual, recreational, and social activity, as well as travel. The program, which was initiated in 1975, offers a week of activities, classes, room and board, and local transportation for the incredible price of around $275. The program at McNeese is usually held the last week in September and the first week of October. It includes courses in Louisiana's political heritage, Cajun cuisine, and Cajun culture (attendance is required at one of the three courses). Housing is provided in a campus dormitory. Hostelers must be sixty years or older (but may bring a companion 50 or over). For more information on the Elderhostel Program, contact the national office at ELDERHOSTEL, P.O. Box 1959, Dept. TN, Wakefield, MA 01880-5959.

Louisiana Peace Memorial N. Lakeshore Dr.

The towering structure on the lakefront in downtown Lake Charles is a 120-foot-tall birdhouse (said to be the largest in the world), constructed as a memorial to veterans who served in Vietnam.

Mass Grave for Hurricane Victims 2700 E. Opelousas St.

Hurricane Audrey, which slammed the Gulf coast of Louisiana due south of Lake Charles on June 28, 1957, was the kind of event that people who experienced it tend to measure all others by. A ten-foot storm surge ripped across the coastal *cheniers* and wiped out homes and livestock 20 miles inland. There were estimated to be over 500 fatalities. Two hundred of these victims are buried in a mass grave at Combre Memorial Park Cemetery in Lake Charles (where relief efforts were based). From I-10, go one block south on Route 14 and take a left onto Opelousas Street. The cemetery is on the left. (318) 436-3341.

Mass grave of Hurricane Audrey victims. (Photo by Julie Posner)

Food

Lake Charles has the full range of fast-food restaurants, but very few really great regional eateries. The best food around town is the seafood, Texas-style barbeque, and boudin.

Acadian Delight/Geyen's Barbecue Local Fave, $. 2007 Moeling St.

Whatever you want, they got it, from fresh gingerbread "stageplanks" to barbeque ribs and stew! Geyen's is basically a soul-food restaurant that happens to have a bakery in the back. You order at the counter but can dine at one of the three tables in the store front. (318) 433-6020.

*Crab Palace Boiled Seafood, $-$$. 2218 Enterprise Blvd.

The Crab Palace serves gumbos, stews, and fried seafood, but the minimalist decor, plastic tablecloths, and line out the door mark it as a classic boiling point. Their boiled crabs are the best I've had west of New Iberia. Fried hard-shell crabs are also popular. The hard crab is actually battered and dropped into boiling grease. Barbequed hard-shells are the same as the fried ones, only drenched in barbeque sauce. These are superbly messy. Crabs cost about $7 a dozen. The Palace is open Tuesday through Saturday from 10:30 A.M. to 9 P.M. (318) 433-4660.

Granger's Local Fave, $-$$. Old Town Rd.

Granger's is a wild joint, serving boiled crawfish, hot tamales, boudin, fresh-ground hamburgers, and a decent etouffée in a tavern-like atmosphere. The dining area co-joins a pool-room bar and jukebox room (with a small dance floor), so there is always a rousing hubbub in the air. The crawfish are a bargain at $7 for 3.5 pounds. We got a beer tray of the mudbugs and two dinners for $15.

Granger's just keeps on expanding. On our last visit they had added a drive-through window for crawfish, boudin, and hot tamales, as well as frozen drinks. Granger's is open from noon until midnight. Go north on Route 14 from Lake Charles approximately 10 miles. At the caution light turn east onto Old Town Road and Granger's will be on the left, half a mile up. (318) 433-9130.

*Hackett's Cajun Kitchen Boudin/Cajun Down Home, $. 5614 Rt. 14.

Charles Hackett grew up making boudin at his daddy's grocery down in Sweetlake. He now offers the traditional family recipe, along with four flavors of his own creation. Try the smoked,

Miller's. (Photo by Julie Posner)

shrimp, or catfish varieties. All have a spiciness that comes on slow but has a powerful afterburn. You can also purchase tasso crusted in red pepper, and chewy strands of beef jerky (popular among hunters). Plate lunches are dished up on Monday through Friday and may be eaten in a small dining area. A plate of pork chops, rice with gravy, corn, and fried okra cost $3.75. Fried catfish is usually served on Monday and shrimp Creole on Friday. Hackett's is open Monday through Friday from 7:30 A.M. to 6 P.M., and Saturday until 3 P.M. (318) 474-3731.

Mr. D's on the Bayou Seafood, $$. 3205 Common St.

Mr. D's serves all manner of seafood preparations, but they really excel with fried food. One out of every three plates is piled high with crisp catfish filets, crusted in a thin cornmeal batter. Seafood dinners range from $7 to $10 and come with baked potato, cole slaw, and cornbread. I recommend substituting a small order of greens for the cole slaw. If you just want fish, Mr. D's accommodates with a one-pound pile of catfish filets for $7. Mr. D's is situated in a building that was formerly a fried fish franchise, but don't be put off by the decor. From the iced tea to the greens and fried shrimp, everything is freshly prepared. Owner John Madison roams the floor, where he greets and is greeted by virtually every patron. Mr. D's is open Monday through Saturday from 11 A.M. to 10 P.M. (318) 433-9652.

*Miller's Cafe Local Fave/Down Home, $. 138 Louisiana Ave.

Miller's Cafe has been serving Lake Charles mountainous plates of soul food and homemade sweet dough pies for over forty years. They are located in a decaying, predominantly black neighborhood one block north of I-10. Folks from all over cut a path to this venerable old cafe for the best lunches and dinners in town. Their business card boasts, "Everything good to eat," and it is a promise fulfilled. I go for the smothered chicken and chops, and steaming crawfish stew. These are heaped beside rice and a choice of two vegetables (three without the rice) for under $4. The vegetables are mostly fixed from scratch and include okra, mustard greens, yams, and highly seasoned black-eye peas. You can dine at the counter or one of a dozen wooden tables, or get a plate to go. In cool weather, I usually snag a go-plate and eat by the lakefront on Lakeshore Drive. They are located just a few blocks east of Eddie Shuler's legendary Goldband Music Store. Miller's is open Monday through Friday from 7 A.M. to 8 P.M., and Saturday until 7 P.M. (318) 433-9184.

Smokey Joe's Bar-B-Que 406 W. McNeese St.

Smokey Joe's won readers' choice honors in *Louisiana Life* maga-

Record man Eddie Shuler. (Photo by Julie Posner)

zine for "best barbeque in south Louisiana." Joe explains, "I just fix barbeque the way I like to eat it." He does all the work himself, cutting the meat into strips and marinating it overnight. The ribs and chopped beef sandwiches here are served Texas-style in a red sauce. It may not be the best in Cajun Country, but it gets my vote for best in Lake Charles. A lot of people go for the cardboard boxes of fried catfish, while kids will enjoy the snowballs. Smokey Joe's is housed in an old hamburger stand, and the smokehouse out back is almost as big as the kitchen. Dining is on outdoor picnic tables. Smokey Joe's is open Monday through Sunday from 10 A.M. to 8 P.M. (318) 478-3352.

Music

Goldband Records 313 Church St.

Goldband Record Store and Recording Studio shares space with Quick Service T.V. Repair in an old wood-frame house on the run-down north side of I-10. Inside, the Goldband shop looks much the same as it did forty years ago. Racks of forty-fives and albums are scattered about a roomful of busted TV's and vintage instruments. There is an old 45 player on the counter where you can "test out" records before buying. Record producer Eddie Shuler opened the shop in the early fifties, when he was recording such well-known artists as Iry Lejeune, Boozoo Chavis, Dolly Parton, and Jimmy C. Newman. Shuler released the first Zydeco record with "Paper In My Shoe" by Boozoo Chavis, and cracked the national Hot 100 charts with the pounding "Sugar Bee" by Cleveland Crochet in 1961.

Shuler is now in his seventies and has had triple by-pass heart surgery, but he still answers the phone with a disturbing "Hello, Quick!" and can be found lugging TV's in and out of the repair room in back. Shuler's energy is boundless and, against all odds, he always has a new recording to play that "is my next hit!" Shuler has kept hundreds of his old recordings in print, including forty-fives and albums which he sells briskly to overseas collectors. There is no telling what you might uncover in the dusty racks of records in his shop, which are remnants from his forty-plus years in business. Among the oddities to seek out are "Puppy Love" by 13-year-old Dolly Parton, "Mummies Curse" by Freddy Fender (with Satan and the Disciples in support!), and collections by Cookie and the Cupcakes. Goldband/Quick Service is one block east of Ryan Street on the north side of I-10. Eastbound on the interstate, exit at Enterprise Boulevard and follow the north access road to Church Street. (318) 439-8839, 439-4295.

Downtowner Motel 507 Lakeshore Dr.

On Friday and Saturday night, the Downtowner hosts Gee Gee Shinn playing a Vegas-style Swamp Pop set for a packed dance floor.

Lloyd's Lounge Country and Cajun bar. 4101 U.S. 90 East.

Lloyd's is a real get-down honky-tonk with a Wild West feel. The tiny room is dominated by a horseshoe bar and pool tables. Every Friday or Saturday a Country-Cajun band occupies a small bandstand in the corner. If you are looking for a night of music off the beaten path in Lake Charles, this is the spot. Lloyd's is located on the east end of town (1.3 miles east of Route 171) on U.S. 90. (318) 436-9160.

Teaser's Country and Cajun bar. 5800 U.S. 90 East.

With a name like Teaser's you would expect a disco with strobe lights. Actually this lounge, popular with the younger crowd, is a honky-tonk and Country-Cajun music haven. It is especially raucous on Friday nights, when there are ladies' drink specials and local stars like Mel "Love Bug" Pellerin command the stage. (318) 436-9140.

★VFW Post Cajun and Country dance hall. 2130 Country Club Rd.

In Western Cajun Country, there are far fewer Cajun and Zydeco dance halls than in the neighboring Heartland region. Dances out here are traditionally held at VFW, church, or community halls. This VFW in southern Lake Charles claims to have the longest continually running Cajun dance, held each Saturday night for over twenty years. The hall featured legendary accordionist Joe Bonsal as a regular for years. Jesse Leger's is now the house band. The hall has a huge dance floor and its walls are festooned with photos of the Cajun Music Hall of Fame musicians. The Cajun music starts at 8 P.M. every Saturday, and country bands play at 9 on Sundays. The VFW attracts an older crowd and serious Cajun music fans. They have a list of rules to keep the peace: no shorts (men or women), no halters or tank tops or mini skirts (shorter than 3" above the knee), no dancing without shoes or with lit cigarettes or drinks in hand, Western attire permissible (but must be clean), and no rubber boots or shower thongs. Take Ryan Street south from I-210. Ryan becomes University Dr. before bending and becoming Country Club Dr. (318) 477-9176.

★Thibodeaux's Hall 626 Enterprise Boulevard.

For twenty-five years Thibodeaux's was known as Walker's Hall. The odd two-story dance hall still features the best in Zydeco

Thibodeaux's Zydeco dance hall. (Photo by Julie Posner)

entertainment a couple of weekends each month. The old hall has an Enterprise Boulevard address, but is actually located a block east of the boulevard in the shadow of I-10. Exit I-10 at Enterprise Boulevard south. Turn left on the south side of I-10 and the hall will be one block down, at the corner of Franklin Street. (318) 433-1190.

Recreation

*Sam Houston State Park, Campground, & Cabins

Sam Houston Park is named for the Texas folk hero of the Alamo, who traveled extensively in southwest Louisiana. The 1068-acre park is situated on the west fork of the Calcasieu River, a wooded area north of Lake Charles. Sam Houston offers the loveliest camping in the Lake Charles area and some great day-use facilities. There are two nature trails (about three quarters of a mile long) which wind through the woods at the river's edge, and boat rentals ($8 for jonboat, paddles, and life jackets) for folks who want to paddle around the area. Many visitors come for the day to picnic along the water and fish from the bank. The day-use area is equipped with a bath house, barbeque pits, and picnic tables.

For those who wish to stay overnight, the park offers twelve vacation cabins and seventy-three campsites ($12 a night), many with views of the water. Campsites have water and electrical hook-ups and the park is equipped with a dumping station. The cabins cost $45 a night and sleep six. They are right on the river bank and have screened porches overlooking the water. Cabins are completely furnished with cooking utensils and linens, and have central air-conditioning and heat. Sam Houston is about 8 miles from Lake Charles. To get there, take Route 171 4 miles north from I-10. Turn left at the traffic light onto Route 378. Go three miles and turn right at the park sign. From here it is a little over a mile to the park and the route is well marked. (318) 855-2665.

Prien Lake Park/Beach Prien Lake Rd.

If you are put off by swimming on a beach directly under the interstate, or with a view of Westlake industries, this is not the place for you. Prien Park is located on Prien Lake Road under the I-210 bridge crossing. There is a man-made sand beach and a rental stand where you can get paddleboats or inner tubes. From I-210, exit north onto Lake Street. Turn left on Prien Lake Road. Admission is $1. The park is open from 5 A.M. to 10 P.M. (318) 477-4344.

North Beach North Lakeshore Dr.

If you are hot enough, you might be willing to swim at this man-made beach beside I-10 (also with a view of Westlake industries). There are paddleboat rentals and a water slide.

*Creole Nature Trail/Hug the Coast Highway

The marshland south of Lake Charles offers wetlands vistas, fishing, and the best bird watching on the Gulf Coast. This area is the primary tourist attraction in Western Cajun Country and is covered in this chapter in the section "Scenic Wetlands."

Special Events

Contraband Days First 2 weeks in May.

This festival celebrates Lake Charles' pirate legacy with sailing regattas, outdoor concerts, food booths, a carnival, and plenty of planned mayhem. The pirate Jean Lafitte allegedly made trading arrangements with early settler Charles Sallier (for whom the city was named). His buccaneers docked at the lakefront near the city and are believed by some to have buried considerable treasure in the area. There is probably not a city in South Louisiana with access to the coast that does not believe Lafitte's men buried treasure nearby, but only Lake Charles has taken to celebrating this belief. The celebration begins with an enactment of buccaneers storming the lakefront area near the Civic Center and throwing city officials into the lake. This is an event worth watching, as the mayor "walks the plank" over the seawall in his suit and tie. (318) 436-5508.

Cajun Music and Food Festival 3rd weekend in July.

Burton Coliseum is the site of this festival, which includes accordion, fiddling, and dancing contests. Dozens of bands play and there are a number of food and crafts booths. Festival hours are 9 A.M. to midnight and until 7 P.M. on Sunday. Admission is $2 for adults. (318) 527-0317 or 433-6522.

Lodging

Motels and Hotels:

Days Inn 1010 N. Rt. 171, $36 to $40 double. (318) 433-1711.

Downtowner Motor Inn 507 North Lakeshore Dr., $44 to $50 double. (318) 433-0541.

Econo Lodge 1101 West Prien Lake Rd., $45 to $48 double. (318) 446-6900.

Lake Charles Hilton 505 North Lakeshore Dr., $60 to $78 double. (318) 433-7121.

Howard Johnson's I-10 at U.S. 171, $46 double. (318) 433-5213.

Lakeview Motel 1000 N. Lakeshore Dr., $25 double. (318) 436-3336.

Travel Inn 1212 N. Lakeshore Dr., $25 to $30 double. (318) 433-9461.

Camping:

Duplantis Campground U.S. 171 and Phil Lane (10 miles north of Lake Charles). Full hook-ups and showers. (318) 885-3985.

Jamie Mobile Campground Rt. 27 and Opelousas St. $8, full hook-ups. (318) 439-4422.

*Sam Houston State Park
The park offers twelve vacation cabins and seventy-three campsites. See the Recreation heading in this chapter for a full description of the campground facilities.

WEST FROM LAKE CHARLES: THE RIO HONDO TERRITORY

During most of the first fifty years of settlement in the Lake Charles area, the territory between the Calcasieu and Sabine rivers was the province of pirates, outlaws, and quarreling squatters. This area came to be known as the Rio Hondo, after the Sabine River, which was called *Arroyo Hondo*. Much of the lawlessness in the region owed to a border dispute that put sovereignty over the land in question. It was alternately claimed by the Spanish, French, Americans, and Mexicans. In 1821, the Sabine River was made the western boundary of Louisiana and the United States. Brazen lawlessness subsided, but the threat of conflict remained throughout the War Between the States, when the Sabine was traveled by blockade runners.

Today the Calcasieu River Bridge on I-10 (built in 1952) bears a striking symbol of the conflict which characterized the region; 10,000 cast-iron buccaneer pistols adorn its guard rails in a criss-cross pattern. An air of the Wild West pervades the roughly thirty-mile-wide strip of Louisiana between Lake Charles and the Texas border. There are rough-and-tumble Country music bars along U.S. 90, a horse track, and a huge cockpit attracting characters from both sides of the Texas-Louisiana border.

Sulphur

The city of Sulphur was laid out in 1878, shortly after the arrival of the Southern Pacific Railroad. It was named Sulphur City for the huge mineral deposits discovered in a salt dome on the west end of town. After scientist Hermann Frasch pioneered a new technique for mining sulphur, the dome became the most productive sulphur mine in the United States. The mine closed in the 1920s and is now used as a storage facility by the National Petroleum Reserve. The big employers in the area are now oil and petro-chemical companies. Visitors to Sulphur, which lies just north of Interstate 10, 7 miles west of Lake Charles, can view artifacts of the mining days at the Brimstone Museum, and get a rib-sticking lunch at Gelner's Red Barn Barbecue. Sulphur is located at the western end of the Creole Nature Trail (Route 27), which wends through the marshes and prime bird watching areas to the south (*see* section on tour of scenic wetlands below).

Frasch Park 800 Picard Rd.

Frasch Park is a small suburban recreational facility which serves as the site of the Brimstone Museum and Visitors Center, as well as a public pool and golf course. The park is named for Hermann Frasch, who developed the process which made the mining of sulphur here commercially viable. To get to the park from I-10, take the Sulphur Exit (#20) onto Route 27 north. Go about a quarter of a mile and turn left on Parish Road. Travel a quarter of a mile and take a right onto Picard Road. The park will be about a half mile down on the left.

Visitors Center and Brimstone Museum 800 Picard Rd. Frasch Park.

The Brimstone Museum and Sulphur Visitors Center are housed in the Sulphur depot of the Southern Pacific Railroad, which was moved to Frasch Park in 1976. A one-ton obelisk of sulphur marks the museum entrance. The museum commemorates the development in Sulphur of the Frasch process of mining sulphur. The Frasch process involved pumping super-heated water into a well, then pumping liquified sulphur to the surface. There is a display in the museum detailing the process, and a number of photographs of the mining operations. Employing the Frasch Process, the Union Sulphur Company began operations here in 1905. The mine produced over 10,000,000 tons of sulphur before it was closed in 1926. Most of the artifacts in the museum are either directly related to the old sulphur industry, or are representative of life in Sulphur during the heyday of the mining operations. The museum is open Monday through Friday from 9:30 A.M. to 5 P.M. (318) 527-7142.

Swimming Pool 800 Picard Rd. Frasch Park.

The small swimming pool is open Monday through Saturday from 9 A.M. to noon and 3 P.M. to 8 P.M. Sunday it is open from 1 P.M. to 6 P.M. Admission is $1.25 for adults. During the evenings children under twelve are allowed only if accompanied by an adult.

Golf Club 800 Picard Rd. Frasch Park.

The 18-hole course at Frasch Park is popular among local golf enthusiasts, and is a well-maintained and manicured facility. The Pro Shop is open from 6:30 A.M. to 5 P.M. (until 7:30 P.M. in the summer). The daily greens fee is $7. (318) 527-8693.

Paragon Drug Store U.S. 90, downtown Sulphur.

Open since 1891, this is the oldest continuously operated drug store in Louisiana. Paragon was the first business in town and was awarded the single-digit phone number, "1." The interior has pressed tin ceiling tiles with floral designs and six-sided ceramic floor tiles. A small museum displays tools used by Dr. D. S. Perkins, who was also Sulphur's first mayor.

*Louisiana High School Championship Rodeo

The cattle industry has shrunk in importance in South Louisiana during the twentieth century, but in Cajun Country the art of riding and roping is still refined and practiced at numerous rodeos. The Louisiana High School Championship is held in Sulphur every summer.

Food

Gelner's Red Barn Barbecue 2250 E. Napoleon St. (U.S. 90).

Mr. Gelner is from Cameron, Texas, and he fixes the meanest batch of Texas barbeque east of the Lone Star State! Gelner smokes his ribs over mesquite for four hours, using a recipe he learned "from an old black man back in 1965," and serves them with or without a spicy red sauce. He has discontinued serving brisket, but ribs are his specialty anyhow. The Red Barn has an all-you-can-eat special on ribs and chicken for $5 at lunch and $6 at dinner ($8 on Sundays). They are open Monday through Saturday for lunch from 11 A.M. to 2 P.M., and for dinner from 5 P.M. to 9 P.M. Sundays they are open from 10 A.M. to 3 P.M. (318) 625-9627.

Lodging

Chateau Motor Inn 2022 Ruth St., Route 27 at I-10, $38 to $48 double. (318) 528-2061.

Holiday Inn 2033 Ruth St., $43 double. (318) 528-2061.

La Quinta 2600 S. Ruth St. $54 to $60 double. (318) 527-8303.

WEST OF SULPHUR

Oak Archway on Old Spanish Trail U.S. 90 between Vinton and Sulphur.

Between Sulphur and Vinton, 14 miles west of Sulphur, may be the single most beautiful stretch of the Old Spanish Trail (U.S. 90). In the 1930s, the W.P.A. planted uniform rows of live oaks on either side of the road. Today these trees have grown to form a long, cool, green tunnel.

Delta Downs Racetrack Rt. 3060, Vinton.

Delta Downs is a small racetrack with all the good-timing atmosphere of a country "bush track." There is ample inexpensive ($2.50) seating in the air-conditioned clubhouse, but many folks bring lawn chairs to set up by the track. Quarterhorse races are held April through August, and thoroughbreds are run September through March. You can bet on the races here or elsewhere at Delta's offtrack betting windows.

The track entered the annals of horse-racing infamy on January 11, 1990. In the great "Race in the Fog," also known as the "Disappearing Horse Race," jockey Sylvester Carmouche and his mount disappeared after falling badly behind on a fog-shrouded track. As the two-lap race came to a close, Carmouche emerged from the fog, and crossed the wire with a 24-length lead! The fog was so thick that even after cameras were consulted, it was unclear whether he had ever completed the first lap! Carmouche was suspended, but there are still some wonderfully foggy races here, and there is no telling what you might (or might not) see. General admission is $1.25 (minimum age 18). Parking is $1. Thursday through Saturday, races begin at 6:30 P.M. Sunday races start at 1 P.M.

From I-10, take exit #4 (Toomey/Starks). Go 3 miles north on Route 109 and take a right onto Route 3060. The racetrack is 1 mile down on the right. 1-800-589-7441 or (318) 433-3206.

Niblett's Bluff Park and Campground Rt. 3063, Texas border.

Niblett's Bluff is 3 miles north of I-10 on the bank of the Sabine

Circle Club Cockpit. (Photo by Julie Posner)

River. I use the term "bank" generously. Although they have been called "bluffs" for a century and a half, the shores of the Sabine actually rise only 2-3 feet above the water. Niblett's Bluff is free for day-use activities such as swimming, boating, fishing, and picnicking. There is a $7 fee to camp on the pine-shaded "bluff" and for $15 one can rent a very simple (modern) one-room cabin. Because the campground is free and has excellent swimming and fishing, it gets very crowded on weekends during the summer. Jet skis and airboats roar up and down the river.

During the working week and in the cooler months, Niblett's Bluff is a fantastic day-use or overnight facility. You can walk the wooded grounds and see the breastworks of a fort constructed during the War Between the States, slip a canoe (bring your own) into the quiet river, and at night, make the short drive over to Delta Downs Racetrack. The park is open for free from 6 A.M. to 10 P.M. Camping with hook-ups is $7. Tent camping is $3. Cabins are furnished with a double bed and bunk beds, air-conditioning, and heat. There are no kitchens, but there are a sink and barbeque pit on the front porch. Bathhouses are located nearby. From I-10, take exit 4 (Toomey/Starks) and head north on Route 109 for 3 miles. Turn left on Route 3063. Niblett's Bluff is 2.6 miles east. (318) 589-7117.

*Circle Club Cockpit Rt. 109 S. (I-10 Exit #4).

The Circle Club is everything you would expect of a big border-town tavern attracting a wagering and cock-fighting crowd from East Texas (it is 4 miles to the state line) and the wild Rio Hondo territory. Actually, folks come from around the South to the big derby weekends here. You know this is cockfighting territory by the training grounds and seventy-five cock tepees in the yard between the club and the interstate. You enter through the bar, a big room where steaks and burgers are grilling and cock handlers and spectators are noisily sharing beers. In one corner, there is a spur concession where handlers can purchase sharpened gaffs to arm their fowl. There is a fee ranging from $8 to $15 to enter the pit area in back, which is a circular arena with tiered grandstand seating for several hundred. In the rear of the pit, there is an area called the "drags" where fights which are not quickly decided in the main arena may continue to a decision. During big tournaments, there are often two or three fights ocurring in the crude dirt-floor drags, while a new match is being consummated in the arena.

If you have never been to a cockfight, you should be warned that the spectacle of two animals engaged in sometimes mortal combat is not for everyone. However, owner Delane Navarre (President of the Louisiana Cockers Association) runs an orderly establishment. Unlike many pits which require memberships, the Circle Club is open to anyone who pays the admission and refrains from troublemaking. No cameras are permitted in the pit area. The cockfighting season runs from the second weekend in October to the first weekend in August. The best time to see a fight is during one of the big "Derbys" scheduled throughout the season. There is a "Powder Puff Derby" featuring all women handlers, a Welcome Derby (usually the second weekend of October), and a Clean Up Derby (usually the first weekend in August). The big derbys can run for twelve hours. Navarre gets the outdoor barbeque pit (which is the size of your typical small-town water reservoir!) smoking, and serves free barbeque and fried fish. Most Saturdays fights begin at noon. Friday fights begin at about 10 P.M. The Circle Club is located immediately south of I-10 on Route 109 (Exit # 4 at Toomey/Starks). (318) 589-2921 or 589-9919.

Louisiana Welcome and Tourist Information Center I-10 Eastbound.

This center, located 2 miles from the state line, has the biggest collection of brochures and maps for South Louisiana attractions. In addition to maps of the parish and Lake Charles, I recommend picking up pamphlets for the Lake Charles Charpentier District and the Creole Nature Trail. The center is located on the edge of Lake Bienvenu, which is bordered by a beautiful cypress swamp. There are picnic tables and barbecue pits by the water and a short elevated walking path through the swamp.

Lodging

Best Western Delta Downs Motor Inn Toomey Exit, $45 to $50 double. (318) 589-7492.

Niblett's Bluff Park and Campground Rt. 3063, Texas border. Cabins, RV, and tent camping. See description above.

SCENIC WETLANDS

The coastal wetlands, Prairie marsh, and beaches of Cameron Parish are the primary attraction in Western Cajun Country, and one of the most remarkably wild areas in all of Louisiana. Until the twentieth century, the area was virtually inaccessible except by boat. Now it is accessed by the Creole Nature Trail, which forms a scenic 100-mile loop south of Lake Charles, and the Hug the Coast Highway (Route 82), which parallels the Gulf Coast for 135 miles from the Texas border to the Central Cajun Country village of Abbeville. The area is home to two wildlife refuges, a coastal bird sanctuary, and miles of sandy Gulf coast beach. It is a prime area for bird and alligator watching, as well as fishing and hunting. Good brochures to the area are available from the Lake Charles Tourist Center and the Louisiana Welcome Center.

Most of the scenic wetlands of Western Cajun Country lie within Cameron Parish. Cameron is Louisiana's largest and least densely populated parish. Its six residents per square mile is less than half the number of the next most densely populated area. Few places in Cameron are over two feet above sea level, with permanently flooded marsh the predominant feature. The area was originally inhabited by Attakapas Indians, who named its two rivers, the Mermentau and Calcasieu, after tribal chieftains. The first white settlers were people of Scots-Irish descent who arrived in the mid-1800s and built homes on the coastal *cheniers*. The *cheniers* are a chain of slightly elevated oak-covered ridges along the coast which comprise the only significant high ground in Cameron. Those who elect to travel the Hug the Coast Highway will pass through the fishing, trapping, and ranching communities of Grand Chenier and Pecan Island, which now occupy the cheniers.

Creole Nature Trail

The Creole Nature Trail (Route 27) plunges south from the city of Sulphur, about 10 miles west of Lake Charles. It may be traveled as a full loop, or as a means of accessing the Hug the Coast Highway between Holly Beach and Abbeville. The whole loop is a hundred miles, and with stops, the drive will occupy most of a day. There are a couple of markets along the way, but you will want to stock up on sun screen and bug spray before leaving. You may also want to pack a cooler with cold drinks or a picnic to enjoy on the beach, after hiking in the Sabine Wildlife Refuge and Holleyman Bird Sanctuary. Those planning on eating out on the trip are advised to hold off for the eastern leg of Route 27, which heads north from Creole to Lake Charles and passes Hackett's Corner's Boudin Factory Restaurant.

Intracoastal Park Campground Rt. 27, 13 miles south of Sulphur.

Thirteen miles south of Sulphur, Route 27 crosses the Intracoastal Waterway and the bridge provides a superb elevated view of the miles of uninhabited marsh. One mile past the bridge is the turnoff for the Intracoastal Park Campground and Recreation Area. When we first visited the park, there was a knot of police cars and a gang of fishermen standing around with guns drawn. A renegade alligator had just eaten the campground manager's dog, and the law was there to settle the score.

This is a primitive facility with outhouses and no showers. Twenty-five camping sites, some with sheltered picnic tables and grills, are on a high bank overlooking the Intracoastal Waterway. Bank fishing is excellent and there is a boat launch ($4). The mosquitoes are likely to provide a greater menace than the alligators. Sites with water and electric hook-ups cost $8 a night. There is no fee for day use. After you pass over the Intracoastal bridge, turn right and pass back under the bridge. (318) 762-3367.

Hackberry About 17 miles south of I-10.

The town of Hackberry claims to be the "Crab Capital of the South." This is the site of a large storage facility of the National Strategic Petroleum Reserve, and home to a couple of popular "gun and rod" clubs. You will find bait and tackle shops here where you can get fishing or crabbing supplies and tips on where they are biting.

*Sabine Wildlife Refuge

The Sabine National Wildlife Refuge, established in 1937, contains 142,000 acres of salt- and freshwater marsh. There are over 150 miles of waterways in the refuge open to boat travel, but most visitors will spend time at the Sabine visitors interpretive center, hiking the elevated Sabine Nature trail, or fishing and crabbing at roadside access points. The refuge was established with the primary goal of protecting the wetlands habitat of the millions of migratory waterfowl that visit the area as they traverse the Central and Mississippi flyways. Bird watchers toting binoculars flock to this area, but many eyes are also turned towards the alligators, nutria, and snakes that abound in its muddy sloughs.

Recreational fishing is permitted from the banks or by boat. Where the Creole Nature Trail cuts through the refuge, there are several small bridges and easements where you can throw a castnet for shrimp or crab, or cast for speckled trout and redfish. There is no camping allowed within the refuge, but sites are available to the north at the Intracoastal Waterway and to the south at Holly Beach.

*Sabine Visitors Center and Headquarters 25 miles south of I-10.

The visitors center for the Sabine Refuge has excellent modern exhibits describing the flora and fauna of the region. Here you will find the world's only Cajun robot! Speaking in a thick Cajun dialect, this figure of an old fisherman tells about life in the marsh as his fishing pole jerks with a strike and an alligator snaps its jaws. Over 50,000 dollars were spent on this lifelike diorama. You will find public restrooms and a number of interpretive brochures are available, describing what wildlife events to look for in different months. You will learn what months are best for fishing and crabbing, which birds to look for, and where to watch for alligators nesting. The center is about 10 miles north of Holly Beach. They are open year round, Monday through Friday from 7 A.M. to 4 P.M. and weekends from noon to 4 P.M. (318) 762-3816.

*Sabine Nature Trail Rt. 27, 4 miles south of refuge headquarters.

Whether you are looking for alligators, roseate spoonbills, or just a scenic walk in the salt air, the Sabine Nature Trail is a fascinating stop. The Nature Trail is a 1.5-mile-long boardwalk through the marsh, leading to a wooden observation tower. I have never seen as many alligators in such a small area as I did one hot August morning on the Nature Trail. A brochure is available at the rest station (public bathrooms) at the trail head. This pamphlet has numbers corresponding to different wetlands features along the trail. The trail begins at a parking area on Route 27, 4 miles south of the Refuge Visitors Center and Headquarters (about 6 miles north of Holly Beach).

Hug the Coast Highway

Thirty-six miles south of I-10 (at Sulphur), the Creole Nature Trail intersects the Hug the Coast Highway at the town of Holly Beach. At this point travelers may want to head west 9.5 miles to the Holleyman-Sheely Bird Sanctuary. Those planning on completing the Creole Nature Trail loop, or traveling the Hug the Coast Highway to Abbeville, will want to turn east on Route 82. Until the construction of the Hug the Coast Highway in 1953, most of the Gulf settlements of Cameron and Vermilion Parish were accessible only by boat. Mail was delivered by water. Electrical and phone service were not established in most areas until around 1960. Along this route you will pass the coastal *chenier* communities with their gnarled oak trees, fields of unfenced cattle, and miles of open marsh.

Holleyman-Sheely Bird Sanctuary Rt. 82, 8.5 miles west of Holly Beach.

This bird sanctuary is located on a quiet, 12-acre *chenier*, just

Sabine Nature Trail. (Photo by Julie Posner)

Holly Beach. (Photo by Julie Posner)

east of the community of Johnson's Bayou. During cool spring months, millions of birds drop into the canopy of oaks. On particularly cool days a phenomenon known as "fallout" occurs, and the sanctuary is filled with the cries of exhausted migratory birds seeking refuge. Record bird sightings of several types have been registered at Holleyman-Sheely. Among the most commonly sought species are warblers, scarlet tanagers, orioles, and rose-breasted grosbeaks. There is plenty of other wildlife to look out for in the area (especially mosquitoes). The Holleyman-Sheely Sanctuary is open daily, free of charge. Eight and a half miles west of Holly Beach (across from the Stingray Plant), turn left on Parish Road 528. Take the second street to the left (unpaved) and continue to the end.

Holly Beach

Holly Beach is known to denizens of South Louisiana by the hyperbolic nickname "the Cajun Riviera." Don't expect any glamorous resorts or a white sand beach. Holly Beach is actually nothing more than a collection of ramshackle camps, fishermen's motels, and a couple of shops tumbling into the warm waters of the Gulf of Mexico. The beach itself is broad and open to the public, but it is better known for its collection of flotsam tossed up by the Gulf than for its sand or water. It seems like everyone that has frequented the area has a story (probably untrue) about relaxing on the beach, sticking their hand into the sand, and finding a dead dog or wild pig! During the summer (the absolute worst time to visit this shadeless strand), the 525 campsites and dozens of rentals fill up with college students and Cajun families hell-bent on enjoying the only beach around. The popularity of the place as a summer destination was obvious from a sign we saw on a restaurant a hundred miles away in Kaplan, which read, "We are NOT going to Holly Beach for the 4th of July!" When the summer crowd departs, Holly Beach returns to its "permanent population level" of 150 residents. This is the best time to visit and roam over six miles of public beach, fish for reds and trout in the surf, and comb the shore for shells and waterborne debris.

Cajun Riviera Festival 2nd weekend in August.

At the hottest and wildest time of summer, Holly Beach throws a festival with beer (and more beer), carnival rides, a rodeo, and performances by popular Cajun and Zydeco bands. There is a daily $1 admission charge for the festivities, which run from 10 A.M. to 11 P.M., Friday through Sunday.

Welcome to Cameron. (Photo by Julie Posner)

Lodging

Be forewarned—most of the lodging at Holly Beach is of the rustic or decrepit variety. A few of the better-looking establishments are listed here.

Motels and Camps:

Tommy's Motel (318) 569-2426.

Holly Beach Motel (318) 569-2352.

Seabreeze Apartments (318) 569-2385.

Joe Nick's Motel (318) 569-2421.

Roy's Cabins (318) 569-2346.

Camping:

Buzzy's RV Park (318) 569-2459.

Daquiri Dayz RV (318) 569-2660.

Roy's Camper Park (318) 569-2364.

Cameron

Free Ferry across Calcasieu Ship Channel

A 50-car ferry across the Calcasieu Pass is the only link between the town of Cameron and the western reaches of Route 82 and the Creole Nature Trail. The ferry runs 24 hours, crossing approximately every 20 minutes.

A sign greets visitors to Cameron, proclaiming its attractions: "No pollution, no traffic light, no big-city life, no city police, no trains (just boats)." That is life as it should be in a city that was isolated to all but waterborne commerce until the 1950s. Cameron is the only deepwater port between the Mississippi and Galveston, and is the seat of Cameron Parish government. Its 3,200 residents work mainly in the fishing and petroleum industries. The isolated existence of the coastal cities in Cameron Parish has made them veritable death chambers when tropical storms have directed themselves at the Gulf coast. Folks around Cameron quit taking chances with "riding out" storms when Hurricane Audrey rolled a tidal wave thirteen feet up the courthouse wall on the morning of June 27, 1957. The storm scattered smashed houses through the marsh, left tangled debris around the tops of telephone poles, and destroyed homes 20 miles inland on the north side of the Intracoastal Waterway. Audrey left 525 dead in Cameron Parish, including 35 in one family, and left its imprint on the memories and lifestyles of those who survived.

Cameron Chamber of Commerce
Open Monday through Friday 8 A.M. to 4 P.M., closed noon to 1 P.M. (318) 775-5222.

Louisiana Fur and Wildlife Festival January.
This has the distinction of being Louisiana's "coolest festival." Celebrants have a great time trying to keep warm. (318) 477-8655, 775-5718.

Monkey Island Ferry
If you ever decide to take every ferry in the state of Louisiana, this little six-car job could easily escape your notice. There is not much on the island except for two miles of roads and a couple of closed seafood plants. At the end of the main road there is a rock jetty that offers some good shore fishing. The ferry is free and located two blocks east of the hand-painted "Welcome to Cameron" sign adorning a building on the Gulf side of Route 82. It operates 24 hours.

Hurricane Audrey Shrine and Monument 3 miles east of Cameron.
Located in front of the Our Lady Star of the Sea Church is a shrine and monument dedicated to the 525 victims of Hurricane Audrey. The shrine was built in 1963 and stood alone on the marsh road until the church was built in 1971. The actual burial location of most of the victims is a mass grave at Lake Charles. The Hurricane Audrey Shrine is located 3 miles east of Cameron and 4 miles west of the Route 27 and Route 82 fork.

Travel Tip

From Cameron, Route 82 and Route 27 east run concurrently for 7 miles and then split into a Y. Route 27 (the Creole Nature Trail) heads north through the city of Creole and Route 82 continues east through Oak Grove. Those interested in following the Hug the Coast Highway may want to skip the following section, detailing the eastern leg of the Creole Nature Trail loop to Lake Charles.

Creole Nature Trail (Rt. 27 north)

At the town of Creole about 14 miles east of Cameron, Route 27 veers sharply northward. There is not a great deal to see on this "eastern leg" of the Creole Nature Trail, since the Cameron

Prairie Wildlife Refuge has not opened its trails or visitor facilities. However, the drive will take you past the Boudin Factory, the best eatery in Cameron Parish. It is about 40 miles from Creole to I-10 at Lake Charles.

Cameron Prairie Wildlife Refuge Rt. 27, north of Creole.

A visitors' interpretive center is planned, as well as walkways into the marsh. At present much of the Cameron Prairie Refuge is accessible only by boat. The refuge is located about 15 miles north of Creole, just north of the Gibbstown Bridge over the Intracoastal Waterway. For information and brochures on the refuge, turn east at the marked road and travel 2.2 miles to the refuge office. Visitors are welcome from 8 A.M. to 4:30 P.M., Monday through Friday. (318) 598-2216.

*Boudin Factory Cajun/Down Home, \$. Rt. 27 and Rt. 384, Sweetlake.

A restaurant this divine does not deserve to be stranded out on the Prairie marsh. Consider it God's gift to the hapless traveler who has driven 80 miles around the Creole Nature Trail without a decent bite to eat. Jimmy and Cindy Fogelman own the Factory and turn out some of the most solidly meaty and slowly hot boudin in Cajun Country. The boudin isn't even the best thing here. Go for a plate of Fogelman's pit-cooked beef ribs, which are smoked to perfection. The outside edges are crunchy and chewy, while the inside is nothing but tender, lean meat. A three-pound serving with baked beans and potato salad is under \$5. Everything here is great, including steaming plate lunches. In the cool-weather months, a plate of red beans with Fogelman's boudin or barbecued sausage will warm your heart and reach those cold extremities in moments. Cindy's homemade chocolate chip, sugar, peanut butter, and oatmeal cookies are just like mom's. They are sold in generous wax paper packets (just like you used to find in your lunch bag in third grade). The front of the Boudin Factory is a country store and the restaurant tables have a commanding view of racks of dry goods, fishing caps, and motor oil. The Boudin Factory is located at the intersection of Route 82 and Route 384, about 17 miles north of Creole. They are open Monday through Saturday, from 7:30 A.M. to 6 P.M. (318) 598-3448.

Travel Tip

From the Boudin Factory, the Creole Nature Trail follows Route 384 west before heading north into Lake Charles by way of Route

385. You may want to take a shortcut by following Route 27 north to Route 14 west into Lake Charles.

Rt. 82: East of Creole

Rutherford Beach
This beach is located immediately south of Oak Grove, the first community east of the Route 27 and Route 82 split. The swimming and beach at Rutherford are much the same as at Holly Beach to the west (debris-strewn sand and warm water), but there are only a few camps here and the crowds are a lot thinner.
Grand Chenier Rt. 82, 9 miles east of Creole.
Grand Chenier is the most heavily populated "oak island" on Louisiana's Gulf Coast, with over 1000 residents. One of two *cheniers* accessible by car, it stretches almost 15 miles from southeastern Cameron Parish into Vermilion Parish. The ridge is about 6 miles inland from the Gulf Coast.
In the early 1800s, the isolated ridge of oaks was a refuge for outlaws. Legitimate settlement began with the arrival of homesteaders of Scots-Irish descent around 1850. These settlers lived in cane and palmetto shacks and raised citrus fruits and subsistence crops on the two-mile-wide swath of slightly arable ground. Hurricanes wiped out the citrus crop, and residents turned to trapping, hunting, and ranching. Since the *cheniers* were connected to the outside world by road in the early 1950's, some residents have found part-time work as hunting guides, or dressing wild game, but for the most part their daily pursuits have changed little in the last century. Cattle may still be seen grazing on unfenced patches of grass floating in a sea of marsh.
*Rockefeller Refuge Rt. 82, Grand Chenier.
Rockefeller has the best land access of all Louisiana's coastal wildlife refuges. Visitors can enter the heart of the marsh by way of Price Lake Road to crab, fish, and scout for wildlife. The refuge sprawls along 26 miles of coastal marsh in Cameron and Vermilion parishes. Its 84,000 acres are sandwiched in the 4- to 6-mile-wide strip between Route 82 and the Gulf. The area was purchased by naturalist E.A. McIlhenny in 1912. McIlhenny sold the land to the Rockefeller Foundation and convinced the Foundation to establish a wildlife sanctuary. Today, water-management and conservation projects are underway to protect the wetlands, which are a landing strip for millions of migratory birds each year. Over 400,000 ducks winter at the refuge, alongside a grow-

ing population of Canadian geese and a huge number of other temporary avi-residents. The Rockefeller Refuge Headquarters is located near Grand Chenier in the northwestern corner of the sanctuary, but is geared towards management rather than public information. The best place to enjoy the refuge and its wildlife is at the Price Road access point and observation tower (closed December 1 through March 1). (318) 538-2276.

*Price Lake Road .5 miles west of Headquarters, Rockefeller Refuge.

As you enter Price Lake Road a sign instructs recreational crabbers, "Limit 12 dozen crabs and 25 lbs. shrimp per day"! They are not kidding. A mile down, the shell road opens on either side to wide shallow lakes, and continues another two miles before dead-ending in the marsh. Crabbers using nothing more than a dip net, rotten chicken necks, and weighted string may be seen filling fifty-gallon garbage cans with crustaceans! I have inadvertently caught twenty crabs in an hour fishing for trout here. Recreational fishermen share the harvest with waterbirds that wade among their lines, while alligators sun in the mud ten feet away. From a three-story observation tower, bird watchers can see clear to the coastal fringe. The Price Lake Road area is closed between December 1 and March 1.

Pecan Island Rt. 82, 40 miles southwest of Abbeville.

Pecan Island is one of two (the other is Grand Chenier) populated *cheniers* accessible by car. The so-called island is a 16-mile-long and 2-mile-wide ridge, 6 miles inland from the coast. It was discovered by Texas cattleman Jake Cole in the mid-1800s. Cole stumbled on the raised earth while looking for a place to graze his cattle. He reportedly found the island covered with bleached bones and Indian burial mounds twenty feet high. Many of the island's mounds were desecrated by treasure hunters (looking for pirate Jean Lafitte's loot) in the 1920s, but a few still remain within sight of the road. From Pecan Island, Route 82 turns north and crosses the Intracoastal Waterway. Here there is a cluster of bars whose names—OK Corral Bar, Little Prairie Hangout, and Cowboy's Hangout—are testimony to the importance of the cattle industry in southern Vermilion Parish. From this point travelers may head due north on Route 35 to Kaplan, or wind northeast 21 miles to Abbeville.

Cowboy's Hangout Bar and Cockpit Rt. 82 at Intracoastal Waterway.

Cowboy's is a rough-and-tumble bar flung out on the Prairie-marsh. Cockfights are held in a crude pit beside the bar on Sundays at 2 P.M. (call first to verify schedule). They are located a quarter of a mile north of the Intracoastal Waterway. (318) 642-5406.

Mardi Gras riders in Mamou. (Courtesy of LA Office of Tourism)

Appendix A

SPECIAL EVENTS IN CAJUN COUNTRY

South Louisiana is the site of at least one fair or festival every weekend of the year. The biggest event is Mardi Gras, which is described in detail following this list. Other events tend to be harvest celebrations, like the Yambilee Yam Festival in Opelousas and Rice Festival in Crowley. Many have a religious component, such as the shrimp festivals in Chauvin, Delcambre, and Morgan City, during which a priest conducts a ceremonial "Blessing of the Fleet." More recently ethnic festivals have sprung up, celebrating Cajun or French culture. The biggest of these are the Festivals Acadiens and Festival International in Lafayette. Some ethnic festivals have a particular food item as their object, including the Boudin Festival in Broussard, the Cracklin' Festival in Port Barre, and the wild Crawfish Festival in Breaux Bridge. Nearly all of the festivals of all types now feature live Cajun or Zydeco music, and good regional eats. This is a list of festivals worth planning a vacation around. Many smaller festivals are listed within the text.

Major Fairs and Festivals

Mardi Gras (*see* Mardi Gras section following this list).

Festivals Acadiens, Lafayette. 3rd weekend in September.

Festival International de Louisiane, Lafayette. 3rd weekend in April.

Zydeco Festival, Plaisance. Saturday before Labor Day.

St. Landry Heritage Festival; Opelousas, Eunice, Washington. 2nd week in May.

Louisiana Cattle Festival and Fair, Abbeville. 1st weekend in October.

Rayne Frog Festival, Rayne. 2nd weekend in September.

Breaux Bridge Crawfish Festival, Breaux Bridge. 1st weekend in May.

World Championship Crawfish Etouffée Cook-off, Eunice. Last weekend in March.

Mardi Gras

Mardi Gras, or "Fat Tuesday," is the day before Ash Wednesday. In this predominantly Catholic area, it is a time of determined abandon as many residents enjoy their last dances, last beers, and last cigarettes before Lenten fasting begins. This is a great time to visit Cajun Country. Crawfish are in season at local restaurants and bars, dance halls, and nightclubs reverberate with Cajun and Zydeco music.

Many cities in South Louisiana have New Orleans-style Mardi Gras parades, with masked riders tossing trinkets from floats. The *Courir du Mardi Gras* which takes place in perhaps a dozen communities in rural Cajun Country is a very different type of celebration, with roots in ancient Roman and Medieval festivals. Masked riders gather on horseback on Mardi Gras morning. They usually meet in the town hall around 7 A.M., where the *Capitaine* (who holds the office for life) reads the rules of the ride. Typically participants must be men at least eighteen years old. For the youngsters, the ride acts as a rite of passage into manhood. The riders form a rowdy procession of horses, flatbed trucks, and beer and band wagons as they ride out of town.

Upon reaching the designated stops, the *Capitaine* receives clearance from the homeowners before allowing his band to charge into the yard. There, the riders dismount to seek their booty, singing, dancing, and otherwise cutting up. Contributions range from rice and money to live chickens, which are thrown into the air and pursued with drunken abandon by the riders.

During the rides, communities (listed below) have daytime dances, food, and beer to entertain those waiting for the riders' return. Excitement builds as the time for the processional return nears (usually about 3 P.M.). Crowds line the streets to watch the inebriated ensemble enter town, often riding backwards on, standing on top of, or falling off of their mounts! The accumulated booty is gathered and a gumbo is prepared for consumption at an evening dance (open to the public). Mamou was the first town to revive the century-old *Courir du Mardi Gras* tradition in the mid-fifties. It is now possible to travel between nearby towns and enjoy several different Mardi Gras celebrations. Those listed below are most recommended. Note that Church Point holds its *Courir du Mardi Gras* (highly recommended) on Sunday before Fat Tuesday.

Mardi Gras Dates:

1993—February 23	1997—February 11
1994—February 15	1998—February 24
1995—February 28	1999—February 16
1996—February 20	2000—March 7

Mardi Gras Mamou: Monday night there is a street party. Tuesday, *Courir du Mardi Gras* riders depart around 7 A.M. and return around 3 P.M.

Mardi Gras Church Point: Sunday, *Courir du Mardi Gras* riders depart around 7 A.M., returning around 3 P.M. A Cajun dance and gumbo take place during the day at the Saddle Tramp Club.

Mardi Gras Iota: Tuesday, *Courir du Mardi Gras* riders depart around 7 A.M., returning around 2 P.M. Food and craft booths and a Cajun/Zydeco bandstand operate throughout the day.

Mardi Gras Eunice: Monday, the Cajun Cultural Center and Liberty Theater host interpretive presentations and performances during the afternoon and evening. Tuesday, *Courir du Mardi Gras* riders depart around 8 A.M., returning around 3. Daytime activities include a children's parade, bandstand, and plenty of great food.

Appendix B

SELECTED CAJUN AND ZYDECO
RADIO SHOWS

KEUN 1490 AM Eunice. *Cajun*: M-F, 5 A.M. to 6:30 A.M.; Sat., 4 A.M. to noon; Sat., 9 A.M. to 11 A.M., *Broadcast from Dup's. *Zydeco*: Sat., 6 P.M. to midnight. 318-457-3041.

KLCL 1470 AM Lake Charles. *Cajun*: Sun., 9 A.M. to noon. *Zydeco*: Sat., 6 A.M. to noon. 318-433-1641.

KSIG 1450 AM Crowley. *Cajun*: Tues-F, 5:30 P.M. to 7 P.M.; Sat., 7 A.M. to noon. 318-783-2520.

KRVS 88.7 FM Lafayette. *Cajun*: M-F, 5 A.M. to 7 A.M.; Sat., 7 A.M. to 10 P.M. *Zydeco*: Sat., 5 A.M. to 2 P.M.; Sun., 6 A.M. to 4 P.M. 318-984-8395.

KSLO 1470 AM Opelousas. *Cajun*: M-F, 4:30 to 7 A.M.; Sat., 9 A.M. to noon, *Broadcast from Toby's. *Zydeco*: Sat., 4 P.M. to 5 P.M. 318-942-2633.

KVPI 1250 FM Ville Platte. *Cajun*: Sat., 9 A.M. to 1 P.M., *Broadcast from Fred's Lounge. *Zydeco*: Sat., 1:30 P.M. to 3 P.M. 318-363-2124.

KROF 960 AM & 104.9 FM Abbeville. *Cajun*: Sat., 8 A.M. to noon; Sun., 8 A.M. to 2 P.M. 318-893-2531.

KAOK 1400 AM Lake Charles. *Cajun*: M-F, 4 A.M. to 8 A.M. 318-436-7541.

KJCB 770 AM *Zydeco*: M & W, 7 P.M. to 9 P.M.; Sat., noon to 2 P.M. 318-233-4262.

KFXY 106 FM *Zydeco*: Sun., 10:30 A.M. to 2 P.M. 318-232-5363.

KALO 1250 AM *Zydeco*: Thurs., 7 P.M. to 8 P.M.; Sat., 10 A.M. to noon. 318-963-1276.

Appendix C

RECOMMENDED BOOKS

Cajun History and Culture

Ancelet, Barry Jean; Edwards, Jay D.; Pitre, Glen. *Cajun Country.* Jackson, Miss.: University Press of Mississippi, 1991.
Conrad, Glenn R. *Cajuns.* Lafayette, La.: USL-Center for Louisiana Studies, 1978.

South Louisiana Music

Broven, John. *South to Louisiana.* Gretna, La.: Pelican Publishing Co., 1983.
Savoy, Anne Allen. *Cajun Music: A Reflection of a People.* Eunice, La.: Bluebird, 1984.
Ancelet, Barry Jean. *The Makers of Cajun Music.* University of Texas, 1984.

Cajun Food

Prudhomme, Paul. *The Prudhomme Family Cookbook.* New York, NY.: William Morrow and Co., Inc., 1987.

Louisiana Travel

Hansen, Harry, ed. *Louisiana: A Guide to the State.* New York, NY.: Hastings House, 1971.

Bayou Country & Teche Country

Kane, Harnett T. *Bayous of Louisiana.* New York, NY.: William Morrow and Co., Inc., 1943.
Uzee, Philip D. *The Lafourche Country.* Lafayette, La.: USL-Center for Louisiana Studies, 1985.
Caffery, Debbie Fleming. *Carry Me Home.* Washington, D.C.: Smithsonian, 1990.

Atchafalaya Basin

Guirard, Greg. *Cajun Families of the Atchafalaya.* St. Martinville, La.: Privately printed, 1989.
McPhee, John. *The Control of Nature.* New York, NY.: Farrar, Straus, Giroux, 1989.

Delcambre, Kenneth P. *Lords of the Basin*. Breaux Bridge, La.: Privately printed, 1988.

Coastal Wetlands

Hanks, Amanda Segrera. *Louisiana Paradise: The Cheniers and Wetlands of Southwest Louisiana*. Lafayette, La.: USL-Center for Louisiana Studies, 1988.

Plantation Homes

Arrigo, Joseph and Dietrich, Dick. *Louisiana's Plantation Homes: The Grace and the Grandeur*. Stillwater, Minn.: Voyageur Press, 1991.

RECOMMENDED VIDEOS

Spend It All Cajun Culture documentary.
J'ai Eté au Bal Cajun and Zydeco music documentary.
Yum Yum Yum Cajun food documentary.
Marc and Ann Marc and Ann Savoy's Cajun love story documentary.
Hot Pepper Clifton Chenier/Zydeco documentary.
Dry Wood Bois Sec Ardoin/Zydeco documentary.
Belizaire the Cajun Fictional account of a faith healer during vigilante days.
Anything I Catch Remarkable handfishing documentary.
Crawfish Crawfish industry documentary.

Appendix D

RECOMMENDED RECORDINGS

Cajun Recordings

Nathan Abshire *Pine Grove Blues* Ace LP CHD 217
Johnny Allan *Sings Cajun Now* Swallow LP 6069
The Balfa Brothers *Play Traditional Cajun Music, Vols. 1 & 2*
  Swallow CD 6001
Cleveland Crochet and the Sugar Bees Goldband GRLP 7749
D. L. Menard *The Back Door* Swallow LP 6038
D. L. Menard *Cajun Saturday Night* (Cajun/Country) LP 0198

Cajun Anthologies

Cajun Saturday Night Swallow CD 102
Le Gran Mamou Country Music Foundation CMF 013D
Louisiana Cajun Music Special Swallow CD 103

Zydeco Recordings

C. J. Chenier *Let Me In Your Heart* Arhoolie LP 1098 Clifton
Chenier
Bogalusa Boogie Arhoolie CD 347
Clifton Chenier *60 Minutes with the King of Zydeco* Arhoolie CD 301
Boozoo Chavis *The Lake Charles Atom Bomb* Rounder CD 2097
Buckwheat Zydeco *People's Choice* Blues Unlimited LP 5017

Zydeco Anthologies

Zydeco Blues Flyright Fly CD 36
Zydeco Festival Maison de Soul MdS CD 101
Zydeco Volume 1 Arhoolie CD 307

Swamp Pop Recordings

Johnny Allan *South to Louisiana* Swallow LP 4001
Bobby Charles *Chess Masters* Chess CH 9175
Cookie and the Cupcakes *Three Great Rockers* Jin LP 9003
Jimmy Donley *Give Me My Freedom* Charly LP CR 30265
Tommy McLain *Sweet Dreams* Ace CD CH 285

Charles Mann *Walk of Life* Gumbo CD002

Cajun and Zydeco Compilations

Alligator Stomp Rhino CD R270946
Jai Eté au Bal Vol. 1 Arhoolie CD 331
Jai Eté au Bal Vol. 2 Arhoolie CD 332

Appendix E

SOURCES FOR RECORDED AND PRINTED MATERIAL ON CAJUN COUNTRY

State Agencies

Louisiana Department of Wildlife
and Fisheries
P.O. Box 9800
Baton Rouge, La. 70898-9000
504-765-2496

Lafayette Visitors Commission
P.O. Box 52066
Lafayette, La. 70505
1-800-346-1958, (1-800-543-5340 in
Canada)

Louisiana Visitors Commission
1-800-33-GUMBO

Southwest Louisiana Visitors
Commission
P.O. Box 1912
1211 Lakeshore Dr.
Lake Charles, La. 70602
1-800-456-SWLA

Houma-Terrebonne Visitors
Commission
P.O. Box 2792
Houma, La. 70361
1-800-688-2732

Iberia Parish Tourist Commission
2690 Center St.
New Iberia, La. 70560
318-365-1540

Music Sources in Cajun Country

Sound Center (Lanor Records)
P.O. Box 233
329 Main St.
Church Point, La. 70525
318-684-2176
(Retail and mail order.)

Modern Music (Master Trak
Enterprises)
P.O. Box 856
413 N. Parkerson
Crowley, La. 70526
318-783-1601
(Retail and mail order.)

Goldband Records
P.O. Box 1485
313 Church St.
Lake Charles, La. 70601
318-439-4295
(Retail and mail order.)

Floyd's Records (Flat Town Music)
P.O. Drawer 10
434 E. Main St.
Ville Platte, La. 70586
318-363-2184
(Retail and mail order.)

Music Sources outside Cajun Country

Arhoolie & Old Timey Records
10341 San Pablo Ave.
El Cerrito, Ca. 94530
510-525-7471
(Mail order.)

Tower Records
408 N. Peters
New Orleans, La. 70130
504-529-4411
(Retail.)

Roundup Records
P.O. Box 154
N. Cambridge, Ma. 02140
617-661-6308
(Mail order.)

Printed Material Sources

USL
Center for Louisiana Studies
P.O. Box 40831, USL
Lafayette, La. 70504-0831
318-231-6039
(Retail or mail order.)

Louisiana Catalogue Store
Route 3, Box 614
Cut Off, La. 70345
1-800-375-4100
(Retail or mail order.)

Bluebird Press (*Cajun Music: A Reflection of a People*)
P.O. Box 941
Eunice, La. 70535
(Mail order.)

Greg Guirard (*Cajun Families of the Atchafalaya*)
Rt. 2, Box 2388
St. Martinville, La. 70582
(Mail order.)

Bibliography

Acadiana Profile magazine. Vol. 13, No. 2, 1987.

Acadiana Profile magazine. Vol. 13, No. 4, 1988.

Ancelet, Barry Jean. *Cajun Music: Its Origins and Development.* Lafayette, La.: USL-Center for Louisiana Studies, 1989.

Ancelet, Barry Jean. *Capitaine Voyage ton Flag.* Lafayette, La.: USL-Center for Louisiana Studies.

Ancelet, Barry Jean. *The Makers of Cajun Music.* University of Texas, 1984.

Ancelet, Barry Jean; Edwards, Jay D.; Pitre, Glen. *Cajun Country.* Jackson, Miss.: University Press of Mississippi, 1991.

Andrepont, Carola Ann. "History of Opelousas" Opelousas, La.: Privately printed brochure.

Broven, John. *South to Louisiana.* Gretna, La.: Pelican Publishing Co., 1983.

Butler, W. E. *Down Among the Sugar Cane.* Baton Rouge, La.: Moran Publishing Corporation, 1980.

Caffery, Debbie Fleming. *Carry Me Home.* Washington, D.C.: Smithsonian Press, 1990.

Calhoun, Milburn and Doré, Susan Cole, eds. *Louisiana Almanac 1988-89.* Gretna, La.: Pelican Publishing Co., 1988.

Center for Louisiana Studies. *Louisiana Sugar* Lafayette, La.: USL-Center for Louisiana Studies, 1980.

Conrad, Glenn R. *Cajuns.* Lafayette, La.: USL-Center for Louisiana Studies, 1978.

Conrad, Glenn R., ed. *The Cajuns.* Lafayette, La.: USL-Center for Louisiana Studies, 1983.

Conrad, Glenn R. *New Iberia.* Lafayette, La.: USL-Center for Louisiana Studies, 1986.

De Hart, Jess. *Louisiana's Historic Towns.* New Orleans, La.: Hamlet House, 1983.

Delcambre, Kenneth P. *First Facts About Breaux Bridge.* Breaux Bridge, La.: Privately printed, 1988.

Delcambre, Kenneth P. *Lords of the Basin.* Breaux Bridge, La.: Privately printed, 1988.

Feibleman, Peter S. *The Bayous.* New York, NY.: Time-Life Books, 1973.

Gahn, Robert Sr. *A History of Evangeline Parish*. Claitor Publishing Co., 1972.

Guirard, Greg. *Cajun Families of the Atchafalaya*. St. Martinville, La.: Privately printed, 1988.

Hanks, Amanda Segrera. *Louisiana Paradise: The Cheniers and Wetlands of Southwest Louisiana*. Lafayette, La.: USL-Center for Louisiana Studies, 1988.

Hansen, Harry, ed. *Louisiana: A Guide to the State*. New York, NY.: Hastings House, 1971.

Hildebrand, Franklin. *As I Remember*. Jennings, La.: Creative Printing, Inc., 1977.

Kane, Harnett T. *Bayous of Louisiana*. New York, NY.: William Morrow and Co., Inc., 1943.

Kniffen, Fred B.; Gregory, Hiram F.; Stokes, George A. *Historic Indian Tribes of Louisiana*. Baton Rouge, La.: Louisiana State University Press, 1987.

Leeper, Clare D'Artoir. *Louisiana Places*. Baton Rouge, La.: Legacy Publishing Co., 1976.

Lewis, Peirce F. *New Orleans: The Making of an Urban Landscape*. Cambridge, Mass.: Ballinger, 1976.

Looney, Ben Earl. *Cajun Country*. Lafayette, La.: USL-Center for Louisiana Studies, 1985.

McPhee, John. *The Control of Nature*. New York, NY.: Farrar, Straus, & Giroux, 1989.

Prudhomme, Paul. *Chef Paul Prudhomme's Louisiana Kitchen*. New York, NY.: William Morrow and Co., Inc., 1984.

Savoy, Anne Allen. *Cajun Music: A Reflection of a People*. Eunice, La.: Bluebird, 1984.

Sonnier, Austin Jr. *Second Linin': Jazzmen of Southwest Louisiana 1900-1950*. Lafayette, La.: USL-Center for Louisiana Studies, 1989.

Stahls, Paul F. Jr. *Plantation Homes of the Teche Country*. Gretna, La.: Pelican Publishing Co., 1979.

Uzee, Philip D. *The Lafourche Country*. Lafayette, La.: USL-Center for Louisiana Studies, 1985.

Vermilion Historical Society. *History of Vermilion Parish, Louisiana*. Abbeville, La.: The Society, 1983.

Index